ITALIAN MOTORCYCLES

ITALIAN MOTORCYCLES

MICK WALKER

Aston Publications

Sole distributors for the USA

Motorbooks International
Publishers & Wholesalers Inc.

Osceola, Wisconsin 54020, USA

Published in 1991 by Aston Publications Limited
Bourne End House, Harvest Hill
Bourne End, Bucks SL8 5JJ
Printed in Hong Kong through Bookbuilders Ltd

ISBN 0 946627 61 4

Designed by Chris Hand

Sole distributors to the UK book trade,
Springfield Books Limited
Norman Road, Denby Dale
Huddersfield, West Yorkshire HD8 8TH

Sole distributors for the USA,
Motorbooks International
Osceola, Wisconsin 54020
United States

Contents

Mick White (seated) and author Mick Walker with the Walker-tuned 175 Formula 3-engined Ducati Sport at Cadwell Park in March 1988.

Acknowledgements

I began my motorcycling career some three decades ago, first on a couple of Lambretta scooters, and then a Ducati Daytona (Diana outside Britain). So perhaps, even though since then I have owned and ridden machines from almost every other country which produces powered two-wheelers, my first loyalty should remain with Italian machinery.

To me, Italian motorcycles have always displayed a particular style — charisma if you will. The same of course can be said of their four-wheeled cousins.

Unfortunately they have also suffered from a Jekyll and Hyde character, in which engineering genius has often been marred by a distinct lack of attention to the ancillaries, such as paintwork, chrome plating ... and electrical equipment.

Certainly up to the beginning of the 1980s, the content in the *average* Italian motorcycle was either brilliantly good (engine, chassis and brakes) or appallingly bad (finish and electrics). But since then a genuine attempt has been made to close this yawning gap, with the result that as we enter the 1990s, the Italian industry seems set to make a more effective challenge in the all-important export markets of the world. Of course this will not be easy, but with domestic sales falling off, it is of the utmost importance if there is to be an effective Italian bike presence as we head towards the next century.

But for all this, the enthusiasm for Italian two-wheelers by a hard core of owners around the world is perhaps stronger than for any other country's products. Names such as Ducati, Gilera, Moto Guzzi and MV Agusta stir passions unmatched by the vast majority of marques from outside Italy. I for one feel this will be *the* deciding factor as the potential motorcycle customer switches more and more from using his machine as a form of basic transport to a vehicle of enjoyment and pride.

This process started back in the early 1970s with the arrival of the Superbike, and now seems set to go even further with the era of the Prestige bike. But the Japanese are there too and are hardly likely to welcome the Italian challenger.

In the world of the Classic bike, Italian machines are already well established and this is shown by the rapid growth of prices paid by collectors over the past few years, so at least there is a firm base to be built upon.

With a book which covers well over 200 manufacturers, it is perhaps to be expected that the number of people to be thanked is pretty large. And so it proved, with an exceptionally long list of names who deserve a special note of thanks.

First the manufacturers themselves. In particular I would extend words of praise for the important co-operation of the following: Aprilia (Placido Gullotta); Cagiva (Luigi Giacometti); Ducati (Nadia Pavignanni, Franco Valentini and, not least, Ing. Fabio Taglioni); Garelli (Roberto Patrignani); Gilera (Guido Miraglia); and Moto Guzzi (Gema Pedretta). Valuable assistance also came from the following British importers: Aprilia, Robert Jackson of USAB; Ducati, Hoss Elm of Moto Cinelli; Malaguti (and Morini), Peter Glover of Harglo; and Moto Guzzi (and Laverda), Keith Davies of Three Cross Imports.

But perhaps most of all I am indebted to the number of individuals who not only provided their time but related personal experiences to make this book more valuable than it would otherwise have been.

My close associate from other titles, Doug Jackson of The World's Motorcycles News Agency, once again opened his extensive archives to me, which not only include priceless information but many rare, often unpublished photographs and brochures. Don Mitchell supplied me with several items of literature from his comprehensive stock of handbooks, parts catalogues and leaflets.

A special mention must go to Denise Preston of the Italian Trade Centre, London, who went out of her way to 'chase' certain individuals (who will remain nameless) for vital information in Italy — thanks Denise.

Then came the marque specialists: Jaap de Jong (Aermacchi), Gerald Gilligan (Gilera), Tim Parker and Phil Todd (Laverda), Amedeo Castilliani (Moto Guzzi), Dave Kay (MV Agusta), Michael Dregni (Parilla), and Roy Pearce (Rumi). And not forgetting my great Italian friend Gerolamo Bettoni — a Ducati enthusiast of considerable note.

Others who helped in some way include the former MV Agusta team manager, Arturo Magni, and former

The author pictured outside the Mick Walker Motorcycles showroom with shop manager John Blunt during the summer of 1973. The motorcycle the pair are standing behind is one of the limited production Walker-Ducati singles. With a Saxon or Spondon-built chassis, these machines gained a reputation for reliability and superb handling.

racing stars Ken Kavanagh, John Surtees, Bill Lomas and Dan Shorey.

Besides the various factories concerned, photographs came from a wide range of sources, including my own collection, and from the Doug Jackson archives. And from the following: Gerolamo Bettoni, Ian Brand, Alan Carthcart, John Dixon, Peter Glover, Terry Ives, Ken Kavanagh, Herbert Namink, Nick Nicholls, Richard Slater, Philip Tooth, Sue Tully and Don Upshaw.

If I have overlooked anyone, I can but apologize, it was not my intention.

Finally, I would like to thank Tony Pritchard of Aston Publications for allowing my idea into print; as I have found with previous ventures under the Aston imprint, it is carried through with both professionalism *and* enthusiasm.

Mick Walker
Wisbech
Cambridgeshire

May 1990

CHAPTER I

Aermacchi

Originally an old-established coachbuilding enterprise, the company was reorganized in 1912 as the Societá Amnima Nieuport Macchi. The purpose of this venture was to build French-designed Nieuport aircraft for the fledgling Italian Air Corps, under licence. By the end of the Great War, the company, now known as Aeronautica Macchi (soon abbreviated to Aermacchi) was the foremost specialist in the country of seaplanes, which accounted for the factory's location, which was sited on the shores of Lake Varese, northern Italy.

In the 1920s and early 1930s the company became famed for their exploits in the Schneider Trophy Contest, and put up a tremendous fight against Britain's Supermarines, designed by Reginald Mitchell of Spitfire fame. One of these – the tandem-engined MC (Macchi-Castoldi) 72 is, in fact, still the holder of the world record for piston-engined seaplanes, with a speed of 440.69 mph, achieved in 1934. Macchi's chief designer was Mario Castoldi.

During the Second World War, Aermacchi, as producers of the *Regia Aeronautica's* best and fastest fighters, found themselves a target of the first importance for the allied bombers, with the result that they emerged into postwar days with production facilities more or less flattened.

Subsequently able to embark on a large reconstruction programme ... and obtain a licence to build Britain's de Havilland Vampire jet fighter, ... Aermacchi were still working under capacity. So diversification first brought about a three-wheel truck. This was unorthodox and very efficient (and is still being produced today by another company). Then, seeing the boom in motorcycle sales and wishing to have a stake in it, the Aermacchi management began the quest for a good designer who could produce a saleable lightweight. Their choice was Lino Tonti (today chief designer for Moto Guzzi), who had worked at Benelli and who had been engaged on aero engines during the war.

Tonti's initial design for Aermacchi, in 1950, was decidedly unorthodox. It was an open-frame lightweight with a 125 two-stroke engine which pivoted in unit with the rear suspension. Of particular interest was a luggage/tool container shaped (and positioned) like a fuel tank. This featured a hinged mounting on the steering column, allowing the rider to grip the dumpy 'tank' with his knees as on a conventional motorcycle. The real tank meanwhile was under the saddle. This machine, which looked like a scooter with motorcycle-size wheels, sold well and a sports version was successfully used as a trials mount, including participation in the ISDT of 1951 and 1952. The 1951 event incidentally was staged around Varese.

Next sporting interest came in 1955, when Tonti designed a record breaker, making full use of the wind tunnel facilities and other resources of the factory's aviation division. Powered by dohc engines of 48 and 75cc these were one of the first examples of a 'flying cigar', being extremely low to the ground and almost 10ft long. Placed behind the rider (pilot?) the engine had the peculiarity of having its cylinder and head inclined *rearward* at an angle of 20 degrees. The overhead cams were chain-driven, bore and stroke dimensions were 48cc: 40×39mm, 75cc: 44.5×43mm, and with a compression ratio of 10:1, power outputs of 7 bhp at 12,000 rpm and 9 bhp at 11,000 rpm respectively. One has to consider that at this time high-octane fuel was not available. The engines, which used wet sump lubrication, were in unit with four-speed gearboxes and final drive was by chain. Weight in running condition was 97kg (214 lb) for both machines.

The record attempts were carried out in early 1956 on the Milan-Varese *autostrada*. Neither weather nor road conditions were particularly ideal for the Aermacchi streamliner. Piloted by Massimo Pasolini (father of the legendary Renzo) the larger model recorded a speed of 100.2 mph over the flying mile and 108.8 mph over the flying kilometre, breaking, by a considerable margin, the records set up only a few months before by Germany's Adolf Baumm in his feet forward NSU 'flying hammock'. With the smaller engine, the 50cc standing mile was also broken, with a marked increase at 51.25 mph.

Soon after the successful record spree Tonti left to join FB Mondial. His place as technical director at Aermacchi was taken by Alfredo Bianchi, previously with Parilla and the famous car company Alfa Romeo. For Parilla, Bianchi had helped design the 250 ohc sports and racing singles which were so successful in the late 1940s and early 1950s.

Bianchi's first task at Aermacchi was to evolve a production model from a sketch of 'the ultimate motorcycle', which had been drawn up by Count Mario

One of the earliest Aermacchis – the Leffino – a mixture of motorcycle and scooter, with horizontal two-stroke engine in either 125 or 150cc capacity sizes.

The futuristic Chimera, the star of the 1956 Milan Show. Produced originally as a 175 and later as a 250, it proved a sales flop.

Ravelli, a notable automobile stylist who had himself been a racing motorcyclist of considerable repute, having had the distinction of winning the 1925 Italian GP at Monza on a GR, a machine of his own manufacture.

The new machine, the fully enclosed Chimera, first appeared in late 1956. With a capacity of 172.4cc (60×61mm) the newcomer aroused a considerable amount of interest, but the Chimera was destined never to prove a good seller, either at home or abroad. It was therefore decided to undress it to produce a more conventional machine. Ing. Bianchi went back to his drawing office, expressly charged to make as few changes as possible in order to keep manufacturing costs down to the bare minimum. And so this proved, with the only real difference in design being to the rear frame and swinging arm. On the Chimera a near horizontal single rear suspension unit was employed, whereas the undressed bike had a conventional swinging arm with twin vertical rear shocks.

At a time when the vast majority of Italian designers regarded overhead camshafts as absolutely imperative even for touring models, Bianchi had given the Chimera a push-rod motor. This was primarily in the interests of simpler maintenance, but he was also of the opinion that, even for sportsters, there was no real need for the ohc layout. And he was soon to be proved right – even for pure racing use.

When it first appeared, the Chimera was offered in only one engine size. But soon a quarter-litre version, 246.2cc (66×72mm), was introduced. But prior to this, in early 1957, a specially tuned 175, giving 15.5 bhp instead of the standard model's 13 bhp, was made available to a few selected riders for use in Italian Formula 3 Sport machine racing.

Like the purely touring models, there was soon a larger 250 variant of the sportster. This went so well that the factory stripped a 250 of its lights and the other road-going equipment and entered it for the Dutch TT at Assen in June 1960, ridden by Alberto Pagani, the son of 1949 World Champion Nello. Pagani Junior and his simple push-rod single came home a very creditable ninth. But even better was to come the following weekend at the Belgian Grand Prix. Held over the ultra-fast Spa Francorchamps circuit in the Ardennes, the combination of Pagani/Aermacchi amazed racing pundits around the world by scoring fifth place in a race won by a trio of MV Agusta twins, headed by World Champion Carlo Ubbiali, with team-mates Hocking and Taveri second and third, whilst Mike Hailwood piloted his screaming Ducati desmo twin into fourth spot.

On the production racing front there was more success, with an Aermacchi winning the important Monza six-hour event, whilst in Britain an Aermacchi Ala Verde (Green Wing) made its début in the Thruxton 500-miler, where, ridden by Arnold Jones and Horace Crowder, it led its class until forced to retire with gearbox trouble. That it left a real impression is summed up by *The Motor Cycle*, who referred to it as 'that fantastic Italian invader'.

These performances were to be just the beginning. At the final event of the year, held at Oulton Park in October, *Motor Cycle News* was able to record: 'In the 250cc class there was no one to touch Percy Tait and he romped away on Bill Webster's Aermacchi to win by a mile from Dan Shorey.' Mention of Bill Webster, known to many as *Websterini*, demands that his place in the story be related. Always an admirer of Italian motorcycles, having raced single-cylinder MVs for many years and sponsored countless other riders, Webster also owned a successful

English rider Percy Tait was one of the very first riders to race an Aermacchi single back in 1960.

motorcycle business in Crewe, Cheshire. The bike Tait had ridden to victory at Oulton was in fact the same bike as Pagani had campaigned in the GPs that year. Webster had obtained the use of it because he was about to become Aermacchi's first British importer.

1960 was also important for another reason, and one which in retrospect history records as not being in the interests of the marque in the long term. This was the 50 per cent stake taken in the motorcycle division of Aermacchi by the American Harley-Davidson concern. This came about for two reasons. The first was that by this time Aermacchi had re-established itself back in the aviation sector, and by then had four plants. Of these the chief one was the main factory in the town of Varese itself and up to this time the aircraft and motorcycle sections shared this facility. Also in the town was the assembly plant for the three-wheel delivery vehicles. Then on the outskirts of Varese, at the lakeside location at Schiranna, was the old seaplane factory, with its slipways into the lake and its lofty hangar,

which provided storage space for both the motorcycles and trucks. Finally, there were the aircraft assembly shops and airfield at Venegono, and a sideline, the *Cantiere Navale di Apuania*. The latter was the shipbuilding division, with four slipways at Marina di Carrara, where ships from 2500 to 16,000 tons were built. The whole operation had become almost unmanageable − for example, in the main plant, motorcycle, delivery truck and aircraft parts were all being produced and worked on alongside each other!

Meanwhile, Harley-Davidson needed a European plant with cheaper operating costs and the expertise to manufacture a range of lightweight motorcycles with which it could augment its Stateside V-twins. So the deal was struck and the motorcycles were from then on known as Aermacchi-Harley-Davidsons. Another facet of the deal was that all the two-wheel production would be transferred to the lakeside Schiranna location, leaving the main factory to produce solely aircraft. That year had also seen the company competing successfully in motocross, both with the horizontal push-rod 250 and a 498cc (88×82mm) dohc single, which featured a *vertical* cylinder!

1961 saw output stepped up appreciably, with many more machines exported than ever before, the vast majority of these going to North America. In Britain Bill Webster's organization now had a separate company, Italian Imports in Nantwich, which not only brought in small numbers of Aermacchi roadsters, mainly the Ala Verde sports model, but had signed up Alan Shepherd to partner Percy Tait for the new season. Back in Italy the factory backed not only Pagani, but also Gilberto Milani. April 1961 saw Alan Shepherd get off to a winning start at the BMCRC (British Motor Cycle Racing Club) annual Bemsee Hutchinson 100 at Silverstone. His victory in the 250 event came amidst controversy − after Mike Hailwood (Ducati) had been black-flagged for not notifying officials of a machine change.

And it was Hailwood who provided the main opposition that year to Shepherd, for when the Aermacchi rider was not winning, Hailwood on either a Ducati or Mondial would. The only other rider to have the regular use of an Aermacchi in Britain during 1961 was John Surtees's brother, Norman, who had made his début on one of the Varese singles at the 1960 Brands Hatch Christmas meeting. Even though an Aermacchi failed to finish in the top six at any of the classics that year, by the end of 1961 the fleet push-rod models had proved almost unbeatable at the national and club level.

So, as 1962 dawned, the Ala d'Oro (Golden Wing) was the bike which competitors worldwide aspired to own. The factory responded to this demand by building some 150 replicas of the machine raced by Pagani, Milani, Shepherd

Besides roadsters and racers, the Varese company also produced motocross bikes. These included an overhead cam 500 with vertical cylinder, and shown here, the more well-known 246cc ohv model with the famous horizontal unit.

and Tait, and virtually all were sold before the new racing season got under way. In Britain some 30 Ala d'Oros were imported that year and eager customers forked out a cool £457 11s. 9d. − or put another way you could have paid £512 8s. 0d. for an AJS 7R or £536 16s. 0d. for a 500 Manx Norton. To put all this more into perspective a Velocette Venom was £279 and a BSA Gold Star £325.

For this the new Aermacchi owner got a competitive quarter-litre machine, but those first over-the-counter racers were *not* as reliable as many may imagine. Quite simply, under the thin veneer of pukka racer was at heart a humble push-rod roadster. And this is where the problems started. Although fast − around 115 mph − these original long-stroke, wet clutch models were extremely fragile − and costly for their owners. Soon, besides the good race results for some, came the horror stories from others, mainly centred around seized big-end bearings and broken connecting rods. In addition, the wet clutch made starting a difficult task even with such a light machine. However, those that kept going were usually up near the front of the field.

Compared with the roadster version, the racer had a downdraught head with 30mm Dell 'Orto SS1 carb and remote float chamber, alloy cylinder barrel, forged high-compression piston, several more minor engine mods, close-ratio gears (but still four speeds), alloy 18-litre fuel tank painted red, single racing saddle, a pair of pukka racing Oldani brake hubs laced to 18in. alloy rims (roadsters had 17in. steel), camshaft-driven 85mm white face Veglia tacho and a chrome-plated shallow taper megaphone. Other differences included exposed stanchions on the 30mm front forks and a glass-fibre dolphin fairing.

Besides the pure racing version, the Ala d'Oro was also available in roadster trim for Italian Formula 3 events, but in this guise it was mainly sold as a 175. (The smaller engine was fitted with a straight pipe rather than a megaphone for racing.)

At Grand Prix level 1962 was dominated by the works four-cylinder Hondas, but even so Aermacchi showed up well. Perhaps the most noteworthy classic result was Pagani's fifth place in the IoM TT. In a race where there were only seven finishers, both Shepherd and Milani had also been well placed before being forced out. Pagani's average race speed was 85.5 mph.

Earlier, at the season opener in Spain, the same rider had finished fifth. Other finishers in the top six at GPs that year were Pierre Vervroegen (sixth in Belgium), Stuart

Graham (sixth in the Ulster race), Milani (fifth in Italy) and Dietrich (sixth in the Argentine).

Besides the real production racer several Ala Verde roadsters were converted into track bikes. These spurious examples can easily be exposed by their roadster polished alloy brakes, steel cylinder barrel, different front forks and several more minor details.

The Ala d'Oro was also sold in the States, as the Sprint. As the roadsters were often referred to under this title, in North America things tended to get a bit complicated. Ridden by several of the top American Harley riders these did well, not just in pure road racing, but also in flat track and scrambles events.

By the end of 1962 it seemed obvious to Ing. Bianchi that no more power could be extracted from the long-stroke 250, so he changed the bore and stroke to an over-square 72×61mm, giving 248.3cc. With this, power went up to 28 bhp at 9500 rpm (previous maximum had been 8000 rpm), and the adoption of a five-speed gearbox enabled more effective use of the power available. In addition, 1963 also saw an improvement in the level of reliability.

The other major change, at least in Britain, was that of importer. Sadly, early in the year Bill Webster died from a heart attack and was replaced in May by Syd Lawton, a notable ex-racer and well-known dealer from Southampton.

1963 also saw an interesting prototype appear at Imola. This had at first been envisaged to allow for competition in 500cc motocross at the end of 1962, by employing a short-stroke piston and cylinder to a long-stroke bottom end. The resulting square 72×72mm bore and stroke dimensions added up to 293cc. In this form it had only slightly more power than the 250, but more torque and less revs — a maximum of 9000. Even so Milani brought it home fifth at Hockenheim, West Germany, the first single behind the multis.

1964 saw it changed to a full 350, with 74mm bore and 80mm stroke, but it was only used by factory-supported riders that year; the highlights were a pair of fourth places by Milani at the West German GP at Solitude and by new signing Renzo Pasolini at the Italian Grand Prix at Monza in September. Yet another fourth place, this time at the Sachsenring in East Germany, was the best a 250 could do in the classics that year piloted by old hand Gilberto Milani. 1964 also saw a 250 Ala d'Oro again take overall victory in the Monza six-hour race during September, with Pagani and Giuseppe Visenzi as co-riders. And the American market was becoming increasingly important, with 75 per cent of the factory's production being shipped to the States.

After being thwarted by rain earlier in the year, Roger Reimann managed to bag a speed record for Harley-Davidson at the Bonneville Salt Flats in early October. Enclosed in a 14ft long shell the record breaker was powered by a specially prepared short-stroke 248cc Ala d'Oro road-racing engine (running on petrol). Reimann averaged 156.24 mph for the flying mile and 156.54 for the kilometre. The records were approved by the AMA but not the FIM, since no recognized observer was present. Hence the speeds constituted American records only.

The factory's racing support programme was much the same for 1965 as it had been for the latter part of 1964. Renzo Pasolini and Gilberto Milani, as works riders-cum-testers performing a similar task to those performed by Norton team men at the end of the 1950s, when the British factory adopted a policy of racing production Manx models. Alberto Pagani, on the other hand, was to ride a semi-private machine with a one-off tubular space-frame that he had built himself. The Aermacchi policy called for the works-supported riders to concentrate on the important international meetings in Italy and abroad, plus the classics, to enable Ing. Bianchi to improve still further the over-the-counter production racers for the following year.

Changes introduced into production examples for 1965 of both the 250 and 350 (the first year it was actually offered for sale) mainly concentrated on the transmission. A dry multi-plate clutch was fitted in place of the wet type previously employed and a more robust five-speed gear cluster replaced the previous year's component.

Around this time the first signs of conflict appeared between the Italian and American ideas of what constituted development. Ing. Bianchi realized that to remain competitive at world level it would be necessary eventually to offer an ohc design (this was in stark contrast to his original thinking of a decade previously, when designing the Chimera). So, to keep costs to a minimum, Bianchi designed a double overhead cam head for the existing flat single. Even though it offered the chance to give a much needed boost in power output *and* future sales chances, the Harley-Davidson faction won the day, saying that they wanted development confined to push-rod motors, so the whole of the ohc programme of engines and spares were sold to Dutch enthusiast André de la Porte. Later they passed on to Swiss enthusiast Yves Liengme, who still owns the dohc machine(s). There were in fact two machines, a 250 and 350. A private venture by factory employee Celestino Piva was also built.

1965 also saw the first interest by outsiders such as the Swiss Othmar Drixl, who began to offer frame kits and complete machines under the Drixton name. This trend later saw others such as the Rickman brothers involved in similar ventures, strangely not because of any real handling problem with the works machines, rather the specialist

Throughout the 1960s Aermacchi not only offered its over-the-counter Ala d'Oro racers to the public, but raced factory development models. Works rider Alberto Pagani is shown on just such a machine during the 1967 Junior (350cc) TT, in which he finished fourth.

frames provided riders with a riding position closer to the old British styles, which were still being campaigned by the vast majority of riders all over Europe.

As the 1965 racing season progressed it became increasingly clear that it was the 350 rather than the 250 in which Aermacchi's racing future lay. The larger engine offered a much superior power-to-weight ratio, and whereas in the quarter-litre class a whole host of machinery was coming on to the market, including Bultaco, Yamaha, Greeves, Cotton and DMW, in the 350 category the opposition, at non-works level, was limited to the ageing British singles, the AJS 7R and Manx Norton. All season the best an Aermacchi could manage in the 250 class at the classics was sixth, but in the 350 category there were a trio of fourth places, Pasolini in West Germany and Holland and Milani in Czechoslovakia.

As 1966 dawned, the top continental Aermacchi rider was, without doubt, the bespectacled Pasolini, who astounded everyone by scoring a sensational third spot at the classic season opener at Barcelona, Spain. Around the twists and turns of Monjuich Park, 'Paso' showed that he was a world star in the making, by finishing with only Mike Hailwood's Honda six and Derek Woodman's MZ in front of him. And old hand Pagani showed that he still was a force to be reckoned with, scoring third in the home round at Monza later in the season. But again the 350 proved superior with a whole string of top six placings at world level, the highlight of which was without doubt the second and third placings gained by Pasolini and Pagani at Monza.

In Britain Dave Degens had his best year to date with a whole string of wins on Syd Lawton's 350 Aermacchi. The Isle of Man Manx GP Lightweight race had made a return in 1964, following a long spell when there had been only the Junior (350) and Senior (500) events. In the 1964 event, Aermacchi had showed up well with 2nd, 3rd, 4th and 6th places, but had slumped to a highest of 8th in 1965. In the 1966 Lightweight TT the marque had scored 8th, 11th and 13th with works entries, but for the first time the Varese factory won a race over the demanding 37¾-mile Isle of Man TT circuit, when Bob Farmer took his privately entered 250 to victory at an average speed of 86.20 mph for the four-lap Lightweight Manx Grand Prix.

As Bianchi had predicted, the push-rod engine was now approaching its limit of development and although superior to the majority of AJS and Nortons in the 350 category, the appearance of the Yamaha TDIC in 1967 killed the 250 stone dead. As the 1967 production racers were the peak of Aermacchi four-stroke development it is worth relating their specification in full. It is also worth noting that unlike the original long-stroke wet-clutch four-speed 250s, which were extremely fragile, the 1967 bikes were generally the very model of reliability. Both the 250 and 350 retained the previous short-stroke capacity, the same bore and stroke, and with compression ratios of the 250, 11.5:1 and the 350, 11:1, and with maximum safe rpm of the 250 10,200 and the 350 8500.

The crankcases were of an improved design, incorporating a 3½-pint wet sump. The 1967 models had only one oil pump, a feed-type, and used a gravity scavenge return system. The oil was filtered through two nylon strainers. A further improvement that year was made to the camshaft oil feed, which was now controlled by small jets. Con-rods were hand forged from solid chrome nickel molybdenum of 85-97 tons per square inch tensile strength. These had the grain running longitudinally and large double strengthening webs around both the big and small ends. The former consisted of a 30mm crankpin, and a high-tensile light alloy cage with double row $\frac{1}{4} \times \frac{5}{16}$in. rollers.

The cylinder head casting had been improved with much deeper finning and considerably more metal around the four holding-down stud holes, providing more support for valve guides and seats. The spark plug was repositioned and was now almost vertical. A 30mm inlet port and 39mm inlet valve head diameter provided increased breathing, particularly at higher engine revolutions. The gearbox was redesigned with larger gear pinions, whilst the dry clutch was improved to free immediately and was lighter to operate. The cycle parts remained much as before, although the rear sub-frame had been modified and there was now a choice of either Oldani or Fontana brakes. Dry weight (without the fairing) was 210 lb. Performance saw the 250 now capable of a genuine 120 mph and the 350 another 10 mph.

The main development with the flat single after 1967 was the introduction of 380 and 402cc engines, enabling it to compete in the 500cc category. There was also a shorter-

Besides its push-rod singles, Aermacchi also produced a range of two-strokes, for both road and track. The first racer was a 125 single. The photograph shows the Mainini-Drixl special. This not only featured a one-off frame, but rotary valve induction, circa 1970.

stroke version of the 350 with a capacity of 348cc. But it was largely the 500 class, plus races such as the Isle of Man TT and the Manx Grand Prix, which was to become the machine's forté. The new breed of Yamaha production racers, the TD2 and TR2, which appeared at the end of the 1960s, effectively made the opposition (including Aermacchi) at club and national level totally obsolete in both the 250 and 350 classes.

At international level riders such as Carruthers, Steenson, Findlay, Milani, Bergamonti and Barnett all did well, even as late as 1970, with perhaps Alan Barnett's near 100 mph lap in the 350 TT being the highlight. But everyone, including Aermacchi, knew in their hearts that the day of the four-stroke, singles in particular, was over. So common sense ruled and the Varese development team decided the time had come for a totally new concept.

During the summer of 1967 Aermacchi produced their first 'stroker' effort designed by West German Peter Durr. This was based on the production roadster which had appeared a few months earlier and was a simple piston ported single-cylinder with air cooling. With a capacity of

Sue Tully of Greenford, Middlesex, with her 1973 Harley-Davidson (Aermacchi) SS350. The last of the famous flat singles were manufactured the following year. The American influence is clearly visible.

Raced as AMF Harley-Davidsons, the Aermacchi two-stroke twins won four world titles in the mid-1970s, ridden by Walter Villa, who is seen here at Imola.

Developed from the original piston-ported 125 of 1967, by 1976 it had become the Harley-Davidson SS125 and besides Stateside styling it had also gained a duplex frame, 12-volt electrics, oil injection and a five-speed box.

123.15cc (56×50mm) and 9.7:1 compression ratio, 27mm Dell 'Orto carburettor and four-speed box, it produced 19 bhp at 9200 rpm. The unit was mounted in a spine-type frame, with the usual Cerani suspension and Oldani front brake (of smaller sizes than the four-strokes) and a standard production component at the rear.

The machine made its début in July 1967, when it was ridden by Pagani into third spot at Zingonia. The following year saw it changed and improved considerably with a brand new double-cradle tubular frame, new cylinder head and barrel, and a five-speed gearbox. Power was now over 20 bhp. Although it was never popular, in the same way as the legendary flat single thumpers had been, the ⅛-litre 'stroker' none the less proved competitive, even at the highest level.

1969 saw the 125 single achieve some good results in GPs, with riders who included Dodds, Bertarelli and Carruthers. In fact, it was the last-named who gained the best result, second place behind 1969 World Champion Dave Simmonds in the Isle of Man TT. Fellow Aussie Johnny Dodds gave Aermacchi their first ever classic win, when he piloted his 125 to victory in the West German GP at the Nürburgring. The breakthrough as regards *real* success at world level was not to come until later, with a

completely new concept entirely for Aermacchi, the two-stroke twin.

The first the outside world saw of this design was when Renzo Pasolini, who had returned to his first love after four years with rivals Benelli, whistled the prototype 250 around Modena autodrome on 25 February, 1971. This new battle iron from the Varese factory was not the work of Alfredo Bianchi, who had retired, but his successor, William Soncini. In fact the design was first initiated two years earlier, in 1969, when the Americans suggested that they needed a 250 to compete with the Yamaha twins.

The engine employed the cylinders of the successful 125 racer (which by then developed 25 bhp) and therefore the bore and stroke remained at an oversquare 56×50mm. Fed by twin 30mm Dell 'Ortos coupled to flat-type rubber-mounted Amal float chambers, electronic ignition by a Dansi system powered by a generator on the nearside of the crankshaft and with a compression ratio of 12.5:1, the 248.06cc powerhouse churned out an impressive 46 bhp at the rear wheel at between 10,500 and 11,000 rpm. In the interests of simplicity (at least that was the official reason) rotary disc valves were not considered necessary (again following the Yamaha formula) and lubrication was by a simple petroil mix. Drive to a six-speed gearbox was by straight-cut primary gears on the offside, where there was also the tachometer drive and dry clutch. The crankcase was split horizontally. The weight of the prototype was 125kg, but within a short period of time the original iron cylinders were replaced by lighter alloy components with a saving of no less than 10kg.

1971 was very much a development year, but Pasolini ended the season with a fifth place at the Spanish GP, but there was no real hint of what 1972 was to bring. When the 1972 season got under way, Pasolini, then the sole factory representative, scorched to wins in Italy, Yugoslavia and Spain against a horde of Yamahas in the 250 class. Entirely new for 1972 was a 347.4cc (64×54mm) 350. The larger-engined bike made its GP début at the West German event in April, where Pasolini came home fifth. Then came two thirds in France and Austria, followed by a second, behind Agostini's MV, on home ground at Imola. Other seconds were gained in East Germany, Czechoslovakia, and Spain. Even so the 350 was never destined to be quite as successful as the smaller twin.

At the end of 1972 Harley-Davidson purchased all the remaining Aermacchi shares (the Italian company was by then firmly re-established in the aviation business). There was a new 65cc mini motorcycle (called the Shortster in the States) and a sporting 350 ohv flat single roadster, the TV, the latter complementing the standard touring Sprint model. On the racing front, in 1973 the two-stroke twins had yet more power and watercooling. Pasolini had two new team-mates, Frenchman Michel Rougerie and Bruno Kneubühler from Switzerland. And both the 250 and 350 were offered as over-the-counter racers for the first time under the prefix RR. Things looked set for a truly great year. But as history now testifies 'Black Sunday', 20 May, 1973, changed all that. At Monza in the 250 Italian GP, Pasolini and Jarno Saarinen crashed and both died. The accident, which was at first rumoured to have been caused by the Italian's machine seizing, was later proved to have happened through no fault of either machines or riders, but oil left on the circuit from a previous race.

The resultant outcry ensured that for eight years the Italian GP was staged at either Mugelo, Misano or Imola, but not Monza. As evidence of how the Italian nation felt about Renzo Pasolini, some 15 years after his death, Ducati (for whom he had never ridden) even named a motorcycle after him!

Immediately after Pasolini's accident, Rougerie proved the most successful of the Varese factory's riders, who now included Gianfranco Bonera. 1974 saw Harley-Davidson Varese back in racing in force and used an improved 250, which was not only fast but also reliable. Bonera had switched to MV Agusta and his replacement was Walter Villa, who backed up Rougerie (at least that is how the season started). Very soon it was Villa who proved that he was the best, not only in the team, but the world, and at the end of 1974 he was 250 World Champion, with wins at Imola, Assen, Imatra and Brno. Meanwhile a third at Imola was the best the 350 could do. By now the 250 was pumping out 58 bhp at 12,000 rpm and the 350, 64 bhp at 11,000 rpm, giving 155 mph and 160 mph respectively.

Mighty Yamaha found it difficult competing in the quarter-litre class for the first time since Benelli had won back in 1969, while on the production side a record number of 45,000 machines were produced, the majority of which were exported to North America, including X and Z 90s, SX 125, SS and SX 350s and the new SX 175 trail bike. Just to prove that 1974 was no fluke, the following year Villa and Rougerie repeated the performance, but not only did Villa win the Championship, but his team-mate came second, soundly thrashing the pack of finely tuned Yamahas.

In 1976 Bonera went back to Harley-Davidson after two years with MV. That year Villa and Bonera rode the 'unbeatable' 250 and a new, more powerful 350, which the Varese team had come up with over the winter. This now produced 70 bhp at 11,400 rpm and around 165 mph. There was also an 80 bhp, four-carb 500cc racer, but this proved unreliable and uncompetitive. Villa retained his 250 crown, making it a hat-trick, but took the 350 title as well, a remarkable performance for such a small équipe.

Then came a quick break-up of an unbeatable team, with 1977 proving a major disappointment. Unknown to outside circles at the time, the Varese factory was by now well and truly in the grip of cost accountants, who knew nothing about motorcycles. This was because the giant American conglomerate AMF (American Machine & Foundry Corporation) which had owned Harley-Davidson both in the States and Italy since the early 1970s, had decided to put the motorcycle company under the microscope.

On the surface the racing season started in much the same way as it had done for the past three years, with Villa winning, this time at the Venezuelan GP (on the 250). Cost cutting had shown its head even before the season started with only two riders, Villa and new boy Franco Uncini, who won the Italian GP at Imola (the third in the series) after taking a third in West Germany. Then came the *real* problems, not only were the 350s totally outclassed (the highest position that year was a fifth by Uncini in Holland), but after his early victory in South America Villa went *six* GPs before even finishing on the 250 and then took a fourth in Holland. By this stage in the season his chance of retaining the Championship for a record fourth term was almost impossible. Even so, at the next round in Belgium he scored his second victory of the year. After this, even though the Varese factory staged a mini-comeback with wins in Finland (Villa) and Czechoslovakia (Uncini), the 250 World Championship went to outsider Mario Lega on a Morbidelli. Strangely Lega only won a single GP, the Yugoslavian at Opitija, but his consistent scoring at almost every round ensured him the title. It was little consolation to the Harley team that Villa and Uncini took second and third places in the championship. If 1977 had been a disappointment, then 1978 can be labelled a total disaster. Except for a third in Belgium and an eighth in Czechoslovakia, Villa either did not finish or was way down the field. Uncini was now aboard a private Yamaha, later to re-emerge in 1979 on a 500 Suzuki and later still to become Champion of the World in the blue ribband class in 1982 backed by Roberto Gallina. The reason for this dramatic change in fortune can be traced back to the decision in December 1977 that all the factory machines should be handed over to the newly formed Team Nolan (Nolan was a helmet manufacturer) and that the riders would be Villa and Claudio Lusuardi. Villa would contest the 250 and 350 world series, with Lusuardi contesting the 50cc world title on a Bultaco and back up Villa in the 250 class. He would also contest the 50 and 250 Italian championships. In retrospect this decision to close the factory's racing department, when there were new designs, a disc-valve monoshock 250 twin and three-cylinder 350, acts as proof that AMF had already set the wheels in motion to kill off the Italian operation.

It is unknown if the sole American still at Varese, Ken Thorpe, the managing director, actually knew of the corporate decision until news broke in May that year that the Italian arm of Harley-Davidson was to be put into liquidation. This came into effect in late July, when the whole of Italy traditionally closes for almost four weeks until the end of August. During this time a company, at that time *almost* totally unknown in the motorcycle world, Cagiva SpA, emerged as clear favourites to buy Aermacchi. And so the era of the Aermacchi–Harley-Davidson marriage was finally over, ending in a total break-up. But as one set of players passed into history, a new star, Cagiva (see Chapter 6), was born.

CHAPTER 2

Aprilia

Although Aprilia (no connection to the infamous electrical concern) is generally regarded as a young company within the Italian motorcycle industry, it was created as long ago as 1956 by Alberto Beggio, the father of the existing president, Ivano Beggio.

Initially the newly created company based its activities upon the construction of bicycles, but in 1960 Aprilia built its first powered two-wheeler, a moped. Until the mid-1970s Aprilia's principal revenue came from pedal rather than engine power. However, by 1975 it began to look as if bicycles were going out of fashion and there had been a rapid decline in sales figures. This proved the moment when a faction at the Noale (near Venice) factory backed a scheme to build a brand new motocross motorcycle. Ultimately made in a variety of engine capacities, this was powered by bought-in engines such as Sachs, Hiro and Rotax, and with the last-named it was to start an association which continues to the present day.

This project proved to the management that it could compete with the best, as Aprilia was soon a force to be reckoned with out on the race circuit. In 1976 Aprilia participated with outstanding success in both national and international motocross competitions throughout the length and breadth of Italy. These racing prototypes acted as development machines for a series of off-road production dirt bikes which followed from the 1977 model year. This resulted in the Noale company winning the 125 and 500cc Italian motocross Championships in 1976 and 1977.

Through to 1982 Aprilia continued to consolidate a position of offering its customers a line which mainly concentrated upon mopeds and the off-road machinery, notably enduro and motocross bikes, which were, provided their riders had the ability, capable of challenging for honours straight from the crate.

That year the company's turnover was some £5½ million, yet five years later this had risen to a staggering £45 million! Sales director Pablo Pizzorni says it's all due to the philosophy 'of staying very close to the young mentality'. In other words the Aprilia management is tuned into what today's youngsters wear, what colours are in fashion, the music they listen to and even what films and TV programmes they watch. For example, whilst other Italian manufacturers were complaining about the helmet law introduced in 1986, Aprilia began marketing their own helmets in outrageous fashion-conscious designs and colours, so effectively turning a problem into a positive advantage. Another factor in Aprilia's sudden success is that they believe in youth; the average age of their employees is under 30 and even the president is only in his early 40s.

There are no 'middle ground' Aprilia motorcycles (the ride-to-work commuter moped has long since been axed). The roadster models are split into three distinct categories; road racer replica, Paris-Dakar on-off road, or glittering chrome and snazzy paintwork custom bike.

Although Aprilia no longer manufacture motocrossers, the company's sporting involvement continues through trials and road racing, both of which are supported at works level, and in the sale of replicas.

In both fields they have been notably successful. Loris Reggiani's performances in the 250cc World Championships between 1985 and 1987 brought attention to the marque from road-race enthusiasts the world over. With the introduction of the Climber in 1988, the company set the pace in the one-day trials market with its watercooled 276.6cc (76×61mm) rotary valve single.

With its small size Aprilia had managed to change direction like a small yacht compared to many other manufacturers who resemble a giant oil tanker. As the company grows bigger it will obviously become more difficult to move quite so quickly, but it appears that Aprilia is determined to stay one jump ahead of its competitors. And unlike many companies the management is alive to the need to incorporate new thinking. But although competition bikes have played a role in the Aprilia miracle, it is the success of the standard production roadsters which has really made things happen.

In 1982 a new street model, the STX125 with liquid cooling, monoshock rear suspension and a fresh style, was launched. The success of this machine convinced the company's president, Ivano Beggio, that this was the way to go. This one model created the knowledge that by combining the latest technical innovation and styling Aprilia could be a winner out on the street, in the same way as it had out on the motocross circuit.

Aprilia first came to notice with some excellent off-road machines in the mid-1970s, with models such as this 125 enduro with German Sachs motor and seven-speed gearbox.

The number of units manufactured illustrates this; 1981 saw 4500 motorcycles, which by 1988 had risen to almost 40,000, 18,000 of which were in the all-important 125cc sector, so placing Aprilia third overall in the Italian market. This was a fantastic achievement for a company which hardly anyone had ever heard of a few short years before.

Aprilia's main object now is to break into foreign markets and they realize that this will mean new models, and presents their most difficult challenge yet. As proof of just how difficult the company's task really is, the 1989 range had only two models above 125cc, the 600 Tuareg Wind trial bike and the specialized Climber Trials bike.

So a massive investment programme costing 60 billion lire (£24 million) is being phased over 1989, 1990 and 1991, with a target of expanding the model range up to and including 1000cc and 25 different models. If this was not a bold enough plan, Aprilia also have the design of an advanced 500 GP road racer on the stocks which could be ready by 1991. But their main concern is the development of five brand new engines, including a five-valve per cylinder 750 V-twin and a 250 V-twin two-stroke which could be slotted into the existing AFI Sintesi chassis. This latter machine has largely been conceived to sell in Japan, where Aprilias are well established and highly rated. There are currently over 90 people working on the new engine designs out of a total workforce of 300. Twenty-five per cent of production was exported in 1988, with the main priority being mainland Europe, Switzerland, France and Portugal being their best markets. There is also a co-operation agreement in force with the Spanish Derbi

Entrance to the Noale factory . . .

. . . and part of its interior, photographed during November 1988.

Aprilia gained considerable publicity through the efforts of works rider Loris Reggiani, shown here in vivid action during the 1985 season. His machine employed a specially tuned Austrian Rotax in-line twin engine, with a capacity of 250cc.

Typical of the current Aprilia model range, the 600 Tuareg Wind. It has every modern innovation, including four valves per cylinder, upside-down forks, monoshock rear suspension and electric starting.

marque (Derbi are Aprilia's importer for that country).

Aprilia also own three other factories besides the motorcycle plant at Noale. One of these manufactures sunglasses, the other two accessories for the motorcycle trade. The latter plants have played a vital role in Aprilia's progress. One of the age-old criticisms of Italian motorcycles had centred around ancillary components. By producing much of this themselves Aprilia have had control over the standard of finish that the vast majority of

Italian manufacturers can only dream of. An Aprilia spokesman told me, 'Reliability, after-sales service and a good parts back-up are vital, but so is a finish which stays good; people judge on what they see out on the street.' Aprilia have also created a new company whose sole business is spare parts, again vitally important but often overlooked.

Then comes performance, for good looks are of no use if the bike does not go. The AFI Sintesi not only looks as though it will do 100 mph, but it can achieve it. It also handles and brakes like a racer. With all these qualities and its superb style it should be a winner. This leaves just one problem, price. If Aprilia are to mount an effective export challenge, somehow they have to get nearer Japanese competitive prices. When this chapter was written in May 1990 the price of the street racer AFI Aprilia was some £1000 more expensive in Britain than the market leader, the Yamaha TZR125.

Aprilia claim to be aiming for a target of some 100,000 machines by the end of 1992. This is a tall order indeed — can they do it? I would not like to bet on it either way, but on the basis of past results they might just surprise everyone and achieve it. President Ivano Beggio must have the last word: 'I have a high respect for the Japanese product. However, Aprilia tries to offer the market something different, which comes to the top of its category.'

I for one will be watching future developments at Aprilia with great interest . . .

CHAPTER 3

Benelli

Six brothers, all still young enough to willingly accept the guidance of an astute and devoted mother, founded a small mechanical workshop in Pesaro, on the Adriatic coast, in 1911. At first the workshop's activities were restricted to the repair of cars and motorcycles, both quite capable of taxing even the most gifted engineering student in those days, and anything else mechanical, including firearms. Soon, however, the brothers began a limited amount of manufacturing on their own account. They began to produce parts for not only cars, but aircraft, and this latter development was accelerated by the outbreak in 1914 of the First World War, during which time the Pesaro workshop was kept at full stretch producing components for the military.

With the end of the hostilities, the Benelli brothers then turned their attention to a new field. In Italy, as elsewhere in much of Europe, there was a new demand for cheap mechanical transport, a demand which gave rise in Italy to the forerunners of autocycles and mopeds. The Benellis produced their first engine, a 98cc two-stroke power unit to be mounted (à la Velosolex of today) in front of the steering column of a conventional pedal cycle. Drive from this auxiliary engine was transmitted, by chain, to the front wheel. Unfortunately the Benelli engine had an inherent problem. Quite simply it developed *too* much power, and rapidly caused the destruction of the hapless bicycle to which it was attached!

There was only one logical step which could be taken: to build a frame which could withstand the engine's performance. And with that in mind came the very first Benelli motorcycle. Introduced in 1921, it featured a full loop frame, with girder front forks. The 98cc two-stroke engine had magneto ignition and transmitted its power via a separate two-speed gearbox and chain drive. Not long afterwards a larger 150cc model was added.

After the war, one of the brothers took very little further interest in the family workshop. As the Lancia car agent in Ancona, Francesco Benelli had quite enough to keep him busy. Of the other five, Giovanni and Giuseppe were the engineering brains, while Filippo and Domenico looked after the financial and commercial sectors of the business and Antonio (soon to be known as Tonino), youngest of the six, had one driving desire in life, to prove

his ability as a road racer.

By 1923, when the 150cc machine had been added to the Benelli list, young Tonino finally got his chance, and no less an event than the Italian Grand Prix at Monza was where he chose to make his début. Far from overawed by the occasion, Tonino finished a magnificent fifth in the hotly contested 175cc category. His machine, although specially tuned, was still based around the company's production 150cc model.

The following year saw his first victory, in the Parma-Poggio di Berceto hill climb. At the time this was one of the most famous motor sport events in the Italian calendar, so the victory was all the more welcome, particularly as it had been achieved on the '150', competing against larger 175cc bikes. There were further successes in 1925 and 1926, but things really began to open up for Tonino in 1927.

By then his elder brothers had built a pukka racing machine for him, a 175 ohc single, which not only had a very competitive performance but was the first of a long line of overhead camshaft models from the Benelli company. That year Tonino, proudly riding the machine bearing his name, had several victories, not only in Italy but also abroad. The 172cc (62×57mm) engine at first had coil valve springs, which were soon replaced by hairpins. Power output was a class-leading 10 bhp at 6500 rpm.

Rival manufacturers attempted to narrow the gap between the performance of their own machines and that of Benelli, but before they had quite managed it brothers Giovanni and Giuseppe had provided Tonino with an even more potent piece of machinery in the shape of the dohc version of the 175. On this the bore and stroke became 'square' at 60.5mm, giving 173.8cc. This appeared in 1932 and from 1935 a 250 version was also developed. When one considers that improved variants of this design were still being raced in the early 1960s one can appreciate just how advanced this particular machine was when it first appeared.

Lone hand Tonino was joined by several other riders, notably Baschieri, who gained the marque's first classic victory when he won his class in the 1931 Swiss Grand Prix. Other Benelli competitors included Alberti, Aldrighetti and the legendary Dorino Serafini (later to win

Photographed on 17 October, 1929, the Benelli brothers, left to right, Tonino, Francesco, Giovanni, Giuseppe, Filippo and Mino.

The Benelli 175 Monza Sport was a popular and speedy mount in the mid-1930s.

worldwide acclaim with the four-cylinder Gilera in the days immediately prior to the Second World War).

1932 was to be Tonino's last season, and together with Baschieri and Serafini the Benelli team swept all before them. In October Tonino scored his last victory at the French Grand Prix at Montlhéry – by over two minutes! But a month later he crashed at speed in torrential rain at the Tigullio circuit, near Genoa. The result was that he broke a·leg, an arm and five ribs and suffered serious internal injuries. Unconscious for some two weeks, he finally recovered, but his racing days were over.

Without their leader, and Serafini who had 'defected' to ·rivals MM, the following year Benelli lost the 175cc Italian Championship which they had held for several years. But Giovanni Benelli applied his magical tuning touch that winter, so the 1934 season saw new team rider Rossetti regain the title for the Pesaro marque. Thereafter, the 175cc title was discontinued for 20 years, but Benelli responded by merely transforming their dohc single into a 250.

By the mid-1930s the Pesaro company had grown to be one of the *Pentarchia* (the famous big five) Italian manufacturers, the others being Bianchi, Garelli, Gilera and Moto Guzzi. But enthusiasm for road racing continued, and in 1935 work was begun on an enlarged version of their existing racer as a contender for the increasingly important 250cc category.

The new engine followed the lines of the original 175

The Benelli équipe at the Italian Grand Prix at Monza in 1938. From the left the riders are Soprani, Martelli and Rossetti, while *Commendatore* Giovanni Benelli is on the right of the photograph.

double knocker very closely with its gear-driven cams, dry sump lubrication and separate transmission. The main difference was that to achieve the increased engine size of 248cc, a long-stroke (62×78mm) solution was used and the exhaust valve had a modified outlet. Its first success was a new world speed record for the flying kilometre at 181.818 kph (around 113 mph). This was not only faster than the existing 250 record, but also the 350.

However, the Benelli 250 could not compete with the latest Guzzis until the following year, when its bore and stroke were altered to 65×75mm, giving 248.8cc. It also suffered a number of mechanical problems, which meant that 1936 and 1937 were largely taken up with further development. Meanwhile the European Championships were totally dominated by Moto Guzzi and the German company DKW.

The new machine's first real racing success came in 1937, when Martelli won the Milano−Taranto marathon. Tonino Benelli, now recovered from his 1932 crash, had made something of a comeback by acting as self-appointed factory tester. And it was during just such a sortie, on the Pesaro-Riccione coast road, that this most enthusiastic and daring of the Benelli brothers was to meet his death, when he was killed in September 1937.

By the middle of 1938 almost every mainland European factory, as well as AJS and Velocette in Britain, had accepted supercharging as something which was there to stay. The Benelli concern was no exception and they attacked the matter from two totally opposed angles. One was with a suitably converted single-cylinder 250, the other a superbly crafted watercooled four-cylinder model, again

of 250cc, which developed 62 bhp. But unfortunately before either could be fully race tested the war came along and with it the end of Benelli's supercharging plans.

However, the Pesaro concern did have the satisfaction of seeing the Irish rider E. A. (Ted) Mellors score an easy victory in the 1939 Lightweight TT in the Isle of Man at an average speed of 74.26 mph. The race was run for the most part in wet, murky conditions and it represented the factory's and Mellors's first TT success.

With the war came the destruction of the Benelli plant, and all the machinery which the brothers had saved from the ruins of their factory was commandeered by the German forces and transported north to the Fatherland for the war effort, together with everything else that might be of use, if only as scrap metal. But the priceless racing machines escaped. They were dismantled and concealed, together with the watercooled four, and hidden for the duration of hostilities in a dried-up well.

With no factory or machinery, Benelli were unable to make an early resumption of production after the war, unlike rivals such as Gilera and Guzzi. Not only this, but there was a family row which saw Giuseppe depart with his sons Marco and Luigi to found the Motobi enterprise (see Chapter 14).

Even if they were not in a position to immediately benefit from the motorcycling boom which swept Italy following the end of the war, from as early as 1945 the brothers had brought the pre-war racers out of concealment for a resumption of the battle with rivals Moto Guzzi. Men such as Ciai, Francisci and Martelli scored a number of victories for Benelli during the period 1945-47, and for

Pre-war, Benelli built this superbly crafted supercharged four-cylinder 250. Post-war the FIM changed the rules, so it was never raced.

Dario Ambrosini, world champion with his double-knocker Benelli single in 1950.

1948 Dario Ambrosini rejoined the Pesaro marque after a spell as a Guzzi rider and almost immediately brought international success. The FIM instituted the new World Championship Series in 1949 and Ambrosini and Benelli responded by finishing second overall in the 250cc title stakes, behind Bruno Ruffo's Guzzi. At the final round in Italy the Monza crowd saw Ambrosini score a sensational victory, with champion Ruffo down in fourth place. A second Benelli piloted by Umberto Masetti was third.

The Monza result was a foretaste of what was to come the following year, when in 1950 Ambrosini took the Championship and won every round, except in Ulster, where Englishman Maurice Cann rode his Guzzi to victory.

In 1951, after winning the Swiss Grand Prix over the

tricky Bremgarten circuit at Berne and finishing a close second behind Tommy Wood (Guzzi) in the Lightweight TT, Ambrosini was killed in a most unfortunate accident during practice for the French GP at Albi, when he skidded and lost control of his machine on molten tar. Shocked by the death of its lone star rider, Benelli withdrew from racing, and did not appear in anything like an official capacity again until 1959.

On the production side, the factory had only really begun to get back to normal in 1950, where at the Milan Show held at the end of that year they displayed pre-war-designed 500 and 250 four-stroke singles in touring guise and a new 98cc two-stroke, in standard and de luxe form, built into a frame distinguished by the absence of any front down tube. A year later the 98 had become a 125, which as the Leoncino (Little Lion) was to win fame following its victory in the 1953 Giro d'Italia (The Tour of Italy), ridden by Leopoldo Tartarini (later to head the Italjet factory).

The highlight of the 1951 Milan Show (actually held in late January 1952) was a 250cc overhead valve vertical twin, the Leonessa (Lioness). Together with the Leoncino, this had a long and successful production life thoughout the 1950s. Interestingly the smaller machine was produced in both two- and four-stroke versions.

But except for these models, Benelli did not have much to shout about as regards standard production models until the line was broadened as a result of an amalgamation in 1962 (following the death of Giuseppe Benelli) of the Motobi and Benelli interests, just one year after the original company had celebrated its Golden Jubilee. The last new Benelli design before this had been the 172cc (62×57mm) ohv single, in either Turismo or Sport form. This made its début during 1959.

In racing it was not until 1959 that the marque felt inclined to pick up the threads again, and that year came back with a considerably revised version of the long-running double knocker 250 single, ridden by Dickie Dale, Geoff Duke and the dashing young Italian Silvio Grassetti. The motor was at last modified to an oversquare 70mm bore and stroke of only 64.8mm (248.1cc), which pumped out 33 bhp at 11,500 rpm, compared to Ambrosini's Championship winning machine which offered 29 bhp at 9400 rpm.

One of the few 1959 successes of the revamped single was in the non-championship Swiss Grand Prix, run over a 'round-the-houses' circuit at Locarno, where Geoff Duke waltzed away from the rest of the pack. It was soon apparent that the single, however expertly ridden, could not hold its own against the latest multis that were beginning to appear at Grand Prix level. So in 1960 Benelli produced its second four, this time air-cooled and, of course, without

Benelli's most successful production bike of the 1950s was the 125 Leoncino. It was offered in both two-stroke (as shown) and four-stroke versions.

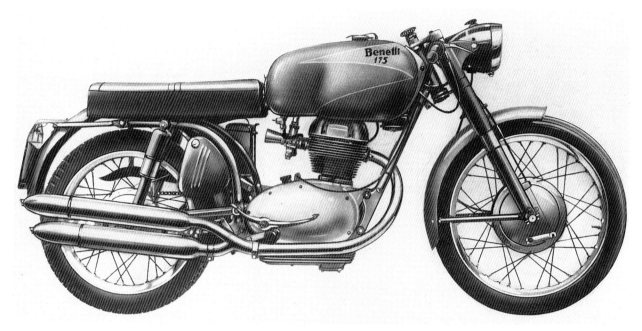

The Pesaro company introduced a brand new model for the 1959 season, the Sport version of this 172cc (62×57mm) ohv single is shown. It has typical Italian style of the period.

Bruno Spaggiari testing the new Benelli 250 four during 1960.

a supercharger.

Designed by Ing. Savelli, initial testing was carried out by Bruno Spaggiari, but it was not until 1962 that the machine was race ready and then the rider was Grassetti. He won his second race with the machine at Cesenatico. Although everyone in Italy thought that this would be the start of a serious challenge, the new four proved incapable of beating either the ultra rapid Morini single ridden by Tarquinio Provini or the latest Japanese four-cylinder Hondas. And even though the company signed Provini at the end of 1963, even this was not enough. For 1964 Benelli made several improvements to its 246.3cc (44×40.5mm) four, but although Provini won the opening Spanish GP at Barcelona's Monjuich Park the rest of the season proved disappointing and the Italian Championship went to Morini and its new rider, Giacomo Agostini.

1965 saw Provini and his Benelli at last take the Italian title, but this was a somewhat hollow victory, because Morini had effectively retired after Agostini had taken up an offer to ride for Count Agusta's MV team. Its one World Championship success that year was when Provini won the Italian GP at Monza in torrential rain, ahead of the East German Heinz Rossner's MZ twin. Remi Venturi on another Pesaro four was third.

Meanwhile Benelli had also been busy preparing a larger 343.1cc (51×42mm) for the 350 class. Together with an improved 250 four Provini had high hopes for 1966, but this was ended, together with his racing career, after a

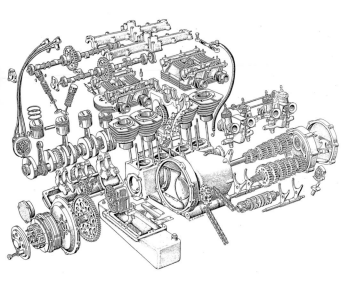

Exploded view of the four-cylinder engine as it was in 1962.
Note the distributor ignition and gear drive to the double
overhead camshafts.

high-speed spill in practice for the IoM TT. Then Benelli signed the Aermacchi star Renzo Pasolini as its new rider to replace the injured Provini. Soon 'Paso', as he was known, was proving his worth. He made his and Benelli's début in the 500cc class late in 1966 by winning at the Vallelunga circuit, north of Rome, with an overbored 350 four, which by now sported a 16-valve cylinder head.

At the beginning of 1967 a larger 491cc model made a race-winning début at Modena in the opening Italian meeting of the season, where Pasolini beat Agostini's MV by a fraction of a second. With this victory came a period, at least in Italy, of a closely contested rivalry between Benelli and MV and Agostini and Pasolini. In the races held along the Adriatic coast, 'Paso' often beat his rival, especially in the 350cc category. This constant competition sharpened the Pesaro-built fours, with the result that they became both more powerful and lighter. In 1968 Pasolini came home second in the 350cc World Championship series, even though he did not win a classic event.

At the end of 1968 the Japanese manufacturers with-

Works rider Silvio Grassetti aboard the Pesaro-built four during the 1962 Spanish Grand Prix at Montjuich Park, Barcelona.

drew and Benelli decided to concentrate its efforts at world level exclusively on the 250 class. The result was that Benelli riders Pasolini and the Australian Kel Carruthers won a total of six Grands Prix that year, with the Aussie finally taking the title after Pasolini put himself out of the running with *two* major accidents that season. The last one in Finland sidelined him for the rest of the season.

Benelli then withdrew once more, with Carruthers going to the USA, where he became Yamaha's top rider and tuner in the States, whilst Pasolini returned to Aermacchi.

Although stars such as Mike Hailwood and Jarno Saarinen both rode Benellis on occasion during 1971, the Pesaro factory was by now in the grip of a deep financial crisis, which was only resolved when, later that year, the Argentinian Alejandro de Tomaso acquired the ailing company. At that time Benelli had a real mixture of standard production models, including a whole range of mini-bikes, various four-stroke ohv singles based on the old Motobi design and the relatively new 650 Tornado. The latter was a 643cc parallel twin, with its cylinders inclined forward 12 degrees from the vertical and with the overhead valve mechanism operated by push-rods and rockers. It featured very over square 84×58mm cylinder dimensions and produced 50 bhp at 7000 rpm. Primary drive was by helical gears and the power was transmitted via the five-speed gearbox to the rear wheel by chain. Maximum speed was around 105 mph.

As in the case of Aermacchi and Ducati, the American market played an important role in the affairs of the Benelli company during the 1960s. But even the efforts of their importers, Cosmopolitan Motors, could not halt the slide into terminal decline of the once great marque.

Australian Kel Carruthers became the next Benelli world champion after Ambrosini, when he took the 250cc title in 1969.

Even though the motorcycle division passed into de Tomaso's hands, the Benelli family still managed to retain control of Benelli Armi, the gun side of the business, which had flourished whilst the two-wheel side had crumbled in the late 1960s. This was located at Urbino, 20 miles or so south-west of the Benelli motorcycle works at Pesaro. Here Benelli could be likened to BSA in England and the Belgian FN company, all three being linked by the fact that each produced bikes and guns...But unlike the other two, Benelli did not start making guns in earnest until 1967, four years before the Pesaro motorcycle factory was sold, whereas the motorcycles were a tradition of 60 years' standing before the de Tomaso takeover. By the mid-1970s it made almost half the frames for Italy's motorcycles, including companies such as Moto Guzzi, Benelli (de Tomaso Pesaro) and the Italian arm of AMF Harley-Davidson at the former Aermacchi plant in Varese. The Benelli Armi factory was run at this time by Paolo, a second-generation Benelli and one time competitions manager of the Pesaro factory, and his cousin Innocenzo Nardi Dei.

The first thing which de Tomaso did at Pesaro after the takeover was to instigate a complete revision of the model line. Only the Mini-Bikes (for North America) and the 650 Tornado were continued and new 125 and 250 two-stroke twins with certain Japanese design features and which the old management had been developing were brought to production status. These shared a lot of common engine and cycle parts. The smaller machine was slightly long-stroke with its 42.5×44mm bore and stroke measurements

Conceived mainly for the North American market, the Tornado was a 643cc vertical twin with push-rod-operated valves and a five-speed gearbox – the photograph shows the 1971 version.

Following the de Tomaso takeover in the early 1970s came the Japanese-inspired 500 Quattro (four) and 750 Sei (six). Although they created lots of interest very few were to be produced.

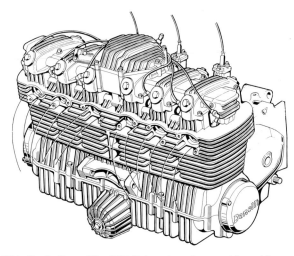

This illustration of the 750 Sei engine gives an idea of its width. The finned protrusion at the front of the crankcase is the oil filter cover. Note also the rocker inspection caps and six plug leads.

(124.77cc). The 250 had in fact a capacity of 231.4cc (56×47mm) and gave 25 bhp at 6870 rpm, the smaller twin producing 15.4 bhp at 7000 rpm. Both had Dansi flywheel magneto electronic ignition, iron cylinder barrels and horizontally split crankcases and also weak 6-volt electrics and dated petroil lubrication. In Europe the 'stroker' twins were marketed as the 2C, while in North America the larger model was sold as the Phantom. Next came a 120.6cc (56×49mm) single-cylinder on-off road model, labelled Cross. Unlike the twins this had points ignition and a vertically split crankcase.

The big news of 1972 was the arrival of the prototype of Benelli's incredible 750 Sei (Six). This de Tomaso creation was produced quite blatantly as an attempt to upstage the Japanese in the superbike stakes. It did not really make it for two main reasons. The first was that mighty Honda brought out their own six, the CBX, not long afterwards. And perhaps more important, except for its six megaphones crowding the rear wheel, the 750 Sei had a conservative, even modest, styling job. With a more adventurous stylist Benelli's road-going six could have become a *real* classic. As it is, its only real claim to fame is because it is still the only modern six-pipe roadster (except for its larger brother the 900) outside Japan.

Performance from the 747.77cc (56×50.6mm) engine was a modest 109 mph, electronically timed by *Motor Cycle Mechanics* in their July 1976 test. The claimed power output was 71 bhp at 8500 rpm. The engine shared much in common with Honda's CB500 four, even its bore and stroke measurements giving the truth to the argument that expediency came before technical independence. But whatever else, de Tomaso managed to get his prestige model on stream in months rather than years, together with its smaller brother, the 500 Quattro (Four). Much of the engineering design work for both the Benelli multis was the responsibility of Ing. Aurelio Bertocchi, son of Guerrino Bertocchi, former chief mechanic for the Maserati Grand Prix car team.

Another problem was the delivery time. It was to be almost two years, and mid-1974, before an export customer could buy the 750 Sei. Perhaps it would have been better to have held back before details of its existence were released, but was the purpose behind the six sales or publicity? Certainly, compared to rivals such as the Ducati and Guzzi V-twins or even Laverda's triple, very few of either the 750 Sei or 500 Quattro were actually produced. Later there was a four-cylinder 350 Benelli and 350/400 badge-engineered Guzzi version offered, but these were no more successful than their bigger brothers. Meanwhile the two-strokes gained chrome-plated alloy cylinders.

In 1976 came perhaps the definitive Benelli four-stroke roadster multi, the 254. 254 did not stand for its capacity, but supposedly 'two-fifty four cylinder'. In practice, as with the two-stroke 2C twin, the 254 actually had a capacity of only 231.1cc (44×38mm). At least this time Benelli couldn't be accused of copying anyone, because the jewel-like 254 was all their own work. And to this very day no one else has been bold enough to copy Benelli with another production 250cc four-cylinder model. With a specification which included 10.1:1 compression ratio, 27.8 bhp at 10,500 rpm, four Dell 'Orto PHBG 18mm carbs, five-speed gearbox, electric starting, 12-volt 12-amp hour battery, alternator, cast alloy wheels, 260mm (10.2in.) hydraulically operated Brembo disc front brake and a dry weight of only 117kg (258 lb), the 250 Quattro appeared to have everything going for it. However, there were two considerable problems. One was the weird styling job, which contrasted wildly with the conservative appearance of the larger multis, and a very high price tag. For example, in Britain the cost during 1978 was at least double that of Japanese four-strokes such as the Honda CB250 Dream and Yamaha XS250 models, at £1299 from importers Agrati Sales of St Marks Street, Nottingham.

By 1980 there was a new British concessionaire in the shape of former BMW importers TKM. Trading as Benelli Concessionaires Ltd, they had their head offices at 361/365 Chiswick High Road, London, W4. TKM brought in not only a revised 254 Quattro, but also the full line of both two- and four-stroke Benellis, from the 49cc G2 step-thru mopeds to the newly released 900 Sei Superbike. The latter not only had a much revised styling appearance compared to the 750 version, but its engine had been updated to combat the gearbox and crankshaft problems of the original. The increase in capacity to 905.9cc had been achieved by not simply boring out the cylinder to 60mm, but also increasing the stroke to 53.4mm. Power was up to 80 bhp at 8400 rpm. Other differences included an electric start, duplex rear drive chain, cast alloy wheels, disc rear brake and six-into-two exhaust system. The latter did not look as nice as the original Basso straight six system, but at least the new Silenium-made pipes did not rot so badly.

Performance – 134 mph was claimed – was also significantly improved. Much of this was due not only to the increase in capacity and power output, but with a lower dry weight of 220kg (485 lb), the power-to-weight ratio was considerably improved. Of all the models imported into Britain by the TKM organization it was the four-cylinder 354 and 504 Sport models which offered the best overall balance of performance, reliability *and* style. These were essentially the same motorcycle, except for having either 345.57cc (50×44mm) or 498cc (56×50.6mm) engines. The smaller four pumped out 38 bhp at 10,200 rpm and had a maximum speed of 99 mph, whilst the 504 Sport produced a healthy 52 bhp at 8900 rpm and 117 mph. Of the two the 504 was the best as it had a much superior power-to-weight ratio, for the 354 Sport suffered a distinct

lack of power. Even so both were attractive machines with their choice of Italian racing red and gold or black and gold finishes. Another TKM import was the 654, a 603.94cc (60×53.4mm) four.

Although not imported, there was also a 123.5cc (45.5×38mm) four-stroke twin, the 124. This sold mainly in Italy and produced 16 bhp at 10,600 rpm and had a maximum speed of 81 mph. But again price was a limiting factor when pitted against the Japanese in export markets.

No doubt price was one of the reasons why TKM never realized its ambitious sales targets and quickly departed the British scene. The remaining stocks of machines were offered through the giant discount dealers Motor Cycle City, who had a string of showrooms in London and the south-east of England, while the remaining stock of spares went north, to Speedscene, based in Huddersfield, West Yorkshire. This company also brought in a small number of machines during 1984-85.

In Italy, Benelli concentrated much of their efforts during the 1980s on building lightweight commuter mopeds and scooters. An early introduction was the 49cc S50 two-stroke. Of modern design, this was very much in the mould of Japanese types, like the Yamaha Pasola and Honda Melody. Later came the Laser, with a very similar appearance to the Honda Stream. Benelli also built a 125 motocrosser, with which they contested the World Championship series during the mid-1980s, eventually offering a production version from 1988 onwards. By this time the last of the multi-cylinder four-strokes were being sold off, the 254 Quattro to West Germany, the 354 Sport to Israel and small numbers of the 900 Sei for general sale.

Benelli stunned the motorcycling world when it announced this jewel-like production 250 four-cylinder in 1976. Its high cost ruled out volume sales in the vital export markets.

At the 1987 Milan Show the company, which by now shared a stand with Moto Guzzi, displayed four new models; the 125 Jarno, 125 BKX, E3 and City Bike. The first two were lightweight motorcycles powered by an ultra-modern single-cylinder liquid-cooled 123.15cc (56×50mm) two-stroke engine with the so-called Benelli Power System, which controlled the exhaust gas flow by an analogical electronic system, and a six-speed gearbox.

The Jarno was an out-and-out sportster of the type so successfully marketed by Cagiva, Gilera and Aprilia and certainly looked the part with its plastic enclosure, sharp racy lines and Grand Prix style. And underneath it was good too, with a sophisticated light alloy double beam frame and square section swinging arm in the same material. The front braking system had dual 240mm discs, with a single unit of the same diameter at the rear. Each brake had twin piston calipers.

The rear suspension was monoshock, with a progressively operating single damper with adjustable trim by means of a pull rod. Other details included a 13.5:1 compression ratio, 28mm Dell 'Orto carb, oil pump lubrication, 16in. tyres, cast alloy wheels, electric starting and Motoplat electronic ignition. Claimed power was 27 bhp at 9800 rpm, giving a 100 mph potential.

The BKX was an enduro-styled bike, which used a slightly detuned (24 bhp) version of the Jarno's engine, but still retaining its main technical features, including the exhaust valve.

The other two machines were mopeds. The E3 used a modern three-speed engine with electric ignition, whilst the City Bike brought back the idea of a folding bike which could be stored in a car boot, caravan or boat.

The 'grand plan' was that Benelli would concentrate upon the design and manufacture of small capacity two-stroke mopeds, scooters and lightweight motorcycles, whilst fellow members of the de Tomaso group, Moto Guzzi, built the larger-capacity four-stroke models. To this end both now came under the GBM (Guzzi Benelli Moto) banner.

The final 'real' motorcycle from Benelli was the 125 Jarno, a 100mph super sports street racer for the modern youth. It made its début at Milan in late 1987.

But by early 1989 it was evident that with ever decreasing sales the Benelli section was becoming a financial liability. Therefore, when the chance came later that year to sell the Pesero factory, de Tomaso grasped it with both hands.

The new owners had no interest in motorcycles, intending instead to utilize the production facilities for general engineering, although limited production of the moped range would continue until existing component stocks became exhausted.

But to all intents and purpose one of Italy's greatest and longest-running marques was at an end, defeated by a combination of a general recession of the commuter market and fierce competition from other companies both in Italy and abroad.

CHAPTER 4

Bianchi

Of all the great pioneers, Edoardo Bianchi, born in Milan in 1865, was without doubt the most famous in Italy's early motorcycling history. In 1885, at the age of 20, Bianchi set up a small machine shop for bicycle manufacture. He moved to larger premises in 1888, when he produced the first Italian bicycles with pneumatic tyres. His business expanded at a great pace during the 1890s, when cycling became as fashionable in Italy as elsewhere in Europe. Edoardo Bianchi's first powered two-wheeler came in 1897, when he built a single-cylinder motorcycle (more accurately a 'clip-on' engine attached to a conventional bicycle). Its most noteworthy feature was an automatic inlet valve. By the turn of the century Bianchi was not only offering tricycles powered by an engine *behind* the rear axle, but also a car of his own design powered by a single-cylinder de Dion engine.

By 1903, with a vast new factory in the Via Nino Bixio, the motorcycle range consisted of a much improved single-cylinder model with such luxuries as magneto ignition, leading link front forks and belt drive. 1905 saw a new design of Truffault fork and by 1910 a brand new 500 made Bianchi the envy of every other manufacturer in Italy. It was the great success of his brilliantly conceived 498cc single that really put Bianchi on the road to success, together with car and even truck manufacture in these early days.

During the Great War Bianchi concentrated on aero engines, but also supplied a 649cc V-twin engine and the purpose-built C75 military models. These were manufactured in considerable numbers. After the end of hostilities the V-twin model was increased in size to 741cc. In 1920 the Milan factory entered into a period of expansion which eventually led to the construction of its own foundry and wheel rolling facilities. The same year one of the V-twins set a new world flying kilometre record of 77.6 mph on the highway near Gallerate. The rider, Carlo Mafteis, was killed the following year racing the same machine at Brescia.

The first real push for international sales came when the marque took a stand at the 1921 Paris Show. Its star exhibit was a new 598cc V-twin, which entered production shortly afterwards. At the same time a new all chain-drive version of the 498cc made its bow. It was the 600 twin, however, which really grabbed the attention with its unit construction ohv engine, three-speed constant mesh gearbox, helical gear primary drive (one of the very first to be fitted to a motorcycle) and a wet multi-plate all metal clutch.

Not long after this a British importer was appointed with prestigious offices in St James's Street, Piccadilly. The company (Bianchi Motors Ltd) presented the 600 V-twin to the British public at the 1922 Olympia Show, together with a 348cc side-valve single. British sales were limited by the extremely high prices; the V-twin, for example, sold for around £150, over double the price of a similar 'Made in Britain' machine.

The following year saw more new models, including a smaller 498cc version of the V-twin. Next came the superbly crafted 171cc (57×67mm) ohv single-cylinder roadster. This was the work of new designer Ernesto Gnesa. 1925 also saw the début of a much improved ohv 348cc single and the superb dohc works racing models. The latter were the work of Bianchi chief designer Ing. Albino Baldi. The racers, built to counter the threat to Bianchi's sales by newcomers Moto Guzzi and Garelli, were ridden by such stars as Mario Ghersi, Luigi Arcangeli and the legendary Tazio Nuvolari and scored an amazing array of victories throughout Europe during the late 1920s. However, their one visit to the Isle of Man TT in 1926 did not prove so successful, for the three entries, ridden by Ghersi, Arcangeli and Miro Maffeis, finished well down the field in 13th, 14th and 20th positions.

With 20 bhp available the early version of the 348.36cc (74×81mm) dohc single not only had its cams driven by shaft and bevels but, unusual for those far-off vintage days, the valve springs were of the coil variety, and enclosed. By 1929 the output was up to 30 bhp, giving a maximum speed of 93 mph on high gearing. The gearbox was a hand-operated three-speed affair. Among the highlights of a glittering career the *Freccia Celeste* (Sky Blue Arrow) could list its remarkable run of five consecutive victories in the Italian Grand Prix, when the great Nuvolari won from 1925 to 1928 and Amilcare Moretti took the 1929 race.

Back in 1925 the Bianchi 350 double knocker also set a number of impressive world speed records: the 3 hours at 76 mph, the 300-kilometre at 78 mph and the 400-kilo-

The Bianchi team for the 1933 ISDT: the riders are (left to right) Pignorini, Bandini and Aldrighetti.

metre at 75 mph.

By the end of 1930 the 350 Freccia Celeste, now with a four-speed gearbox, was retired in the face of the more advanced Velocette, Norton and Swiss Motosacoche machines. However, the 350 was bored out to 500cc, which resulted in yet more victories, particularly in the demanding long-distance events such as the Milan-Naples and the Lario races. In the latter event Bianchi took victory in both 1934 and 1935. The 500 also came back to win the 1936 Milan-Naples event, but it was by then completely outclassed by machines such as the Norton singles, Guzzi V-twins and the Rodine (later Gilera) four-cylinder.

Judging that the four-cylinder route was the way to go, Bianchi then commissioned Ing. Baldi to design just such a machine. The result was a 493cc (52×58mm) supercharged model, which represented the pinnacle of pre-Second World War motorcycle development, even though unlike the Rondine/Gilera and Benelli fours of the period it was air cooled rather than liquid cooled. The cylinders were set vertically across the frame, and had close-fitting short finning. The double overhead cams were driven from a vertical shaft on the offside, with the camshafts working directly on valves angled at 90 degrees in hemispherical heads. The power output of the Baldi-designed Bianchi four was almost 80 bhp at 7000 rpm. The supercharger was a Cozette, fitted to the rear of the cylinder

assembly, and there was a Solex carburettor. The gearbox was a four-speed unit and the power unit was housed in a truly massive frame which sported girder forks and plunger rear suspension. But even though it was displayed at the Milan Show in November 1939, Italy's entry into the war the following June sealed its fate.

After the conflict was finally over, its designer was dead and superchargers were banned by the FIM, and so this most interesting of Bianchi motorcycles was abandoned, although the engine has survived.

On the production front not only motorcycles, but cycles, cars and trucks had continued to pour out of the Bianchi plants throughout the 1930s. As the decade progressed, however, Bianchi found it increasingly difficult to compete with the industrial might of Fiat in the four-wheel sector. Meanwhile sales of cycles and motorcycles were booming, and a new factory at Desio was opened to manufacture these exclusively in 1939, the year that Bianchi passenger car production came to a halt. With the encouragement of the Fascist government vast contracts were awarded for a new range of military trucks powered by licence-built German Mercedes-Benz diesel engines. These were made in large numbers during the war years, as were generating sets, motorcycles and motorcycle-based three-wheelers.

With the return of peace, Bianchi were soon back or

The frontal view of the fearsome 493cc supercharged four. Designed by Ing. Baldi it first appeared at the Milan Show in November 1939. Italy's entry into the war the following June sealed its fate.

the civilian motorcycle scene and by the time the 1947 Milan Show was staged that December, could truly claim to have retained their pre-war spot in the 'top three', along with rivals Gilera and Moto Guzzi. Like these manufacturers Bianchi chose to play safe, by restricting their efforts to just two models, a 125 two-stroke and a 250cc four-stroke which *The Motor Cycle* described as 'both nicely turned out and quite solid jobs, but nothing to get excited about'. By 1949 there was also a 175cc four-stroke, and this, like the other models in the range, was largely based on pre-war technology, including pressed steel blade girder fork and rigid frames. By 1951 the four-strokes had been dropped and a Turismo Lusso version of the existing 125 two-stroke offered. Both these came with telescopic forks and swinging arm rear suspension, the latter with vertical hydraulically damped shocks. Bianchi's main line of business was now bicycles and they had become the largest cycle manufacturer in Italy.

September 1952 brought the news that Alfonso Drusiani had moved from FB Mondial to Bianchi. As Mondial had just scored a trio of 125cc World Championship victories, everyone automatically expected Bianchi to field a 125GP mount in 1953, but it did not happen. Drusiani soon left to mastermind the Moto Comet 175 ohc twin.

November 1953 saw a new 174cc two-stroke of conventional and unexciting design. About all that could be said of it was that it had two wheels and went! But more, much more was needed to enable the old-established company to fight for a strong share of the all-important home market. With new firms and new designs springing up almost every month Bianchi had to have something new, and something different – and as the opposition was mainly four-stroke, Bianchi needed a 'thumper'.

Their answer was to launch a pair of brand new 174.73cc (60×61.8mm) models. Both cylinder and head were cast in light alloy, with Austentic iron liners and steel valve seats. The single overhead cam was driven by a chain running in an enclosed compartment on the offside of the cylinder. Ignition was by coil and battery with the contact breaker in the offside of the outer crankcase cover. Primary drive was by enclosed chain and the four-speed box was in unit with the engine. Designed by Ing. Colombo, the 175 was to eventually be known as the Tonale (Tone). The sports version, complete with flyscreen, clip-ons, racing seat and racing numberplates, produced 14.5 bhp and could reach 90 mph. This was obviously intended for use in events such as the Giro d'Italia and looked every inch what it was, a clubman's racer.

But in many ways Bianchi had left it too late and in 1955 Feruccio Quintavelle, a Milanese industrialist, created a new joint venture company involving not only Fiat and Bianchi, but also the tyre manufacturers Pirelli. The purpose was to relaunch the passenger car side of the company under the name Autobianchi SpA and the first results of the new accord came two years later with a small car called the Binachina. This was a two-seater coupé based on the Fiat 500 floorpan and was soon joined by various other versions, including an estate car and van. Autobianchi was taken over completely by Fiat in 1963 (Edoardo Bianchi's son Giuseppe had sold his shares in the venture in 1958) and still survives today in name alone under Lancia management, now themselves a subsidiary of the giant Fiat empire.

One of the very first of the post-war Bianchi roadsters was this 125 two-stroke single. Unlike the rival Mondial in the background, the Bianchi sported telescopic forks and swinging arm rear suspension.

When Autobianchi was being formed, the motorcycle (and cycle) divisions of Bianchi were separated into an entirely autonomous company, Edoardo Bianchi SpA, with production facilities at Taliedo, Milan. In a belated attempt to catch up lost ground, Bianchi's two-wheel enterprise not only commissioned another four-stroke to complement the 175 Tonale, but decided to re-enter sporting events, albeit with roadster-based machines. The first signs of this came during the 1956 Milano-Taranto race with the appearance of a 203cc (65×61.5mm) oversquare version of the 175 chain-driven ohc engine. Running on a 8.5:1 compression ratio the enlarged Tonale produced 18 bhp at 7800 rpm. With several components in alloy, such as the tank, the little Bianchi was good for a shade over 100 mph. The new machine gave evidence of its potential by finishing in second place in the Milano-Taranto, behind a Gilera Saturno in the overall classification and easily winning the 250 category.

The 203 Bianchi was a machine in the same mould as the Ducati 175 Formula 3, in other words a racer in all but name, but equipped with the bare minimum of road-going components such as lights and battery to meet the FMI (Italian Motorcycle Federation) regulations to enable it to compete in the 'sports' class racing so popular (and prestigious) at the time.

The rules stated:
1. The manufacturer must have the model 'approved' by the FMI.
2. In order to get this approval, the same manufacturer must show that he had built already ten units of the model, and,
3. He must build at least 50 other units of the model, at a monthly rate of ten, and exactly the same as the original.
4. The price of the later models must be as quoted when the bike was submitted for FMI approval.
5. The carburettor choke must not exceed the following dimensions: 50cc two-stroke, 17mm; four-stroke 15mm; 75cc 20/18mm; 100cc 23/20mm; 125cc 25/22mm; 250cc, 30/28mm.
6. The machine must be fitted with a starting device.
7. Generators for ignition and lighting must be integral with the power unit.

Although the regulations appeared simple, some manufacturers soon found ways to 'cheat'. And in any case success was so important to sales that soon the idea of the Formula 3 sports category was largely lost through the

Factory brochure of the Amalfi autocycle. It used a 47cc two-stroke power unit (this brochure was issued in 1958).

majority of the machines being pukka racers under another heading. For example, the Bianchi 203 had a vast number of special bits, even a different frame!

Ing. Colombo of Bianchi also developed an even larger Tonale-based racer to compete in open class events. This made its début during the summer of 1957 when, ridden by Gino Franzosi, it put up a good show to hold third berth behind the MV duo of Ubbiali and Taveri at Locarno before being forced out with mechanical trouble. Unlike the production bike, primary drive was by gears, a 9.5:1 compression was employed and a 30mm carburettor fitted. Bore and stroke were a square 66×66mm, giving a capacity of 235cc. Power output was stated to be 23 bhp at 7800 rpm and maximum speed around 112 mph. Another Bianchi rider, Osvaldo Perfetti, who had won a sports race at Monza on 31 August, 1957, on the 203cc F3 model, crashed a few weeks later at the Lesmo Curve while testing a dohc prototype Bianchi single which Ing. Colombo had been developing for Grand Prix events. This project was not developed further.

Shortly before the Milan Show opened in November that year Bianchi hit the headlines by claiming two 175cc world speed records. After waiting some 48 hours because of poor weather, Bianchi wheeled out a fully streamlined 175 at Monza for attempts on medium and long-distance records on Saturday, 9 November. The sky was dull and overcast and there was a slight breeze when works rider

During 1959 Bianchi raced 175 and 250 singles, but good results were hard to achieve. The engines were based on the overhead cam units employed in the successful Bianchi motocrossers.

Gino Franzosi climbed into the streamliner and set off. During his first one-and-a-half-hour spell, both the 100 kilometre and hour records fell, the former in 32 minutes 20.4 seconds (115.25 mph), the latter at 116.20 mph. The old records stood to Carini and Ciceri on a 98cc Ducati (see Chapter 8). A fine drizzle was falling when Alano Montanari took over from Franzosi and conditions were steadily worsening as Franzosi re-entered the machine after another hour and a half for a second spell.

By this time the drizzle had turned to rain, which reduced visibility and roadholding to such an extent that Ing. Colombo interrupted the attempt after 4 hours 19 minutes and 20 seconds, when 476 miles had been completed. The fastest lap (by Franzosi) had been made in a time of 1 minute 20.8 seconds (118.13 mph). The record machine was derived from the standard Tonale; it used the 60×61.8mm bore and stroke of the roadster, but also employed a number of special parts from the 203 and 235cc racing versions. Running on alcohol, with a compression ratio of around 10:1, the power output gave 17 bhp at 8000 rpm. The frame was that used on the 235cc racer. The wheels carried 2.50×17 tyres and only the rear one was fitted with a brake.

Because of the full enclosure, which was extremely narrow, there was almost no steering lock, the machine having to be lifted around by a metal bar which slotted through the streamlining. A pair of air intakes looked after engine cooling. The weight of the complete machine was 120kg (265 lb).

The highlight of the Bianchi display at the 1957 Milan Show, the record breaker apart, was the new 125, the Bernina, shown in two forms. This was an ohv design with the valves disposed transversely across the head. Compression was 6.5:1 and a power output of 6 bhp at 6500 rpm was claimed. Primary drive to the four-speed gearbox was by helical gears and final drive by exposed chain. Its capacity of 123.64cc (53×56mm) was unfashionably long-stroke. The frame was tubular with the engine unit joining the front down tube with the rear sub-frame. There was also a sports version. This was essentially similar to the standard version except for straight bracing tubes, one each side, from the base of the steering head lug to the rear swinging arm pivot. *The Motor Cycle* commented: 'Anachronisms as exemplified by the Bianchi frame struts do appear in Italian designs occasionally and seem to be accepted. An associated facet on the same theme is the fact that while Italy produces many of the neatest and most stylish machines in the world a few of her models are distinctly untidy.'

When the Bianchi range was announced in early 1958 for the forthcoming sales season, however, it comprised

In April 1960 the world's press was shown this brand new 248cc (55×52.5mm) dohc twin. Designed by Ing. Lino Tonti this was subsequently developed into first a 350 and later a 500cc model.

only four models: a pair of 48cc mopeds powered by the same 47.8cc (39×40mm) two-stroke engine; the 123.176cc (52×58mm) Mendola, a neatly styled two-stroke single with a conventional single down tube, full cradle frame and 50 mph maximum speed; and finally the latest version of the chain-driven ohc Tonale 175. The Bernina had gone back to the design shop for a new frame, which would delay its official launch date for several months.

Bianchi was making a great effort to improve its share of the motorcycle market for 1959. On the production front several new designs were laid down which would come to fruition over the next few months, while in the sporting sphere there was a three-pronged attack on trials, moto-cross and road racing. For trials Bianchi constructed six special 125 models for use by selected riders entered by the leading Bianchi dealers, including Premoli of Varese and Dall 'Ara of Bergamo. The engines of these trials irons were based on the new ohv Bernina model, which had just gone on sale. This now sported a full double-cradle frame and was of far more conventional appearance than the original prototypes displayed at Milan over a year earlier. With a maximum speed of 52 mph the first production model, the LV (Lusso Veloce), was not only noticeably faster than the two-stroke it replaced, but was more economical, able to exceed 150 mpg comfortably.

Bianchi's best-known roadster of the 1950s and 1960s was the Tonale. It used a chain-driven ohc engine with a capacity of 174.73cc.

1959 saw a whole series of machines prepared for motocross action. These were all based around a neat unit construction five-speed engine, with single overhead cam driven by shaft and bevel running up the near side of the cylinder. Although this was initially built as a 250, by the Moto Cross des Nations in late August, three of the four Italian team men rode Bianchis, but larger 350 and 400cc versions. These were outwardly identical. The 400cc models were in fact simply bored-out 350s, for the bore and stroke dimensions were 77×74mm (350) and 82×74mm (400cc). The machines were fitted with small megaphones with reverse cones, and, although high revving, also offered good power further down the scale.

After the Moto Cross des Nations, the 1958 World Motocross Champion Belgian René Baeten put in some laps on one of the Bianchis and voiced himself highly impressed. The machine seemed perfectly tailored for the Champion, who proceeded to put on an impressive display, and his control of the Bianchi can be judged from the fact that he was able to change from first to fourth gear while 'wheeling' from the start line!

Success earlier in the year with the quarter-litre machine in the hands of Vincenzo Soletti had convinced Bianchi management that they had a potential challenger: the result was the bigger class bikes. These had elektron crankcases, twin-plug ignition and the engine was safe to 10,000 rpm, although the maximum power of 35 bhp came at a lower 8000 rpm. Soletti ended the year as the 1959 250cc Italian Motocross Champion on Bianchi machinery. The man responsible for the design was Ing. Lino Tonti, formerly with Aermacchi, Mondial and Paton, who had been appointed head of the Bianchi racing and development department a few months earlier.

During bench testing Tonti was impressed by the power curve of the motocross unit and had the idea of tuning it for road racing. The result was an extremely neat 250. With a new frame, brakes and other cycle parts, the machine was ready for the 1959 Swiss GP (a non-Championship event) at Locarno, where Gianfranco Muscio turned in good lap times despite persistent valve spring trouble which eventually forced him to retire. There was also a 175 version, exactly the same except for bore and stroke measurements, and intended for Italian use.

The oversquare power units, 65×52.6mm for the 175cc, and 77×53.4mm for the 248cc, had twin overhead camshafts and fully enclosed valve gear (primarily for motocross use, where mud and dirt could have caused havoc). The claimed power outputs of the road racers were 20 bhp at 10,500 rpm for the 175 and 30 bhp at 10,000 rpm for the larger unit. Like the motocrossers the primary drive was by straight-cut gears with the multi-plate clutch in an oil bath on the nearside of the heavily finned crankcases. Twin ignition coils were attached to the front tubes of the double cradle frame, which had orthodox suspension and Oldani twin cam brakes of 220mm (front) and 180mm (rear) diameter. Further development was cancelled and the 175 and 250cc singles sold off after Ing. Tonti got the go-ahead from the company's management to carry out the design for a brand new twin-cylinder dohc 250 engine for Grand Prix racing.

At least one of the singles ended up in South America, but development continued on the motocrossers, with Emilio Ostorero enjoying a considerable run of success throughout Europe during 1960 and 1961, on both the 250 and 400. In addition one of the latter was exported to Terry Hill in Belfast, Northern Ireland, during March 1960 for use by grass-track and motocross ace Noel Bell at selected meetings.

By 1959 Bianchi had a British importer, Longford (Automotive) Ltd of King Street, Hammersmith, London W6. The same company handled NSU sales in Britain. One of the first machines imported was the new Falco (Hawk) moped. This was what could be termed a luxury model, with front and rear suspension and a three-speed gearbox. Maximum speed of the 49cc (38×43mm) piston ported two-stroke engine was 34 mph. But *The Motor Cycle* found in their test published in their 22 October, 1959, issue that although it 'would cruise steadily at 30 mph without complaint from the engine, at its 34 mph maximum, however, there was a good deal of vibration'. Price including purchase tax was £79 9s. 1d.

A change in Italian law during July 1959 had seen a spate of new scooters, mopeds and ultra-lightweight motorcycles of under 60cc. The changes to the *Codice Stradale* (Highway Code) meant that 50cc machines of not more than 15.5kg (35 lb) engine weight, 1.5 bhp maximum power and 25 mph maximum speed were exempt from the normal tax and driving licence provided they carried only one person. At the same time several tiny motorcycles, hitherto of 50cc, had been blown up slightly in capacity and power to qualify as passenger-carrying machines not restricted in speed or obliged (as were the tax-free models) to use cycle tracks where available. Into this latter category came a new 50cc ultra-lightweight Bianchi motorcycle and a restricted version of the Falco moped to qualify for the no tax, no licence rules. April 1960 saw Bianchi join the scooter-producing league with a small 71.5cc model called the BiBi. Power was supplied by a horizontal 3 bhp two-stroke engine via a three-speed gearbox built in unit and twist-grip controlled. Primary drive was by gears linked with a multi-plate oil bath clutch transmitting power to the rear wheel by a totally enclosed chain on the left-hand side. Air ducts on the front mudguard helped cool the engine, which breathed through a 16mm carburettor. Suspension was by telescopic fork at the front, carrying a 3.50×8 wheel, and by swinging arm at the rear. Maximum speed (with passenger) was a claimed 43 mph.

Another newcomer was the Gardena 75. This was an ultra-lightweight motorcycle powered by a 71.5cc (46×43mm) single-cylinder two-stroke engine developed from the unit fitted to the BiBi scooter, and shared the three-speed, hand-operated gearbox. Maximum power was 3.4 bhp at 6500 rpm. Frame construction was of pressed sheet-steel, with the swinging arm manufactured in the same material. Dry weight was 60kg (132 lb). Bianchi claimed a maximum speed of over 46 mph, but *Motor Cycle Mechanics* only got 44 mph in their test. Interestingly, *MCM* found that the most surprising thing about the Gardena 'is the lack of noise − both mechanical and exhaust'.

In October 1960 the British importers announced that its model range for 1961 would comprise three machines: the Gardena 75, Tonale 175 and Falco moped. The recently announced Orsetto 80 lightweight scooter, at least for the time being, would not be brought in. The Orsetto was a development of the BiBi and its 77.8cc (48×43mm) was a bored-out version of the latter. Power output was 3.7 bhp at 6250 rpm. Later this machine was to be marketed in Britain, but not as a Bianchi. This was under a licence agreement which saw Raleigh Industries of Nottingham offer it as the Raleigh Roma.

The really big news in 1960 for the famous old Milanese marque came on the last day of March, when Bianchi held a dinner in Milan and officially announced their comeback to Grand Prix racing after many years' absence from the big time. The machine with which this

challenge would be undertaken was the Tonti-designed dohc parallel twin mentioned briefly earlier. Developed over the preceding months, this had a bore and stroke of 55×52.5mm and the gear drive to the double overhead camshafts lay between and to the rear of the two cylinders. The valves were closed by totally enclosed hairpin springs and the maximum revs were stated to be 12,000, when the power output would be on a par to that produced by the existing MV 250 twin. The team leader was to be the English rider Derek Minter, who had agreed to race the bike even though it had thrown him off whilst being put through its paces at Monza when the engine seized at maximum speed. He escaped with a broken right collarbone, which put him out of racing for over a month. Minter said that, even at this early stage of its development, the Bianchi twin was almost as quick as Provini's 1960 Morini single, which had been circulating at the same time.

It is worth looking at the prototype Bianchi double-knocker twin in greater detail, as it was to lead to not only a whole series of racers from the factory, but ultimately its successors were to be the final racing machines to bear the proud Bianchi logo. Supported in two ball and two roller bearings, the built-up crankshaft assembly included four flywheel discs. Between the inner two was a pinion from which both transmission and valve gear were driven. The pinion meshed with a gear on an intermediate shaft, at the left-hand end of which was a pinion driving the exposed dry clutch; the final drive was taken from the right-hand side of the unit. A train of gears housed in an upward extension of the crankcase between the cylinders took the drive from the intermediate gear to the inlet camshaft, while a further train led forward from there to the exhaust camshaft.

Another model which enjoyed sales success during the same period was the 75 Gardena. This racy little two-stroke was good for around 50 mph.

Bianchi's star performer during 1963 and 1964 was Italian rider Remo Venturi. He not only put up some magnificent performances in the classics, but also took the Italian Senior 500cc championship in 1964 on his 482cc twin.

Magnesium alloy was used for the cam boxes, clutch housing and integral oil sump; the crankcase, cylinder barrels and heads were in aluminium alloy. Each head contained a pair of 12mm sparking plugs fired simultaneously by Bosch six-volt double-ended coils mounted behind the steering head. The contact breakers were driven by the off-side end of the crankshaft. With its 55×52.5mm dimensions the engine was slightly oversquare; the two Dell 'Orto SS1 carburettors had a choke diameter of 27mm. There were *two* oil pumps; one fed the crankshaft bearings, the other the valve gear; oil return was by gravity.

An interesting feature was the strong family resemblance between the frame and that of the motocross models, except that some of the triangulation tubes on the racer were of smaller diameter, while there was an additional, over-section tube connecting the top of the steering head to a cross-member at the seat nose. This arrangement would not have been practicable on the off-road frame because of the extra height of the single-cylinder engine. A 13.5-litre (3-gallon) aluminium petrol tank was held in place by a quick-release strap. The front fork was unusual in two respects. First, the top and bottom yokes were manufactured of light alloy, and the wheel spindle was mounted in lugs extending forward of the sliders (this arrangement allowed the use of straighter, stiffer yokes). Both these features are relatively commonplace today, but were far less common three decades ago. Both front and rear suspension had two-way hydraulic damping of Bianchi design, manufactured by

specialists Ceriani. Tyre size was 2.75×18 front and 3.00×18 rear. Both Oldani hubs were heavily ribbed and featured cable-operated, two leading-shoe brakes of 210mm diameter.

Straight off the drawing board the new Bianchi twin pumped out 34 bhp at 11,500 rpm and was capable of over 130 mph. There were early plans to produce a 350 by boring the cylinders to 65mm. Weight was 120kg (264 lb) complete with streamlining. But all was not sweetness and light. A hint of things to come came with the news that Minter had received a cable in early May to say no machine would be available for him to ride in the North West 200 in Northern Ireland.

Worse followed. Of several riders entered for the TT on the brand new Bianchi twins only Perfetti was destined to finish, ninth of 17 in the Lightweight (250cc) race at an average speed of 77.56 mph. This was some 15 mph slower than the winner. Team leader Minter had a miserable time with his engine seizing as he sped down Sulby Straight at full chat during practice, and yet again in the race on the second lap!

There followed a number of similar retirements that season. But undaunted Tonti carried out a redesign to 348cc (65×52.5mm) by increasing the size of the cylinder bore. This was necessary because, as a 250, the Bianchi twin was grossly overweight and it better fitted the 350 class.

The new bike, now with a choice of five- or six-speed box, made its bow at the 1960 Italian GP. At Monza, Ernesto Brambilla (Minter was out of the race due to an accident in the preceding 250 event) created a sensation by leading the MV fours for several laps before his petrol tap vibrated shut and team-mate Gianfranco Muscio took over before he too was forced out, with a fractured oil pipe. Another Bianchi limped home in 12th place. But at least Monza had proved that as a 350 the Bianchi had real potential.

Over the winter there were two significant developments: the signing of Scottish star Bob McIntyre, and the bench testing of a new half-litre engine, in reality 386cc. The other half of the 1961 team was to be Monza star Brambilla. When Brambilla had an easy win in early April at Cesanatico in the 500cc race on his new 350 twin, Bianchi seemed set for a more successful season. Brambilla's victory had been through speed and reliability. But in the classics it was a different story, with the season opener at Hockenheim only too typical. Here McIntyre and Brambilla stormed into a one-two lead, but only as far as the third lap, when both bikes retired with blown-up engines. Then, in the Junior TT, McIntyre snarled away from the start line at a fantastic pace, and by Sulby Bridge (some 18 miles out) he led Hocking's MV four by a full ten seconds. Then the gremlins struck again and the Scot was forced to retire with a broken gearbox lay-shaft. (This was hollow, but Tonti modified later ones to solid shaft.) Things did get better, however. McIntyre scored a superb second as Assen, with Brambilla fourth, then at the Sachsenring in East Germany the pair were third and fifth. McIntyre's fellow Scot and racing pal Alastair King took another second with Tonti's twin at the Ulster GP, whilst Alan Shepherd was the only Bianchi finisher at Monza in September, fourth behind a pair of MVs and a Czech Jawa. McIntyre finished the season in fifth place in the Championship table with Brambilla becoming the 500cc Italian champion.

September 1961 saw Ing. Tonti's latest experiment: a twin with *four* carbs! With one of the works 350 engines bored out to an experimental 386cc, the cylinder head had bifurcated inlet ports. The cunning did not end there, though, for the carburettors in each pair were of differing choke sizes and one opened before the other. The chief aim was better acceleration; but when South African rider Paddy Driver tried the machine during practice for the Italian GP the timing and carburation seemed to go haywire, with the result that the engine never performed as hoped for. With other developments in the wind the four carbs project was shelved.

The 1961 season had shown the latest 350 twin to rival even the *best* MV fours on the fastest circuits, but a host of teething troubles, notably broken valve springs, and far from perfect handling on bumpier sections of the circuit restricted its true potential. In an attempt to solve the valve spring trouble Tonti designed desmodromic cylinder heads, but ultimately plumped for a reduction in maximum revs from 12,000 to 10,400 to solve the problem.

An interesting facet of the Bianchi 350 twin was that the valves seated directly into the head, and to permit this arrangement the material of the cylinder heads was of high-duty casting alloy. The 'seats' were work-hardened by prolonged hammering with a two-diameter steel drift. Finally, the closing contours of the cams were so shaped as to allow the valves down comparatively gently on to their seats and therefore keep impact loadings low.

At Hockenheim McIntyre's machine had been timed at almost 150 mph on the fastest section of the circuit, quick enough to be competitive even against half-litre rivals. Early hopes that McIntyre would be out again on a Bianchi were dashed when he signed to ride for Honda in 1962 — the bike he had principally been attracted to was a larger (285cc) version of the all-conquering Japanese 250 four and was to prove a serious threat. Without the services of the Scotsman, Bianchi recruited the dashing young Italian

Silvio Grassetti, who repaid them by scoring a couple of places at Assen and Monza. Notably, Grassetti did not beat any MV or Honda fours — only the Jawa twin and various privately entered singles.

The veteran Remo Venturi was signed in January 1963 to replace Grassetti, who had gone to MV. Early in the season he put up some truly remarkable performances. This was the year of the Gilera return (see Chapter 10). So the Bianchi man faced three makes of four-cylinder rivals that year, but even so Venturi achieved some excellent results. For example, at Riccione in late March he led the 500cc race on a 422cc version before falling, breaking his windscreen and losing a minute. However, he restarted to ride the remaining 26 laps of the 68.87-mile race holding his fairing in place by hand and still managed to finish third! Then at Imola a month later there was real drama. The *Motor Cycling* headline said it all: 'Shock Win By Bianchi At Imola.' The sole Bianchi ridden by Venturi gave Gilera a rude shock by snatching the 350cc laurels in the important international Shell *Coppa d'Oro* (Gold Cup) at Imola.

In fact, Bianchi themselves had been so overawed by the opposition that the twin was almost scratched from the race! It was only Venturi's performance during practice, when he had lapped a second faster than the Gileras, which had forced Tonti into letting him race. Making a brilliant start, Venturi rocketed into an early lead and even when Gilera team leader Minter caught him he refused to give up. For eight laps they diced wheel to wheel until Minter heeled his Gilera over too far, and crashed. After this Venturi roared on to a famous victory well ahead of Gilera number two John Hartle. In the 500cc event Venturi finished fifth behind the Gileras of Minter and Hartle and the MVs of Hailwood and Grassetti.

To prove the results were no fluke and that at last the

Race kitted Tonale roadster seen at a recent CRMC (Classic Racing Motorcycle Club) event at Cadwell Park.

Bianchi was reliable, Venturi went on to finish second behind World Champion Jim Redman's Honda at the West German Grand Prix at the end of May. Venturi's average race speed was 120.30 mph, compared with Redman's 121.85 mph. Only the Bianchi man finished on the same lap as the winner and in front of Read (Gilera), Havel (Jawa) and Milani (Aermacchi).

With Bianchi opting not to contest the TT, there was then a lull on the classic front. One of Venturi's finest performances during this period, was at an international meeting at the end of June, over the 2-mile seafront San Remo circuit. The 500cc race provided the packed ranks of sun-bathed spectators with a really thrilling climax to the day, for it turned out to be a terrific dice between Venturi, the hero of Imola, on his 422cc Bianchi and Grassetti's MV four. Grassetti's mount seemed to have the edge on maximum speed, but Venturi was in great form on the lighter Bianchi, outriding the MV man on the many curves and corners. At roughly the halfway stage Venturi managed to break away, and from then on the Bianchi gained steadily on the MV to score a magnificent win.

A week later came the Dutch TT at Assen. The 350cc race, which started the day's programme, promised an intriguing struggle, with one second covering the best training laps of Redman (Honda), Hailwood (MV) and Venturi. But disaster struck on the very first lap. From the start Hailwood had shot away, only to be passed by Venturi and Redman. And when the Italian held his advantage, the race looked like developing into a great struggle. But then, as Venturi cranked the Bianchi into a fast right-hander, it broke away − some observers suggested that cars crossing the road at that point had deposited a layer of sand − and he crashed heavily. The accident effectively ruined Bianchi's title challenge and Venturi was out for some few weeks with a badly sprained back.

Venturi's forced inactivity gave Ing. Tonti a chance to update the twins still further. When they reappeared at Monza in September, again ridden by Venturi, they put on an excellent performance in both the 350 and 500cc races. There were completely new frames which had reduced overall height considerably and the larger engine had been increased to 452cc (70×59mm). Venturi finished third on the 350 and in the 500cc race, as *Motor Cycling* put it, 'simply steamed away from the Gileras, but retired at the pits after 24 laps while holding second spot behind race winner Mike Hailwood'.

October saw France's veteran speed ace and record breaker Georges Monneret win the 350cc class at Montlhéry. Then aged 54, Monneret had been specially loaned a works 350 Bianchi for this his last ever race.

For 1964 more development work was carried out, with the capacity of the larger machine being increased still further, to 498.06cc (73×59.5mm), while maximum power had been increased to 77 bhp at 10,200 rpm. The smaller engine now gave 50 bhp at 10,600 rpm. Venturi was again the rider. Highlights of the year were a second (500cc) and third (350cc) at the Dutch TT and a win in the 500cc Italian championships.

Grassetti replaced Venturi in 1965, but his only finish of note in the world title series was second behind Agostini's new three-cylinder MV at Monza. The Bianchi camp did, however, have the satisfaction of beating Provini (Benelli four), Stastny (Jawa), Woodman (MZ) and Pasolini (Aermacchi).

By now Bianchi was struggling, with decreased sales which had led to financial problems and the lack of resources to go racing properly. Added to this Tonti had left the company. Shortly afterwards the contents of the race shop were sold off to buyers from Italy and Germany. The last Bianchi rider to score World Championship points was Grassetti, with a fourth place at Monza in September 1966.

Time was fast running out for the motorcycle division of Bianchi, and the following year, 1967, saw the final machines come off the production line. The name was not to be lost, for it was carried on by Autobianchi on four wheels and Bianchi bicycles. The cycle business, part of the defunct motorcycle company, was eventually taken over by the giant Piaggio group, manufacturers of the famous Vespa scooter. Today Bianchi is Italy's leading cycle manufacturer and exports all over the world. So the spirit of Edoardo Bianchi lives on, although sadly not as a motorcycle manufacturer.

CHAPTER 5

Bimota

Very much the glamour boy of the modern Italian motorcycle industry, one of the company's early brochure quotes puts things nicely into view: 'It wins on the race track and flies along the world's roads.' But just how many enthusiasts know Bimota's history? To find its origins one has to go back to the early 1970s. It was then that the now legendary name first made its entry into the motorcycling world.

Massimo Tamburini owned a heating business at Rimini on the Adriatic coast. This area of Italy had long been a centre for both racing and bike manufacturing. The long-established Benelli factory was just down the road at nearby Pesaro, whilst the streets of Rimini itself had often been the battleground for some of Italy's hottest racing in the early post-war period.

As a hobby Tamburini modified several of the local riders' machines to make them not only quicker, but lighter and better handling. The results were obviously successful, because before long his work on one particular machine, an MV Agusta 600 four, became known throughout Italy. The transformation of what had previously been an ugly and slow touring bike into something which looked and handled like a real Superbike was truly impressive. It no doubt pleased those who wanted a full road-going replica of the Gallarate 'fire engine', but one person who did not appreciate this transformation was Count Domenico Agusta. This was because the Count had decreed that the 600 four was to be a de luxe tourer and not something that could be converted by its owners into a private replica of the real thing.

It was another event which was the real key to the creation of the Bimota company. This was a routine test session at Misano race circuit in the summer of 1972. Tamburini, his friend Giuseppe Morri and the racer Luigi Anelli were testing a Honda 750 four, with one of the special frames. A journalist was also there and he wrote an article about Tamburini's Honda. This one article which appeared in Italy's best-selling motorcycle magazine created such a wave of interest that a commercial company was set up to meet the influx of orders. The company was named after the three partners who set it up, Bianchi, Morri and Tamburini, and began trading on 1 January, 1973.

Following the huge amount of publicity generated by the racer's début, Bimota also received many requests for a road-going replica. Eventually this appeared in the shape of the HB1 (Honda-Bimota 1). Like the racer, this used a CB750 engine. However, the main intention in those early days was to supply frame kits, not complete machines. The HB1 was therefore a kit, not a motorcycle. This consisted of a chrome-moly frame and box-section swinging arm, with eccentric chain adjustment in the swinging-arm spindle section, rather than the conventional rear wheel spindle. There was a glass-fibre tank, seat assembly (incorporating the rear light and mudguard) and front mudguard. It also included an oil radiator pan, clip-ons, footrests, electron wheels, silencers, Ceriani forks, Marzocchi twin rear shocks, triple Scarab disc brakes and a full set of instructions.

In addition to the Honda 750, Tamburini had just finished building a pukka racing machine powered by a rapid twin-cylinder Yamaha TR2 motor. The chassis weighed barely 6kg (13 lb), and the design was both original and revolutionary. When the Bimota-Yamaha made its début in the hands of Luigi Anelli at Modena in early 1973, it soon became clear that each one of the innovations counted for something. Tamburini had left nothing to chance, every aesthetic element and every technical detail was there for a clearly defined purpose. It can in retrospect be seen that although the Bimota-Honda led directly to the road-going Bimotas which were to follow, it was the Bimota-Yamaha which facilitated much of the technical assessment and testing under the most competitive conditions − out on the race circuit.

Another of the early Bimotas was a 500 Paton four-stroke twin ridden by Amando Corecca. This used a developed version of the venerable dohc unit designed by ex-Mondial engineer Giuseppe Pattoni some ten years before and raced by the Hannah team in the late 1960s with Fred Stevens and Billie Nelson as riders. The engine unit, rather than its handling abilities, ultimately restricted the Bimota-Paton's success.

1974 saw Anelli replaced by Giuseppe Elementi as the official Bimota factory rider. Relatively unknown at the time, Elementi was soon producing race-winning results against the very top riders of the day. These included a

The machine which launched Bimota: the Honda-engined HB1. The prototype is seen here in the summer of 1972 at Misano race circuit. Massimo Tamburini (dark overcoat) designed the chassis and the rider was Luigi Anelli. A journalist who was at the circuit wrote an article on the machine for one of Italy's leading magazines. This resulted in a massive influx of enquiries for replicas and led to the formation of Bimota on 1 January, 1973. The company was named after the three individuals who set it up. Bianchi, Morri and Tamburini.

seventh place in the Italian GP, held that year at Imola. Another rider who gained several successes on Bimota machinery that year was none other than Roberto Gallina, later to win worldwide acclaim as the man behind the HP Suzuki team, and World Champions Marco Lucchinelli and Franco Uncini in 1981 and 1982, respectively.

The following year heralded a big influx of competitors using the Bimota chassis. One was Yamaha star Johnny Cecotto. Entered by the Venezuelan Yamaha importer, the South American became Champion of the World, with victories in the 350cc class in France, West Germany, Italy and Finland in the eight-round series.

One big thing in favour of Bimota was the ability to construct one-off frames as well as larger batches for series production use. At that time the roadster Bimota was in its infancy and the company's main revenue came from racing.

To illustrate this, in Cecotto's championship year much of Bimota's success revolved around Yamaha-powered machines ridden not only by Cecotto, but also by Bruno Kneubuhler, Otello Buscherini and Mario Lega. In all, over 60 frames were made and sold during 1975.

Cecotto's championship resulted in even more business for the Rimini concern. 1976 saw a whole host of Bimota-framed prototypes from a variety of factories. The new year got off to a flying start when the Italian Suzuki importers, Saaid, placed an order for 50 special frames for its batch of 492cc water-cooled twins. These TR500-based machines boasted 83 bhp at 9000 rpm. With Ceriani forks, 18in. magnesium wheels and the Bimota monoshock frame they weighed in at an amazingly low 145kg (266 lb dry).

Even though the HB1 had been a sales success, the racing programme always came first in those early days of

The Bimota production facilities in the summer of 1977.

Bimota's history. But the Suzuki-Italia connection changed all that. Although originally a 'racing only' venture, it was to prove so successful that Saaid came back with an order for 200 GS750-powered Superbikes. This was not only the first truly mass-produced Bimota motorcycle, but also its first roadster offered as a complete package. The first glimpse the public had of this sensational-looking projectile was at the Bologna Motor Show in January 1977. To enable this sort of production to be undertaken the workforce was increased from 16 to 30. It was reported at the time that Suzuki technicians had flown specially from Japan before the show opened to look at the new bike and give their approval. It was also planned from an early stage that an endurance racing version would follow later.

The SB2 was nothing if not unorthodox. The 18-litre (4-gal) fuel tank was mounted *under* the engine, with an electric pump to lift fuel to carburettor height. The tank position lowered the centre of gravity by some 14 per cent compared to a standard GS750. In the performance stakes the Bimota had a definite edge on the original, with a maximum speed of 143 mph. Much of this was due to the

efficient streamlining and its lighter 180kg (396 lb) weight. This was around 20 mph more and 41kg (90 lb) less than the standard model. The steering column of the SB2 was inclined at 25 degrees, which gave great manoeuvrability, but also greater sensitivity to the rider. The 35mm Ceriani racing-type forks were inclined by 29 degrees to improve roadholding over fast sections and, because of its lever effect, also hold down the rear of the bike during hard braking. Both the frame and the square section swinging arm were made exclusively from chrome moly tubing. Setting a trend was the single, vertically mounted de Carbon racing car-type monoshock suspension unit. By the standard of the day the respective weights for the frame and the swinging arm of 8.5 and 3.5kg (19 and 7½ lb) were truly light.

On the racing front the Tamburini-led team had helped with the construction of a chassis for a brand new four-cylinder two-stroke Paton GP racer. This had been tested for the first time in early February 1975 by Virginio Ferrari. The 90-degree V-four produced 90 bhp at some 11,000 rpm, but race results never matched its performance figures. Again this used a Bimota monoshock frame, with a Dutch Koni rear shock.

Designer Tamburini had another project, one very special to him, but which ultimately was to prove one of his few white elephants. This was the unique four-carburettor, twin-cylinder 500cc Harley-Davidson. At that time, the Italian arm of Harley-Davidson, based in Varese, were on a high. For two years running they had taken the 250 world title away from mighty Yamaha and for 1976 planned a triple assault at the championships, in the 250, 350 *and* 500 classes. In the end Harley-Davidson took both the smaller titles but not the blue ribband. Even though the new design was not a success, this was not really down to Bimota, but rather Harley, who just could not cope with the rigours and cost of competing in all three classes. Nonetheless, much that was learnt in coping with its near 100 bhp power output was to be later incorporated in the large-capacity sports roadsters.

Like his earlier designs, Tamburini's Bimota-Harley bristled with novel ideas. The rear swinging arm embraced the gearbox so that the chain retained the same tension whatever the position of the rear wheel. The single rear shock was fitted in an almost vertical position with the bottom fixing just forward of the rear wheel. A balancer was fitted in the middle of the chrome-moly frame with an adjustable arm, which was used to determine the height of the rear suspension. Even the 38mm front forks were fully adjustable and of Tamburini's own design. Riders of the ill-fated 500 HDS were Vanes Francini and Paulo Scattiolari. Both riders débuted the machines at Modena during March

Inside the machine shop at Bimota in 1977.

1976, and used them in that year's Italian championships.

Meanwhile Harley's team leader and double World Champion Walter Villa used Bimota frames for part of the 1976 season, making his début with the Bimota chassis during practice for the Yugoslav GP in May. This brought Villa into open dispute with the Harley-Davidson team manager, Gilberto Milani, and was ultimately one of the reasons for the eventual break-up of the team. Even so, at the start of the following season it was reported that for their 1977 GP effort Harley had ordered 11 of the Rimini-built frames for the works 250 and 350cc machines.

Another leading GP team to use Bimota was Morbidelli. The Bimota-framed Morbidelli made its début at the 1976 Dutch TT. Designer and team manager of Morbidelli, Jorg Möller, stated after the début: 'There are are still some modifications to be made, but I am certain we are on the right lines with this frame.' Bimota were also asked to help MV Agusta sort out their handling problems that year, but the famous marque were already in terminal decline, and except for wins at the Dutch TT (350) and the company's last GP appearance at the Nürburgring for the West German (500) even Agostini and Bimota could do little to stem the two-stroke takeover at Grand Prix level. Future World Champion Marco Lucchinelli rode a 350 Bimota-Yamaha during 1977 to gain some of his first victories and start the climb to fame and fortune.

The next development in the evolution of the Bimota Superbike came at the bi-annual International Milan Show, staged at the end of November 1977. Once again Tamburini had come up with a mouth-watering cocktail of technology and flamboyant style. The newcomer was the KB1, housing either the 900 or 1000 Kawasaki dohc four. The KB1 made full use of the three key Bimota features proven on the race circuits of the world. These were variable steering geometry, the space-frame, and monoshock rear suspension. Variable steering geometry was a Bimota exclusive. Just as on the SB2, the fork legs (now 38mm) and steering column were at slightly different angles. By featuring eccentric upper and lower steering-head bearings, the trail could be changed to suit the rider's requirements, either for fast or twisty conditions. The KB1 steering column was inclined at 24 degrees, and the fork legs by 28 degrees, while the trail could be varied between 3.9 inches and 4.7 inches.

Unlike the Suzuki frame, that for the Kawasaki did not feature the 'split' design of the main side tubes. This was because, on the Kawasaki, the engine was mounted that much higher. Another major difference was that the single rear suspension unit was now mounted in the horizontal position. Although heavier than the SB2, the KB1 still retained a useful weight saving over the standard production Kawasaki 900/1000, at just 193kg (426 lb) dry.

The 1979 Bimota KB2, powered by a 550cc Kawasaki four-cylinder engine. Not the trellis-type chassis, monoshock rear suspension and aggressive style. It set new standards for middleweight multis.

The bike which saved the company, the Ducati Pantah-powered DB1 of 1985.

Cost of a complete KB1 upon its launch in Italy was £4216, whilst a 'do-it-yourself' frame kit without the power unit was listed at £1686.

By this time Bimota had gained a British importer, ex-*Motor Cycle* journalist David Dixon. Operating as Dixon Racing of Godalming, Surrey, his first imports were frame kits for the Suzuki GS750, but when the KB1 chassis kit became available in Britain during July 1978, the asking price was £2495.

Even with this continued success out on the street, Bimota proved that it could still be a force on the race circuit and attract future stars. In 1979 the young American Randy Mamola stormed on to the Grand Prix scene with a fifth place on a 250 Bimota-Yamaha in the opening round at San Carlos, Venezuela. Even better placings were to follow: second in West Germany, second in Italy, eighth in Spain, tenth in Yugoslavia, seventh in Holland, second in Britain (Silverstone), fifth in Czechoslovakia and fourth in France. Mamola in his first GP season finished a highly creditable fourth in the final World Championship placings. Other top riders who used Bimota-framed machines in 1979 were Eric Saul, Maurizio Massiniani, Michel Rougerie, Patrick Fernandez and Loris Reggiani.

The crowning track glory for the now well-established

Bimota rider Davide Tardozzi (3) became Formula 1 Italian champion in 1987.

The Bimota YB4 ridden by Mark Phillips in one of the supporting races at the British GP staged at Donington Park, August 1988.

Rimini concern came the following year when South African privateer Jon Ekerold took the 350 world title on his Bimota-Yamaha YB3 with wins in France, Holland and West Germany. Known as the 'hard man of international racing', Ekerold finished second in 1981 behind the works-supported Kawasaki rider Anton Mang, whilst Fernandez on another Bimota-Yamaha snatched fourth spot in the Championship. By this time, however, Bimota had expanded considerably and had made a management decision to concentrate their production on exclusively going machinery.

Next in the Superbike line-up had come the SB3 in 1980, using the new 1100 Suzuki motor and a revised version of the original SB2 called the SB2/80. It was with these machines that Dixon Racing established six British national speed records at Elvington in autumn 1980. The records were set in the Pro-street class over the flying quarter-mile, kilometre and mile. The SB3's fastest one-way of 160.19 mph over the flying kilometre was the first time 160 mph had been broken by a road bike anywhere in Europe. Amazingly, neither machine was new and both were in the 'well-used' category. The SB3 was Dixon's own demonstrator and the motor had already covered over 20,000 miles.

The SB2/80 chassis housed a three-year-old GS750 motor with the standard 65mm bores increased to 73mm, giving a capacity of 944cc. Both engines used Yoshimura cams, valve gear, pistons and 29mm carbs. Alterations for

Elvington were race exhaust systems and higher gearing. The machines could not run in the Production class, because the rules did not allow 'non-original' frames, thus the pair of Bimotas were forced to run alongside the highly specialized turbocharged Pro-stockers.

Bimota's second Honda-powered machine was a long time coming, but the wait was well worth it. The CB900F-engined HB2 appeared at the 1981 Milan Show. Its existence owed much to lessons learned from designing another Bimota, the lightweight Kawasaki 550-powered KB2 Laser. This introduced 16-in. wheels, adjustable 40mm Forcella Italia forks and several other innovations.

The HB2 departed from traditional Bimota practice in only having a semi-space-frame design in which the engine was cradled by two detachable tubes which bolted up to the front multi-tube steering-head structure. This was cross-braced for rigidity and equipped with 40mm versions of the KB2 fork legs. At the rear two cradle tubes bolted up to a pair of alloy plates which were attached to the upper frame structure by a mixture of bonding and bolts; if damaged or detached for any reason these plates, milled like many alloy parts on the bike from a solid piece of high-tensile Avional 14 aircraft alloy, had to be reassembled in a special jig to get the correct relationship between the steering head and the swinging arm. The HB2 was superseded at the end of 1982 by the 1162cc CB1100-engined HB3.

Milan 1983 saw Bimota commit the cardinal error in the world of motorcycle sales. The golden rule is *never,*

never make your existing stock obsolete by displaying a new machine which you do not have ready to sell or plan to have in the immediate future. But Bimota did, and almost paid the ultimate penalty: that of going out of business. The machine which almost destroyed the Rimini company was the futuristic Tesi. This was not simply state-of-the-art engineering, but with its hydraulically operated central hub steering made everything else on the stand old-fashioned. In the months after the show this had a disastrous effect on sales. Quite simply all the customers who had been considering purchasing one of the models which Bimota already had in production changed their minds. What concerned them was that their imminent purchase was soon to be made instantly obsolete (the Japanese could well learn something from the Tesi saga). So quite simply they did not buy, in fact almost no one did. Within a few months (by July 1984) Bimota were bankrupt. The famous name was only rescued by the saving grace of Italian company law, 'controlled administration'. In Britain Bimota would have gone to the wall, but in Italy companies are given a 24-month breathing space to recover from a deep financial crisis.

With all debts frozen, and assistance with management skills, Bimota were able to concentrate on what they knew best, design and development. Enter the first Italian-powered road-going Bimota, the DB1 with 750cc Ducati Pantah engine. Thanks to the worldwide success of this machine, when the 31 July, 1986, deadline came around, the company was back in profit and in a position to convince creditors that all debts would soon be repaid. And by the end of 1986, Bimota had sold some 600 DB1s worldwide.

The man responsible for the creation of the DB1 was Ing. Fredrico Martini, who by then had succeeded Tamburini — the latter had quit after a management disagreement. A sad reminder that in the hard commercial world even a company's creator cannot always remain at the top, or even with the company! As covered elsewhere (see Chapter 6) Tamburini eventually resurfaced as a consultant with the giant Cagiva organization and was largely responsible for the creation of bikes such as the Ducati Paso and Cagiva Freccia.

The DB1 was sold in both street and racing (DB1RS) versions. Besides this Bimota also offered a wide range of 750 Ducati engine tuning parts for sale, including con-rods, pistons and camshafts. With these goodies the racing RS pumped out 80 bhp at 9000 rpm, compared with the standard 70 at 8500 of the DB1. Even if it was the Ducati-powered DB1 which provided the breathing space, the real foundations for the company's long-term future was to be with the Japanese Yamaha concern.

Although in Bimota's early days there had previously been a number of Yamaha-powered models, these had been exclusively racing 'stroker twins'. The new agreement created the FJ1200-engined YB5 and FZ750-powered YB4 models. Unlike the YB5 and all previous Bimotas, the YB4 was to be produced in both roadster and endurance racing versions. Bimota saw both these Yamaha-engined types forming the mainstay of their range, certainly until the end of the 1980s. As for Yamaha, they saw their part of the agreement benefiting themselves in the same way as various other Japanese and American corporate bodies had from involvement with small prestigious car firms such as Lotus and Aston Martin.

Autumn 1987 saw the unveiling of the 989cc Genesis-powered YB6 at the Tokyo Show, followed shortly afterwards by two more new models at the 50th Milan Show in November that year, the YB4EI and YB4EIR. The same year also saw Bimota win the TT F1 World Championship (Virginio Ferrari) and F1 Italian Championship (Davide Tardossi).

But what of the project which so nearly caused Bimotas downfall, the Tesi? Since the financial crisis, development of this has been largely placed on the back burner, although development is still continuing (now *very* quietly).

Perhaps most amazing of all is that Bimota, with only 34 full-time employees, is one of the smallest motorcycle producers in the world. But at the same time one of the most prestigious, with a worldwide reputation for its technical expertise.

President Bruno Passerini oversees a closely knit team of specialists, where high promotional penetration and a research and development department, whose investment accounts for 15 per cent of the factory's turnover, is a vital factor in the Rimini company's future health.

Currently over half the entire production is exported to Japan and perhaps explains why the Japanese 'Big Four' of Honda, Suzuki, Kawasaki and now Yamaha have been so keen to supply engines and be associated with the Italian marque.

CHAPTER 6

Cagiva

In a few short years the name Cagiva has come to be a symbol of corporate power, innovative engineering and quality workmanship within the Italian motorcycle industry. These factors have helped it become a respected name, not just at home but around the world. Born in September 1978, the Cagiva motorcycle operation has grown rapidly to establish itself as *the* major force in Italian motorcycling. Just how they have done it is a complicated story, 'a phoenix which has risen from many fires', as one journalist called the company's climb to power. The phoenix is in respect of earlier occupiers of Cagiva's original, and still existing, Varese factory location, Aermacchi and Harley-Davidson (see Chapter 1), for Cagiva took over the Schiranna, Varese, lakeside facilities when AMF finally pulled the plug in the summer of 1978.

The Cagiva name is an amalgam of CA for CAstiglioni, GI for GIovanni, the father of the two brothers who now control the business, and VA for VArese. The factory's logo is an Italianized version of Harley-Davidson's Number 1 motif, with its central section dominated by an elephant. The latter was taken from the emblem of the company's original metal-stamping business. This venture, formed by Giovanni Castiglioni, was already well established as one of the region's largest employers. The Castiglioni name had been established through the manufacture of locks, belt buckles, clasps and all those dinky bits of metal work one finds on luggage and handbags. The Castiglioni metal-pressing operation was so efficient that it could actually beat the foreign competition on both price and quality.

When interviewed shortly after they had acquired the former Aermacchi-Harley-Davidson facilities in 1978, Gianfranco, the eldest of the two sons (the other is Claudio), was reported to have said in reply to a question as to why the family had purchased the plant, 'Because we love motorcycles, of course!' Indeed no one could accuse the Castiglionis of lack of interest in their new venture, because the Cagiva name was to be seen on the heavily modified Suzuki RG500s of Franco Bonera and Marco Lucchinelli, sponsored by the brothers, before they became motorcycle manufacturers in their own right. This enthusiasm for the sport has remained a feature of the Cagiva enterprise to the present time, not just road racing,

but a notable presence in the off-road sector, trials, motocross and enduro.

As proof of this interest, one of the very first projects laid out by the new Cagiva management in the autumn of 1978 was the authority for the development of a water-cooled motocrosser. The prototype 125 was tested in 1979 and went on sale the following year, several months before the Japanese came up with a similar bike at the end of 1981. Called the WXM125, this trend-setting liquid-cooled off-road racer had a capacity of 124.63cc (56×50.6mm). Other features included reed valve induction, air *and* water-cooling, a six-speed gearbox, magnesium outer engine covers, Japanese electronic ignition, 35mm leading axle forks, Corte Corso rear shocks, an American-made alloy swinging arm, alloy petrol tank and a dry weight of 90kg (198 lb). The remainder of the Cagiva model range for the first couple of years were rehashed Harley-Davidson designs, all two-stroke singles, including a motocross and enduro air-cooled 250.

An enduro version of the six-speed 125, albeit air-cooled, was the next 'new' Cagiva in the spring of 1981. Amazingly, although the factory has no real experience of modern two-stroke dirt bikes, both the Cagiva 125 motocross and enduro models were the equal of anything in the world when they appeared, being both fast and reliable.

A 500cc racer was constructed by a small band of ex-MV Agusta technicians during 1980. This appeared at the final GP of the year at the Nürburgring. Although it sported Cagiva stickers it was nothing more than a modified production Yamaha four. Ridden by Virginio Ferrari it failed to qualify for the race.

Mid-way through 1981 a completely new 500cc two-stroke across-the-frame, four-cylinder road racer made its début. Ferrari was once again the pilot. And this bike was destined to be the first true Cagiva GP racer. The frame designed by Nico Bakker was a relatively conventional steel affair, with de Carbon rear shock and Suzuki forks, but the engine was revolutionary. It was unique, being a transverse four with disc valve and it overcame exhaust problems by reversing the outer cylinders, permitting two pipes on each side, after the style of Kenny Roberts's 1980 Yamaha. Dell 'Orto carbs fed four disc valves which were placed on the top of the gearbox and driven by rubber-

When Cagiva first took over the former Harley-Davidson (Aermacchi) Varese plant during autumn 1978, they constructed a couple of prototypes using the old Aermacchi ohv flat-single engine, but these never went any further.

toothed belts. The Cagiva GP bike used cylindrical exhaust power valves akin to those of the then current works Yamahas. Maximum output of the 498.52cc engine, which used the same 56×50.6mm dimensions as the single-cylinder 125 motocrosser, was a claimed 120 bhp at 12,000 rpm. But although producing plenty of power, the design was not a success. Induction problems and a decision to scrap the exhaust power valve as overcomplicated did not help.

For 1982 a Suzuki-style square-four was designed as a replacement for the ill-fated across-the-frame layout. The Varese team, managed by former Aermacchi works rider Gilberto Milani, had recruited Dutch engineer and two-stroke tuning wizard Jan Thiel, and it was Thiel who designed the new square-four. An aluminium square-section frame was introduced along with revamped suspension. The engine still retained the 56×50.6mm dimensions and featured disc valves. 118 bhp and 11,500 rpm were, *lower* than the 1981 figures, but at least these were usable horses. Riders were Buet Van Dulman and later Jon Ekerold. Van Dulman scored the company's first World Championship points with a tenth place at Hockenheim − not a great deal of return for so much effort.

All this development proved expensive, but, so what,

as the Castiglionis proved that unlike most non-Japanese teams they really did seem to possess a bottomless pocket. This wealth of capital had also enabled Cagiva to press on with production development. In fact, money was a vital factor in the rapid growth of the marque. Another has been the Castiglioni brothers' will to succeed backed up by the fact that they are not only enthusiastic motorcyclists, but, far more importantly, successful businessmen. By emphasizing the fundamentals, efficient manufacturing, high quality, competitive pricing (by Italian standards) and authorizing new models, the fledgling company was able to achieve the seemingly impossible task of growing from nothing to be a world power within a decade, something no one except the Japanese have managed in recent times.

August 1981 witnessed two new speed records for Cagiva, when a 24-year-old Dutchman, Bart Smith, broke both the 125cc world record for the flying kilometre at 137.02 mph and the mile at 136.77 mph. The record-breaking session, between 1 and 4 August, was staged at Lalistad in Holland with a cigar-shaped projectile powered by a specially prepared WMX125 motocross engine. The previous month Smith had tried to beat the records (previously held by NSU) in the United States at the Great Salt Lake in Utah, but the bad weather conditions prevailing at the time ruled out any chance of making an

Production was concentrated upon the Harley-conceived range of two-stroke singles, such as the SST 250 shown here.

attempt, so the team returned to Holland. The Lalistad venue was over a stretch of motorway which was still under construction and special permission had to be obtained from the Dutch authorities.

During the first three years of its existence, there is no doubt that the new business not only had the advantage of being able to capitalize on the vast stock of spares and former Harley designs which existed at the time of the takeover, but also one of these former Harley-Davidson models became the best-selling motorcycle on the Italian market in the all-important 125cc sector over the period 1979-82.

This was the SST125, which had been considerably updated prior to AMF's decision to close the Varese facilities. By simply giving it cast alloy wheels, better switchgear and, finally, in 1982, electronic ignition, Cagiva were able to sell large numbers of these 123.15cc (56×50mm) piston-ported five-speed models on the home market.

However, when ranged against the Japanese in export markets, the SST125, together with the rest of the former Harley-Davidson range, was woefully outclassed as Cagiva entered the 1980s. Unlike much of the Italian motorcycle industry, Cagiva was not content with simply marking time and, perhaps most important of all, they were not too proud or limited by tunnel vision to examine, in detail, all the latest Japanese technology. This policy not only kept them abreast of the opposition, but also meant they were always fully aware of the competition. To illustrate the great success of this 'open mind' approach, Cagiva built 6000 bikes in 1979, 13,000 in 1980 and, by 1982, this figure was increased still further to 40,000. This also showed in the number of staff; from the original 130 workers in late 1978 the figure had increased to 300, of which 50 were employed in R&D, by the beginning of 1982.

The previous year had seen the opening of the first foreign plant, when a factory in Venezuela began producing Cagivas for the South American market from kits produced back at Varese. This was followed by several other overseas projects, and as early as 1981 talks had taken place with the Soviet government into the feasibility of supplying Cagiva expertise to the USSR in the same way as Fiat had done earlier in the four-wheel sector. But to date the only concrete results of Italian-Russian co-operation came in 1982, when Russian riders rode the new 500 motocross bike in the World Championship series. A tie-up in the future should not, however, be ruled out.

The 1981 Milan Show marked an important milestone in the company's progress because it was here that a number of brand new models made their public bow. These included an up-to-the-minute six-speed 125 trial bike, which shared many of its technical features with the successful dirt bikes. There were also a number of off-roaders, including a water-cooled enduro; an enlarged version of the WMX125, the WMX250 (actually 190.3cc (67×54mm)); a 500 motocrosser, and the company's first ever four-stroke design, the Ala Rossa. This was a single-cylinder trail bike with its overhead cam driven, as on the typical modern Japanese engine, by simplex chain. The Ala Rossa was to spearhead the company's initial four-stroke challenge.

However, the Castiglioni brothers had even bigger and grander ideas. They dreamed of the true 'Italian Alternative' − a motorcycle line which would stretch from the smallest moped to the biggest Superbike. For this to become a reality it needed larger-capacity multi-cylinder models which, if developed from scratch, would take many years to come to fruition and billions of lire. So, instead, the Castiglionis scoured Europe in the search for a partnership deal which could speed the process, and

Another design which did not progress beyond the prototype stage was this water-cooled high-performance sportster, which used a detuned version of Walter Villa's championship-winning 250 Harley two-stroke twin. Its only appearance was at the 1979 Milan show.

therefore not only really broaden the range, but *cost* a whole lot less.

They even sent sales director Luigi Giacometti to England in 1982. Giacometti's brief was to take a detailed look at the ailing Hesketh company, which went into liquidation that summer. But this contact came to nothing when the Hesketh receiver revealed that all the Daventry factory had to offer was a pile of drawings, for the vast majority of components which comprised the V1000 Superbike came from outside suppliers. After all the searching abroad it was perhaps ironic that the Italian state-owned Ducati concern should make contact with Cagiva. This came in early 1983. At this time the Bologna factory was finding things very hard going, and so both parties proceeded with intense behind-the-scenes discussions.

The result of these meetings came on 2 June, 1983, when Cagiva and Ducati executives called a joint press conference. Held in a Milan Hotel, this announced to the world that Ducati would supply Cagiva with engines for the latter's new range of larger-capacity motorcycles (from 350 to 1000cc) and that the agreement was to run for seven

Cagiva's WMX 125 motocrosser was an instant success when it appeared in 1980. It was also the world's first production water-cooled dirt racer. The radiator was mounted at the front top of its forks.

ELEFANT 350

CAGIVA LA MOTO ITALIANA

Elefant 350: it was machines like this which came as the result of co-operation in 1983 and later, in 1985, the takeover by Cagiva of the legendary Ducati marque. The engine was the 349cc version of the Pantah 90-degree V-twin.

years. The Ducati name was to remain on the engines, but the bikes were to be marketed by Cagiva. The press conference had a completely opposite effect to that which the two parties had envisaged. Instead of a harmonious relationship, the ink on the 'agreement' was hardly dry when rumour and counter-rumour about just who was doing what and when began to circulate. This was not helped by some wild press speculation, particularly in export markets such as Britain and North America. For example, the British specialist weekly newspaper *Motor Cycle News* had a headline screaming 'It's the end for Ducati'.

As events were to prove this was way off the truth. Ducati continued to build bikes and in fact they *speeded* up development of new models, including the bevel-driven Mille V-twins (in Mike Hailwood Replica and S2 form) and the all new F1 sportster. Cagiva pushed ahead with its own Ducati-engined vees, such as the Alazurra middleweight sports tourer and the Elephant trail bike.

For almost two years there was an uneasy peace between the co-organizers of the 2 June, 1983, accord, with Cagiva buying batches of engines and Ducati continuing to build complete bikes. Then came the news on 1 May, 1985, that Cagiva had bought out Ducati for a reported £3 million, and so a new era in Italian motorcycling was born. Initially the plan was to retain the Ducati name for a short period only, as had been the case with Cagiva's buy-out of AMF Harley-Davidson, but it was soon realized that 'Ducati' was worth just too much hard currency to drop, so except for a small grey elephant the Ducati name lives on, and is destined to do so for many years to come.

The brothers now had a comprehensive range of

machinery from 125 to 1000cc, but felt they still needed one thing, style. Again a bold step was made. Massimo Tamburini, co-founder of Bimota and its chief designer for over ten years, was recruited to the Cagiva team and charged with the task of creating individual exciting designs. Tamburini's skill was soon evident, with a whole stream of superbly executed creations, including the Ducati Paso and Cagiva Freccia.

The next target was North America, but here Cagiva, and even Ducati, had a problem: lack of reputation and an efficient dealer network. In typically simple and effective style the Castiglioni brothers solved it by purchasing the world-renowned Swedish Husqvarna concern in 1986. This solved another problem too. By then Cagiva were having to build their off-road bikes at the former TGM factory at Parma. With 'Husky', the brothers not only now owned a famous and respected name, but one which also possessed a well-established dealer network across the Atlantic. Then, in 1987, yet another string was added to the fast-growing Cagiva empire, that of Moto Morini.

Once again there was a well-thought-out strategy behind the move. Both Ducati and Morini were in Bologna. The Ducati factory at Borgo Panigale was ultra-modern and had excess capacity, whereas the Morini facilities at Via Bergami were splitting at the seams and in need of modernization. Morini had a new water-cooled V-twin with belt drive to single overhead camshafts and four valve heads at an advanced stage of development. And whereas the latest generation of Ducatis with eight valves were intended as 750s or larger, the new Morini engine was envisaged as anything from 250 to 500cc.

Another development in 1987 was the opening of Cagiva Commerciale, a company to oversee the entire Cagiva motorcycle operation, including a centralized parts division under a single control, and based within the Ducati factory complex.

The 50th Milan Show, staged at the end of November 1987, saw the four marques, Ducati, Husqvarna, Morini and of course Cagiva, dominate the show with a massive stand and premier position. There were a dozen full-blown Cagivas, as opposed to motorcycles produced by other names under the Cagiva umbrella, for 1988. These were: 50 Cocis (named after a famous American Indian chief) and 125 Tamanaco. Both of these used a hi-tech liquid-cooled reed valve two-stroke single-cylinder engine with Paris-Dakar styling, twin headlamps, disc brake front and rear, monoshock rear suspension and a striking multi-colour finish. Then came the Cruiser, Blues and Freccia. These used the same basic 124.6cc (56×50.6mm) engine as the Tamanaco, but differed in purpose and state of tune. The Cruiser was a development of the Alleta Rossa trail

For over a decade Cagiva has poured vast sums of lire into a Grand Prix road-racing programme, which to date has produced very little in the way of results. The 1985 version of the 500 V-four is illustrated.

bike of the mid-1980s, the Blues a custom cruiser with masses of chrome and a garish *purple* paint job and the star of the show, the Freccia super sportster, with its all-enveloping plastic work, and 27 bhp, 100 mph performance.

Then came a quartet of ultra-modern enduro-styled trail bikes powered by either 343.27cc (82×65mm) or 452cc (94×65mm) four-valve single-cylinder, five-speed engines developed from the earlier two-valve Ala Rossa.

Only two Ducati-powered V-twins remained in the line-up, the 350 Elefant and 750 Lucky Explorer. Both these were Paris-Dakar-type bikes, but much better suited for street rather than dirt use. The bigger version with over 70 bph was a real handful off-road. All the other V-twins had been discontinued (except a specialized police machine) now that it had been decided to retain Ducati's separate identity. Bringing up the balance were a pair of pukka motocrossers, the WMX125 and WMX250. They were direct descendants of the actual works bikes which had won the world motocross title in 1985 and 1986 (both 125s) and finished second twice in 1987 (125 and 250cc). The WMX250 now had a full-size engine, 249.3cc (70×64.8mm), and both bikes could match the performance of any production machine currently on offer from rival manufacturers, including the latest offerings from the Japanese 'big four'.

The big news for 1989 was the introduction of the latest version of the street-racing Freccia. Not only had the power been upped to 30 bhp and a claimed 106 mph, but it now boasted seven speeds! This was in direct response to the serious challenge being mounted by both Aprilia and Gilera in the all-important 125cc class of the domestic market. These two rivals had Cagiva fighting tooth and nail for the lion's share and had seen a frantic race in the development stakes.

One can only hope for Cagiva's sake that they are more successful in the 'battle of the street' than they have been out on the Grand Prix road-racing circuit with their elusive quest for 500cc honours. After Boet Van Dulman and Jon Ekerold had come the French endurance champion Hervé Moineau in 1984, then the Spanish star Juan Garriga in 1985. That year saw the introduction of a new engine layout. This was a 90-degree V-four, but retained the usual 56×50.6mm bore and stroke measurements. Garriga proved this was more competitive by finishing eighth in Spain and tenth in Holland. But then the Spaniard quit and most of 1986 was spent looking for a replacement. By the beginning of 1987 the Belgian Didier de Radigues and the Frenchman Raymond Roche had been recruited and the pair put up some good performances at the end of that year. For 1988 Cagiva made headlines by signing the American superstar Randy Mamola. Roche stayed as his co-rider, but

Typical of Cagiva's hi-tech range of small-capacity two-stroke models is this 1988 125 Tamanaco trail bike.

de Radigues left to ride for Yamaha.

After the promising end to 1987, 1988 with Mamola and Roche was expected to at least result in some leaderboard places, but the opening rounds were a total disaster with a whole series of retirements, several through crashes. The crashes were largely blamed on Pirelli, who had just signed a two-year contract with the team. However, the Italian tyre giant headhunted the best tyre technician in the business and by mid-season, when Mamola gained a superb third place in a very wet Belgian GP, everyone started to believe that the Varese team had cracked it. But no, this run of success was soon brought to an end, and by the time the British GP took place in August Mamola was to be lapped and finally finished in ninth spot, whilst Roche retired in around 17th position.

The year also saw a new racer produced to meet the new set of rules which the FIM had introduced for the 1988 season, which limited the 125cc class to singles. However, even though they had managed to build a succession of world-beating motocrossers in that engine size, the racers used by former champion Pier Paolo Bianchi and Ian Maconnachie were simply not fast enough to get anywhere near the class-leading Derbis and Hondas.

For 1989 the competition effort was pruned back drastically. The motocross team was all but axed, and only

Mamola was retained to contest the 500cc world title series. The team also switched to Michelin tyres. The 125 single-cylinder racer project was abandoned.

And so to 1990. This got under way for Cagiva in dramatic fashion when in January it blitzed the Japanese opposition to win the prestigious Paris-Dakar Rally. Unfortunately this success couldn't be transferred to the Grand Prix road racing team, who with a team of three riders (Mamola, Haslam and Barros) had a disastrous season.

So what of the future? The Castiglionis seem to have made only one serious error, that of pouring vast sums of money into a road-racing Grand Prix challenge that at best can be described as disappointing, and at worst throwing good money after bad for a decade. In virtually every other area they have guided Cagiva into a leading position in the same period from almost nothing, which is an outstanding achievement. But whatever has been gained in these first ten years will not count for much if this level of progress cannot be maintained or even starts being reversed. As with Aprilia, my own feeling is that on past form the marque with the little grey elephant *should* make it, but in the fickle world of motorcycle manufacturing no one can be entirely sure what the future holds.

CHAPTER 7

Capriolo

The Capriolo marque is able to trace its ancestry back back to the year 1908 when Count Gianni Caproni founded what was ultimately to become one of Italy's largest industrial complexes of the inter-war years, the giant Caproni group. The First World War had seen Caproni produce a line of heavy bombers which were considered so advanced for their time that they were even purchased by the fledgling US Army Air Corps, which used them to form its very first heavy bomber squadron in 1918. During the twenties and early thirties, Count Caproni's various subsidiaries produced over 100 different types of aircraft, many of which were outstanding in their day. Besides the aviation side, the Caproni muscle was behind several other ventures, including the Isotta-Fraschini automobile plant, which apart from turning out many famous cars, also produced aero, industrial and marine engines.

By the Second World War the aviation division of Caproni was fading fast. The majority of its designs were obsolete, consisting largely of Colonial police types, notably lumbering tri-motors, which were totally unsuited to the demands of modern warfare. Although it was still a massive organization its only successful products of the war period were a range of twin-engined light bombers and the Reggiane 2000 fighter series. Mention should also be made of Italy's first (the world's third) jet aircraft, the Caproni Campini of 1940. With much of its wide-ranging produc-tion facilities badly affected by the conflict, times were hard for the Caproni organization in the immediate post-war era.

One of the few undamaged factories was Caproni's former aircraft plant in Trento, north-east Italy. This was situated in an area of outstanding natural beauty close to the Austrian border. The deer and mountain range displayed in the design of the original Capriolo insignia illustrated its birthplace to perfection, with the word Capriolo, meaning the male species of a small deer in the Italian language. Like many other companies whose wartime production was unwanted after the conflict, Caproni realized that motorcycles would be an excellent way of keeping its workforce occupied. The Trento factory was therefore re-equipped for its new role and the company's name changed to Aeromere SpA, with its products marketed under the Capriolo brand name. Besides motorcycles, there was also

to be the production of three-wheel light trucks.

Its first two-wheel product was a 73cc (47×43mm) face cam model in which the crankshaft ran in line with the frame. It also used full unit construction, a foot-operated four-speed gearbox and a pressed steel square-section frame. Known as the Capriolo 75, this unusual design together with a steady demand for the company's three-wheelers placed the newly reformed Trento operation on a sound financial footing. The year 1950 saw an abortive co-operation venture with Ducati of Bologna to produce a new lightweight motorcycle. Ultimately both companies decided to go their own way.

Encouraged by the success of the Capriolo operation, another part of the Caproni group made a move into the two-wheel sector. This was Caproni-Vizzola of Milan. Production commenced in 1952, but unlike the Trento operation, Caproni-Vizzola not only retained its original company name, but fitted bought-in engines, mainly from NSU in Germany. A 247cc Max-powered machine, the Cavimax, made its début at the Milan show in late November 1953. Except for the engine the Cavimax differed considerably from the German original. A spine frame was retained, but the mid-section pressings were modified and the rear suspension fork was of a cleaner design, while the front fork, though still a leading-link layout, bore little resemblance to the Neckarsulm pattern. The stanchions were more upright and their merged upper portion did not partially embrace the steering head. Also the links were pivoted in front of the stanchions instead of behind. The deeply valanced mudguards and totally new shape of both the tank and dual seat helped set it apart from its German brother, even though the massive Eberspacher silencer was retained. This attractive machine was helped by having a mass of polished alloy, including the full-width brake hubs and wheel rims. Later the Caproni-Vizzola company increased its use of NSU engines to include the 173cc Cavilux.

At the same show as the NSU-powered Caproni-Vizzola had made its bow, Capriolo provided one of the real surprises with their Cento 50. This featured a horizontally opposed 149.2cc (using the same 47×43mm dimensions of the 75 single) ohv transverse twin. Like the already well-established single, the Cento 50 had a pressed-steel frame,

The first model offered by the former Caproni aircraft factory at Trento, in north-east Italy, was the 75. This featured a crankshaft which ran in-line with the frame, but the relatively rare face cam was to become a Capriolo hallmark.

but with full swinging arm, twin-shock suspension. Unlike its smaller brother, however, the new twin was equipped with an Earles-type front fork, with single-tube static members and a welded-up pivoting section which utilized pressed-steel arms similar to those employed at the rear.

Of exceptionally neat design, the power unit had an integral four-speed gearbox, with the drive taken through 90 degrees internally to permit the use of chain final drive. Each of the alloy cylinders was provided with its own ignition coil, mounted neatly within the angles of the frame's front down members. Running on a 7:1 compression ratio, maximum power output was 7.5 bhp at 6000 rpm. Other details included 17in. diameter tyres and a dry weight of 103kg (227 lb). No changes were made to the existing single-cylinder 75, but a sports model, with engine tuning including a redesigned cylinder head, was added to the range.

A year later and the Cento 50 had been updated for the 1955 season with the replacement of the Earles forks by more conventional teles and full-width brake hubs. Otherwise the specification remained unchanged, as did the Turismo and Sport versions of the popular 75.

1952 had seen the first sporting successes for the Trento marque, when one of the little Capriolos had won its class in the famous Milano–Taranto race. Two years later this success was followed up when Claudio Galliani had

ridden one of the new 75 sport models to victory in the same event, averaging 82.725 km/h (51.40 mph) for the entire distance. More success came when Galliani won his class the following year in the Giro d'Italia at 88 km/h (55 mph). The same rider also became 1955 Italian Junior racing champion. But after these successes the 75cc category became the preserve of Laverda and Ceccato.

It was perhaps because of this that Capriolo began their interest in the trials scene, with Jolas Strenghetto representing his country in the 1956 ISDT as a member of the Vase A squad on a specially prepared 75. Strenghetto and two non-team members on 75 Capriolos all retired, hardly an encouraging first venture in the world of long-distance trials for the factory.

The Milan Show that year saw the début of a brand new engine size for Capriolo, a 125. Like the earlier singles this used the interesting face cam layout. The 123.5cc (55×52mm) single-cylinder unit was of particularly clean design. And significantly its output of 7.5 bhp at 6000 rpm was identical to the much-more-costly-to-produce flat-twin 50 Cento that it replaced. The cycle parts of the newcomer were very similar to the 50 Cento, but at 95kg (209 lb) it was considerably lighter.

The 1957 model line-up saw four machines offered: three versions of the 75: Normale, Turismo Speciale and Sport, plus the new 125 Turismo Veloce. Prices ranged from 148,000 to 193,000 lire.

For 1958 a smaller version of the face cam model was introduced; this had a slightly inclined 74.6cc (47×43cc) cylinder and produced 4.5 bhp at 6000 rpm. Much of the balance of the specification closely followed its larger brother with four speeds, unit construction, helical gear primary drive and wet multi-plate clutch. It was with one of these new machines (still using the pressed steel chassis) that Strenghetto was to become one of the heroes of the ISDT that year; when riding the smallest machine in the trial he won a Gold medal. Strenghetto was an official member of the Italian Vase B team, along with Sergio Moscheni and Vargilo Crippa on 125 Capriolos. Besides Strenghetto, team-mate Moscheni also went home from Bavaria with a 'Gold', but Crippa was forced to retire.

Encouraged by its success, for 1959 Capriolo announced it would be supporting a four-man squad in long-distance trials that year: Manfe, Casagrande, Bertoli and Strenghetto. And by the time of the ISDT selection in August they had put up such an excellent run of results that the Italian selectors picked two 125s for the Trophy effort and a trio of 75s for the Vase teams. This confidence was rewarded with Italy finishing second in the all-important Trophy contest, thanks in no small part to the efforts of Capriolo riders Strenghetto and Moscheni, but because of its small engine size it was the 75 rather than the 125 which created the most media interest. Its success in the 1958 and 1959 ISDTs, and the manner in which it dominated other events in Italy, resulted in such a clamouring at the Aeromere factory's doors at Trento that it was decided to build a batch of replicas.

The oversquare engine developed 5.5 bhp at 6500 rpm and like the roadster version featured the most interesting Capriolo hallmark, the face cam valve gear system. The face cam (also referred to as the disc cam) was carried at the top of a vertical shaft in the left-hand side of the cylinder; at the base of the shaft a worm gear on the crankshaft, supported in three ball race bearings, provided the method of operation. Poppet-type valves, set at sixty degrees, were returned to their seats by coil springs. Incorporated in the helical geared primary drive was a centrifugal flywheel which acted as a sludge trap for the lubricant, which had already passed through a wire gauze filter. The gear-type oil pump, driven by the lower end of the camshaft, forced oil to the big end and, by pipe, to the face cam and camshaft, from where it was returned by gravity to the centrifugal flywheel and back to the integral sump. A flywheel magneto was enclosed in the offside of the crankcase, where there was also an ingenious 'blower' system to assist cooling under heavy engine loads. A pair of HT coils were housed in a waterproof metal box attached

The Cento 50 was one of the surprises of the 1953 Milan Show. It featured a horizontally opposed 149.2cc ohv transverse twin engine. The first version had Earles-type forks. The model shown is the 1955 type with telescopic forks and swinging arm rear suspension.

to the nearside of the front down tube; failure of one therefore meant nothing more than a temporary halt while the rider switched the load over to the sound coil. Carburation was by an 18mm diameter Dell 'Orto instrument and specially constructed filter. As with the roadster, there was a four-speed gearbox in unit with the engine controlled from the offside; the selector mechanism, positioned outside the gear housing, also featured an

The flat-twin engine from the Cento 50 was of exceptionally clean design. The single Dell 'Orto carburettor was almost hidden from sight. Unlike the similar BMW design, the Capriolo had chain final drive.

Capriolo 125

economia + prestazioni + sicurezza + estetica TOTALE = Capriolo 125

MOTORE 4 tempi · alesaggio mm 55 corsa mm 52 · cilindrata 123,5 rapporto di compressione 1:7 · distribuzione: camme in testa comandate da albero verticale · lubrificazione: forzata con pompa ad ingranaggi · accensione: a volano magnete · trasmissione primaria ad ingranaggi elicoidali con parastrappi · cambio a 4 velocità con ingranaggi sempre in presa · frizione: a dischi multipli in bagno d'olio potenza: cv. 7,5 a 6000 giri.

TELAIO a culla in lamiera stampata forcella anteriore teleidraulica · forcella posteriore a braccio oscillante con ammortizzatori oleodinamici · ruote 2,50 x 19 · freni a frenatura centrale diam. 160 x 30 · peso in ordine di marcia Kg. 95 · impianto elettrico con batterie 6 V.

PRESTAZIONI
velocità 95 Km/h
consumo lt. 2,2 per 100 Km.
pendenze superabili 30%

AEROMERE - TRENTO
Affiliata Stabilimento AEROCAPRONI - TRENTO
CANTIERE AERONAUTICO DI GARDOLO
OFFICINA MECCANICA DI ARCO

A completely new 123.5cc face cam single made its bow at the 1956 Milan Show, but still used square tube chassis.

external handle on top of the crankcase with which the rider could swap cogs in the event of the pedal control being damaged. Like the road-going version 19in. diameter wheels were used, but knobbly competition tyres were obviously fitted to the trials mount, a wider 2.75 section at the rear, a standard section 2.50 at the front.

In ISDT trim the 75 Capriolo was good for a shade under 50 mph and illustrates the effectiveness of the egg-cup size power unit; it was possible to go down as low as 22 mph in top gear if necessary. The larger face cam trials model could top 60 mph and was in essence a scaled-up version of the smaller bike in almost every detail. Both replica ISDT versions were displayed a couple of months

after the ISDT at the Milan Show in November 1959, where they received an enthusiastic reception.

Perhaps it was a good thing that Capriolo had decided to produce these bikes as that had produced a lighter, neater frame. The company's trials involvement paid off commercially when a version of this frame (albeit still of pressed steel construction) was adopted for the standard production roadster models. And besides the 75 and 125 a new 100 class model was added to the range. This used a 98cc (49×52mm) version of the successful face cam design.

In late 1960 Aeromere established a subsidiary in Britain with which they hoped to make a considerable penetration into the market. The company traded under the title Capriolo Ltd and was based at 66 Southbridge Road, Croydon, Surrey. Initially only the 75 and 125 were imported and it was one of the latter which was tested by *Motor Cycling* in their 12 January, 1961, issue. Except for an over-optimistic speedometer and near solid operation of the front forks, tester Bruce Main-Smith was full of praise for the newcomer to the British market, summarizing his report up in the following manner: 'This Capriolo is definitely one of the better examples of modern Italian design – very lively, manageable, safe and, provided the

Details of face cam engine from the 1960 Capriolo 125.

The Capriolo 75: based on the models campaigned in the ISDT during the late 1950s. The road-going version was both speedy and economical. It also heralded a more conventional frame, but was still made from pressed steel.

Top of the range, the 1960 Capriolo 125 De Luxe.

Special one-day trials model converted by the Rickman Brothers on show at Earls Court, 1962.

rider remembers that a crisp exhaust does not delight the populace at large, equally suitable for open road and town work.'

If anything the 75 TV model tested some three months later by *Motor Cycle News* (19 April, 1961, issue) received even more praise, Peter Howdle commenting: 'If any parent asked me to suggest a good "buy" for a 16-year-old itching to own his first bike, I would place the "75" Capriolo very near the top of my short list. At £123 it represents top value. It is light, safe and easy to ride. That amazing ohc engine packs enough steam to satisfy any red-blooded youngster − irrespective of age − and is ultra-economical.' With their electronic test equipment, *MCN* recorded a speed of 54 mph over the flying quarter mile, but like the vast majority of other makes imported into Britain at the same time, Bianchi, Parilla and even Guzzi, for example, Capriolo never really made any significant impact.

There was even a pukka one-day trials version constructed by the Rickman Brothers. Launched at the 1962 Earls Court Show, this was a superbly crafted little

mount. Its specification included glass-fibre tank and lightweight seat, high-level exhaust system, Girling rear shocks, alloy wheel rims (21in. at the front), Avon Trials Supreme tyres, trials bars, alloy mudguards and a completely new tubular rear sub-frame and swinging arm assembly.

Capriolo were imported into North America by Cosmopolitan Motors, the same company which also handled Bianchi, Parilla and Capri scooters. Stateside, three models were sold; the 75 Antelope, 100 Gazelle and 125 Cheetah − these names were applicable only on the American market. However, as in Britain, they largely failed to make any real impact.

With declining home sales, Aeromere (Capriolo) closed their Trento operation in mid-1964, following in the footsteps of Capriolo-Vizzola, who had ceased production five years earlier in 1959. Today any Caproni group motorcycle is a rare sight indeed as very few of either factory's two-wheelers seem to have survived, even though several thousand examples were manufactured.

CHAPTER 8

Ducati

Today the name Ducati means two things, expensive large-capacity V-twins and the company's legendary desmodromic valve operation. However, this has not always been the position, for Ducati Meccanica rose out of the ashes of Societa Scientifica Radiobrevetti Ducati, which was founded in 1926 by two brothers, Adriano and Marcello Ducati, and specialized in producing radio equipment. Throughout the 1930s the company prospered, due in no small part to the role played by the radio in the Fascist Party's propaganda machine, and by 1939 the Ducati company employed 7000 people.

When Italy's dictator, Benito Mussolini, an open supporter of Adolf Hitler and the Nazi regime, took Italy into the war on Germany's side on 10 June, 1940, it was a fateful decision for both Italy and Ducati, as subsequent events were to prove. At that time, Ducati were mainly producing military equipment, which apart from radios included gun sights and other artillery optical parts.

By September 1943, when Marshal Badoglio successfully negotiated a cease-fire with the Allies, Italy was a split country; the Allies were firmly established in the south of the country, while the Fascists (and Germans) remained entrenched in the north. Thus Bologna, the home of Ducati, being a major industrial and railway centre, in the very heart of the Fascist part of Italy, suffered from much heavy bombing.

By mid-1944 it was evident to all but the most committed Fascist that their cause was lost. One such realist was the Turin-based engineer Aldo Farinelli. Turin, some 200 miles north-west of Bologna, was still in German-held territory, but Farinelli, like many Italians, was sick of the war and was already speculating on what would happen in a devastated Italy when the war finally ended. It was then that he realized that one of the country's major problems was going to be basic transport. Not only would civilian vehicles be in short supply, but perhaps more crucially the fuel to power them would be even scarcer.

Farinelli worked at the time for a small but successful engineering company, and during 1944 he and several colleagues began to investigate various ways in which to combat the problem. Their solution was simple; a clip-on, low-compression, four-stroke engine which could be produced in large numbers and fitted to conventional bicycles. But perhaps most important of all, it achieved amazing fuel consumption figures – up to 280 mpg! The 48cc engine was named Cucciolo (puppy dog) and was unusual in having pull rather than push-rods operating its valves.

Societa Italiana per Applicazione Techiche Auto-Aviatore (Siata), the company for whom Farinelli worked, announced plans to begin production of the engine in July 1945. When the engine went on sale, in the autumn of 1945, demand soon exceeded supply and by the beginning of the following year it was evident that a merger with a larger company was the only way of solving this problem.

Back in Bologna, Ducati also had a serious problem, but of a different nature, a wrecked factory and over 9000 workers idle. However, a government body, Instituto per la Recostruzione Industriale (IRI), originally set up by Mussolini, was now employed by the ruling Christian Democrats to solve just such problems. The IRI's funds were limited, but working with the Vatican as a business partner, it identified and then assisted key businesses which had before the war employed workers on a large scale – Ducati was one such company.

So Ducati received help, but the price was high – total government/Vatican control. The Ducati family were 'paid off' and, with the necessary funds and help, the factory was rebuilt and a research organization formed. The relaunched company's first products were radios and cameras, but more significantly for its future a deal was made between the IRI/Vatican, Ducati and Siata in Turin for Ducati to produce the Cucciolo.

The Cucciolo 'clip-on' engine was originally sold as a proprietary unit, either for customers to fit to their own pedal cycle, or to other manufacturers who built a complete machine around it.

But soon Ducati realized that it too could produce a complete vehicle, their first effort appearing at the 1948 Milan Show; this, however, was not a two-wheeler, but a three-wheel lightweight truck, which was powered by a bored-out Cucciolo engine and code-named T3. Although this was not a big seller, it did prove that the company could build something other than just the engine.

The next step was an abortive partnership agreement

One of the main centres of attraction at the Milan Show which opened on 12 January, 1952, was the Ducati Cruiser scooter. This innovative design employed a four-stroke engine and automatic transmission. Sales were disappointing.

with the Trento-based Capriolo concern to build an ultra-lightweight motorcycle, powered by a modified version of the 60cc Cucciolo-based unit used in the T3 truck. However, Ducati and Capriolo decided to part company in May 1950 to go their own ways.

By the Milan Show held in November that year, the Bologna company had its own machine. This was the 60 Sport, powered by a 59.57cc (42×43mm) ohv engine and which again showed Cucciolo influence. Equipped with teles and swinging arm suspension, the little machine had a definite advantage over the majority of other Italian machines of the same capacity. Its success was to be instrumental in convincing the management that the company's future lay with the manufacture of lightweight motorcycles. The next project consisted of an increase of capacity for their 60 Sport to 65.38cc (44×43mm) and which became known as the '65'. This was to be offered in various guises, not only Sport, but T and TL (Turismo Lusso), and another project was the development of a brand new scooter. It was this latter machine which was to be the sensation of the next Milan Show, held some two months later than normal, in mid-January 1952. Known as

the Cruiser and styled by the famous design house of Ghia, it was powered by a highly innovative 175cc (62×58mm) overhead valve engine which was mounted horizontally, with the cylinder head towards the nearside. A flexible coupling took the drive to a hydraulic torque converter, from which there was a shaft and bevel drive to the stub-axle-mounted rear wheel.

The housing of the converter and shaft formed the pivoted arm of the rear suspension, which was controlled by pull-rods actuating coil springs and rubber cartridges in horizontally placed cylinders. With the torque converter eliminating the orthodox gearbox and operating mechanism, controls were few. Once the Cruiser was on the move, it was driven entirely by using the throttle and brakes. A 'clutch' lever was provided to lock the transmission to the engine, so that, should the electric starter fail, the Cruiser could be bump-started and when it fired the transmission lock could be disconnected and the machine driven through the converter.

With the Mondial scooter (see Chapter 12), which was introduced at the same show, the Cruiser can lay claim to the distinction of probably being the world's first scooter

The rider in the foreground is Leopoldo Tartarini at the start of the 1955 Giro d'Italia with his Ducati 98 Gran Sport. This was the first of Ing. Fabio Taglioni's designs for the company.

equipped with the luxury of an electric start and the very first to use an automatic gearbox. Although most elegant in appearance and lavishly equipped, the Cruiser was destined to prove a massive flop, being taken out of production in late 1953, after only 2000 had been produced. This was partly due to its expensive price tag (half again more than an equivalent Lambretta or Vespa). Also its weight was significantly higher because of its heavier four-stroke power plant and complex specification. Originally the engine gave a healthy 12 bhp, but on production models this was restricted to 8 bhp due to a government ruling which resulted in the machine having too much flab to haul around without enough muscle to cope. The lesson of the Cruiser's expensive failure was a bitter one for Ducati, but it was one which they took note of, with the result that for many years afterwards it concentrated on motorcycles rather than scooters.

The Milan Show was yet again the setting for the launch of the next Ducati, the '98'. This was a particularly

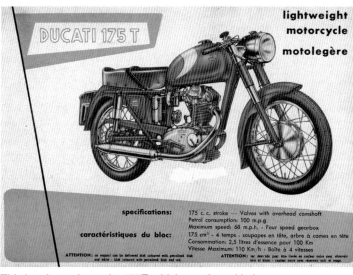

This brochure shows the 175T, which together with the more sporting "S" model became an instant best-seller when it went on sale in early 1957.

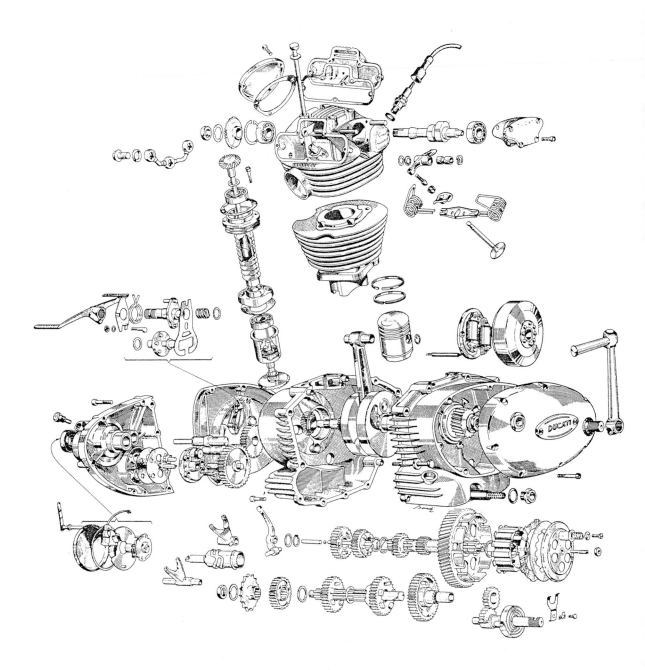

Exploded view of 174cc (62×57.8mm) overhead cam single engine.

neat ohv model with bore and stroke dimensions of 49×52mm respectively. Its cylinder was inclined forward 20 degrees from the vertical, and running on an 8:1 compression ratio it gave 6.5 bhp at 7000 rpm. An unusual feature on the 98 Sport model was the use of an oil cooler mounted in the front of the crankcase. Unlike the 60 and 65, the gearbox was a four-speeder. Together with a later 125 version of 124.443cc, with bore and stroke of

(55.2×52mm), the 98 became a best-seller.

By this time (1953) an interest in sport had begun to develop inside the factory at Borgo Panigale on the northern outskirts of Bologna, an area of Italy where there is quite exceptional enthusiasm for motor and motorcycle racing. But participation in trials and racing, particularly long-distance races like the Milano-Taranto and Giro d'Italia was rewarded with only modest success, since the

Most famous of all the early (narrow-case) Ducati overhead cam singles, the Mach 1. This was – manufactured between 1964 and 1966.

First of the production 750 GT V-twins as it appeared in 1971.

machines used by Ducati were far too standard to be able to compete effectively with their specially prepared rivals.

Determined to have a real go, the directors of the factory called in Fabio Taglioni in April 1954. A racing enthusiast whose hobbies, flowers and photography, have brought him considerable fame, Ing. Taglioni had worked for both Ceccato and Mondial. Only at Ducati, however, making full use of the factory's considerable technical resources, could he completely exploit his mechanical skill.

As the Bologna factory was at that time mainly interested in sports racing, having abandoned trials, Taglioni began by designing a sohc 100cc model, which became known as the Gran Sport. Attractive in appearance, it was orthodox in design. Sturdily made and inexpensive to buy, it was fast, reliable and easy to maintain and, like the subsequent 125cc version, it sold in quite large quantities in Italy and abroad. This Gran Sport served to put such famous riders as Francesco Villa, Bruno Spaggiari, Alberto Pagani, Giuseppe Mandolini, Alberto Gandossi and Franco Farné on the road to fame.

The engine had bore and stroke dimensions of 49.4×52mm, giving a capacity of 98cc. Its light alloy barrel, with cast-iron liner, was inclined slightly forward. Driven by a bevel shaft on the right-hand side of the engine, its sohc valve gear had exposed rockers and hairpin valve springs. The gear primary drive and multi-plate clutch were on the left, transmitting the power to a four-speed gearbox. The crankshaft, with full-circle flywheels, carried a small flywheel magneto on its drive-side extremity, supplying current for the battery of the coil ignition system; and at the opposite end, outside the timing bevel, a gear with straight-cut teeth provided the drive for

the oil pump (the Gran Sport had wet sump lubrication) and also for the contact-breaker. Adjustment of the contact-points could be made through a spring-retained inspection cap at the front of the crankcase cover. An initial power output of 9 bhp at 9000 rpm, with the engine running on an 8.5:1 compression ratio, was later boosted to 12 bhp at 10,500 rpm, with the maximum speed going up from 80 mph to 87 mph as a result.

The 125cc version (55.5×52mm) produced 14 bhp at 10,000 rpm and had a top speed of over 90 mph; and the 175cc version (62×57.8mm) gave 16 bhp at 9000 rpm and had a top speed of 100 mph. Weighing 190 lb and 200 lb respectively, as against the 180 lb of the 100cc model, the 125 and 175 later appeared with enclosed rockers and valve springs, and another modification was the use of 18in. wheels instead of the original 17in. A further version of 250cc capacity (74×57.8mm), which produced 25 bhp at 9000 rpm, was raced with considerable success in America by Francesco Villa. These Taglioni Ducatis were extremely successful in long-distance races and also in sports category events on closed circuits. Further evidence of their worth came in 1956, when one of the 100cc machines, suitably streamlined, set up new one-hour, 100km and 1000km world records on the banked circuit at the Monza Autodrome, at over 100 mph for the shorter distances and 96 mph for the 1000km.

It was in 1956 that the factory decided to widen their racing activities by having a go for Grand Prix honours and Ing. Taglioni evolved a double-knocker version of the 125cc Gran Sport. Apart from the two camshafts every-thing was left unaltered; this one modification had the immediate effect of boosting the power output to 16 bhp at 11,500 rpm on a 9.5:1 compression ratio. This was still not good enough to match the fabulous MVs and Mondials, nor the very fast new Gilera twin. So the following year

Introduced in 1975, the 900SS soon became the factory's most popular model. The machine illustrated is a 1977 model raced under the Mick Walker banner by Dave Cartwright.

Taglioni designed the famous desmodromic single. The engine layout was very much like that of the Gran Sport and its twin-cam successor, the Grand Prix. In fact the only noticeable differences were the massive desmodromic gear case over the cylinder head and the dual ignition with the usual 14mm plug on the left supplemented by another 10mm plug near the bevel shaft on the right. The flywheel magneto was discarded and reliance placed on a single battery to supply energy to twin coils. Later, the frame was modified from single-cradle to double-cradle pattern. Valve diameters of the single-cylinder 125cc 'desmo' were 31mm inlet and 27mm exhaust. Carburettor choke was normally 27mm, but was increased to 29mm for very fast circuits, and depending on course requirements, five or six cogs were tucked into the gearbox. Dry weight was just over 90kg (200 lb).

Prototype engines were tested over a long period, on the bench and on the track, power output was 17 bhp at 12,500 rpm and the desmodromic valve gear worked well and was reliable. Hundred-hour bench tests on full throttle caused no drop in the engine's performance, and no ill effects resulted from over-revving even though the track testers were at times letting the revs soar to above 15,000 — a fantastic figure at that time. Ing. Taglioni's new brainchild appeared to be capable of a brilliant performance.

Its first success came in the 1957 Swedish GP at Hedemora, with the works rider Gianni Degli Antoni winning the 125cc class. A few weeks later, at the Italian GP, the Ducatis seemed ready to threaten MV and Mondial supremacy; but a multiple crash on Monza's notorious first Lesmo bend, on the very first lap, completely eliminated any hopes of another success.

The most successful, yet still unlucky, racing season for Ducati was 1958. Running on a 10:1 compression ratio and with its power output bumped up to 19 bhp at 13,000 rpm the single-cylinder 'desmo' would top 110 mph, even though dolphin fairings were all that the FIM would now permit, instead of the full-enclosure streamlining of

The 900 GTS, developed from the 860 GT/GTS, used valve spring heads, not desmo. It was Ducati's idea of a touring machine.

previous seasons. In the Italian championship, Ducati riders were completely successful against an MV team which included Carlo Ubbiali and had been strengthened by the addition of Tarquinio Provini.

In the World Championship, honours were more evenly shared, with MV winning the TT and the German, Dutch and Ulster Grands Prix, while Ducati took the Belgian, Swedish and Italian Grands Prix. The first five places went to the desmodromic Bologna models in the home meetings: Bruno Spaggiari, Alberto Gandossi, Francesco Villa, Dave Chadwick and Luigi Taveri! It had been bad luck for Ducati when Spaggiari crashed in a mid-season national championship race for, even though he remounted and overhauled Ubbiali to win, he had a broken collar-bone which forced him to rest for a few vital weeks. In Northern Ireland Gandossi fell after tearing into the lead and setting a new lap record, but remounted to finish fourth.

The 1958 Italian GP saw the new twin-cylinder 125cc racer introduced. With bore and stroke dimensions of 42.5×45mm, it again had desmodromic valve gear, driven by a chain of gears accommodated between the two cylinders. Compression ratio was 10.2:1 and the engine developed 22.5 bhp at 14,000 rpm and could be allowed to touch 17,000 rpm on the over-run without disaster. It had coil ignition, with a single 10mm plug for each cylinder. A six-speed gearbox was fitted.

The five Monza finishers were joined by Mike Hailwood for 1959, and, with the single and twin-cylinder

'desmos' and six top riders, it looked a promising season for Ducati. Continual bad luck made it quite the contrary, however, and the factory had only one Grand Prix win, in the Ulster, where Hailwood came home first on one of the singles. At its début the twin had been ridden into third place at Monza by Villa; 12 months later it achieved exactly the same result, with Taveri as rider, after a race-long tussle with Ernst Degner (MZ), the eventual winner, and Ubbiali (MV). Discouraged by these results, and influenced no doubt by the general fall in motorcycle sales in Italy, Ducati withdrew from racing at the end of 1959. The desmos were sold to leading Italian and foreign riders, among them Mike Hailwood, who enjoyed considerable success on one of the singles the following summer. In 1961 Franco Farné, with another of the singles, won the first three rounds of the Italian championship and the 125cc class of the international Imola Gold Cup meeting, in which he had to fight all the way with Degner (MZ) and Tom Phillis and Jim Redman on Hondas. Then, however, Farne was put out of action for a long spell as the result of a crash.

Other racing equipment went to the Spanish Mototrans factory, which made Ducatis under licence and also maintained its own race department. With the help of some of the Ducati works mechanics, the Spanish factory developed a lighter, revised version of the twin-cylinder 'desmo' and Spaggiari was down to ride at Monza in 1963. It failed to materialize, however, possibly because the Honda four and the Suzuki twin were by then capable of such discouragingly high speeds. It is worth adding that in 1960 Ducati built a 250cc desmodromic twin to Mike Hailwood's special order. On exactly the same lines as the 125cc twin, it had the 55.5×52mm bore and stroke dimensions of the 125cc single. The power output was 43 bhp at the crankshaft, 37 bhp at the rear wheel, at 11,500 rpm, but the machine was too heavy, close to 300 lb, and its engine was too temperamental. Virtually a prototype which needed full factory development, it was also tried in over-bored form for 350cc events. This larger version was the idea of the former Norton and Guzzi star, Australian rider Ken Kavanagh. Kavanagh, then based in Italy, had successfully campaigned a 125 GP throughout Europe in 1959, and the results gained had encouraged Taglioni to build him a special 220 (actually 216cc) dohc model based on the production 175 Formula 3 for an Australian tour during the winter of 1959/60.

Upon his return Kavanagh entered into an agreement to buy a 350 Desmo twin from the factory, but his experiences with the machine finally convinced him that he should quit racing after the Italian GP at Monza. Hailwood fared little better with a similar machine and so both the Kavanagh and Hailwood bikes, plus Mike's 250 twins, were sold off, most going to John Surtees. In Surtees's hands they were equipped with a new, lighter frame and Reynolds forks for his brother Norman to ride. Again the results were none too good and the machines were moth-balled.

As far as standard road going machinery was concerned an important date had been the Milan Show in November 1956. Developed from the sports racing Gran Sport, this was a 174.5cc (62×57.8mm) single, available in touring or sports form. It therefore used the now classic bevel-driven single overhead cam configuration, with the all-alloy unit construction engine incorporating a deeply finned sump. A major difference was that the valve gear was now enclosed. Although the 84 mph Sport won on looks and performance, its less glamorous brother, the 175T, won fame with an around-the-world trip which was made during part of 1957 and 1958 by Giorgio Monetti and Leo Tartarini (the latter rider was later to become the boss of Italjet).

During 1958 and 1959, Ducati, thanks to Taglioni's design genius, were not only able to mount the racing attack already related, but undertake a considerable expansion of the production model range. The first newcomer to appear was a smaller version of the 125 Sport, which had reached dealers' showrooms late in 1957. The 100 Sport was virtually identical to its larger brother and proved particularly popular on the home market. Then in an attempt to offer a more creditable export challenge, Ducati introduced their largest motorcycle to date, the Elite. This was essentially a larger 175, achieved by boring

the cylinder out to 67mm while retaining the 57.8mm stroke of the original engine. Like the 175, the 203.783cc model was a success not only in Italy but around the world. By now the 175 and the 200 were also being offered in Motocross (Street Scrambler) and Americano (US Custom) styles.

By 1959, when the larger ohc model made its bow, Ducati had already begun to meet with success in the task of finding overseas distributors, notably in North America (Berliner of New Jersey) and in Britain (the Kings of Oxford Group). There was a vast range of models to choose from: 85T, 85 Sport, 98TL, 125T (all push-rods); 100 Sport, 125 Sport, 175T, 175 Sport, 175 Americano, 175 Motocross, 200 Elite, 200 Motocross and the strange Il Muletto (The Mule), a three-wheeler motor truck, powered by a 199.259cc (62×66mm) ohv engine. Apart from the Mototrans factory in Spain, the Bologna company controlled a branch office in Portugal (Lisbon) and other representatives included the Soosan Trading Corporation, Teheran, Iran; Enrique Blasco, Buenos Aires, Argentina, and Radyo-Mekanik of Istanbul, Turkey.

The big breakthrough came with the launch of a full-size 250 in early 1961. In Britain this was marketed as the 250 Daytona (Diana in other markets) and the Monza, not imported till much later. The new 250s were vastly oversquare with their 74×57.8mm bore and stroke. Other details included crankshaft flywheels in which the near-side shoulder was wider, altering the width of the crankpin. The clutch, introduced on the 1960 version of the 200, featured bearings within its drum rather than in the casing. Much of the balance, however, was similar to the first ohc singles.

With a top speed for the Daytona electronically timed at 84 mph it was no faster than the 175 Sport, but the extra capacity showed itself in the form of more effective torque. In addition, the British importer, Ducati Concessionaires (Kings of Manchester), offered a race kit comprising a high-compression piston, sports cam and 27mm Dell'Orto carb, which gave 100 mph performance. In the United States *Cycle World* timed an American version (fitted with the kit as an optional extra) at 104.1 mph during a 1962 test session at Riverside Raceway, California.

The tuned Daytona was almost a racer with lights. Certainly it had the performance and it looked the business. Strangely enough, although it was supplied with clip-ons, it did not have rear-set foot rests, which the high-speed road rider or budding track racer wanted. Even though the bike remained a good seller between 1961 and 1964, Ducati realized that it could improve both the performance and ancillaries. The result was the Mach 1 and with it a legend was born. It was an out and out sportster in the same mould

Mike Hailwood seen in action during the 1979 TT at Quarter Bridge. He finished fourth, and could not repeat his famous race victory on a similar machine a year earlier.

as that king of the café racers, the BSA DBD34 Gold Star. For the sum of £269 you bought a tuned motor which boasted a hefty 10:1 forged three-ring Borgo piston, hot camshaft, shim set tappets, 29mm Dell 'Orto carb, five-speed box, exposed spring rear units, full rear-set controls and a bright red and silver finish. Although the Mach 1 was shown in period brochures with a single racing-style seat, most came with an ugly reverse-waisted dual saddle. Other changes included larger valves, stronger valve springs and other more minor differences to detail specification.

In its road-test *Motor Cycle News* said: 'In a Lightning jet fighter, Mach 1 (plus a bit) takes you through the sound barrier. The new-for-1965 Ducati Mach 1 takes you through the "ton barrier" and it's a two-fifty! There's a supercharger-like whine from the single overhead cam-shaft, the gears snick home as quickly as you can move your foot, then with the magic "100" on the clock you can make heads turn by dropping it into fifth!'

Of course no bike is perfect and certainly not the Mach 1. Many riders had trouble achieving the speed recorded by *MCN*. This was not surprising, because, 'as delivered', the Mach 1 came with an 18-tooth gearbox and a 40-tooth rear wheel sprocket. This gave a theoretical maximum of 106 mph, but in almost every situation it was over-geared. Lower ratios would have been more suitable, while still allowing 100 mph to be attained. The curved kickstarter, mounted as on all Duke singles on the left, was almost impossible to operate. The 150 mph Veglia speedo was

grossly inaccurate and its undamped needle tended to swing about more like a rev counter. Lighting was hardly up to the standard of a 125cc commuter bike, let alone a 100 mph sportster. Last, but by no means least, the finish of the paintwork and chrome left a lot to be desired. In addition the spokes were painted silver and were prone to rusting, contrasting with the superbly finished alloy brake hubs.

Most of the Mach 1s imported into Britain ended up on the race track. One of the first to campaign a Mach 1 on

Close-up of the 1979 Darmah SD Sport engine assembly. Note the cranked kickstarter, the oil filter housing and electric starter motor between the vee of the cylinders.

1981 saw the Bologna factory introduce the much improved Pantah 600SL. This was not only larger than the original, but had uprated gearbox and hydraulic clutch.

British short circuits was Londoner Brian Jefferies, who purchased one of the early bikes from dealer Vic Camp (later to become the British distributor). Without doubt, however, the most successful of all Mach 1 racers in the first few months was production specialist Mick Rogers. Although only having sight in one eye, Rogers was the man to beat throughout the 1965 season in the 250 Production class. Spurred on by this, Vic Camp produced the first of his Mach 1 racers. Initially this was quite simply a standard bike, less lights but with add-on glass-fibre. The following year the 'racerized' Mach 1 gained more attractive glass-fibre, a 30mm Dell 'Orto carburettor', twin-plug ignition and alloy rims. Otherwise it was still standard.

Camp signed up leading short-circuit star Tom Phillips for the 1966 season. The same bike was also ridden to second place in the Manx GP that year by Ken Watson, but it was not in standard trim. Besides its Oldani front brake, the motor had several special parts, including a works cam, slipper piston and titanium con-rod. The paying customer did not get anything like the Phillips/Watson bike, even though it may have looked the same. I bought a brand new Camp Mach 1 'racer' myself for the 1966 season. During the second practice lap for the Manx GP the con-rod snapped. After I kicked up a fuss Mr Camp eventually sold me some special parts similar to those in the Phillips/Watson machine. 1967 saw an immediate improvement in my fortunes, including wins and places at both club and national level. Sadly the bike was burnt out after finishing a waterlogged Manx GP that year. Other Ducati riders followed suit, resulting in the fact that today around two-thirds of a classic grid in the 250 races are Ducatis.

Back on the street the Mach 1 remained unchanged throughout its short life of some 2½ years, except for a supposed strengthening of the kickstarter gears shortly after the start of production. However, together with other five-speed, narrow-case 250s, and even more so on the 350 Sebring, this remained an area of weakness. Very, very few original road-going Mach 1s have survived. Production was small and although they were popular in Britain, they were in less demand in other countries. Most of the bikes sold ended up on the track, so original parts such as tool boxes, mudguards, tanks and seats are virtually unobtainable. This is a pity because, although the single-cylinder spares picture is not as good as it was, the majority of engine parts are still available. Prices have risen quite rapidly recently. I have seen road and racing Mach 1s advertised in the British press for around £2500. If you want to buy one, always make sure you are getting what is advertised. A Monza can be made to *look* like a Mach 1, but they started life very differently. A pukka Mach 1 will have the prefix DM 250 M1 and an engine number starting with two or three zeros. If it simply says DM 250 and then a number 8 or 9 you've either got a Daytona GT or Monza (five-speed) or Daytona four-speed. But *don't* bother with a Mach 1 if all you want is daily transport. I cannot think of a more unsuitable motorcycle for this task. The Mach 1 is all about hard riding over winding roads, preferably on a hot summer's day with light traffic − which in itself is almost as rare as a Mach 1 these days!

Then there were the two-strokes. These had come about because of a planned expansion in the early 1960s. With much of Ducati's production going overseas it was felt important to widen the model range still more to include mopeds, ultra-lightweights and even scooters. The first two-strokes were launched in 1961, both 50cc mopeds: the Brisk, a single-speed automatic, and the Piuma three-speeder. The management then came up with a new scooter design, utilizing the Piuma engine suitably modified. The name given to this project was Brio, a name which was to be retained for all the two-stroke scooters produced by Ducati. The first Brio was the '48'. The single-cylinder piston port two-stroke engine differed from the earlier mopeds in that it was equipped with fan cooling. This consisted of a series of blades attached to the flywheel magneto rotor. The air was directed on to the cylinder barrel and head by means of an alloy cover through which the air passed. The 48 Brio engine produced a mere 1.5 bhp at 5200 rpm, so fan cooling would seem to be the least of its priorities! The actual engine capacity was 47.633cc (bore and stroke 38×42mm) and the compression ratio was 7:1, giving a top speed of 31 mph. Strangely as the British moped law stands today the 48 Brio would have been ideal, but back in 1963 it was underpowered. Other details included a six-volt 18-watt flywheel magneto for ignition and lighting, three-speed hand-operated gearbox, primary transmission by helical gears and final drive by chain in an enclosed oil bath. The frame followed conventional scooter design. The steel split wheels were 9in. with brake diameter 105mm front and rear, in alloy hubs. Several accessories were available as optional extras; spare wheel, front carrier, two types of rear carrier, a speedometer (not fitted as standard) and a steering lock.

The following year, 1964, saw the introduction of a larger improved Brio, the '100'. This used the same 93.969cc engine unit as the Cadet and Mountaineer lightweight motorcycles, which were launched at the same time. Again fan cooling was used. However, unlike the smaller Brio, the newcomer was much more sprightly with a maximum speed of over 50 mph and 6 bhp at 5200 rpm, the same as the motorcycles, as was the 51×46mm bore and stroke and the 8.5:1 compression ratio. Although the three-speed hand-operated gear change was retained the rest of the engine was substantially improved, including the output of the flywheel magneto, which was now six-volt 30-watt. There were improvements to the general specification as well. Replacing the single seat of the '48' was a much more stylish dual saddle, wider 3.50×8 tyres, larger 105mm headlight (formerly 95mm) and much larger rear body-work. The side panels were longer, but still detachable by turning a single alloy handle each side. The rear light was improved by fitting one from the 250cc motorcycle which had an oblong alloy body. A speedometer was now standard.

Both Brios remained in production until 1968, and, although unchanged, both were retitled 50 and 100/25 respectively in their final production year. None of the modifications made to the motorcycles and mopeds which used the same engines were carried out to the scooter and so these finally died out. Today the scooters are almost forgotten by all but the most enthusiastic supporter of the marque, but both the Brio and the earlier Cruiser were important steeping stones in the evolution of Ducati Meccanica.

Other machines produced for similar expansionist reasons were the 160 Monza Junior, a 500 parallel-twin and the massive 1260cc Apollo V-four. Of the three, only the smaller bike entered production, and although several thousand were produced in some 3½ years, it could not be described as a popular bike. Its 151.968cc (61×52mm) engine was based on the 100/125 series rather than a scaled-down bigger unit. Unlike the vast majority of the Duke ohc singles, the 160 was solely built as a touring mount.

Both the other projects were largely conceived for the American market. The twin first appeared at the Berliner dealer convention held immediately after the US Grand Prix in March 1965. The 497cc (74×57.8mm) push-rod overhead valve engine had an electric starter and was coupled to a five-speed gearbox. Power was a claimed 40 bhp at 6000 rpm. It never left the prototype stage, nor did other Ducati parallel twins built in the same period: another 500 and an 800cc intended mainly for police work. The Apollo had its origin in the desire by the Ducati American importers, the Berliner brothers, to offer a suitable bike for Stateside police work. 'Suitable' meant cylinders, preferably with a V configuration, at least 1200cc, and with a tyre size of 5.00×16! At the time, the late 1950s, Berliner was already the importer of the German Zündapp and British Matchless and Norton and more importantly in this context, Ducati.

It also happened that only the Italian factory was interested in the proposal. Negotiations between Joseph Berliner and Ducati's managing director, Dr Giuseppe Montano, began as early as late 1959, but the government-appointed officials in Rome, who controlled the Ducati purse strings at the time, back-pedalled on the idea. Talks and yet more talks dragged on for literally years, before Bologna was actually given the green light following Berliner's eventual agreement to fund the cost of producing a prototype. The American company also agreed to under-write part of the finance required to meet tooling costs of the production model. The result was a 1257cc V-four with the extremely oversquare bore and stroke measurements of 84.5×56mm with push-rod operated ohv. The single camshaft nestled at the base of the vee and was gear driven by the crankshaft. There were four sets of points, four condensers, four ignition coils and four 14mm spark plugs. Power was transmitted through a five-speed gearbox and seven-plate wet clutch and helical primary drive gears to the rear wheel via a duplex final drive chain. Berliner had wanted shaft-drive, but Ing. Taglioni was against this because it would have increased production costs unnecessarily. A 12-volt, 32-amp hour battery provided the sparks and looked after an electric starter and 200-watt generator. It was also needed for the various police equipment, such as radio, extra lights and siren.

Built in 1962, the prototype was first tested in 1963. This revealed the bike's Achilles' heel, the tyres. In those days tyre technology was simply not advanced enough for the kind of performance that the awesome Ducati V-4 was capable of, so the power was dropped from around 100 to 67 bhp, but this brought its own problems, as it no longer offered any real advantage over the home-grown Harley V-twins, which already equipped the bulk of the police forces throughout the States. Even so it was hoped that a solution would be found and production was scheduled to start in 1965. This never happened, not because a solution to the tyre-shredding problem could not be found, but because

A year later, 1982, and the 600TL tourer made its bow. Although a competent machine, sales did not match expectations.

the bureaucrats in Rome once again put the block on the project. All that remains today is the prototype in North America and an engine unit back at the factory in Bologna.

Life had to go on at Ducati and Ing. Taglioni was requested to carry out a major redesign on the long-running ohc singles. This resulted in a new family of one-lungers, commonly identified by the feature which most distinguished them from the previous singles and are known today as the 'wide-case' Ducatis. Unlike all the earlier models these are characterized by having the rear engine mounting bolts and crankcase mountings some four times wider than the front ones, whereas on the original all were the same 'narrow' width. The first model with the new wider rear crankcase mountings made its public début at the bi-annual international Cologne motorcycle show in West Germany during September 1967. This was a 350 (340cc) styled in Mark 3 roadster form. Except for the different paintwork on the tank and side panels, the new production Mark 3s were launched in June 1968 and were essentially the same as the prototype. Also launched around the same time was an on/off-road version, the 350 Street Scrambler.

Soon these two were joined by a pair of 250s (identical except for capacity) and muted touring versions, called the Monza and Sebring, which were soon taken out of

production. It is worth noting that the latter were *not* the Monzas or Sebrings which were built between 1965 and 1967 and sold in both North America and Britain (in the latter market from 1968 onwards) and were of the earlier 'narrow-case' design.

By the end of 1968 a further two models had appeared and these were now famous Desmo models, again offered initially in 250 and 350 form. On these early Mark 3 and Desmo models, only the method of valve operation and more chrome on the Desmo placed the two models apart. Besides the wider rear engine mounts, the new frame was stronger at the rear, although the front and rear suspension on the early 'wide-case' models was the same as the original singles, with the 31.5mm enclosed spring forks and three-position chrome spring Marzocchi rear units. The brakes were also unchanged.

But it was in the engine department that the major changes (and improvements) occurred. The head design of the Mk 3 followed that of the super sporting Mach 1 (as did the carburettor), while on the Desmo (marketed as the Mk 3D) the actual design of the desmodromic system for mechanical valve opening and closing was very similar to the one that Ing. Taglioni had devised for his early racing machines. The difference was that the roadster's valve closing was assisted by springs (off the 125/160 models), unlike the racers, which had none at all. Other engine changes from the earlier models affected the bottom end, which had been a source of problems. An important alteration was to the kick-start gear, always a weak point on the narrow-case models. The big-end had also proved fragile, unless the machine was maintained and ridden by an experienced rider. Here it was vital on the older models to have regular oil changes and not to allow the engine to labour at low revs, particularly on a high gear. Even so the big end was often found wanting. With the new engine the con-rod and big-end bearing were beefed up and the wet-sump lubrication capacity increased from 3¾ to 5½ pints. There were also a host of minor changes, including the gearbox and selector box. The electrics, although still six-volt, were uprated from 60- to 80-watt and a larger 13-amp hour battery installed. Events were to prove that in its search for even better big-end life the diameter of the big-end was increased on three separate occasions: the last change to a 32mm crankpin was in 1974, which was also the final year of production. Earlier, from 1969, an even bigger version of the single theme had been introduced, the 450, actually 436cc (86×75mm).

1971 saw an update with several cosmetic changes, which led to the more sporting Mk 3 Special and the externally identical Desmo, nicknamed the 'Silver Shotgun'. This was in reaction to the metallic silver finish of the tank, seat and mudguards. These two continued until the end of 1972, as did another machine, the Mk 3 Tourer. The sportster had introduced the double-sided Grimeca-made front brake and 35mm Marzocchi front forks, later a feature of the final blue and gold Mk 3s imported into Britain from November 1973. Hardly any of the 1971-72 bikes reached Britain because, at that time, importer Vic Camp was in dispute with the Italian factory over prices, as were the American importers, Berliner. From the end of 1973, although slightly earlier in Italy, came the definitive single. There were three types: Mk 3, Street Scrambler and Desmo. The last mentioned were truly striking machines with their yellow/black finish and had a choice of disc or dual drum front stopper, and like the other models were offered in 250, 350 and 450cc versions. Finally in mid-1974 came a special 239cc (72.5×57.8mm) model for the French market. Some of these reached Britain during 1975, after the production of the singles had come to an end following a production run which had begun with the 175 way back in early 1957. Somehow, although they are more widely known today, the V-twins which replaced them never quite seemed the same type of bike, at least in this writer's personal view.

Prior to 1970, Ducati had almost entirely restricted their designer Ing. Fabio Taglioni's brief to single-cylinder engines. The only exceptions were parallel-twin prototypes and the abortive V-4 Apollo project. Following the replacement of the long-serving *Doctore* Giuseppe Montano as factory boss in 1969 by the combination of government-appointed officials Arnaldo Milvio and Fredmano Spairani, the Bologna company set out on a new path.

Although the long-established overhead cam singles were to continue for the time being, Milvio and Spairani firmly believed that the future lay in the trend towards bigger machines, and therefore one of the duo's first tasks was to instruct Taglioni to design a 750 as soon as possible. Perhaps in retrospect his choice of a V-twin was to be expected and can be explained in relatively simple terms: cost effectiveness (at least from a development time point of view) and the need for a unique design which could carry the marque into the next decade and beyond. It was also a configuration which he had personally admired for a long while. The heart of the newcomer was the engine. This was a 90-degree angle V-twin and, as the front pot was nearly horizontal, the rear cylinder was provided with its own supply of cool air, compared to say models such as the Harley-Davidson or Vincent vees which, with a much narrower angle vee, tend to suffer from overheating of the rear cylinder. The most important reason for the choice of the wide angle was that it provided the best primary balance factor. Italy's other 90-degree twin was the Moto Guzzi (see Chapter 15), which avoided the cooling problem entirely by turning the engine so that both cylinders were in the airstream and by utilizing shaft final drive.

Taglioni had an altogether more sporting approach than the designer of the Mandello V-twin, for he used the more sporting rear chain drive and the narrow engine profile allowed a more sporting stance. The narrow frontal angle endowed the Ducati with not only the best possible penetration, but also greater angles of lean for its rider. In many ways the Ducati 750 was a pair of the famous overhead cam singles in a common crankcase. Because of this, the engine assembly, at least of the prototype, when it appeared in mid-1970, was substantially the same as the production models which began to flow off the Bologna line the following year. As on the singles, this was a full unit construction design with wet sump lubrication and shaft and bevel drive to the overhead cam gear. The first model, the GT, employed conventional ohc valve operation, and not the desmodromic positive system as used on the most sporting of the singles by this time. It had a capacity of 747.95cc (80×74.4mm), and the drive was transmitted via a helical geared primary drive, a wet multi-plate clutch and five-speed gearbox. The factory claimed a maximum speed of 122 mph, but in reality top whack was more like 112-115 mph. Its greatest asset was the unit's huge torque and

Mechanic Pat Slinn working on the 600 Ducati F2 racer of four times world champion Tony Rutter, circa 1982.

instant throttle response in any gear. This was one modern 750 which did not need revving to the heavens, unlike Honda's CB750 or to a lesser extent the BSA and Triumph triples. The only major change between the prototype and the first production version was the front brake, which was changed from a massive 240mm dual drum to a 300mm hydraulically operated disc.

The majority of the journalists who tested the bike were impressed, both inside and out, as the following quote from *Motor Cycle Mechanics* reveals, 'Whilst I was at Mick Walker's shop I had the chance of seeing inside one of the V-twin engines, and to anyone who likes seeing crafts-manship at its best the big V is an eye-opener. The crankshaft is massive and the con-rods that swing from it wouldn't look out of place in a drag bike. All the way through the engine there are signs of attention to detail, the little things that make all the differences between a good bike and an average machine. Crankshaft main bearings are suitably large and the cages that keep the rollers apart are made from a nylon-type material. The reason for this is that ordinary caged roller bearings are normally noisy. The nylon section helps to keep this noise down. All the shafts in the engine are individually shimmed − a process that takes up a lot of time during manufacture but pays off in longer life and silent running. The bevels that drive the top-mounted camshafts are driven by gears that look strong enough to have come out of the back axle of a car. Even the gears are carefully matched to ensure precision running. What it amounts to is an engine that is blueprinted as standard.' As on all Ducatis the standard of the alloy casting work was truly superb. But, of course, in a contrast so

familiar to the majority of Italian motorcycles of the period the paintwork and chrome plating of the 750GT were far from perfect. In stark contrast to the already mentioned alloy work, the awful painted wheel spokes acted as a reminder that once again Ducati had skimped on some details. Built around the engine was a duplex frame, which, in traditional Ducati practice, used the engine as an integral stressed member. And although it did not look anything special (in fact at a glance the GT looked large and felt large) it was extremely efficient in operation.

This was not only important for the road rider, but also played a significant role in what was to prove one of the major racetrack upsets of all time, the 1972 Imola 200-mile event. This took place on 23 April, 1972, and resulted in the now almost legendary 1-2 victory for the Bologna factory with a pair of 750 V-twins, ridden by Paul Smart and Bruno Spaggiari. Ranged against the cream of the world's superbikes from such names as MV Agusta, Moto Guzzi, Honda, Norton, Triumph, Laverda, Kawasaki, Suzuki and BMW, the pair of Ducatis showed a clean pair of heels to everything on the Imola track that day. Behind this famous victory lie some unexpected facts: that Imola had not been the real target, but instead Daytona; and it was only because the Americans had insisted upon the minimum 200 replica rule that Ducati had not contested the Stateside classic the month before. Then there was the saga of the riders who said 'no'. Men like Jarno Saarinen, Barry Sheene and Renzo Pasolini, to name but three. And it is a well-known fact that the eventual race winner, Smart, would have also turned down the offer if his wife had not agreed in his absence! Ten machines were actually built for Daytona/Imola in 1972 and ridden at the latter by a total of four riders: Smart, Spaggiari plus Ermanno Giuliano and the Englishman Alan Dunscombe.

The Italians Spaggiari and Giuliano had already campaigned the 500 V-twin racer which Ducati had used in Grand Prix events with little effect for the past couple of seasons, whilst Smart was already a seasoned international competitor. The strangest choice was Dunscombe, who was having his first ever ride outside Britain. Even so he was the 'official' pilot for British importer Vic Camp and had tested the 500 GP machine the previous year, when Phil Read and Spaggiari had raced them at Silverstone. Also at Silverstone the great Mike Hailwood had practised on another Ducati, a 750, but based around the 500, and not the production-inspired Imola machines. As if to add confusion to the scene Milvio and Spairani also commissioned a 3-cylinder 350 GP bike, but this was never to turn a wheel in anger and the project was soon aborted.

For a relatively short period after the Imola victory the Ducati management team professed an appetite for even greater things. There was mention of a full Grand Prix effort, but in reality the success of the larger V-twin in Formula 750 events effectively put to an end optimistic dreams of classic glory. Whatever else may be said it was this one victory in April 1972 that effectively started the legend of the Ducati V-twin, at least the variety with desmo valve gear. This allowed the engines to run up to 10,000 rpm in the lower gears and provide a maximum power of 85 bhp at 8800 rpm. Other features of the Imola engines were high-lift cams (later offered to private owners), forged 10:1 Mondial pistons, 40mm Dell 'Orto pumper carburettors and stronger connecting rods. However, the five-speed gearbox, wet clutch and standard roadster crankcase differed from the more specialist racing machine which the factory entered for Imola the following year. This also featured a new frame and swinging arm and central axle forks. Conversely it never achieved the success of the original.

Out on the street 1972 had seen the introduction of the 750 Sport. This differed from the GT not only in its distinctive yellow and black paint job but also larger 32mm carburettors (the GT had 30mm instruments), open bellmouths (instead of air filter boxes) and higher-compression pistons. However, the camshafts remained the same.

For 1973 both the GT and Sport were given a visual uplift, although the engine specifications were unchanged, except for the replacement of the British Amal Concentric Mk 1 carburettors with round slide Dell 'Orto PHF instruments. On the racing front, 1973 had not only seen new Imola Formula 750 machines (Spaggiari finished second overall in the two-leg event), but the début of a larger V-twin. This had a capacity of 863.9cc (86×74.4mm) and made its public bow at the Barcelona 24 Hours marathon, held at the Monjuich Park circuit during July. The 860's arrival could not have been better, as the new engine not only lasted the full distance but, ridden by Benjamin Grau and Salvador Canellas, recorded a race victory which also included new lap and distance record speeds.

In November, four months after the Barcelona triumph, the standard road-going version of the 860 made its first appearance at the bi-annual international Milan Show, in the shape of the prototype, with the title of 860GTI. Unfortunately as events were to prove this was not a machine modelled around the Barcelona race winner, but instead a rather ugly touring mount with angular styling and a small nose fairing. The production version which came on stream a year later in November 1974 was essentially the same machine, but without the headlamp surround, featured a different colour scheme, had re-

Ing. Taglioni and his grandson Luca with the last of his creations for Ducati, the 1985 1000cc Mille Replica.

angled louvres in the side panels and lost the Borrani alloy rims, and was now called 860GT. The 860GTI/GT was the work of the well-known car stylist Giorgetto Giugiaro of the Ital Design Studio in Milan, which just goes to prove that two-wheelers require a somewhat different approach to vehicles with four. If this was not bad enough the Ducati management, changed yet again after Milvio and Spairani had been replaced the previous year, made a monumental series of errors by deleting all the existing models (the singles and well-loved 750 vees) and instead introduced a couple of middleweight parallel twins and, of all things, a 125 two-stroke enduro bike!

Needless to say the company and its dealer network paid the price, as 1975 was to prove a sales disaster. Ducati distributors and the dealer network, both in Italy and abroad, were stuck with models which no one wanted to buy and had frequent requests for models which were no longer available. And I can vouch from personal experience!

Strangely, in 1974 there had been unparalleled demand for the company's range, which then consisted of 239, 248, 340 and 436cc singles in Street Scrambler (SCR), Mk 3 or Desmo form, 750GT, 750 Sport and the strictly limited production hand-built 750SS. The latter bike was almost a road-going street-legal version of the 1972 Imola race winner. A race kit was available to those customers wishing to enter their machine in Formula 750 events.

In contrast the 1975 range consisted of: 125 ISDT, 350 and 500 GTL and 860 GT. The brightness at the end of a very dark tunnel was provided by the machine which Ducati saw as a replacement for the 750SS, the 900SS.

New breed: the 750 F1 first appeared in 1985.

This quickly became the company's most popular model. But initially only a handful had been built, in contrast to the thousands of unwanted 'standard production' referred to above.

The 1975 crisis really lasted until 1977, when Ducati at last got its priorities right. This saw not only totally restyled 350 and 500 parallel twins, but the 900SS was treated as an important series production model in its own right and, most important of all, at least in terms of sales, the introduction of the new Darmah. The Darmah combined the style of the new super sporting Desmo Sport parallel twins (both were the work of the same man, Leo Tartarini, the Italjet boss) and the use of the Desmo engine from the 900SS. As if this was not enough the Bologna factory also put a considerable amount of thought into the area it had neglected most in the past, that of ancillary equipment. Gone were the dreadful Aprilia electrical components and equally poor Ducati Electronica items. In their place came Bosch, Nippon-denso and Lucas parts. The result was a machine which could at last attract a wide audience and resulted in sales figures improving dramatically. For 1978 the 900SS received much of the Darmah improvements, including the Bosch/Nippon-denso electrics.

Mike Hailwood's legendary Isle of Man comeback victory in the 1978 Formula 1 TT provided Ducati with not only their first World Championship, but an almost endless stream of publicity. It also led the following year to the introduction of the much-admired Mike Hailwood Replica. Again, as with the 750SS and 900SS before it, the MHR was originally seen as a limited production machine. And of course once again Ducati got it wrong, because by the early 1980s it was the company's best-selling model.

1979 was also important for other reasons. There was the lovely Darmah SS, a sports version of the SD, with clip-ons, rear-sets, 900SS-type fairing and a superb ice-blue metallic paint finish. The first of the new breed Pantah V-twins, the 500SL, also made its appearance that year, but not generally for export. The main talking point of the Pantah was the belt drive to the overhead cams. Although it shared the earlier bevel driven V-twin's 90-degree configuration there were a number of other very important changes, including the plain bearing big-ends and screw-in car-type oil filter canister.

The original plan was for both single- and twin-cylinder belt-driven engines. But both the 350 Utah (trail) and Rollah (roadster) singles never got beyond the pair of prototypes, which made a fleeting appearance at the 1977 Milan Show, together with a prototype 500 V-twin.

The 1979 500SL Pantah had a capacity of 498.89cc (74×58mm) and like all the 1979 range now featured desmodromic cylinder heads. The last valve spring model was the 900GTS of 1978, which ran alongside its replacement, the Darmah, for several months (probably for the reason that Ducati needed to use up its excess stock of 860GT components upon which the GTS was based).

As the new decade dawned all seemed bright, with the other part of Ducati Meccanica also doing well – this comprised the stationary engine and diesel section, both of which had full order books. From 1981 onwards, however, the going got ever tougher for the two-wheel division, even though a number of new models appeared, including the 600 SL (1981) and TL (1982), both 583.08cc (80×58mm); 350 SL and XL (both 1982), 348.96cc (66×51mm); a revised 900SS (1981) and finally its replacement, the 900S2 (1983).

The Bologna factory also had the glory of winning a further four world championship titles (in the Formula 2 TT category) by stint of the efforts of the Englishman Tony Rutter (who was champion in 1981, 1982, 1983 and 1984). By then the sales recession around the world had hit Ducati hard, although its many fans found it difficult to believe Ducati Meccanica SpA was on its corporate knees. As related in Chapter 6, part of its plight was answered in June 1983, when an agreement was reached between the Bologna company and the Cagiva concern. This saw the Castiglioni brothers sign up to buy a contracted number of Ducati V-twin engines for a new range of Cagiva motorcycles. At the time the press generally foresaw the end of Ducati as a manufacturer in its own right. This was not strictly true as for the next two years it continued to produce complete motorcycles, including the introduction of the new Mille. Besides being the largest of the classic bevel-driven models to be offered, 973.14cc (88×80mm), the Mille was the last design by Ing. Taglioni to actually reach production status. It featured a similar high-pressure lubrication system to the Pantah, which allowed the use of plain bearing big-ends and a canister-type oil filter. Other improvements included the stronger gearbox first fitted to the 900S2, and a hydraulic clutch. At the same time the outer engine covers lost the 'square' appearance. And in terms of both performance *and* reliability the Mille engine was the best of the bevel-driven vees. It was offered in both the S2 and Replica versions, although the latter was built in larger numbers, surviving until early 1986. Another Taglioni design of the 1980s was a 1000cc V-four, but this never left the prototype stage.

By this time Cagiva had purchased Ducati Meccanica from the Italian government and the actual date of the transaction was 1 May, 1985. Since then the factory's fortunes have been transformed, first by the F1 750 and F3 350 during 1985-87, then quickly followed by a mass of new models, including the 750 Paso in 1986 and 906 Paso in 1989. In between came other important models, including the 851 Superbike and 750 Sport, with Taglioni finally going into retirement in the mid-1980s (although he remained on the company's payroll as a consultant until May 1989). The models introduced since the Cagiva take-over have been the responsibility of his successor as chief designer, Ing. Massimo Bordi. Bordi was born on 9 May, 1948, and joined Ducati in January 1978 after gaining a university degree in 1974. Other people who have played an important role in the engineering side of the company since the Cagiva takeover are Franco Farné, a former racer of considerable repute and a Ducati employee since as far back as 1950, and his right-hand man in the racing/experimental department, Giorgio Grimandi. As this chapter was being written it appeared that Ducati's fortunes are once more on a high, with their 1990 model range consisting of: Indiana (custom), 851 Superbike (in Standard and SP versions), 750 Sport, 900 Super Sport and the Paso in 750 and 906 engine sizes.

The Castiglioni brothers have invested heavily since their purchase in 1985, with the result that today the Bologna factory is the centre of Cagiva's motorcycle empire (which currently consists of not only Ducati and Cagiva, but also Husqvarna and Moto Morini). Another innovation has been to centralize the spare parts for all these four marques under the same roof next door to the old Ducati Meccanica factory on the site previously owned by Zanussi, who in turn used the facilities of the former Ducati Electronica company.

The latter had split away from Ducati Meccanica as far back as 1953. So at long last Ducati's commercial expertise would appear to match their engineering skill. Long may this state of affairs continue and one can but wonder at what the future has in store for one of Italy's most illustrious marques.

CHAPTER 9

Garelli

To the vast majority the Garelli marque is synonymous with mopeds. However, this has not always been the case. Founded just after the First World War by Ing. Adalberto Garelli, the factory quickly established itself and became well known in the 1920s for its 350cc split-single two-strokes. These were production and racing versions based on Ing. Garelli's original machine which he built in 1913, but by the time production commenced in 1919, many details of the design had been improved.

Garelli first thought out the idea of a two-stroke split single during 1912. It consisted of two cylinders cast in a single block, with a common combustion chamber, the two pistons working in parallel, both connected by a long gudgeon pin and single con-rod. Each piston had a capacity of 174.6cc, making a total of 349cc. Other specification details included a bore and stroke of 50×89mm.

To prove his design in 1914 Adalberto Garelli decided to 'climb' the Moncenisio Pass in northern Italy, and was the first person to achieve it on a motorcycle. Besides the mechanical victory it was also a personal one, for the conditions were extremely poor, with bitterly cold winds and heavy snows making his journey very hazardous. To mark this event the Commander of Caserma Ospizio Capetavo handed Garelli a signed statement of confirmation. This document was dated 10 January, 1914, the day of the actual climb.

Adalberto Garelli was born in Turin in 1886. In 1908, at the age of 22, he gained his degree in engineering and, from 1909, dedicated his work to the study and perfection of the first two-stroke engines at Fiat. Fiat did not share his enthusiasm for two-strokes, and he left the company in 1911. In 1914, the same year as his memorable climb over the Moncenisio Pass, he joined Bianchi as head of their motorcycle division. Garelli's next stop was at Stucchi, another important motorcycle factory of the period. He remained with them for three years, 1915 to 1918. During this period he won a competition organized by the Italian Army for a military motorcycle with a special version of his 350 split single. Finally, with the 1914-18 War over, in 1919 he was able to realize his dream and set up his own factory, at Sesto San Giovanni, near Milan.

Almost from the outset, his design drew public attention and admiration, thanks to a victorious début in the Milan-Naples road race. This was a remarkable win from a manufacturer who had only just commenced production. The race took place over an 840-kilometre route linking two of Italy's major cities. In those days the roads were mostly hard earth, not tarmac, but for all that the distance was covered in 21 hours 56 minutes 2 seconds at an average speed of 38.296 km/h. The rider was Ettore Girardi.

During this time the Sesto San Giovanni factory was fully occupied with the mass-production of its first two models, the 'Normale da Turismo' and the 'Raid Nord Sud'. The Turismo was the touring version capable of 50 mph, while the sporting Raid would reach 75 mph and was produced to capitalize on the Milan-Naples race win. The racing 350s were entered by Garelli on circuits throughout Europe and were ridden by such legendary competitors as Nuvolari, Varzi, Gnesa, Vailati, Fergnani, Magnani and many other famous names of the period.

Apart from racing, Garelli was also actively involved in attempting to break world records. On 7 September, 1922, Visioli and Fergnani broke eight world records. Following this success a second record attempt was made in the autumn of 1923 with Gnesa, Sbaitz, Fergnani and Maghetti. This was brilliantly successful, with no less than 76 world records broken, some over long distances and times up to 12 hours. Speeds gained included an average of over 66 mph. The final attempt was in 1926, when three motorcycles were ridden by 14 riders alternating with each other. The result this time was an incredible 138 hours, with speeds of up to 81.5 mph.

Besides the Milan-Naples race of 1919, many victories were recorded, amongst these the Circuit of Lario in 1921, the international Grand Prix at Monza in 1922 and the first-ever victory by an Italian motorcycle abroad, at the Strasbourg circuit in 1922. The first national racing champion of Italy was Ernesto Gnesa, who won his title aboard a 350 Garelli at Monza in 1922.

One 350 racer was the first to be equipped with a very large oil tank for separate lubrication. Like the most sophisticated modern two-strokes of today the oil was automatically mixed with the fuel, in a quantity accurately proportioned to the throttle setting. Another milestone in two-stroke technology was the use of an expansion chamber-type exhaust system.

Adalberto Garelli.

A beautifully restored example of the glorious 350 racer is kept as a fitting tribute to Garelli's early history in the Garelli Museum. The final 1926 model developed 20 bhp at 4500 rpm and had a maximum speed of over 87.5 mph. It had a two-speed gearchange with the control lever on the back of the petrol tank. The oil mixture ratio was 17 per cent and its weight was less than 100 kg.

From 1927 onwards Garelli became less and less active in the motorcycle field and by 1928 they were heavily involved in the manufacture of military equipment, to such an extent that in 1936 Garelli no longer appeared on the list of Italian motorcycle factories.

It was not until after the Second World War had passed, and with it the demand for military items, that the name reappeared, initially with an engine providing auxiliary propulsion for ordinary bicycles. Called the Mosquito, it was designed by Adalberto Garelli with assistance from Ing. Gilardi. Like the earlier 350 split-single it was an instant success. In fact this is an understatement, as during its life-span over two *million* Mosquitos were sold throughout the world. In its original form it had a capacity of 38.5cc, with an external flywheel, roller drive, 0.8 bhp power output, a 5.5:1 compression ratio and a maximum speed of 20 mph. As was to be expected it was a two-stroke, but with a horizontal cylinder layout, weighing just over 4kg and able to run for 40 miles

on one litre of fuel. It was easily fitted to a conventional bicycle and power was transmitted to the rear wheel by means of a friction roller.

In 1952 over 400,000 Mosquito engines were produced and sold in Italy and abroad. The following year the original model was replaced by the 38B. 1955 saw the most substantial change to the Mosquito, when capacity was upped to 49cc (40×39mm) and the use of the Centrimatic clutch was adopted. In principle this type of clutch was the forerunner of all the centrifugal clutches used on fully automatic mopeds today. This continued success of the engine led Garelli to develop into other motorcycling areas, not limiting itself solely to auxiliary engines, but also into complete powered two-wheelers with chain-driven transmission. In the same year the Velomosquito was produced, a complete machine which today can be classed as one of the first modern mopeds.

The year 1956 saw the début of the 315, a three-speed variant of the Mosquito, opening up the road to further improvements, which in turn led to larger engines of 70, 98 and 100cc. It was in the late 1950s that Garelli made its first contacts with the Agrati organization, which had factories at Monticello. The first co-operation was limited to Agrati providing certain cycle parts. This was followed by Garelli supplying Agrati with engine units to be installed in their own machines. This increasing participation led in 1961 to

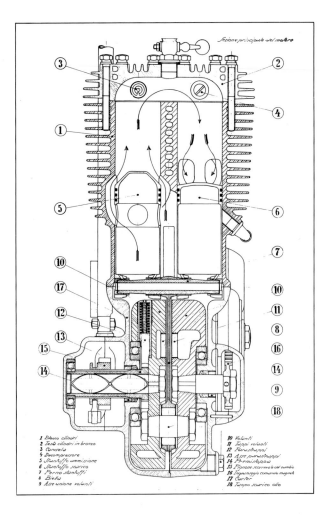

Sezione principale del motore

③ ②
④
①
⑤ ⑥
⑦
⑩ ⑩
⑰ ⑪
⑫ ⑧
⑬ ⑯
⑮ ⑭
⑭ ⑨
⑱

1 Blocco cilindri
2 Testa cilindri in bronzo
3 Candela
4 Decompressore
5 Stantuffo sommissione
6 Stantuffo scarico
7 Perno stantuffi
8 Biella
9 Asse unione volanti

10 Volanti
11 Tappi volanti
12 Perno rinvaspi
13 Asse rinvaspi
14 Premistoppa
15 Pignone scarrico e del cambio
16 Ingranaggio comando magneti
17 Carter
18 Tappo scarico olio

Technical drawing showing details of the 1920 Garelli 350cc
split single engine.

Agrati and Garelli joining forces. With the formation of the
Agrati-Garelli group, the combine was considerably
strengthened, for not only were mopeds being produced,
but also engines for go-karts, agricultural use, outboard
motors and light vans. The merger also allowed Garelli to
return to its sporting origins with the capture of several
world records.

Antonio Agrati, who had founded the company
bearing his name, was a skilled blacksmith in the small
town of Brianza, Cortenouva di Monticello, in the province
of Como. For many years the main Agrati-Garelli plant was
located there. Antonio Agrati died in 1924 at the age of 92
and his original workshop was left in the hands of his three
sons, Clodoveo, Luigi and Mario, who set out to change the
activity of their father's business into something more
modern. At first this was by repairing agricultural steam
engines. By 1925 the business had expanded to such an

extent that it was decided to build electric motors of varying
capacities and these were an immediate success. In order to
make full use of the tools required for the cutting of the
rotors, they utilized them for the manufacture of gears and
various bicycle parts.

Then disaster struck: all three sons died prematurely
within a short space of time. Not one to give up, Mario
Agrati's widow, helped by Carlo, the 16-year-old son of
Clodoveo, decided to continue the company. In this
difficult situation the construction of electric motors was
reluctantly abandoned and with the help of the workforce
the bicycle business survived. Ever since that time Agrati
has been manufacturing cycling equipment. Throughout
the 1920s and 1930s the Agrati enterprise continued. Like
Garelli, Agrati survived the war, and by 1955 it was
decided to produce frames for motorcycles, scooters and
mopeds.

The year 1958 was important, as steps were taken to
make mopeds with the Agrati name. Agrati introduced the
Capri scooter, which had a 70cc two-stroke engine. This
was followed by the very interesting Como in 1960, which
was a 50cc machine, the first scooter in this class. The
Capri was also produced in 125 and 150cc form, both with
four-speed gear changes. It was exported in considerable
numbers all around the world.

After the 1961 merger the ranges of both marques were
rationalized, with only the more popular models being
continued. This was also because motorcycle sales
worldwide were depressed after the record sales of the late
1950s. Besides various mopeds, they produced a very
attractive 50cc sports motorcycle, the Junior. Originally in
three-speed form, it was later equipped with four gears and
named Record, after the record-breaking Monza visit of
1963. Factory engineer William Soncini and other
personnel prepared two 49cc machines for the record-
breaking attempts in the 50 and 75cc classes. The two fully
faired machines were ridden by a team of riders in
atrocious weather conditions on 3-4 November, 1963. The
team consisted of Marchesani, Pastori, Patrignani,
Pernigotti, Spinnello and Zubani. The following results
were achieved: six hours recorded at the average speed of
75.7 mph (50cc only), 1000km at 72 mph and the 24 hours
at 67 mph. The 24 hours record is still intact, in spite of
numerous attempts since to break it.

Another interesting part of Garelli's history is the
relatively unknown fact today that a four-stroke motorcycle
was produced. This appeared in 1960, just before the
merger, and in many ways was a typical Italian product of
the period. Simply called 'Garelli 125', it used a single-
cylinder ohv engine designed by the Parilla factory, with a
capacity of 123.6cc. Bore and stroke were both 54mm and

One of the great success stories of the immediate post-war years was the 38cc Mosquito auxiliary engine unit.

maximum power was 7.5 bhp at 7500 rpm. Other features were a Dell 'Orto UB20 BS carburettor, four-speed gearbox and helical geared primary drive. Maximum speed was a brisk 62 mph. It was one of the models carried through as an Agrati-Garelli group product, remaining in production until 1964, by which time it had been restyled, although the engine remained unchanged during its existence.

During the 1960s the fall in demand for motorcycling products saw much of the Agrati-Garelli production capacity utilized in other fields, such as chain-saw motors, go-kart engines and even a small truck with a 49cc power unit for light urban transport. In 1969 a decision was taken to concentrate the group's energies completely back into motorcycling. This meant entirely new designs, one of which was the forerunner of the successful Tiger Cross and Rekord Sports mopeds sold in Britain from 1973 to 1976. From these came the later KL series, which was still as late as 1987. 80cc versions in road and trail bike configuration were also constructed.

In 1972 a new step-through moped with a flat cylinder engine was introduced. This powered models such as the Eureka and small-wheeled Katia, of which over half a million were sold worldwide. Another technically interesting machine (although a sales failure) was the Electric Katia moped, produced in 1974, designed by Ing. Benso Marelli, who in 1966 succeeded Soncini as chief designer.

During August 1980 a journey was undertaken by Italian journalist Roberto Patrignani, the same ex-racer who had been part of the Garelli record-breaking team of 1963. This was a coast-to-coast moped ride across the USA starting in Charleston, South Carolina, on the Atlantic Coast and ending on the Pacific Coast in Los Angeles, California. He covered 2860 miles in 16 stages and the average distance travelled per day was 177 miles. During that time only 19.4 gallons of petrol were consumed, an average of 147 mpg. The machine, a Garelli Noi automatic, proved just what had become possible with a modern moped.

During 1981 several brand new models began to appear in addition to Garelli's main production of conventional mopeds. These included the GT80, also available with a 50cc engine. This sporting lightweight motorcycle had a disc front brake, cast wheels, square headlamp and a built-in rear carrier. Another was the RGS, a full-blown enduro mount even though its capacity was only 49cc. Garelli's most interesting new bike was one for the enthusiast, even though it was only a 125. This was the café racer water-cooled 125 TSR, a match both in performance and styling to anything currently on sale from the might of Japan. This employed a single-cylinder watercooled 124.8cc (57×52.8mm) six-speed engine which pumped out 22.5 bhp at 8750 rpm.

In 1982 Garelli made a triumphant return to road racing, and the results were shattering (for the opposition) in both classes they had chosen to enter, the 50 and 125cc; they won first and second places in the 125cc World Championship with riders Angel Nieto and Eugenio Lazzarini and added to this was the World Constructor's Championships in the same category. They also obtained second place in the 50cc class with Lazzarini. In 1983, Nieto repeated his performance and again became World Champion. Anyone who saw him clinch the 125 title at the Silverstone GP in 1983 would have been left in no doubt either of his ability as a rider or the speed and reliability of his mount. The reliability factor cannot be overstated, as in almost 30 starts during the 1982/83 seasons there were only two retirements, one attributable to lack of sparks. Unlike the larger classes, where other features come into their own, 50 and 125 racing places the emphasis firmly on power output.

For many years 125s had been limited by the FIM, the sport's governing body, to a twin-cylinder, six-speed formula. So if one compares a Yamaha 125 V-four of the late 1960s, which was a no-holds-barred 40 bhp rocket ship, and one of the most exotic Grand Prix bikes of all time, the Garelli's 47 bhp on its water-cooled twin-cylinders was even more amazing. The engine originally was the work of ace two-stroke designer Jorg Möller. It was

Garelli marketed this 125 four-stroke model from 1960 until 1964. Its ohv engine was a Parilla design.

In 1963 Garelli used this 49cc machine to break a number of speed records at the Monza Autodrome.

**Junior Tiger Cross
Junior Rekord**

Before the government brought in new laws to restrict their speed, machines like the Garelli Tiger Cross and Rekord sold in relatively large numbers to British youngsters during the mid-1970s.

designed by him for Minerelli, under whose banner it won its first Grand Prix way back in 1978, ridden by Pier-Paolo Bianchi. Other features of the Garelli 125 included a dry weight of 172 lb, magnesium 29mm Dell 'Orto PH SA carburettor, duralumin monocoque frame with conventional twin Bitubo gas-filled rear units, an alloy swinging arm, Marzocchi 32mm front forks with a mechanical anti-dive system and Campagnolo magnesium wheels. Angel Nieto joined Minerelli towards the end of the 1978 season, but MBA's Eugenio Lazzarini took the title; Nieto, however, was Champion in 1979. The team continued until the end of 1981, when Minerelli decided to retire from the Grand Prix scene. This is when Garelli appeared in the shape of Daniel Agrati, who took over the complete team. The one exception to this was the frame designer Dutchman Martin Mijwaat, who chose to return home to his native Holland.

Mijwaat's fellow Dutchman Jan Thiel, who replaced Möller when the former's contract expired at the end of 1979, steadily continued engine development, which included a new crankshaft and work to increase low-speed torque. The chassis, however, remained virtually unaltered, but even so the roadholding and cornering ability was reportedly the best in the class. By 1983 the 50 was reported to have a maximum speed in excess of 120 mph, and the 125 of 145 mph! Also that year worldwide production of Garellis reached 130,000. This was helped by

the opening a year earlier of the company's third Italian plant, but there was also an assembly facility at Curitiba in Brazil. Success on the racing circuit continued in 1984, with the first three places in the Riders' 125 World Championship. In fact, in spite of a fall during the final round at Mugello, Nieto won the 13th title of his long career with a total of 90 points, ahead of Lazzarini (78) and newcomer Fausto Gresini (51). It is worth noting that Garelli also won the Constructors' World title and that previously only Mondial (1950 and 1951), MV Agusta (1955) and Honda (1962) had taken the first three places in the 125 championships. The 50 had to be retired, as the class had changed to 80cc.

By 1985 the Agrati-Garelli empire was feeling the financial squeeze of the recession which had swept the motorcycle business around the world since the beginning of the 1980s. Even so it continued with its sports programme, which saw two new developments that year: a 250 V-twin racer and a 320cc trials bike. The new racer was entrusted to Fausto Gresini and Ezio Gianola. The team was sponsored by the FMI (Italian Motorcycling Federation) and managed by Eugenio Lazzarini (who had hung up his leathers at the end of 1984). The trials effort saw the factory support Danilo Galeazzi on a works version of a production 323 model, which had an exact capacity of 321.53cc (80×64mm).

At the Milan Show in November 1985 the factory

presented four new production models, the Tiger 50XLE and 125XLE trail bikes, the F1 Formuno moped and a revised version of their 'best-selling' 125 GTA sports roadster, now with double front disc brakes. In addition the company displayed the reborn Mosquito 35cc auxiliary engine. This was offered either as a kit or in complete versions known as the Bicimosquito and Velomosquito. This return to a concept of over three decades previously might seem strange when one realizes that by 1985 Garelli were also offering their top-of-the-range mopeds with such innovations as electric starting, water-cooling and oil pump lubrication.

With powered two-wheeler registrations falling, the Agrati group had come to rely more and more heavily on its Torpedo bicycle division and some 60 different models were offered. In Britain its subsidiary, Agrati Sales Ltd of St Mark's Street, Nottingham, had been forced to close its doors through falling sales. Established over many years, this was ample proof, if any were needed, of the depressed state of the market.

For 1986 the FMI continued its sponsorship deal and Lazzarini continued in his role of race manager. Much of the emphasis was centred on the new 250 V-twin, to be ridden by Maurizio Vitali. The trials efforts at factory level were divided between Galeazzi and new signings Carlo Franco and Donato Miglio. The team's goal was victory in the Trials World Championship Series. Although the dirt boys failed to win the title, Garelli's top rider in the 125 road racing Championship, Luca Calalora, became the 1986 title holder, with team-mate Fausto Gresini in second spot. By contrast the larger twin was way down in 15th place in the 250 hunt. In fact the 250 V-twin was to prove a real flop, with Vitali only managing 18th in 1987, a year in which Garelli once again took the 125cc Championship with Gresini and new boy Bruno Casanova. This meant Garelli had won the title five years in succession.

By the time the 50th Cycle and Motorcycle International Show was staged in Milan during November 1987, it was evident that Garelli was suffering badly from a depressed market. Not only had a new General Manager, Cesare Befani, been appointed as part of a major reshuffle at top management level which had seen the Agrati family leave the scene, but the two existing plants at Sesto San Giovanni and Monticello Brianza had been relocated completely at the latter site and the former closed completely. Production had been cut back to concentrate on just six mopeds (including the Mosquito project) and three motorcycles: the GTA 125 'Gresini', Tiger 125 XLE

Garelli entered Grand Prix racing in 1982. The Spanish star Angel Nieto promptly took the 125cc title for the company in both 1982 and 1983 on his ultra-rapid twin-cylinder two-stroke.

The 1985 Garelli works team.

By 1985 Garelli had also developed a 250 twin, but it was destined to never reap the success of its smaller brothers.

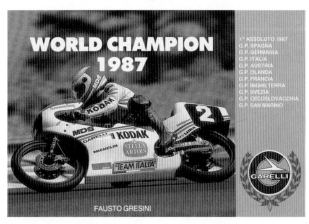

Postcard proclaiming the victories of the 1987 125cc world champion Fausto Gresini.

Although the 1985 Garelli GTA 125 had every modern convenience it could not match similar machines from Aprilia, Cagiva and Gilera in the all important Italian domestic market. Combined with a general downturn in the market, its lack of success prompted a financial crisis for the company.

and Trial 323. Even so it was announced that the company would be building a new single-cylinder 125 racer to conform to the new FMI rules introduced for the 1988 season. Riders were named as Gresini and the Spanish pilot Reyes, with Paulo Casoli to ride the 250. As history has recorded Garelli found themselves unable to match the speed of the Spanish Derbi or even the new single-cylinder production Hondas and again the 250 was very much out of contention. So as it enters the 1990s Garelli is holding on . . . just. On the production front and with reduced costs it looks like surviving the crisis, but on the race circuit its glory days now seem to be over, at least for the present.

CHAPTER 10

Gilera

Gilera is one of the truly great names in Italian motorcycling and is today once again a vibrant force within the industry, after years of decline and stagnation.

The famous Arcore marque was founded by Giuseppe Gilera, who was born on 21 December, 1887, at Zelobuonpersico, a small village to the south-east of Milan.

The well-known Italian journalist Carlo Perelli once described him as 'an ingenious man with an alert mind, evergreen enthusiasm for mechanical things and for the sport and a mild temperament which has made him universally liked'.

Brought up in a working-class family, even as a schoolboy the young Giuseppe was fascinated by all forms of mechanized transport, which were then in their infant stage of development; he went to work in the Bianchi factory in Milan at the age of 15.

Displaying an aptitude far above his age and upbringing, Gilera soon moved on to work as a mechanic with the Italian branch of the Swiss Moto Rêve concern.

After a spell in Geneva with the engineering firm of Bucher and Zeda, he finally returned to his native Italy in 1908.

By now Giuseppe Gilera had also proved his worth as a most competent road racer, particularly in hill-climb events. Racing though, was no more than a spare-time activity. His real love was his work as an engineer with an ultimate aim of becoming a motorcycle manufacturer in his own right, and by 1909, at the age of 22, he was ready to take the leap which was to alter his life. So Gilera founded his own marque in a small workshop at 42 Corso XXII Marzo, in Milan.

The first model was a 317cc (67×90mm) pedal-assisted single-cylinder device, with both the inlet and exhaust valves mechanically operated. Such a layout was quite rare in those days, when it was customary to have a side exhaust valve, mechanically operated, and an automatic overhead inlet valve kept closed (at least in theory) by a light spring and opening when the depression created within the cylinder as the piston descended before becoming strong enough to overcome the spring pressure. Gilera was one of the very first Italian manufacturers to provide his machines with a gear-change.

Realizing the importance of competition success very early in his business career, Gilera not only took part himself, but supported other riders on his machines. In fact he gained the marque's first victory when he won at the then well-known Circuit of Cremona in 1912. The gruelling 118-mile race was completed at an average speed of 28 mph, which was better than might at first seem the case when one considers the appallingly bad road surfaces of the period. Then came the Great War, during which Gilera's fledgling business turned its attention to the production of bicycles for the Italian army.

After the ending of hostilities there was a massive demand for motorcycles in Italy, but it was not until 1920 that Gilera was able to capitalize on this — after moving out of Milan to a much larger factory at Arcore, a few miles away on the main road from Milan to Lecco, and not far from Monza park, where the famous autodrome was later to be constructed. In order to look after the new facilities, with particular attention to the design and experimental departments, Giuseppe Gilera decided to give up active participation in the sport. However, before this happened he was involved in an accident while riding out in the country at night, when he collided with a stationary and unlit wagon. His injuries included the loss of a lung and meant that he was hospitalized for some considerable time.

His younger brother Luigi not only looked after the business in his absence, but also kept the family's sporting flag flying. Luigi Gilera not only competed in trials, including the ISDT, but became quite a famous sidecar driver, actually winning his last sidecar race at late as 1946.

Throughout the 1920s Moto Gilera achievements were mainly in long-distance trials, with 350 and 500cc side-valve machines. In 1925, however, Gino Zanchetta used one of the supremely well-built and reliable, but not very fast, side-valvers to win the 500cc category of the Milano—Naples road race.

Just how sturdy these bikes were was proved in 1930, when Luigi Gilera, with a 600cc sidecar outfit, and Maffeis and Grana on 500cc solos, won the International Trophy for Italy in the ISDT, based that year around Grenoble in France. There was a repeat performance the following year at Merano in Italy; and again in 1932 an all-Gilera team represented Italy — losing the trophy contest by a matter of

In April 1939, Piero Taruffi set a new world record for the hour by covering 204 kilometres (127 miles) on the Bergamo–Brescia autostrada. The photograph shows the designer Ing. Piero Remor (centre in suit) with Taruffi astride the supercharged four-cylinder Gilera.

seconds in the speed test to the British trio of Perrigo (BSA), Rowley (AJS) and Bradley (Sunbeam and sidecar). By then the name Gilera had become internationally famous, and home sales had increased to such an extent that the factory had become one of Italy's largest.

The policy of taking part in long-distance trials continued, with the occasional foray into road events, such as 1936, when ISDT rider Grana won the 500cc sidecar class of the Milano–Taranto at an average speed of almost 50 mph for the 800-mile event.

Factory boss Giuseppe Gilera was by this time already considering the possibility of entering the international Grand Prix circuit to challenge rivals such as Moto Guzzi and Bianchi. As far back as 1933 an experimental sohc 500cc single-cylinder racing engine with bevel gear cam drive was designed. Two years on, another 500cc was proposed, but with a train of gears instead of shaft and bevels for the cam drive.

But all this proved unnecessary when, at the end of 1935, he was offered a ready-made machine. This was the *Rondine* ('Swallow'), a water-cooled, supercharged 4-cylinder machine developed by a team of Rome-based engineers which included Piero Remor, Carlo Gianini and

Count Bonmartini. In fact the roots of the project could be traced back to 1924, with the formation of GRB (Gianini, Remor, Bonmartini). The name changed in 1927 to OPRA (Officina Precisioneromana Automobili) with an injection of fresh capital from Count Lancelotti.

By 1933 the name had changed once again to CNA (Compagnia Nazionale Aeronautica) and a new 4-cylinder engine designed, which, when it was first tested in 1934, was given the name Rondine. After taking part in a few races during 1935, the leading player of the CNA organization decided to get out of the business and sold the company to the giant Caproni organization, which had its head offices in Milan.

Caproni's main line of business at this time was aviation, so they simply wanted to dispose of the motorcycle section of CNA, which itself had primarily been allied to the aircraft industry, hence Caproni's purchase. Gilera was quick to seize the opportunity of taking the Rondine over, together with rider-technician Piero Taruffi. Within a year the machine had been partly redesigned as a result of a joint effort by Remor, Taruffi and Gilera, with its rigid, pressed-steel frame replaced by a tubular one incorporating swinging arm rear suspension.

The engine was to set the pattern for not only the Gilera racers which were to follow, but many others, including, notably, MV Agusta and Honda. The four side-by-side cylinders, mounted transversely in the frame, were inclined slightly forwards and had a train of gears driving the twin overhead camshafts set between the two middle cylinders. Bore and stroke dimensions were 52×58mm, giving a capacity of 492.7cc, which at first gave 80 bhp at 8000 rpm − quite sensational in those days!

Its main problems centred around handling all this power, and early riders Taruffi and Giordano Aldrighetti had their work cut out controlling the beast. However, to prove power is not everything, the pair, who first appeared on their new mounts in the middle of 1937, had only one success that year. This came in the Italian Grand Prix at Monza when, in the face of strong Guzzi and BMW opposition, Aldrighetti won at record speed, despite having stopped *three* times at his pit with ignition faults.

The same year Taruffi achieved outstanding success in establishing a number of new short- and long-distance world records, with a fully streamlined version of the four on the newly constructed Bergamo-Brescia *autostrada*. First he raised the figure for the flying kilometre to 170.15 mph, which just beat Eric Fernihough's 169.79 mph on a

995cc JAP-engined Brough Superior, to become the holder of the absolute world's record for a short time. This soon fell to Germany's Ernst Henne using a 493cc BMW with a speed of 173.68 mph. He then set a number of new longer-distance records. Although gaining less publicity these were arguably of greater significance. These longer-distance attempts were not as simple as they may have seemed, because not only was the road dotted with several bridges, which caused aerodynamic difficulties, but the machine had to be turned round at both ends of a measured course several times during each attempt.

The development work on the racers and record breakers did not mean the production models were neglected, and in 1938 the famous Gilera 500 VT-SS appeared. A very popular bike, this 498cc single was affectionately known as the 'eight-bolt', and featured a light alloy cylinder head with inclined valves. The gearbox was a four-speeder and it retained the unique Gilera rear suspension system and used the engine unit as a stressed frame member.

In road racing, the 'four' got away to a flying start, with Aldrighetti winning the 1938 Milano−Taranto race at an average speed of 73.2 mph. The same rider then followed this up by winning the famous Lario event, with new team-

One of the blown works Gilera fours − except for the Second World War, it could well have dominated racing at that time. Dorino Serafini was European Champion on just such a machine in 1939.

A 1948 Gilera 500 Saturno. First developed immediately prior to the outbreak of war, it became one of the Arcore company's best-loved models ever.

than peacetime bikes. In 1942 a new military side-valve model appeared. This was the 500 VL *Marte* (Mars) and it was the first Gilera model to use shaft drive.

When the war was finally over, Gilera made a return to racing. With the four deprived of its supercharger to meet the FIM regulations, Nello Pagani still managed to win the 1946 500cc Swiss Grand Prix over the tricky Bremgarten circuit at Berne. Despite this win, however, it was soon apparent that the pre-war machine, shorn of its blower, but still heavy and suffering poor handling, would have to be greatly improved if it was to keep up with the times. To meet this challenge, Giuseppe Gilera hired Ing. Remor, who joined the Arcore racing department in early 1947.

In late 1946, the first post-war Milan Show had been staged and Gilera displayed only 250 and 500cc single-cylinder models. These were the *Nettuno* (Neptune) and *Saturno* (Saturn), respectively. The *Nettuno* had a square 68×68mm bore and stroke (246.95cc), while the larger machine was a long-stroke 84×90mm unit with a capacity of 498.76cc; both were ohv.

The *Saturno* had been redesigned just prior to the outbreak of the war by Ing. Giuseppe Salmaggi, from an original design by Mario Mellone back in 1933, and the prototype Saturno had won the last Targa Florio before Italy's entry into the hostilities. The *Saturno* in particular was to become a mainstay Gilera production model of the immediate post-war period, being built not only as a sporting roadster, but racer and even as a motocross machine. Because of this it can lay claim to having been Italy's answer to the BSA Gold Star. Like the British bike, the *Saturno* was developed over a number of years. The original model sported girder forks and Gilera's well-known rear suspension, embodying a swinging fork and horizontal compression springs. In 1950, the *Saturno* Sport was presented at the Milan Show with oil-damped telescopic front forks and in 1952 the various variants received a brand-new frame with swinging arm and twin-shock rear suspension.

The pukka racing *Saturno* was referred to as the *Competizione* (Competition) up to the end of 1948, the *San Remo* (after the race circuit of the same name) from 1948 to 1951, and as the *Corsa* (Racing) from 1951 to its final demise in 1959. The *Saturno Cross* off-road racer was offered between the years 1952 and 1956, and all versions of this model featured teles at the front and twin-shock swinging arm at the rear.

An interesting double knocker works *Saturno* road racer designed by Ing. Francesco Passoni made its first public appearance at the 1952 Italian Grand Prix at Monza. Even though it looked an impressive bike and pushed out a promising 48 bhp at 8000 rpm, it lived very much in the

mate Dorino Serafini second, but then suffered an accident in the Swiss Grand Prix, putting himself out of action for the remainder of the season. Mechanical problems kept Serafini out of the results.

But 1939 was to be Gilera's year. Serafini won in Sweden, Germany and Ulster, the last victory giving him the all-important European Championship. Taruffi, who had by now retired from racing, continued his record-breaking activities, raising the one-hour figure to 127.7 mph, which was to remain unbroken until 1953, when Ray Amm clocked 133.5 mph using the Norton 'kneeler'.

The onset of the Second World War came at a particularly bad time for the Arcore factory. Much money had been poured into the racing and record-breaking projects, including the design of a brand-new air-cooled 250 four. This latter machine had the supercharger mounted in front of the crankcase instead of behind the cylinders. Although never actually raced, it did set the pattern for the post-war 500cc four.

However, Giuseppe Gilera and his staff made the best of things, with production continuing with military rather shadow of the faster British single-cylinder Nortons of the era, let alone the latest version of the Arcore 4-cylinder 'fire engine'.

When Remor had joined Gilera in early 1947 the FIM's newly introduced ban on supercharging meant that the power of the original Gilera four had dropped by *half* from 90 to 45 bhp. Not only was its top speed greatly reduced, but its sheer bulk and weight were no longer compensated for by power. So it was quickly decided to build a new 500 which would incorporate the design advances featured in the 1940 250.

Designed by Ing. Remor, the new model was ready for testing by the end of 1947. Its air-cooled engine shared the earlier unit's dimensions, but with cylinders inclined some 30 degrees forward from the vertical produced 55 bhp at 8500 rpm. With an in-unit 4-speed close-ratio gearbox it was housed in a pressed-steel frame which had blade girder-type front forks with central coil spring and torsion bar swinging arm rear suspension. The machine had 20in.

wheels and weighed 295 lb. Other changes from the earlier supercharged model included its lubrication system. The oil tank was no longer separate, but occupied a lower chamber of the engine's crankcase assembly. A single Dell 'Orto carburettor fed each pair of cylinders.

Teething troubles stopped the new four when on its way to winning at its early appearances and it was not until the Italian Grand Prix of 1948 that its first classic victory was achieved, when Massimo Masserini took the chequered flag at Faenza (Monza was still out of commission following war damage). A few weeks earlier the same rider had given the machine its first ever win at Bergamo.

In 1949 Nello Pagani won the Dutch TT and the Italian Grand Prix, but was beaten by a single point by Les Graham (AJS) for the newly introduced World Championship. At that time, Gilera were extremely active in the sidecar class with such drivers as Erole Frigerio, Ernesto Merlo and the brothers Alfredo and Albino

New for 1949 was this 125 ohv model. Its engine was to form the basis for the vast majority of Gilera's production for the next 15 years and be produced in a variety of sizes from 98 to 202cc.

Works rider Nello Pagani in action with the 1950 version of the 500 four-cylinder.

Prix by Alfredo Milani.

In a year which had seen the Arcore factory take both the riders' and manufacturers' titles, it had become evident to all that Gilera possessed the finest all-round racer in the world. 1952 had seen the company's first use of a non-Italian rider, when Cromie McCandless won the 500cc Ulster Grand Prix.

No doubt all these factors were instrumental in what followed, as 1953 saw Norton's two top riders, Duke and Reg Armstrong (together with Dickie Dale), 'defect' to the Italian team. This paid off for both the factory and the two riders concerned, when Gilera scored a 1-2 in the 500cc Riders' and Manufacturers' Championships, with Duke winning the Riders' title and Armstrong finishing runner-up.

The ex-Norton riders were also instrumental in the further development of the machine's cycle parts which was undertaken by Ing. Francesco Passoni. The only real disappointment that year was the Isle of Man TT. This was the factory's début in the event and the team took no fewer than eight machines, a vast stockpile of spares and equipment and four riders: Duke, Armstrong, Dale and Milani. After a trouble-free practice week, the highest placed Gilera finisher was Armstrong in third spot.

But with Duke scoring wins at the Dutch TT, and the French, Swiss and Italian Grands Prix, Gilera retained their dual Riders' and Manufacturers' Championships.

Observers perhaps thought that Gilera could afford to relax their development programme somewhat, but team manager Taruffi and Ing. Passoni knew better. Not only were the British singles, in the shape of Joe Craig's Nortons, still menacing, but MV were now beginning to make real progress with their own four, although team leader Les Graham had been tragically killed in the 1953 Senior TT.

So, for 1954, Passoni set to work to create an even more competitive machine. The engine was made lower in the frame by modifications to the sump. The included angle of the valves was increased and important detail improvements carried out to the cylinder heads. There were now separate cylinder barrels in place of the paired units previously employed and a new five-speed gearbox fitted. In power terms the changes added up to 64 bhp at 10,500 rpm.

Because of the engine alterations, a new lower and narrower frame was introduced, which transformed the bike's appearance *and* improved handling and roadholding. Finally the diameter and design of the brakes were improved, with a fully ventilated, full-width two-leading shoe device used at the front.

All these alterations, together with the undoubted

Milani. Even with the greater power at their disposal, however, they could never quite get the better of Eric Oliver and his Norton single.

Although Ing. Remor left to join rivals MV Agusta that winter, new signing Umberto Masetti became the 1950 500cc World Champion with wins in Belgium and Holland, together with runner-up positions in Switzerland and at Monza and a sixth in the Ulster Grand Prix. Again the title was gained by a single point, but this time it was Geoff Duke and Norton who lost out.

In 1951 it was Duke and his British single which took the title, but the following year a number of changes to the Gilera design paid off when Masetti became Champion for a second time. The improvements included more horsepower, four carburettors in place of two and the running gear, including the frame, suspension and aerodynamics, improved. Gilera had adopted streamlining for the first time on their road-racing machines, and it comprised a small fairing which blended in with the fuel tank. This was first race-tested in the 1951 Italian Grand

1950 world champion Umberto Masetti keeps his Gilera in front of Lorenzetti's Guzzi V-twin during the 1951 Belgian Grand Prix.

mastery of the maestro Duke's riding, ensured yet another 500cc world title for the Arcore factory in 1954, when Duke finished a full 20 points in front of his nearest challenger, the Rhodesian Ray Amm, on a Norton.

On 14 October, 1954, as if to prove that Gilera could even challenge the mighty car world, Taruffi brought out a four-wheel machine named the *Tarf*. It was basically two cigar-shaped booms linked together with two wheels in each section. Taruffi sat in one (the left), with a works 500 four-cylinder engine in the other. At Montlhéry Taruffi blasted the Gilera-powered device around the French circuit's banking to such good effect that he went back to Italy with a significant number of records, including those for the 50 and 100 kilometres, with speeds in excess of 135 mph.

For 1955 the four was left almost unaltered, except for detail improvements to the front brake. Duke and Armstrong were retained, and the promising Libero Liberati signed up to replace Umberto Masetti, who had joined MV.

Except for Monza, which was won by Masetti with his new MV, Gilera cleaned up the 1955 blue ribband classic events; Duke won four, including Gilera's first ever Senior TT, Armstrong one (Spain) and another new signing, Giuseppe Colnago, one (Belgium). It was also the first year in which Gilera experimented with fully enclosed streamlining.

However, all was not as well as it may have seemed. The Dutch TT at Assen had witnessed a mass protest by private owners over poor conditions and starting money. The following November the FIM suspended the licences

The sensation of the 1953 Milan Show, the exceptionally clean Gilera 305cc ohv vertical twin.

of 14 riders, *including* Gilera stars Duke and Armstrong, preventing them from riding in international events in the first half of 1956 (even though they had not been directly involved!).

In addition, team boss Taruffi parted company (on good terms) with Gilera at the end of 1955 and his place was taken by the young Ferruccio Gilera, the only son of founder Giuseppe Gilera. Ferruccio had worked with the racing team from early 1954 and when he took over control was 25 years old. This new blood was responsible for the introduction of both the 125 twin and 350 4-cylinder models, though the actual engineering work was undertaken by Ing. Passoni and his team of assistants.

The small twin was designed in 1955, and was Ing.

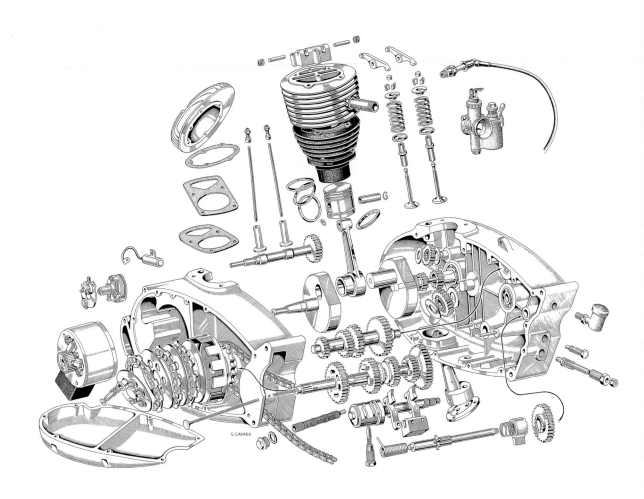

Exploded view of the 150cc Gilera ohv single. Like the 305 twin, this employed parallel valves and four-ring pistons.

Passoni's first completely new racing design for the company. Surprisingly, the 40×49.6mm dimensions were decidedly long-stroke, but nonetheless the 124.656cc power unit revved to 13,000 rpm; maximum power output was 20 bhp at 12,000 rpm. The double overhead camshafts were driven centrally by a train of gears between the cylinders and there was a six-speed gearbox. The original prototype featured leading link front forks, but these were soon changed for telescopics, similar but obviously smaller than the 4-cylinder.

Although ready to race at the end of 1955, the twin was not actually used in anger until 1956, when Gilera signed the lightweight star Romolo Ferri; in fact it was Ferri who suggested changing the leading link forks for teles. With full streamlining the 125 'Gillie' was capable of a genuine 120 mph, making it the fastest machine in its class. When running properly the twin was in a class of its own, but various troubles, including overheating and piston failures,

meant that it retired more times than it finished. However, Ferri did have the satisfaction of setting a new lap record at the fastest of all Grand Prix circuits, Spa-Francorchamps in Belgium, with a speed of 100.85 mph before retiring, and later won the German Grand Prix at Solitude, beating both Ubbiali (MV) and Provini (Mondial). Sadly for the company, and most of all the Gilera family, Ferruccio died of a heart attack while on a business trip to the Gilera subsidiary in Buenos Aires in 1956. In retrospect one can see in the chain of events which were to follow that his untimely passing affected not only his father's interest in racing but the Gilera factory itself.

Forced by the FIM to wait until mid-season before it could field its two main stars, Gilera's hopes of retaining the 500cc Championship titles soon began to fade when MV's new signing, John Surtees, began to pile up the wins. Hopes faded even more when, with a mere two laps to go, Duke was forced to retire in the Belgian GP after a piston

Comm. Giuseppe Gilera and his beloved son, Ferruccio, pictured together at the 1956 Belgian Grand Prix.

had disintegrated while he was leading comfortably. At the German Grand Prix Duke's chances took another nosedive when he was again forced to retire. With Duke falling in Ulster and Armstrong going out with a burnt-out clutch, Gilera's hopes were over; Surtees and MV were the new Champions.

However, pride, if nothing else, was salvaged at Monza in September, when Gileras took the first four places: Duke, Liberati, Monneret and Armstrong. Also at Monza, Liberati débuted a smaller version of the four, suitable for the 350cc class. This had a capacity of 349.664cc (46×52mm) and a power output of 45 bhp at 11,000 rpm and was again the work of Ing. Passoni, but inspired by the will of Ferruccio for the company to dominate at all levels. Although it was to win several races, its power-to-weight ratio was considerably inferior to that of its bigger brother. Over the winter the 500 four was revamped, with the main modification being an increase in capacity to 499.4cc, achieved by increasing the stroke by .8mm.

On to the 1957 season, and Gilera's ill-fortune continued. The team now comprised Duke, Liberati and the Scot Bob McIntyre, the last-named signed to replace Reg Armstrong, who had retired. Duke suffered a heavy crash at the non-championship meeting at Imola before the classics even got under way and was side-lined.

In the Isle of Man the 50th anniversary of the TT saw McIntyre totally dominate the opposition, winning both the Junior and specially extended Senior TT, and he became the first man ever to lap the famous 37¾-mile Mountain Circuit at over 100 mph (the precise speed was 101.12 mph). Then ill-fortune took over once again, with McIntyre falling while chasing Surtees in Holland. Liberati, who won in Belgium, was disqualified because the new Gilera team manager, Roberto Persi, failed to register a change of

1957 500cc world champion Libero Liberati and his dustbin-faired Gilera four.

machine! Even so, Liberati became 500cc World Champion with wins in Ulster and Italy, to add to his victory earlier in the season at Hockenheim. He was also runner-up in the 350cc class.

After the final classic at Monza came the real sensation of the 1956 season, the joint announcement that Moto Guzzi, FB Mondial *and* Gilera would be retiring from competition. In the case of Guzzi and Mondial there is no doubt that this was caused solely by financial considerations, but with Gilera at least some of the cause was the effect of Ferruccio's death a year earlier . . .

At the end of November, most of the Gilera team took part in a record-breaking session at Monza, which culminated in Bob McIntyre taking the all-important Hour at 141.37 mph to break the record set by Norton and Ray Amm four years earlier. *The Motor Cycle* called McIntyre's performance with a streamlined *350* four 'Magnificent'. A number of other records were also smashed by McIntyre and, in the sidecar category, by the Milani brothers, and by Romolo Ferri in the 175 and 250cc classes, riding a 175 Formula Two twin (developed from the 125 GP racer). This last bike had a capacity of 174.8cc (46×52.6mm) and pumped out 23 bhp at 11,200 rpm. Ferri

After announcing their retirement, together with Mondial and Guzzi, from racing, Gilera went on a record-breaking spree at Monza. The photograph shows Romolo Ferri setting off on his fully streamlined 125 twin on 13 November, 1957.

also rode a 125 twin on its last competitive outing.

On the production front the immediate post-war models, the *Nettuno* and *Saturno*, had been joined in 1949 by an ohv 125, in Turismo or Sport form. However, a year or so prior to release of this model the Arcore company had displayed another '125' at the Milan Show in November 1948. This featured side valves and had the appearance of a two-stroke, but was destined never to reach production. Much of the chassis of this prototype was used on a later 125cc model. This featured a 123.67cc (54×54mm) single-cylinder engine with three-speed unit gearbox and parallel valves. The basic layout of this engine, including the valve layout, was to be incorporated into a succession of models which were to follow, including both singles and twins.

During the early 1950s, Gileras were very much carbon copies of the rival Guzzis; the company produced highly innovative track-winning Grand Prix bikes, but their production range was generally lacking flair and decidedly conservative in styling. Occasionally Gilera managed a surprise or two, such as the B300 twin introduced at the 1953 Milan Show. Mechanically it was a fairly straightforward design, with a four-speed gearbox in unit with the engine, blending into a smoothly contoured 'power

egg' as *Motor Cycling* described it. The separate cylinders, of cast-iron, were similarly of clean external appearance, while the light-alloy head had no excrescences at all, the rocker boxes being cast in, and covered by a finned lid. Unusual was the choice of capacity, 305.3cc (60×54mm). Following a sensible approach, however, Gilera had refused to allow themselves to be cramped by arbitrary capacity limits, and had chosen instead to design according to the requirements of the job in hand. In any case, this had the added advantage of being able to employ several components from the well-developed 150cc model, which also shared the same bore and stroke measurements.

In general appearance it followed the smaller models with its telescopic forks, twin shocks, swinging arm rear suspension and full-width polished alloy brake hubs. The wheel rims were of light alloy, and so, too, were the Gilera-built silencers. Although lacking any real power (12.5 bhp at 5800 rpm on the original version), it did have the advantage of being exceptionally smooth, easy to start and very flexible. When *Motor Cycling* tested a B300 in their 9 December, 1954, issue, they recorded a maximum of exactly 70 mph, hardly breathtaking, but this was intended as a tourer *not* a sportster.

For many years Gilera relied on machines such as this 125cc Six Days for the bulk of their revenue.

Nothing really new appeared from Gilera until the 1956 season, but at least when the newcomer appeared it was destined to become one of the factory's best ever sellers. This was the 175 single, which was built in a number of guises and remained in production for many years. Originally produced as either the Sport or Super Sport, it had the almost square engine dimensions of 60×61mm, which gave 172.47cc. The Sport engine offered 7.5 bhp at 6000 rpm, the Super Sport 9.1 bhp at the same revs. The '175' was clearly a development of the earlier 125 and 150 models and, like them, and for that matter the 300 twin, used parallel valves.

From 1957 onwards the Sport and Super Sport were also offered as the Extra and Rossa Extra respectively, with more deeply valanced mudguarding and a few other smaller detail changes to specification. There were also Regolarita (1957) and Motocross (1958) versions. From 1956 there was also an Extra version of the 300 twin. This featured an uprated engine, which gave 15 bhp and 500 extra engine revolutions, with maximum velocity boosted to 77 mph.

To celebrate its Golden Jubilee anniversary, 1959 saw Gilera introduce a new 98cc lightweight motorcycle appropriately named the *Giubeleo* (Jubilee). There were two versions, the Normal and the Extra, the latter with a higher specification. At first sight the Giubeleo might have appeared to be simply a smaller version of the existing ohv singles from the Arcore plant. In truth its engine was somewhat different. In particular, the camshaft was mounted on the nearside of the crankcase and in front of the cylinder. The contact breaker, easily accessible from the outside, was keyed to the gear-driven camshaft, while the nearside wall of the cylinder contained a tunnel for the push-rods. However, the parallel valves were retained. The diameter of these valves were: inlet 19mm, exhaust 17mm. Unlike the 300 twin, for example, which had a duplex primary chain, the new 98 used gears and these also actuated the oil pump for the wet sump lubrication system.

The square 50×50mm (98.173cc) engine developed 6 bhp at 7000 rpm and with a 7.8:1 compression ratio offered maximum torque of 4700 rpm. Cycle parts, including the duplex frame, telescopic forks, swinging arm rear suspension and full-width hubs followed conventional Gilera lines, as did the emergency electrical system, which could be employed if the battery was flat. Like the majority of Gilera standard production models, the 98 Giubeleo was not in the sporting class and therefore did not have speed as a priority. A shade over 50 mph was possible, but it would hold this figure for many miles with no sign of stress from the power unit. Like the other singles, Gilera also produced a Regolarita version, some of which factory riders employed in long-distance trials, such as the ISDT, with considerable success.

By 1960 Gilera had a British importer, Motor Imports Co. Ltd. of 158 Stockwell Road, London SW9. This was an offshoot of the massive Pride and Clarke dealership. The top model offered was the 175 Extra, which cost £210 15s. 3d. At 60 mph with the rider prone (*Motor Cycling*, 21 April, 1960) performance for what was described 'a sporty Italian 175cc lightweight' was disappointing. Remember that the 175 ohc Ducati Sport of the same period was good for at least an extra 20 mph! Three specially prepared 98 Giubeleo Regolarita models secured an impressive trio of gold medals in the 1960 ISDT held in Austria, when, together with 125 versions, a Gilera team won the Silver Vase for Italy.

The 'Jubilee' theme spread to the new 125 (123.15cc, 56×50mm) later in 1959 (it retained the original engine dimensions), a year later, a new 150 (158.33cc, 60×56mm) and finally the 202 version in 1966. This last capacity was achieved by boring the 175 cylinder out to 65mm, with the stroke remaining as before at 61mm. So by now all Gilera singles were oversquare.

The largest of the unit singles (the 246cc *Nettuno* had been discontinued in 1954, followed by the 498cc *Saturno* in 1959) was only ever offered in Giubeleo Super form. This, like later versions of the 125 (from 1965), featured a five-speed gearbox. The year 1962 had seen the appearance of the G50 scooter, which was soon followed by a larger version, the G80. Both employed a remarkably economical push-rod engine (again with parallel valves!). The smaller unit had a capacity of 49.9cc (38×44mm) and the G80 76.44cc (44×44mm). Both used a twist-grip-controlled three-speed gearbox and primary drive was by helical gears.

In early 1963 came headline news when Gilera announced it was returning to the Grand Prix circuit, with a team managed by its former star, Geoff Duke. The riders were to be Derek Minter and John Hartle. The results, however, failed to match the speculation. First Minter crashed in a non-Championship British meeting before the classic season got under way. Duke then brought in Phil Read, but neither he nor Hartle made any real impression.

The following year the Argentinian rider Benedicto Caldarella rode for the Arcore factory, but after a bright start his challenge also soon faded.

Besides the scooter project, Gilera brought out the Gilly two-stroke moped in 1964 and the Cadet 50 two years later. The latter featured an ohv 47.63cc (38×42mm) engine with a vertical cylinder. None of these designs proved particularly successful and it was largely left to the by now ageing singles, together with the long-running 300 twin to prop up the by now rapidly ailing Arcore company's fortunes.

Seven Gilera models were offered for sale in the USA during 1964 by C & N Enterprises of 750 Long Beach Boulevard, Long Beach, California, including the 98, 124 and 175 singles and 300 twin. But even though the importer took full-page advertisements in *Cycle World* they never sold Stateside in any real numbers, if for no other reason that Honda and the other Japanese manufacturers had already begun their massive sales march in the North American market.

With an ever worsening balance sheet the factory back in Arcore, still with *Commendatore* Gilera at the helm, struggled on. No doubt they did their best, as the ultra-lightweight models described above testify. In a market suffering from rapidly falling sales what could they do when saddled with a massive plant, which the Gilera facilities at Arcore had become over the years. One answer seemed to be to follow rival Moto Guzzi's lead − military contracts. So when the Italian government issued tenders for a new high-performance motorcycle to replace its ageing Guzzi *Falcone* flat-singles, Gilera entered the race, together with Guzzi and Ducati. The Gilera design was a 483.02cc (71×61mm) sohc chain-driven vertical twin, the B500 5V, the last part of the designation indicating that it had five speeds.

Initial work on the project began in early 1966 and when the prototype was completed a year later it produced 32 bhp at 7000 rpm and appeared a robust and neatly styled machine. Right from the start Guzzi, however, had the upper hand with their 700cc V7 model, and both the Ducati (an 800cc vertical twin) and Gilera's offerings were soon sidelined in the contest.

After having spent considerable time and expense on the big twin, Gilera produced a 'civilianized' version, the B50. This was almost the same machine, but without the military drab finish and a few styling changes, plus more power: 40 bhp at 7500 rpm. Dry weight was 180kg (397 lb). Both machines were the work of that gifted designer Ing. Giuseppe Salmaggi.

Unfortunately, by the time the B50 was finally ready to enter production in early 1969 Gilera was in deep financial

The prototype 498cc twin, originally intended for police or military work, was developed during the late 1960s for civilian use. A financial crisis saw the company pass into the hands of the massive Piaggio empire and with it all hopes of this interesting parallel twin being put into production.

trouble, and so the project was shelved.

With all these financial worries, Comm. Giuseppe Gilera had finally had enough of the enterprise for which he had worked so hard for so many years, and when the same year an offer (reputed to be some £2 million) was made by the giant Piaggio organization, he willingly accepted. Unfortunately his retirement was to be relatively short-lived, and on 21 November, 1971, just before his 82nd birthday, the great man passed away.

Against a backcloth of uncertainty and recession in the two-wheel world in the late 1960s, Piaggio stood like a beacon of success. Its Vespa scooters and mopeds were selling well, and its other divisions, including aeronautics, were performing strongly. This was in stark contrast to companies such as Gilera, who had relied, perhaps too heavily, on two-wheelers alone.

Piaggio was also looking to the future and an improvement in motorcycle sales. A more healthy market was forecast soon, but there was no way that Piaggio could build up a reputation and range of suitable products from the ground up in enough time to take full advantage of the projected upsurge in business during the early 1970s.

Not only this, but in Italy at least, Gilera was still a household name, respected and admired. Piaggio was also

an extremely efficient business organization, and although it valued tradition and reputation, it could also see that, with Gilera, it would have all the ingredients to take full advantage of an upturn in motorcycle sales. So in November 1969 the Piaggio group became the new owner of Moto Gilera Arcore.

For 1970, many of the long-running models, such as the 300 twin, were discontinued, and a provisional model range assembled: the 98, 124, 150 and 202 four-stroke singles. Most of that year, and 1971, was spent reorganizing the factory and in the design of new models, but sadly the 500 twin did not feature in these plans.

It was also in 1970 that the Frigerio-Gilera model made its début. This was a specialized (and expensive) limited production trail or enduro bike built by the Frigerio brothers of Treviglio, near Bergamo, sons of the famous Gilera sidecar star Ercole, who crashed fatally on the last lap of the Swiss Grand Prix in May 1952. Based on the 202, but bored *and* stroked to 63×72mm (giving 230cc), the Frigerio-Gilera soon built itself an enviable reputation for finishing even the toughest event. The Frigerios manufactured their own sand-cast cylinder head, which featured larger valves, 28mm exhaust and 32mm inlet, a special widely finned light alloy cylinder barrel, with

Piaggio reorganized Gilera, resulting in machines such as this 50 Enduro of 1974 – profit before prestige.

austentic liner, a new crankshaft, special five-speed gearbox and heavy-duty clutch. Carburation was taken care of by a 28mm instrument. Other details of the special included a 10.2:1 compression ratio, dual ignition system, a specially fabricated oil feed to the rear chain and a comprehensive air filtration system. The changes to the engine gave 21 bhp at 7900 rpm, almost double that of the production 202 unit! Some 11 models made up the new 1972 range, from 50cc through to 175cc.

The smallest engine was a brand new 49.7cc (38.4×43mm) piston-ported two-stroke of modern design and completely unrelated to anything which had preceded it from the Arcore factory. Originally a four-speeder, it was later developed into a five-speeder and sold in a number of models, touring, trail and enduro, over the next few years at home and abroad.

Another important model was the Arcore 5V, in 125 or 150 engine sizes. These were developments of the earlier single-cylinder four-stroke models and retained that hallmark of the Gilera production roadster, parallel valves. In fact, certainly as regards the power plant, critics could

argue that the new engine was little more than the old unit, but with squared-off outer engine covers, cylinder barrel and head finning.

Even if this could be levelled at the mechanics, the running gear *was* completely new and much more modern in appearance. For example, there were Grimeca brakes, new forks with gaiters instead of metal spring covers, higher bars, chrome-plated headlamp and tail lamp, matching speedo and tacho, large side panels and a full duplex frame. Another notable change was the use of the latest square slide Dell 'Orto carburettor (VHB 22 on the smaller engine and VHB 23 on the 150 model).

Realizing the importance of motorcycle sport, but at the same time knowing a full return to Grand Prix road racing was completely out of the question, the new Managing Director of Gilera, Enrico Vianson (appointed when Piaggio had taken over in 1969), decided that Gilera's only way of re-entering the sporting world was through trials. In fact, as related earlier the factory was no newcomer to this sector, having participated in off-road events for many years.

Gileras off-road activities were hived off to the Elmeca concern, who proceeded to build both enduro and motocross machines powered by high-performance two-stroke engines. This is just such a machine competing in 1977.

This posed a problem, however, as the existing four-stroke production models, although well tried, reliable and good fun to ride, simply were not competitive enough for international events, such as the ISDT. So, although always a four-stroke factory at heart, the new management were above all realistic and so plumped for a brand new series of *two-stroke* competition models. And competitive they certainly were. Built in conjunction with the Elmeca concern, they were manufactured in 50, 75, 100 and 125cc engine sizes.

The speed at which these new models appeared is a tribute to the dedication of the Piaggio-appointed management team, headed by Enrico Vianson. In an article a few years ago, my friend and fellow-journalist Doug Jackson said, 'Most of their success in the commercial and sporting fields is attributable to him [Vianson]. Indeed he has looked after the company as if he were a son of Mr Gilera himself.'

1973 saw the new machines in action in most European events, with some of the best Italian riders of the day contracted to ride them. Success came immediately in the European Two-Day Enduro Series. The ISDT was

approaching and the factory was looking forward to equipping the Italian National Team in the Trophy contest. A bitter disappointment was in store, however. The FMI (Italian Motorcycle Federation) decided to field a team mounted on Austrian KTMs, probably because they feared that, as a new design, the Gileras might suffer teething troubles.

However, not only was the performance of the Gileras exceptional but they were also reliable. Gilera had therefore to concentrate their efforts on the less prestigious, but nonetheless gruelling, Silver Vase event. Ultimately some unlucky incidents prevented outright success, but the new machines still showed up well. Although they only won the 50cc class outright, on the fifth day they had led the 50, 75 *and* 125cc classes! Building on the high amount of publicity generated by their showing in the ISDT, the factory launched some new off-road models for public sale, a pair of 50s and a 100cc model, all two-strokes, plus a new 100cc roadster.

Competition activity continued into 1974 and a new larger model was added to the team, the 175. This gave no less than 27 bhp at the rear wheel and was a match for any

Today Gilera's fortunes are on the way back, headed by modern machinery such as the MX1. This 100mph plus 125 has become a best-seller on the Italian market.

other machine in competition at that time. More top-class riders came into the team, and the results reflected their own and Gilera's capabilities. The first two-day event in the European series, for instance, had Gilera riders first in the 50cc class, first in the 75, fifth in the 100, first in the 125 and third in the 175. Results like these continued throughout the season, and Gilera was nominated for the Trophy team in the ISDT, and also equipped a Silver Vase team.

After three days both the Trophy and the Vase teams led the events on Gileras, then problems set in and they finished third and second, respectively. The result was still a good one, however, remembering that even at this stage Gilera had not yet been in serious competition for two years! To take on the West Germans and Czechs so strongly was no mean achievement. Then came the bombshell — Piaggio decided that Gilera should withdraw from competition. 1975 ought to have been a fantastic year for the factory, but it was not to be. Instead the factory was to concentrate on developing more production machines, the first being the 50RS, a progression from existing models.

The experience gained in the ISDT and other events was not lost, however, for engines were built to the 1974 specification and supplied to Elmeca, who built them into competition models very similar to the previous Gileras.

The range of production models remained virtually unchanged, although the new CBI commuter moped came on to the scene. Behind the scenes more work was going on with a new 125cc model, a two-stroke designated the 125 Tour. Seen by careful observers around Arcore in early 1976, it was not until the beginning of 1977 that it was launched officially. The models were the 125 TG1 and 125 GR1. The same two-stroke engine was installed in both machines, the TG1 being for pure road use and the GR1 for off-road use. The single-cylinder two-stroke motor gave 14.5 bhp at 7200 rpm, had 12.5:1 compression and five gears. Very well styled and constructed, the TG1 came complete with front disc brake. Pure sports models continued under the Elmeca name in trial and motocross competitions. In 1978 much up-dated 250cc cross and trial machines were produced. Elmeca models were made by

Gilera themselves, signifying a growing interest again in competition; Elmeca for the moment handled only marketing.

Again Gilera became directly involved in trials and motocross. Production was not forgotten, however and a new 200cc four-stroke single went into production. Jan Witteveen, the Dutch two-stroke expert, joined Gilera and became responsible for the design of competition machines. The new production 125cc Cross model was just one of the machines he was connected with, this one giving 28 bhp at 10,200 rpm, very close to works model design and performance. The 1979 Milan Show was a suitable occasion for Gilera to announce more activity in motocross. They signed a top-class team for the 1980 World Championships, including the Belgian Gaston Rahier.

Throughout 1980, 1981 and 1982, Gilera contested the 125cc World Motocross Championships, finishing second twice. Although they pulled out in 1983, the experience gained was put to good use, first with production 125cc motocross and enduro bikes and finally a brand new line of two-stroke roadsters. This included the RV 125, 200 and 250 Super Sports roadsters and RX 125 and 200 trail bikes. All these boasted the very latest in styling and performance, matching the best that Japan could offer.

The future looks secure for Gilera now; since 1969 there have been great advances in design and general stability, and most important there is a greater share of the two-wheel market. Piaggio has had much to do with this rebuilding, and in fact with its own production and Gilera's produces more motorcycles, scooters and mopeds each year than two of the big four Japanese companies.

1985 witnessed a revival in Gilera's fortunes, with a host of new production models. Chief amongst these was the excitingly styled 125KZ. This miniature café racer alone sold over 16,000 units in Italy during 1986, making it the top seller in its class.

The 1985 Milan Show emphasized that Gilera was back as a major force, with the company having one of the biggest and best stands at the exhibition. On show was a complete line-up of ultra-modern two- *and* four-strokes. Machines such as the 125 RTX (trail), the best-selling KZ, the 250 Arizona Rally (a street-legal enduro mount) and the 250 NGR (a supersports roadster). All these were powered by reed-valve water-cooled single-cylinder two-stroke engines. But perhaps most interesting of all was the all new 350 Dakota, a brand new hi-tech four-stroke enduro-styled trail bike. This featured a 349cc single-cylinder engine with four valves, five-speed gearbox and 33 bhp at 7500 rpm.

At Milan two years later the Gilera line appeared even more modern and was, with rivals Cagiva and Aprilia, dominating sales in the home market, together with Honda Italia, notably in the all-important 125 sector. For this the KZ, although still available, had been upstaged by the superbly-styled MX1. This offered 100 mph performance from its 28 bhp, 124.38cc (56×50.5mm) six-speed motor. A trail version, the XR1 was nonetheless stunning.

The real excitement, at least for older enthusiasts, was the return of the famous *Saturno*, at least in name − the *Nuova Saturno Biabero* (the new *Saturno* double overhead cam). Perhaps most amazingly this project was born from a request from the *Japanese* trading company C. Itoh. They wanted a modern single for sale to the by now wealthy Japanese who wanted to capture the spirit (Itoh called it 'old racing fashion') of the 1960s. Like the majority of the modern Gilera designs, the *Saturno Biabero* was the work of Ing. Sandro Columbo, in co-operation with Itoh representative Mr N. Hagiwara.

From this project stemmed a wider production of the newly reborn big sportster single, and it is now produced not only for Japan but also for other markets such as West Germany and Spain. Over 4/5 June, 1988, a team of riders with a pair of the new MX1 125 single-cylinder sports bikes took part in a number of successful record attempts at the Nardi circuit. Foremost of these was the prestigious 125cc 24 hours record. This had been held since May 1979 by Honda. The Gilera team of Curti, Cusi, Ricco, Iotti, Ballardini, Rivola and Braglia easily broke this with a speed of 155.43 km/h over 3729.928 kilometres (97.12 mph, 2317.820 miles). The same riders also set a new record for 12 hours, 6 hours and 1000 kilometres.

Currently there are over 30 different Gilera models, ranging from humble 50cc mopeds through to the 600 XRT, a 569cc (99×74mm) Paris-Dakar-styled trail bike, developed from the Dakota. In 1990 the Arcore company employed some 720 workers, 508 of whom were directly involved on two-wheeler production. The others are responsible for the general engineering side (in the same plant), which manufactures various components, including the steering racks for certain Fiat cars.

But although now firmly re-established in their own right, the famous old marque does not seem likely to re-enter the Grand Prix scene in the foreseeable future − if ever. However, they do look likely to make a return to the export markets of the world now that the ground work has been done so successfully at home. Enthusiasts around the world will wish the Arcore factory every success.

CHAPTER II

Laverda

Breganze lies in the shadows of the Dolomite mountain range in north-east Italy, and is only an hour's swift motoring from Venice. It is also the home of Laverda, a marque which stirs passions with lovers of Italian motorcycles, like few others can. The Laverda name first appeared in the commercial world way back in 1873, when Pietro Laverda founded a company to manufacture farm machinery. In 1948 his grandson, Francesco, decided to build his own lightweight motorcycle. Originally this was not intended for production, but just for his own personal use. Unlike the vast majority of small bikes in post-war Italy, Laverda's creation was a four-stroke. This first effort had a single-cylinder push-rod 74.75cc (46×45mm) engine, with three-speed, foot-change gearbox. This was operated by a rocking pedal on the offside of the machine. It was a clever design with an integrated engine, transmission and rear suspension. It took Francesco Laverda some twelve months to create his prototype, which included casting the piston in the kitchen of his house!

However, we had not reckoned on the enthusiastic response from the locals. In a country recently ravaged by war, personal transport was at a premium. At that time people did not aspire to own anything more than a small cheap and economical runabout, as not only was the motorcycle in short supply, but so was the *benzina* to power it. Five replicas then appeared, manufactured to meet the demands of his closest friends.

One of these friends was a priest, and this, so the story goes, accounted for the fully enclosed chain drive to the rear wheel. Quite simply the man of the cloth was worried that his cassock might become entangled in the said chain.

Other details of those very first Laverda two-wheelers included an all-alloy engine unit, with the cylinder barrel having an austentic iron liner and a power output of 3 bhp at 5200 rpm. The pressed-steel frame was in the form of a sloping spine, with pressed-steel blade forks and a kidney-shaped fuel tank. The crankcase of the inclined cylinder power unit was slung underneath the frame with the head and barrel poking out between the bottom frame tubes. For 1951, when some 500 machines were produced, Laverda's 75 had acquired a somewhat neater appearance with redesigned frame and ancillary equipment. Another difference was that the latest model now sported a pillion saddle, the footrests for which could be unbolted and used as tyre levers. To publicize its products further Laverda then prepared a machine for the 1951 Milano−Taranto road race. However, the bike stopped in Rome with a punctured carburettor float. As the class-winning Guzzi two-stroke only got as far as Naples, Francesco Laverda was not too disappointed with the outcome.

The following year the factory entered a team of four specially prepared 75s, but even though Capriolo scooped the class win, all four Laverdas finished and in doing so created a lot of interest, the resultant favourable press coverage doing sales a power of good. In 1953 the 75cc Milano−Taranto bikes were even more highly tuned and Laverda claimed an optimistic 10 bhp at 12,500 rpm. By now the engine featured a forged high-compression piston, a special cylinder head with larger valves, higher-lift camshaft and a larger carburettor. This paid off in headline-grabbing fashion, for Laverda took the first 14 places in the 75cc class of the Milano−Taranto!

Then came a significant development with the 75 becoming a '100'. This was achieved by boring and stroking the engine dimensions to 52×42mm, respectively. Laverda continued its domination, now extended to the 100cc class as well, of the Milano−Taranto. The 75 continued to be manufactured and both it and the new 100 now sported a neat full duplex swinging arm frame and telescopic forks. There were three versions of the basic 75 in production at that time in touring, sports and Milano−Taranto forms. The touring model produced 3.7 bhp at 6500 rpm and had a top speed of 40 mph, whilst the 'customer' Milano−Taranto 75 pumped out 5.5 bhp at 8600 rpm. (Note the difference between this and the works models!) The Milano−Taranto, unlike the touring models, now came with a four-speed box. In a contemporary test of the production Milano−Taranto bike, Italian journalist Enrico Benzing found that the little Laverda could be kept 'against the stop for hours upon end' and that 'vibration was pretty well non-existent'.

By 1956 Laverda's days in the Milano−Taranto (and Giro d'Italia) were coming to an end, with the push-rod 75 and 100s outclassed by newer overhead cam models such as the Ducati ohc Gran Sport and Cettaco 75. However, even as late as the 1957 Giro, Silvangni on a 75 and Pastorelli on a 100 won their respective production classes, while Montesi took the 75 Sports category. The period between 1958 and 1960 saw the 100 remain in production, while the 75 was finally dropped.

With the new decade came a couple of important new machines, the design of which was supervised by long-time employee Luciano Zen. The first to appear was a scooter, which made its bow at the Milan Show in late 1959. With a capacity of 49cc, this was a particularly neat four-stroke design aimed at the recently introduced no tax, no licence market created by a revised highway code. Initially it had two speeds, but by the time serious production got under way a few months later it had another gear. A second, two-seat version with an increase in capacity came next. Its 40×47mm bore and stroke measurements gave 59.032cc. Power output was 3 bhp at 6000 rpm. In this form it was also built under licence from 1962 to 1965 by the Spanish Montesa factory, which called it the Micro.

Next came the first Laverda twin. This was the *Bicilindrica*, which appeared for the first time in public at the 1961 Milan Show, where it was considered one of the exhibit's highlights. The twin failed to sell in the hoped-for numbers, but Laverda certainly *thought* it would as they had dropped all their other models except for the 60 Scooter. Dressed in a rather plain set of clothes, neither the frame nor other cycle parts of the twin showed much innovative thought. The engine, however, had several interesting features. The camshaft, for example, had a central bearing and the complete engine and gearbox assembly was lubricated from a wet sump mounted in the base of the crankcase, with a gear-driven oil pump located in a downward extension of the central-bearing housing. The overhead valves were push-rod-operated from a single camshaft located at the rear of the cylinder barrels. Bore and stroke were an oversquare 52×47mm. Maximum speed from the rubber-mounted 11 bhp engine obtained by *The Motor Cycle* in their 23 August, 1962, issue was found

Laverda machines were very successful in long-distance road races such as the Giro d'Italia. Here a couple of 75cc models from the Breganze factory are flagged off at the start of the 1954 event in Bologna's main square.

By 1956 the overhead-valve single was also being produced with the larger 98cc engine, such as this 100 Sport model.

to be 63 mph, whilst the same source recorded an impressive 97 mpg over the 600-mile test period. Imported by Eric Sulley (later to become head of sales at Honda UK), the *Motor Cycle* test of the 199cc Laverda twin read: 'Robust, pleasant Italian overhead valve mount with good all-round performance and excellent quality.' Other notable features included a two-leading shoe full-width hub front brake, 'bathtub' rear enclosure and trailing axle telescopic front forks.

Besides Britain, limited numbers also reached North America, where it was sold through the Agrati-Garelli organization. Even though never produced in anything like mass production the 200 twin ran for some seven years. A sport version, with tuned (16 bhp) engine, twin 18mm Dell 'Orto carburettors and new styling (without the 'bathtub' rear enclosure) appeared at the 1963 Milan Show, but never entered production. Laverda claimed an optimistic 87 mph for this interesting prototype. By the mid-1960s the Italian motorcycle industry was facing a major crisis, brought about by the arrival of small cars such as the Fiat 500 and 600.

Luckily for Moto Laverda, unlike the rivals such as Capriolo, Parilla and Rumi, they were part of an industrial group and could fall back on combine harveters, caravans and foundry work or, more accurately, underwrite the lack of motorcycle activity, as Laverda's two-wheeler business was minuscule compared to its much longer-established agricultural section.

A new Laverda 125 sports model, which followed the classic example of Guzzi, Rumi and Aermacchi, appeared at Milan in 1965. This was a very neat near-horizontal 123cc (52×54mm) ohv single. Very soon afterwards a smart trail version appeared and it was offered in both guises for 1966. In 1969 the 125 trail version came to the US first as a Garelli and then as the American Eagle 150. Few were sold. Power output of both versions was a healthy 14 bhp at 8500 rpm. Transmission was via a four-speed box and multi-plate, wet clutch.

1965 had seen Francesco's oldest son Massimo go to North America for further education. While he was there he noticed how well Honda's 305 CB77 Hawk was selling and, for that matter, the larger British vertical twins such as the Triumph and Norton. So the concept of a big twin Laverda was born. Initially this was to be a 650 (later increased in size to 750). Although he did not do the detailed design work, it was Massimo's basic layout that was used. This comprised the ingredients of three separate machines, the CB77, the Norton 650SS and BMW's R69S. First news of this project was leaked at the 1965 Milan Show and in their show report *Motorcyclist Illustrated* commented: 'Another new Laverda, a 650cc twin, could not be got ready in time.' For those pundits who thought this rumour was just another show 'one-off' snippet, the proof positive that the big twin Laverda was not a figment of the imagination came when the Breganze company displayed the prototype at Earls Court in November 1966.

Clearly stated to be 'aimed at the USA market' this was its first ever public showing. The 654cc (75×74mm) engine had a four-bearing 180-degree crankshaft, a duplex chain-driven single overhead camshaft with a triplex chain for the primary drive, a five-plate clutch and five-speed gearbox. Laverda claimed 115 mph and 52 bhp. Drive to the forward-mounted dynamo was by belt, while the electric starter motor was at the rear with the distributor mounted above it. Both the engine assembly and frame showed considerable Honda CB72/77 influence. The engine (or at least the top end) was slightly inclined and featured a single light alloy cylinder casting, with iron liners. The cylinder head was also a one-piece casting, with hemispherical combustion chambers and the valves at angles of 32 degrees (inlet) and 37 degrees (exhaust). A pair of 26mm Dell 'Orto SSI instruments were fitted.

Car practice was evident in the electrical system, with grouped fuses in a compartment beneath the saddle. Behind it was a massive 12-volt battery and air filter box. The ignition switch was tucked away on a lug on the nearside seat tube. The rest of the bike was obviously of European parentage, and as it was the only truly new design at Earls Court, the Laverda created a lot of interest. A company spokesman said that he hoped 'first deliveries would be made in around six months at a price (in Italy) of slightly less than 600,000 lire'. With the American market in mind, there were already plans for a larger version, originally stated to be of around 800cc capacity.

At the time Laverda, and particularly Massimo Laverda, were heavily criticized for copying the Japanese, but Laverda were in on the ground floor of the superbike boom which was soon to engulf the motorcycling world. By the 1967 Milan Show it was clear that the production Laverda big twin would be a 750. This had been achieved by increasing the bore size to 80mm, giving a capacity of 743.9cc. Although much of the mechanics remained the same the machine had been given a considerable restyle

During the 1960s Laverda built this 350cc 2-stroke twin prototype, but it never went into production.

(the tank, seat and silencers in particular) and the front brake diameter had been increased in size and twin-leading shoes were fitted, although the dual drum principle of the original remained.

Another new Laverda at the 1967 Milan show was the *Regolarita Corsa* (Competition Trial). This was a pukka enduro version of the horizontal 125 single. Top Italian enduro rider and 1966 international champion Luigi Gorini had spent much of the year developing the bike. Offered for sale in small quantities (batches of 30 were constructed), the Laverda enduro was to be ridden during 1968 by the 1967 champion Edoardo Dossena, and it was hoped that a five-speed gearbox (from the 750 twin) would ultimately replace the four-speed unit, which was also fitted to the production roadsters. Another development at this time was a 349cc two-stroke twin, which never left the prototype

The original 650 twin which appeared in 1966 was inspired by three machines: the Honda CB77, the Norton 650SS and the BMW R69S.

stage. This used crankcases similar to the smaller 200 twin. Laverda also had developed the Laverdino, a basic commuter moped. This was in production for many years during the late 1960s and early 1970s and used a 49cc two-stroke engine.

Just as they had done years earlier with their little singles, Laverda decided to re-enter the road-racing arena to publicize their new 750 twin. The team's début came unofficially in 1968 at the Oss 24 hours race in Holland. Because this event was organized outside the confines of the FIM, the riders, Massimo Laverda himself and Augusto Brettoni, had to enter under pseudonyms to protect their FIM licences. Massimo's was 'Islero' after his Lamborghini car, whilst Brettoni's was 'Otis' because he was engaged as an elevator maintenance engineer. All this was to no avail, as after building up a massive lead the pair suffered a holed piston, but after repairs they still managed to finish second behind the winning Honda.

This was to herald the start of a long period which saw Laverda take part in endurance races throughout Europe. In 1969 a Laverda 750S won the Oss 24 hours and it achieved this again in 1970. Then came the first 500-kilometre race for production bikes at Monza. Organized by the Italian Federation, this was won by the Laverda team of Brettoni and Angiolini (by now Massimo had quit racing to concentrate on business affairs). The machine used at

Monza had been the new 750S. It was around this time that Roger Slater came on to the scene as British importer and was instrumental in creating much of Laverda's reputation as a speed machine *par excellence* in the British Isles over the next decade. Across the Atlantic ex-Triumph and Suzuki man Jack McCormack tried, but ultimately failed, to launch Laverda in the North American market. In 1971, the 750SFC was put on sale. Like the later Ducati 750SS, the 750SFC was a truly hand-built motorcycle with the express purpose of winning production machine races; it made a winning début at Zeltweg, Austria, with Brettoni in the saddle. After this it did not always win, but did gain a fine reputation for its staying power. With its orange bodywork and silver frame it was a stunningly beautiful motorcycle, which no one could ignore. The original SFCs turned out some 70 bhp at 7500 rpm and were good for just over 130 mph on optimum gearing.

On the production front the early GT and S were followed by the SF, SF1 and SF2. Some SF2s came with single and dual front discs, but these were very few with the former. The final variant was the SF3, which was slightly restyled to look like the Jota (see below) and fitted with cast alloy wheels. There was also the GT (Gran Turismo) model. This was sold not only to the dealer network, but also the police and government authorities in Italy and abroad. The various years of the production of the SFC saw

LAVERDA 750 G.T.

CARATTERISTICHE

● **MOTORE:** Bicilindrico a quattro tempi con albero a cammes in testa □ Cilindrata totale 743,92 cc. □ Potenza massima 52 CV. a 6.700 giri □ Impianto elettrico BOSCH - Batteria 12 V - 24 A/h □ Avviamento elettrico □ Cambio a cinque marce □ Velocità massima 184 Km/h.
● **TELAIO:** Tubolare; posti N. 2 - Peso Kg. 215 □ Sospensioni CE-RIANI □ Freno anteriore a doppia espansione Ø mm. 230x30 □ Freno posteriore a semplice espansione Ø mm. 200x30.

SPECIFICATIONS

● **ENGINE:** Four stroke twin with single overhead camshaft □ Displacement 743,92 cu. cm. □ Maximum output 52 HP. at 6.700 r.p.m. □ Electrical equipment: BOSCH - Battery 12 V - 24 Amp/h □ Electric starting □ Five speed gearbox □ Maximum speed 184 Km/h.
● **FRAME:** Tubular frame: Two seats - Weight 215 Kgs. □ Suspensions: CERIANI □ Front brake: double expanding shoe brake Ø 230x30 mm. □ Rear brake: single expanding shoe brake Ø 200x30 mm.

MOTO LAVERDA - 36042 BREGANZE (Vicenza) - Tel. 83110 - 83241

By 1969 the vertical twin had grown into a 750. Produced in various forms this used a 743.92cc engine with five-speed gearbox. Period factory brochure illustrates the 750GT.

similar changes of drum brakes being replaced by discs and finally wire wheels by cast alloy components. The twins were finally axed in 1976 after some 18,000 of all versions had been produced, making it Laverda's most prolific model series ever.

The first the world saw of any Laverda with more than two cylinders was late in 1969 at the Milan Show. The new machine aroused much public interest, but in many ways it was shown far too early. It was very much a special built from the parts bins of earlier models and Piero (Massimo's younger brother) later commented: 'It was very smooth with a lot of low-speed power. It sounded beautiful, but it was too heavy and too slow. We wanted a sports bike not a luxury tourer.' Its gear ratios were identical to that of the 750, but with a higher final ratio. The compression ratio was 9:1. The camshaft was straight off the GT model with a couple of extra lobes. Bore and stroke also followed an earlier Laverda design, the 650, at 75×74mm, giving a capacity of 980.76cc. Five ball-race main bearings supported the crankshaft plus a needle roller outrigger,

borrowed from the twins, in the primary chaincase. Unlike the twins, the camshaft chain drive was not duplex and located between the cylinders, but a single-row chain driven off the right off-side end of the crank.

Throughout 1970 more development took place with an experimental machine. This had a new full loop frame and a toothed belt-driven twin-cam engine. Through this bike the Laverda design team learned enough to begin building the first limited production models. These featured single overhead camshafts, but although Laverda tried to play things down, the world's press were soon beating a path to their door. Even so, Laverda made various excuses and attempted to undertake more experimentation during the following couple of years. By the end of 1972, the trade too was hammering at Laverda's door. One more year would probably have seen the three near to perfection, but under increasing pressure, Laverda rushed into production with models that were not perfected. They almost got away with it, except for the ignition system. Whatever the previous reputation of Bosch as a manufacturer of

The magnificent 750SFC. Intended as a long-distance racer, this is usually held up as the marque's most beautifully styled motorcycle. The photograph shows an early version made in 1971.

Barcelona 24 Hours, 1974; 750SFC-mounted José Maria Palamo leads Ducati rider Alejandro Tejedo.

The 1963 Aermacchi 250cc Ala d'Oro over-the-counter racing bike.

Phil Read at the start of the 1969 Isle of Man 250cc TT race with the Benelli Four.

The 1973 Benelli 750 *Sei* – the world's first production six-cylinder motorcycle.

The 1964 Ducati 200 Elite; this is the author's own bike photographed in Aden that year.

The 1974 Ducati 750 Super Sport 'Desmo' in its rare and highly desirable 'Imola Replica' form.

Mike Hailwood with his 864cc Ducati at Union Mills in the 1978 Formula 1 TT race.

The 1987 'Paris-Dakar'-styled Gilera XR1 trail bike powered by a 600cc single-cylinder overhead camshaft engine.

The 1990 Gilera *Nuovo Saturno*, a 'cafe racer'-style 500 single, originally inspired by an order from a Japanese customer.

In 1975 Laverda introduced the 246cc Chott. Although a piston-ported two-stroke single, it was nonetheless an expensive machine to build with its magnesium crankcases and brake components.

quality electrics, the type fitted to the new model, known as the 3C, was absolutely awful. The newly devised transistorized system endowed the triple with unreliability of the highest order and lumpy running. For the next couple of years 3C owners around the world had cause to abuse both Laverda and Bosch for a set of electrics which made Lucas and their early alternator seem superb by comparison. The 1973-74 models of the 3C were fast, mechanically noisy and handled reasonably well. The forks were 35mm Ceriani with gaiters and a massive drum at the front with an immensely powerful twin-leading shoe rear drum. Very few of the original 1973 models with the double-sided drum and Lucas switchgear were actually built and today are very collectable. Besides the shortcomings of the Bosch ignition box, which failed every time it came near anything damp, the camshaft pillars crumbled when torqued down, the instruments were too rigidly mounted, causing needles to vibrate off, front mudguard stays were prone to cracking and cam buckets stuck in their sleeves when cold. Last but not least there was a truly awful 123-watt charging system. Most of the problems were cured, except the charging system, by the time the 1975 models were produced. British importer Roger Slater forced the factory to send a team of

mechanics to England and change all the ignition boxes for the later type (with the plug underneath) in an attempt to overcome the dampness problem. 1975 models built from September 1974 also saw the instruments and front mudguard more efficiently mounted and an oil cooler included in the specification. The cam buckets now ran directly in the aluminium head. The cam pillars had been strengthened though were still not perfect, and stronger 38mm forks with twin Brembo discs were fitted. In the same year, the 3C(E) was introduced. This was the standard 3C model rebuilt by Slater with the 750SFC fork yokes, high-compression pistons, wider profile cams and a Slater-designed, less restrictive exhaust system featuring a larger-diameter collector pipe and near open silencers!

Roger Slater was also the man behind the Jota. This exciting sports model was first imported in January 1976. To many enthusiasts, even to this day, this is the ultimate Laverda. It was the factory's answer to the 3C(E). In engine specification it was identical to the 3C(E), but with cast alloy wheels, triple discs, flip-up seat with rear fairing, needle roller swing-arm bearings and was the best triple yet to roll out of the Breganze factory's gates. The Jota was the bike which dominated the prestigious British Avon production race series, winning it in 1976, 1978 and 1979, with Pete Davies (PK) being the star of the proceedings. Other Laverda names were Mick Hunt, Ray Knight and Roger Winterburn. These proddie Laverda racers were usually pretty standard, the only real modification being close-ratio gears on some bikes. Early 1977 witnessed few changes to either the popular Jota or 3CL with its standard motor and exhaust system. The rear cush drive bearings were increased in size and the rubbers swapped for a harder-compound variety, in an attempt to cure premature bearing failure.

Then in September 1977 the 1200T was launched on to the British market. This was essentially a touring model with its increase in capacity to 1115cc achieved by giving the cylinders an additional 5mm on the bore size. There was also a higher-output oil pump, different tank, seat and screw-on side panels. In keeping with its touring guise (or at least Laverda saw it that way) a set of high and wide bars and standard exhaust were fitted. Colour schemes were a choice of metallic red or blue. By now the charging system was improved by an increase to 140 watts, although this was still not enough.

Except for an orange paint job the Jota remained unchanged for 1978. In the same year the Mirage was announced, basically a 1200T with Jota exhaust, cams, lower bars and a green metallic paint job. Two other 1200s were also introduced, but only in small numbers: the Mirage VC (another Slater version) and the Anniversary 1200. Many observers believed these two offerings were made for the sole purpose of shifting unsold stock. Towards the end of 1978 the CDI system was replaced by the much more reliable, if not perfect, BTZ type. At the same time the Jarama became generally available. This was an Americanized version of the 3CL with a left-sidegear change, lower gearing and all the Stateside emission junk, and 'reimported' from North America it was offered at a bargain price (£1999 in Britain) and was soon a firm seller.

The best year ever should have been 1979, with sales

Massimo Laverda with the ill fated V6 endurance machine. It was only raced in anger once, at the 1978 Bol d'Or, but retired after some eight and a half hours with a broken universal joint. Prior to this it had been clocked at almost 180 mph – over 20 mph faster than the winning works Honda.

Brochure for the popular Jota says 'a legend in its lifetime'. It certainly was, with a maximum speed of over 140 mph and a whole crop of race victories to prove it. The bike was conceived by the British importer rather than the factory. First deliveries arrived in Britain during January 1976.

very much on the increase, but in reality it was a disaster. Because of the factory's need to pacify the bureaucrats, who were just starting to voice opinions on noise legislation, Laverda reacted a shade too promptly and changed the centre main bearing from a slip ring roller to a caged ball type because it meant a few less decibels. Unfortunately in their haste the factory did not carry out enough long-term testing. The result was that all triples from engine number 6204 to 6675, excluding numbers 6595-6634, but including 6598-6603, and for 1200cc models with numbers 1519-1566 and 1833-2533 plus 2564 were equipped with the new type of bearing. Not only this, but at around the same time the cylinder head was fitted with a cast iron 'skull', which had the valve seats cut directly into it, the same as the original models, which were no trouble at all. This was done in an attempt to avoid the problems of 1977/1978 models, which had alloy heads with steel valve seats and were prone to cracking across from the seat to the plug hole. The net

result of these seemingly minor changes was a financial disaster for both the factory and its agents. The centre mains fell apart, sometimes after as little as 3000 miles, often causing ultra-expensive damage to the whole bottom end. Apart from this the iron skulls proved too soft, with the result that the valves soon shrunk into them, causing massive cam and head damage. Perhaps 1980 was the high point of these problems when, with the help of the factory, the British importers carried out a nationwide rectification programme. In retrospect this was probably a major reason why the original Roger Slater business foundered in 1982 and also the start of the factory's own financial problems.

Although 1980 was a bad year for all concerned, the bikes themselves produced that year had no problems as the faulty bearings and valve seats had been rectified. The Jota had very few other changes for 1980. The valve sizes had been increased, but this only led to them tangling, so they were machined down. Exhaust pipes were changed to

One of a number of the Formula 500 machines built for a race series in Italy during the late 1970s. It was developed from the Alpino production model.

36mm at the cylinder head and a 630 O-ring chain was fitted. Unfortunately this American product was prone to breaking and was soon changed to the DID equivalent. A hydraulic clutch was also fitted. The original Mirage was discontinued to be replaced by the Mirage TS. This latter machine featured a standard 1200 engine with Jota head and down pipes. To reduce primary drive noise, a couple of springs joined the rear two clutch friction plates of which there were now eight instead of seven, and it seemed to do the job well enough. The Mirage TS had an all-silver finish with body panels.

Some eight years after its launch, in 1981, Laverda finally got round to fitting a 240-watt Nippon-denso alternator to the offside of the engine, while the ignition was moved to the primary chaincase. At the same time the clutch outrigger support was moved from the chain case and became a three-legged spider mounted on to the crankcases in an effort to further reduce clutch noise. The oil filter had a finer mesh and a metal cowl fitted over it. The only small problem was a tendency for the alternator to sheer its mounting bolts. This was easily rectified by fitting extra dowels, a modification done by the factory from early 1982.

The Milan Show in late 1981 had seen not only the launch of the show-stopping RGS, but the 120-degree range of triples. Several changes to the British Laverda connection took place in 1982. First Slater Bros, the

importers since the early 1970s, gave way to Three Cross Motorcycles (although Slater still continued to be involved with spare parts). The various 1200s were discontinued and finally the 120-degree Jota was launched. Many consider this model to be the best of the Jota line. Externally the 120-degree motor was quite similar to the late model 180 it replaced, but with a left-side gear-change and six heavy rubber mountings. The crankshaft now ran in needle roller bearings housed in special sleeves, the crankcases had baffles and the old triplex primary chain was replaced with two simplex chains. The gearbox was different and the cylinder liners were shortened to allow more lubricant to reach the now overworked small ends. The gudgeon pins fitted directly into the con-rod (previously the small end was bushed) to aid engine balance at low rpm. These modified engines ran extremely well except for a light rumble at tickover and an ignition surge around 2750 rpm. There were some small-end problems, but generally they proved trouble-free.

By mid-1982 the long awaited RGS arrived in the showrooms. I tested one for *Motorcycle Enthusiast* a year later. There were lots of changes to the cycle parts and the RGS was also notable for having the fuel filler cap in the offside fairing, which always surprised pump attendants! The motor was the same as the 120-degree Jota except for milder cams, lower compression ratio, revised gear ratios and quieter silencers. A touring kit of factory-fitted extras

Works rider Marco Balbi in vivid action at the Misano circuit in the summer of 1982. The machine is a genuine 'factory' RGS1000 racer.

including streamlined panniers was soon announced, to make the RGS Executive. This was followed later by various other bikes based on the RGS. These included the RGA, RGA Jota, Corsa and even a version with special paint job commissioned by the British importers.

Then finally in 1985 came the SFC1000. When I tested this for the October 1985 issue of *Motorcycle Enthusiast* I was impressed enough to award it the title of 'Europe's most exciting motorcycle of 1985'. Compared to the RGS tested two years previously, the SFC was superior in almost every department. The only real complaints centred around the black exhaust system, a spongy rear brake and an instrument facia which shook violently at tickover. Laverda claimed 156 mph, but during my time with the machine I did not have a chance of track testing it to verify these claims. This level of performance would comfortably exceed that of the original Jota, which had been electronically timed whilst on test by *The Motor Cycle* at 140.04 mph during August 1976, making the Laverda triple the fastest standard production motorcycle of its day. Compared to the latest hi-tech Japanese hardware this may seem quite tame, but fifteen years ago it was the pacesetter. This performance and its race track success made the Laverda triple a cult motorcycle, a position it still holds today.

Why then, did Laverda get itself into a financial mess? The answers are many and varied. First it is important to understand the company's structure and moves behind the scenes. Laverda's original motorcycle 'factory' was based at the family's homestead in downtown Breganze. Then in 1973 a brand new purpose-built factory was constructed in a different location on the outskirts of the town. The

following year Francesco Laverda died, leaving the business in the hands of his sons Massimo and Piero. They made various decisions, including commissioning 125 and 175cc roadsters powered by Zündapp air– and, later, water-cooled engines bought in from West Germany. The brothers also entered into a new co-operation agreement with the Swedish Husqvarna concern (Laverda was the Husqvarna importer for Italy), whereby Laverda would use Husqvarna motors in a pair of new enduro bikes which superseded the earlier 246cc two-stroke single-cylinder Chott. The Chott used an engine of Laverda design with magnesium cases, enclosed rear-drive chain and adjustable steering head angle. Very expensive to make, it was a specialized, street-legal, enduro-cum-trail bike. Laverda also owned the massive agricultural machinery business, a caravan manufacturing company on the site of the old Capriolo factory at Trento and their own vineyards. In 1978 the first of these, Ditta Laverda SpA, 'the agricultura', passed into the hands of Fiat and is still going today. In Italy it is known under the title of Fiat-Laverda-Hesson, whilst in North America the name 'Allis' is tagged on the end. In any case, from the early 1970s the motorcycle plant, 'the moto', Moto Laverda SpA, had to stand on its own two feet commercially.

Another piece in the Laverda commercial jigsaw was the building of the awesome V6. This machine must have cost many millions of lire and was built with the assistance of former Maserati car engineer Giulio Alfieri. Alfieri was employed as a consultant by Laverda and worked with the company's design chief, Luciano Zen. The machine was constructed over a two-year period and made its public début on the Laverda stand at the 1977 Milan Show, followed by its only track appearance at the Bol d'Or the following year. Riders Cereghini and Perugini retired after some eight and a half hours with a broken universal joint in the drive-shaft. Prior to this it had been electronically timed at almost 180 mph, over 20 mph faster than the winning works Honda!

Although Massimo Laverda was later quoted as saying the V6 was 'only built as a design exercise', such a project was way outside the realms of such a small company and without doubt was a considerable drain on Laverda's financial resources. Rumours abounded of various production motorcycles, including a water-cooled four, which would make use of the V6 technology, but none was ever to appear. Instead the triples became older and therefore at a bigger disadvantage as every year passed in the face of faster and better-handling megabikes from the land of Nippon. Instead Moto Laverda SpA sought its salvation in a new range of two-stroke motorcycles. At first this seemed like a good idea with a series of variations of the 123.6cc (54×54mm) six-speed, water-cooled machine proving a good seller in the early 1980s. However, with companies such as Cagiva, Gilera, Garelli and Aprilia joining the contest with new designs, Laverda's early lead in the 'Super 125' streetbike race was soon overtaken.

Another commercial flop was the prestige middleweight. Laverda's first attempt was the 350 and 500 twins in the late 1970s. Like similar parallel twins from Ducati these were doomed to failure. Quite simply they were too near the Japanese in everything except the most important factor, price. Unlike the bigger bikes, the buyers of middleweight twins, at least of the vertical variety, had cost as their priority, not exclusivity. The only bright spots were the Formula 500 racer and the Slater-inspired Monjuich sportster. Yet another project which cost the company dear, but this time did not even get past the prototype stage, was the ill-fated 350 three-cylinder Lesmo. This, together with an engine assembly, made its only public appearance at the 1985 Milan Show. With an engine layout pioneered by the 350 DKW racers of the mid-1950s, the GS 350 Lesmo was intended as Italy's answer to the recently introduced Honda NS400, Laverda saying 'the real jewel of our Company is the long-awaited 350cc two-stroke street bike'. Besides its engine layout, it featured reed-valve induction, electronic

ignition, Gilnisil plated alloy cylinders, electric starting, six speeds and pumps for both the lubrication and cooling systems. There was also an aluminium beam-type frame, triple floating discs, monoshock rear suspension and a comprehensive fairing. Laverda claimed over 200 km/h (125 mph). Although listed in the 1986 model programme, the three-cylinder 'stroker never made it to the production line. Instead the Laverda range, in a year which saw the company enter controlled administration (receivership), comprised: 50 Atlas (trial bike), GS125 Lesmo (sports), CU125 Ride (custom), 600 Atlas (twin-cylinder four-stroke trail bike) and 1000SFC.

Another unsuccessful project for Moto Laverda SpA was the company's venture into the four-wheel world, in the shape of the off-road Laverda 4×4. Intended for both civilian and military use, at least this project did enjoy a level of development support from the Italian government. This truly go-anywhere vehicle was powered by a four-cylinder 2445cc diesel engine fitted with a five-speed gearbox.

Just how much any one particular project affected the company is hard to tell, but collectively they brought Moto Laverda to its knees and finally to a point, during much of 1988 and 1989, where production was at a standstill and the

An Italian Honda NS400, this Laverda 350 Lesmo appeared in prototype form at the 1985 Milan Show, together with a separate engine unit. By then the company was in financial low water, with the result that it never reached production status.

Produced in strictly limited numbers from 1985 onwards the 1000SFC looks like being the last of the Laverda three-cylinder superbikes.

outlook looked grim indeed.

Initially a joint venture company named Imola attempted a rescue act in early 1988. This soon failed. Then came a rumoured workers takeover. And ultimately in mid-1989 this latter faction were successful in gaining control, helped by a group of merchant banks and a Government-run co-operative organization.

The new concern is called Nuovo Moto Laverda, and the man in charge, Dr Ugo Holzer, has deemed that the first models will essentially be where the old Laverda company left off − in other words, the 1000SFC, 600 Atlas, 125 Lesmo in both custom and sports versions and the 50 Atlas. There are also plans to offer a special 40th anniversary limited (1000 machines) edition of the SFC, which only previous Laverda owners will be eligible to purchase.

Plans in the pipeline include a new 600 street bike, and further down the road an entirely new large-capacity touring mount to challenge BMW and Moto Guzzi. Before this dream can become a reality a new designer has to be found. The capital to finance the Laverda re-birth comes from the 65 factory workers, who have formed a co-operative themselves and the state co-operative organization, which has invested three times what the workers have put in whilst the merchant bankers Gruppo Zanini have put up £7. 1 million sterling.

Dr Hozer has stated that Nuova Moto Laverda aims to manufacture around 3500 motorcycles in 1990, and 5500 in 1991. There are also plans to produce the 4×4 off-road four-wheel vehicle. So it seems that at last Laverda enthusiasts can breathe a sigh of relief, secure in the knowledge that, at least for the near future, their marque is alive and kicking.

CHAPTER 12

Mondial

The Mondial story began back in 1929, when four brothers (Carlo, Ettore, Giuseppe and Luigi) founded the FB (*Fratelli Bosselli* – Brothers Bosselli) dealership in Milan, initially to sell GD two-stroke lightweights and then four-stroke CM motorcycles. One of the Bosselli brothers, Giuseppe, gained distinction by riding a CM to win a gold medal in the 1935 ISDT. By 1936 FB had acquired an industrial workshop in Bologna and began to manufacture three-wheel delivery trucks, including a model powered by a 600cc single-cylinder long-stroke ohc engine which fired every other lamp post!

When war came to Italy in June 1940 FB were allowed to continue production of their lightweight trucks, but this ended forcibly in 1944 when the retreating *Wehrmacht* razed the site to the ground before departing the area in the face of the Allied advance. However, one of the brothers, the same Giuseppe who had won an ISDT 'gold', realized that the need for basic transportation in a shattered post-war Italy would be vital. Obviously new production facilities were needed and Giuseppe, who had now succeeded to his father's title of Count, decided to start his new venture in Milan, the commercial and industrial capital of the North.

Like his fellow nobleman Count Domenico Agusta, Giuseppe Bosselli appreciated that an important stepping stone to being recognized by the motorcycling fraternity was through racing and so it was that the first product of the new marque, known as FB Mondial, was to be a racing machine. The FB prefix remembered the former Bosselli enterprise. The man chosen to design what was intended as a source of all-important publicity was none other than Alfonso Drusiani, the brother of Oreste Drusiani, chief designer and co-founder of the CM marque. The new machine appeared in early 1948 and incorporated considerable input from its sponsor, Giuseppe Bosselli, who was also a competent technician and later responsible for many interesting innovations on both the touring and racing models which were to follow.

The new racer, a 125 class machine, was ready in time to begin trials for the 1948 season. It was totally against convention – for, in a field dominated by two-strokes, the Mondial was a four-stroke, but it employed twin overhead camshafts which were driven by a vertical shaft with bevel

gears on the off-side of the engine and the 80-degree inclined valves used exposed hairpin springs. Both cylinder and head were in light alloy, with an austentic liner and steel valve seats. The piston was highly domed with three rings and forged to withstand high engine revolutions. The Marelli magneto was mounted at the front of the crankcase and gear-driven, like the oil pump, to which the lubricant was fed via a container mounted on top of the fuel tank, à la Moto Guzzi. A cover on the nearside concealed the outside flywheel. Primary drive to the four-speed close-ratio gearbox was by straight-cut gears in unit with the engine. On a 9.7:1 compression ratio, the maximum possible with the 80-octane 'pool' petrol available in those days, the 123.5cc (53×56mm) engine gave almost 11 bhp at 8600 rpm. At the time the leading two-strokes such as the Morini and MV Agusta were pushed to put out more than 10 bhp.

Count Bosselli and Alfonso Drusiani saw their handiwork make its début at the 1948 Italian Grand Prix at Faenza. With the former 500cc Italian champion Francesco Lama in the saddle, the little Mondial showed a clean pair of heels to the factory Morinis and MVs and Lama had the satisfaction of setting the fastest lap before retiring because of a leaking petrol tank. A month after the Faenza début, still completely unstreamlined, it was taken out in appalling conditions (heavy rain) on a piece of straight road near Cremona for Gino Cavanna, nicknamed the 'Flying Monk', to break the world records for the 125cc flying and standing start kilometre and mile distances with a fastest run of 80.8 mph over the flying kilo.

By the autumn of 1948, Monza was again back in serviceable condition and the final round in that year's Italian Senior Championships was staged there. This meeting had drawn all the country's leading riders and machines, but the Mondial, now in the hands of the highly experienced Nello Pagani, completely dominated the 125cc category. With a maximum speed of 90 mph the Mondial had a performance undreamed of before, and received a terrific reception from both press and public alike.

For 1949, the power was upped to 13 bhp at 9500 rpm and the two-strokes were left even further behind, with Pagani having no difficulty at all in winning the first 125cc world championship series, with victory in all three rounds in Switzerland, Holland and his native Italy. That same

October 1948 saw Gino Cavanna (nicknamed the 'Flying Monk') break world records for the 125cc flying and standing start kilometre and mile distances with a works Mondial racer. The attempts, on a piece of straight road near Cremona, were carried out in truly appalling weather conditions, including heavy rain and even snow!

year, but now with streamlining, Cavanna hoisted his flying kilo record to over 160 km/h − 100 mph plus. Unable to find a suitable stretch of road in Italy, the Mondial team used a section of the Brussels−Ostend highway.

As it was obvious by now that the FB Mondial had a clear speed advantage, both Morini and MV responded by designing their own four-strokes, but Drusiani countered by developing his engine still further and with 15 bhp at 11,500 rpm the opposition was again crushed in the 1950 world series. Again staged over three rounds, a Mondial won each race, but with three different victors: Bruno Ruffo at Assen, Carlo Ubbiali in Ulster, and Gianni Leoni on home ground at Monza. The title went to Ruffo, who also became Italian national champion that year in both the 125 and 250cc classes, riding a Moto Guzzi in the latter category.

Former fighter ace Leoni owed much of his Monza victory to his mount being equipped with comprehensive streamlining. Unlike the later dustbin type this had the front wheel exposed, but did include total enclosure of the

rear section, plus a frontal fairing more akin to the Dolphin type used from 1958 onwards. On the straights this gave Leoni up to 10 mph more speed than the other Mondial riders, but even so this form of streamlining did not appear on later Mondials. This was probably because of the effect which high winds would have had on the handling, and except for perfect conditions, as at Monza, would not have been worth the risk.

1950 also saw the début of the first Mondial production roadsters, a trio of push-rod four-stroke 125s with many similarities to the racing model. Offered in touring, sport and super sport trim, each had identical frames, pressed-steel blade-type girder forks and plunger rear springing. Even though they were very expensive, they were also sturdy and fast, and soon in great demand by sporting riders. In their 1950 Milan Show review *The Motor Cycle* described the Mondial roadsters as 'distinguished by a sort of spidery elegance that is not at all unsuitable for a family of lightweights'.

In fact the pukka Mondial GP racers' only real failing in the early 1950s was its anachronistic cycle parts, exactly the same double cradle frame with plunger rear suspension and pressed-steel blade girders at the front, as on the roadsters! Even so, during 1951 its jewel-like double-knocker engine, now with power boosted to 16 bhp at a heady 12,000 rpm, was once again more than a match for the, by now, four-stroke Morini and MV opposition, as it screamed out its victorious war cry throughout Europe. That year, for the first time, Count Bosselli included a foreign rider in his team. This was because two of the rounds were held in the United Kingdom, in the Isle of Man, the very first time that 125cc machines had competed on the famous 37¾-mile Mountain Course, and the Ulster Grand Prix. The man chosen to uphold Mondial honour in these two events was Cromie McCandless, brother of Rex, the designer off the legendary Featherbed Norton chassis. McCandless proved his worth by winning both events. Unfortunately for him and Mondial, the Ulster event was then dropped from the world championship points table because insufficient riders had taken part and so Ubbiali gained the world as well as the Italian title. Englishman Len Parry, also drafted into the squad, was destined not to reap the success gained by McCandless. Once again all the races counting towards the World Championship were won by Mondial machines, making a total of eleven (if one includes the 1951 Ulster GP) over three years. Besides Ubbiali, McCandless and Parry, other Mondial factory riders that year were Leoni, Alberti, Pagani, Ferri and Spadoni.

For 1952 Mondial made a big effort on the production front with the introduction of a number of new models.

1950 saw the début of the first Mondial production roadsters; these were push-rod rather than ohc, but otherwise had many similarities to the factory racers of the period.

Heading the list was a 125 'over-the-counter' racer priced at 590,000 lire. This was substantially similar to the world-beating works job *except* for the engine; it was single rather than double overhead cam and it featured gear drive to the camshaft rather than the shaft and bevel used on the factory bike. Other new Mondial motorcycles comprised a 200cc push-rod (a straight development of the earlier 125 ohv) and two-strokes with 125 and 160cc engines. These latter models had telescopic front forks and swinging arm rear suspension. Perhaps most interesting of all was the company's first scooter. This used an adaptation of the new 160cc two-stroke four-speed unit construction engine. On the scooter version of the engine the symmetrical, pear-shape crankcase covers which enclosed the primary transmission, generator and starter motor for the electric start (not employed on the motorcycle) extended to the rear and formed the swinging arm rear fork. Therefore, the engine, the transmission and the rear wheel were a sub-assembly pivoting under the control of the two rear shock absorbers. A duplex frame was made up of tubes welded at the joints, and steel pressings were employed for the weather shield,

floor and partial rear enclosure. The price was 250,000 lire. Even though it was technically advanced the Mondial was to suffer a similar fate to Ducati's Cruiser, introduced at the same time, both small-wheel designs failing to sell in any real numbers.

Compared with their previous years of glory, the 1952 Mondial racing season was a non-event, with the marque failing to win a classic. Ubbiali came nearest with a quartet of seconds at Assen, Solitude, Monza and the TT, to give him second place in the Championship behind Cecil Sandford and MV. The only consolation was that Ubbiali was able to retain his Italian title, but even so Mondial's leading star realized that, certainly for the present time, the Milanese company's GP bike just was not competitive any more and so he quit the team to ride for MV Agusta. In 1953, with Ubbiali gone, there was even less success for the Mondial factory. In Italy it was Mendogni with the Morini who swept all before him, whilst abroad, as was to be the case in 1954, the mighty NSU organization dominated the class.

But even though they had lost ground on the racing

In 1951 Count Bosselli included a foreign rider in his team for the first time. This was the Ulsterman Cromie McCandless, who is shown here on his way to fourth place in the Italian GP at Monza that year.

Besides their works machines, Mondial also produced a production racer, but this had a single, rather than double, overhead camshaft head. The 1952 version is shown.

At the Milan Show in January 1952, Mondial introduced this new scooter. Powered by a 160cc two-stroke engine, it featured electric start and plunger rear springing. The engine and chaincase unit pivoted with the rear wheel.

front, the production side was benefiting from an increased level of development. At the 1952 Milan Show a new ohv 200cc model had pride of place on the company's stand. This had a capacity of 198cc (62×66mm), which, on a 6:1 compression ratio, provided 12 bhp at 6000 rpm. The frame was a neat double-cradle affair with swinging arm rear suspension and telescopic front forks. Unusual features were the forward-operating kickstarter and the twin tail pipes on the silencer. Another newcomer was a sports version of the 160cc two-stroke. Except for the single-knocker 125 over-the-counter racer, all the Mondial production machines by now featured telescopic forks and swinging arm rear suspension. It was with one of the production racers that the then unknown Tarquinio Provini from Cadeo in northern Italy was to take his first steps along the road to stardom. In 1953 he won every race in which he competed, a performance which gained him a place in the works team for 1954. That year he was first in the 125cc class of the Giro d'Italia and Mondial won the eight-stage marathon outright with Remi Venturi on a specially adapted double overhead cam 175.

With NSU's withdrawal at Monza in September 1954 following the death of its 125 World Champion Ruppert Hollaus after a practice crash, Provini split a horde of MV Agustas to take second place behind the race winner Sala.

Then at the final round in Barcelona, Provini gave Mondial its first classic victory for three years with a magnificent win in front of the entire MV Agusta and Montesa factory teams. By now the 125 double knocker was revving to 13,000 rpm and producing 17 bhp. With a dustbin fairing the maximum speed was almost 110 mph.

Provini followed his success by defeating Ubbiali and the MV team for the Italian 125 championships the following year, but failed to capitalize on this success in the world title series. Much of the reason for the lack of success at the higher level was a completely new racer which Drusiani had been working on. This was a 250 twin, essentially a pair of the dohc 123.5cc cylinders giving a capacity of exactly 247cc, grafted on a common crankcase. Although claimed to turn out 35 bhp at 10,000 rpm, which was almost equal to the all-conquering NSU Rennmax, the Drusiani creation at 136kg (300 lb) was far too heavy. In addition the high 11.5:1 compression and fiercer cam profile meant a much narrower power band, which demanded a six-speed box. Although two bikes were eventually built, the whole project proved to be a costly failure. Quite simply, against machines such as the NSU, MV Agusta (and even the NSU Sportmax production racer) it was totally outclassed and soon withdrawn.

As Drusiani had already built a 216cc model out of the

175cc of the type used by Venturi to win the 1954 Giro d'Italia he soon realized that a full-blown purpose-built *lightweight* single would be a much better bet than the gargantuan twin. Most of 1956 was spent not only designing and building this, but also a new 125. That year saw Provini take the 175cc Italian title, although in the 125cc class he had again to give best to his great rival Carlo Ubbiali.

So to 1957, perhaps the greatest in the company's history. Count Bosselli's team not only had the great Provini, but also the Englishman Cecil Sandford and Irishman Sammy Miller in its line-up. The redesigned 125, now fitted with a *seven-speed* gearbox and a twin-plug head with the second 10mm plug tucked away to the rear of the bevel shaft column, pumped out 19 bhp at 13,200 rpm. There had been experiments with a totally new frame. This was a highly innovative space-type design, but was

Remi Venturi in the process of winning the second Giro d'Italia with his 175 Mondial. He is shown here at Verbania, near Milan, on 11 April, 1954, shortly before being declared the winner at the finish in Bologna.

ultimately discarded and an adoption of the more conventional double-cradle tubular type used instead. To lower the height 18in. wheels were employed.

The real technical interest centred around the new 250. Unlike the 125, the 249.1cc (75×56.4mm) single had the drive to its dohc by gears, like the latest 175, rather than bevel-shaft. The vastly oversquare engine dimensions gave the Mondial an ability to achieve 11,400 rpm, although the maximum power output of 29 bhp was produced at 10,800 rpm. Both the 125 and 250 Mondial sported streamlining fore and aft. The front dustbin fairing was particularly beautiful *and* effective. So much so that with only 29 bhp the 250 was timed at Monza at an amazing 137 mph! The larger mount also had the choice of five, six or seven gears, depending upon rider preference and circuit requirements.

The season started with a magnificent double at the Golden Jubilee TT in the Isle of Man, with Provini taking the 125cc race and Sandford the 250. The unluckiest man was Miller, who led the 250 race going into the last corner, Governors Bridge, on the final circuit, only to be thrown off when his gearbox locked up. Shocked and cut, Miller bravely pushed in to finish fifth. With a superb display of riding skills and machine reliability the TT winners went on to soundly thrash the mighty MV team throughout the season, which concluded with Provini becoming World Champion in the 125cc category and Sandford victor in the 250cc class; in addition Provini was Italian champion in both classes.

The month after the Italian GP Mondial announced, together with Gilera and Moto Guzzi, that it was quitting racing. Sad, sad news, but with the domestic motorcycle industry in recession it was the only possible alternative to financial collapse. Sandford promptly retired, whilst Provini went to MV and Miller to Ducati and CZ before embarking on a career in trials. He was destined to become the greatest 'feet-up' rider in history.

Another victim of the Mondial withdrawal was an exciting new 125 racer, which had been seen in the factory's pit area at Monza during practice for the Italian GP. This was a twin-cam model with desmodromic valve operation. Factory sources claimed it was already producing 21 bhp at 13,500 rpm ... one can only wonder what might have been.

The prospects for the Italian motorcycle industry had changed. The cost of works participation had increased dramatically, whilst the returns were diminishing. Mondial also pulled out of moto-cross, after Osterero had won the 250 and 500cc titles in Italy during 1957 and the 250cc in 1956. For Count Bosselli it was back to the much more humdrum life of production targets and balance sheets. But as he still recalls 'the Grand Prix racing era was the greatest period in my life'. Not that the production models had been neglected, as the period 1955-57 had seen unparalleled activity on that front in Mondial's Milan facilities.

The 1955 Mondial range, launched at the Milan Show in November 1954, had seen several new arrivals, notably the Mondialino, the first under-125cc machine the factory had ever produced. This had a pressed-steel, beam-type frame with hydraulically damped swinging arm rear suspension. It was unique in having the front mudguard incorporated with the legs of the swinging bottom link front forks in a single pressing. Power was supplied by a 49cc (40×39.5mm) two-stroke engine with three-speed gearbox. A similar unit, but with only two speeds, powered a cheaper, rigid-framed model. Other newcomers were the 158cc Sogno (wishful thinking), a motorcycle-cum-scooter-like machine with 3.50×15 tyres, comprehensive protection and a unique style. The Constellation was an updated version of the 200cc ohv model, as was the Metropol 160cc two-stroke motorcycle. The brand new Meteor and Gran Sport both used a chain-driven ohc engine derived from the lessons learnt on the Grand Prix circuit. The more sporting Gran Sport was capable of over 85 mph, making it one of the very fastest 175cc roadsters of the time.

A year later and the Milan Show was the scene of the launch of the Champion. This featured a near-vertical push-rod four-speed unit construction engine, slotted into a lightweight chassis, in which the engine was used as a stressed member. With a low selling price, it was clearly aimed at customers who had previously shied away from

Cecil Sandford riding his fully streamlined 250 Mondial to victory in the Lightweight TT, 7 June, 1957. Later that year, after taking the 125 and 250cc world titles, Mondial quit the sport.

The 175cc ST sports model of the early 1960s. This push-rod machine was capable of around 80 mph with handling and braking to match. Note double-barrel silencer.

the marque on price grounds.

The 1956 Milan Show saw Mondial display its 1957 models. The main attraction, certainly for casual observers, was an interesting 'scrambler' powered by a modestly tuned version of the 198cc Constellation push-rod engine. The frame of this closely followed that of the famous Norton Featherbed.

The only new Mondial for 1958 was a sporting 250, which used a bottom end similar to the works single-cylinder racer, but had push-rod valve operation and only four speeds. It was considerably more sporting than the majority of previous street bikes from the company, and factory tester Silvano Rinaldi, who had also been a racer in more minor events for the Milan-based concern, reported the top speed to be almost 100 mph without the silencer but with no other special tuning. This was soon followed by a similar sporting version of their well-known 175 push-rod model. This gave 11 bhp at 7000 rpm and was good for around 75 mph.

For the following year the 250 was dropped and an impressive ten-model line-up was offered. A completely new ultra-lightweight was the 75cc Scugnizzo (Street Urchin). This had a 75cc two-stroke engine, with three speeds and produced 3.6 bhp at 5500 rpm. The Scugnizzo

was offered in two versions: Turismo and Sport. There were also two 49cc two-stroke two-speed models, the Lady moped and Turismo sports moped. Then came a trio of push-rod 125s. All used the basically similar 124cc, four-speed unit, but with different levels of tune, the most potent of which was the Special with 8 bhp at 7500 rpm. There were also three 175s. By far the most attractive, and quickest, was the Sprint. Finished in an eye-catching metallic cherry red with gold forks, frame and tank panels, the Sprint looked every inch an Italian thoroughbred. In style and colour scheme it was very similar to the Ducati 175 Sport. But unfortunately, unlike the Duke, the Mondial Sprint had ohv rather than ohc.

The 1959 Mondial catalogue said: 'Mondial High *Level* Production'. But this was not strictly true, because the company's production figures never approached the numbers turned out by the other well-known marques, such as Guzzi, Gilera, Ducati or even Parilla. Even though their production output was relatively small, Mondial still continued to introduce new models, as the 1959 Milan Show was to prove. Here there were newcomers in the under 100cc class, 88 and 98cc, a 150cc touring motorcycle and flashy 75cc Lady Scooter. This latter product was obviously aimed at the teenage market with twin orna-

The company returned to racing in 1963 with a single-cylinder disc-valve two-stroke. Rider/designer Francesco Villa is seen in action on the machine at Imola early the following year.

mental chrome-plated pipes on each side of the body. The front forks had trailing links; the rear fork was pivoted. Tyre size was 3.00×12 and the final drive from the three-speed gearbox was by enclosed chain. In appearance it was similar to the Capri scooter offered by the Agrati-Garelli organization.

In many ways 1960 saw the high point in the company's fortunes and from then on it was downhill all the way, albeit very slowly. In retrospect the real reason was Count Bosselli's decision to retire to his 'seaside' retreat, leaving everything in the hands of, as he put it recently, 'My playboy nephew, who just managed to destroy everything I had built up'. Initially this was not entirely obvious and probably not even those on the inside realized what was happening. Helping mask the downward spiral was a re-newal of racing activity for a number of years in the early 1960s. Much of this renewed interest in the sport centred around the Villa brothers, Francesco in particular, and it was he who persuaded the new Mondial boss to let him race the 1957 mounts. The 250cc model, up against more recent machinery, did not give particularly good results, even though a similar bike had taken the young Mike Hailwood

to a number of victories in Britain during 1959 and 1960. The 125 proved to still be good enough, at least in Italy, and Villa rode it to victory in the 1961, 1962 and 1963 Italian senior championships.

Francesco Villa was also involved with Mondial in building some interesting new race machinery around the same time. The first was constructed in 1962. This was a dohc 'fifty' with six-speed gearbox and dry clutch. Weighing only 56kg (124 lb), this 39×40mm miniature racer produced 7 bhp at 14,000 rpm. At world champion-ship level it was hopelessly outclassed by the leading contenders, such as the Suzuki and Kreidler two-strokes. Villa was assisted in this project by ex-Mondial race mechanic Omer Melotti. The next design came in 1963, with a single-cylinder disc-valve two-stroke. Like the similar Parilla this was inspired by the success of the East German MZ. And like the Parilla, the Mondial's cylinder was horizontal. Although the head was air-cooled, there was a water jacket for the cylinder and large radiator mounted on top of the crankcase assembly. Equipped with a seven-speed gearbox the machine was prepared for the Italian GP that year. Although it appeared during the

By the late 1970s Mondial was finding the going ever more difficult. One of the few bright spots was the excellent V778 enduro. This sported a 250cc German Sachs engine, with seven speeds, Motoplat ignition, magnesium fork sliders and gas rear shocks. The photograph shows the 1978 version; the following year the factory shut its doors.

training period, and seemed to perform reasonably well, it was decided that the time was not yet right for an actual race début. With several improvements the machine was exhibited at the Milan Show at the end of that year, but did not make its racing début until 1964.

The planned programme called for participation in the Italian national championship races with Francesco Villa, Giuseppe Mandolini and Francesco's brother Walter (later to become a multi-world champion with the Italian arm of the Harley-Davidson team). Producing 24 bhp at 11,000 rpm it was fitted with an *eight*-speed gearbox and weighed 84kg (185 lb). This excellent combination of lightweight and good power output provided Francesco Villa with a machine capable of winning the 1964 Italian title, which he proceeded to do. This result, however, hid the fact that the bike was extremely difficult to ride. Not only did it possess a narrow power band and demanded the rider's left hand to hover over the clutch lever in case of an engine seizure, but the pilot had the task of continually operating a hand-pump for supplementary lubrication in addition to pressing a cut-out button each time a gear was changed. Because of this a major redesign was carried out in the close season. In search of an easier ride and a more reliable mount, the

engine had its cylinder repositioned vertically and the water jacket discarded to provide only air cooling. Although the power dropped fractionally to 23 bhp at 11,500 rpm, this was not a handicap, as the weight had been pruned down to 70kg (155 lb). Most important of all, it was now much easier to ride, with a wider spread of power and less complication. That year Francesco Villa, Mandolini and Giuseppe Visenzi took the first three places in the Italian championship.

Late in 1965, at the Italian championship meeting at San Remo, Mondial introduced a twin-cylinder 250 of 248cc (56×50.5mm) with mixed cooling and double rotary disc induction. Lubrication was by a combination of 20:1 petroil mixture and a supplementary oil pump which ran off the crankshaft, so obviating the need for the awkward hand pump of the earlier single. The 250 was improved in detail for the 1966 season − producing 48 bhp at 11,500 rpm and capable of close on 150 mph, and a similar 124.88cc (43×43mm) twin-cylinder smaller model was also built, albeit with air cooling. At this stage, however, Mondial began to face financial problems, and Francesco Villa left the company, first to work in Spain for Montesa, and later to form his own company (see Chapter 20).

The 1987 Milan Show saw the rebirth of the Mondial marque. The author is seen here with the 125 GP World Challenge single-cylinder road racer.

Brother Walter reverted back to the earlier 125 single-cylinder Mondial and won the Italian championships in both 1966 and 1967.

Meanwhile production of the single-cylinder two-strokes and ohv four-strokes ranging from 49 to 198cc had continued. But by the middle of the 1960s this was on a much more limited scale, hence the decision to pull out of racing in 1966. Mondial had always intended their bikes for the home rather than the export market and a drop in the sales of two-wheelers in Italy during the mid/late 1960s therefore affected the company more than it would one with an export plan. However, production continued and by the mid-1970s Mondial were even manufacturing off-road machines with bought-in West German Sachs engines. At the smaller end of the scale their Matic moped and Mini Cross fun bike both used not Mondial power units, but proprietary Minerelli units.

By the start of 1977, their range was down to just three bikes, the 50cc Matic Mk 2 moped, a 250cc enduro iron and a model of the same engine type and size as those which had given the company its initial fame within the motorcycle industry, a single-cylinder 125cc four-stroke. Things drifted from bad to worse, with the result that if it had continued much longer the once great marque would collapse around his ears, so on 31 December, 1979, Count Bosselli's nephew took the only decision open and closed the FB Mondial motorcycle manufacturing operation. However, this was not to be the complete end of the story, as almost eight years later, the Milan Show, held in late November 1987, witnessed a mini rebirth of the famous company. This was led by the Villa brothers, but with the Count's blessing (he was then over eighty years old). A small but well-presented stand displayed several brand new models, bearing the legendary name, and a couple of the works racers from the 1950s, one complete with its dustbin fairing.

Most exciting of the 'reborn' Mondial range was the 125GP World Challenge. This was a single-cylinder liquid-cooled disc valve over-the-counter racer with a capacity of 124.6cc (56.3×50mm). No power figures were stated, but from its specification, which included a 38mm Dell 'Orto carburettor, Nicasil cylinder bore, Deltabox aluminium frame, Marzocchi MIR 35mm forks, triple Brembo discs and Marvic wheels (17in. front, 18in. rear), it looked every inch a winner. Price was a whopping 14,998,000 lire! The 125 Super Sport was an ultra-modern, fully-faired sportster which, with a maximum speed of 168 km/h (106 mph), made it arguably the fastest standard production ⅛-litre machine in the world at the time. The initial prototype had bore and stroke measurements of 56×50mm, but these were soon changed to the 56.3×50mm dimensions of the road-racer. Running on a 14.5:1 compression ratio the Super Sport pumped out 27.5 bhp at 10,500 rpm. Carburation was by a PHBH30 Dell 'Orto instrument. The remaining model displayed on the stand was the 250RG. This 247cc (68×68mm) device was a full-blown enduro mount and owed much to similar Villa models.

Count Bosselli had teamed up with the Villa brothers, Francesco and Walter, because, in his own words, 'I want one final go at getting Mondial back on top to leave something to my 34-year-old son! The Mondial organization of the late 1980s was based at the Villa factory in Crespallano, some 15km from Bologna. In early 1988 a visit to the facilities revealed that inside there was a vast array of history from both Mondial and the Villas, cups, trophies, and posters detailing past glories. Unfortunately it seems very few actual production versions of the *nuovo* Mondial range were built, with the result that the 'relaunch' would seem to have been less successful than all parties would have hoped.

CHAPTER 13

Morini

A native of the university town of Bologna, Alfonso Morini was born in 1892, and could well be described as a self-made man. Apprenticed to a local blacksmith, Morini saved everything towards the time when he would be able to open his very own workshop facility for the repair of bicycles and motorcycles. This particular ambition was realized shortly prior to the outbreak of the First World War. Although already enthusiastic about motorcycles, Alfonso Morini had been in no position to actually own one and had to rely upon borrowed machines for his initial experiences out on the road.

Luckily his fledgling workshop had gained a good reputation so that by the time he was called up for military service in the Italian army, Morini was able to get a posting to the automobile and motorcycle repair section at Padua. Undoubtedly this helped improve his technical knowledge and skill, so that by the end of the war, when he was at last able to return to his workshop in Bologna, Morini was ready to advance beyond the mere repairing of machines.

He found a partner in the shape of Mario Mazzetti, another enthusiastic and skilled engineer, and pooling their financial resources they formed the MM (Morini-Mazzetti) concern. The story of that enterprise is related in Chapter 20. It is, however, worth mentioning that the partners' first model, a 125cc two-stroke, was launched in 1924 and that it was with one of these that Morini became MM's first official works rider. Success was not immediate, but in September 1927, Morini and the little MM caused a big upset by winning the Italian Grand Prix at Monza. After 1930, the 125cc category became far less popular because of changes in the Italian Highway Code, and MM switched from two-strokes to four-strokes. At first these were ohv, but, later, ohc models appeared. MM continued to patiently develop these and other machines, including side-valve versions, until its ultimate closure in 1957.

Alfonso Morini had severed his connection with the MM concern some 20 years before, in 1937, to start another business under his own name, with Moto Morini becoming a famous name in its own right. Alfonso Morini, always something of an individualist, had always dreamed of his own factory, but in 1937 times were difficult for the Italian motorcycle industry and, although he was soon ready with new designs, was forced to devote the factory to the making

of three-wheel trucks rather than two-wheelers. With the commencement of the Second World War, production was switched to military equipment, including aircraft components, which were mostly made from cast aluminium. The factory, situated in Bologna, was at the very heart of one of the world's principal centres for non-ferrous foundry work and was subjected to constant aerial attack by the Allies as they moved up into the body of Italy. Late in 1943 the Morini plant was partly destroyed by aerial bombardment, for although Italy had surrendered, Bologna was still in a part of the country controlled by the Germans.

In 1945, with the war over, Morini could at last organize the task of rebuilding his partly wrecked factory exclusively for motorcycle production. In fact he was one of the very first Italian manufacturers to put a model on to the market. Launched in 1946, this had an engine capacity of 123cc and was clearly based on the pre-war German DKW 125 design. Like the 'Deek', the new Morini had piston port induction and a unit construction engine with three speeds and flywheel magneto ignition. The specification also included girder front forks, plunger rear suspension and 19in. wheels.

A natural step from this was the production of a racing model for the 125cc class, which was just beginning to figure at international level. With a degree of engine tuning, including a racing carburettor, four-speeds, open megaphone exhaust, revised riding position and alloy rims the *Competizione*, as it was called, entered production in 1947. Selling through to 1949 it was used by many young Italians to get their first taste of the sport. One rider in particular soon carved a name for himself on the Morini. This promising newcomer was Umberto Masetti, later to become 500cc World Champion with Gilera in 1950 and 1952. Another rider to have an early success on the two-stroke Morini was the young engineer Dante Lambertini, who was destined to become head of Morini's racing development and the man chiefly responsible for the fastest single-cylinder four-stroke 250 ever built.

One of the first Italian manufacturers to participate in racing outside Italy after the war, Morini had the 125cc class of the 1948 Dutch TT almost in the bag when a cooked spark plug stopped Masetti's bike. Dutchman Dick Renooy

Morini's first design was this 125cc two-stroke single, which went on sale during 1946.

on an Eysink (fitted with a much modified British Villiers engine with rearward-facing exhaust) went on to win, with Nello Pagani on another Morini second.

Later that year, work began on the design of a new 246cc Jawa-like single-cylinder model, with twin exhaust ports. Introduced in 1949, this was intended as a strictly touring machine, the engine of which was also used to power an array of small three-wheel commercial vehicles. Even though the engine had never been conceived as anything other than a simple utilitarian hack, it had several advanced features, including a unit construction four-speed gearbox and geared primary drive. Its success was another step up the ladder for the Bologna factory.

1949 was also the first year of the newly introduced 'official' World Championship road racing series. In the 125cc class the championship was contested over three rounds; Berne in Switzerland, Assen in Holland and Monza in Italy. Although rival FB Mondial machines won all three rounds and the Championship, Morinis were their most serious challengers, taking a pair of second places, Magi at Berne and Masetti at Monza. Magi also finished second in the series overall behind World Champion Nello Pagani's Mondial, with Masetti fourth. Masetti had also become the first Italian Senior Champion for the 125cc class the previous year with the Morinis clearly faster than their main rivals MV Agusta, also two-strokes at this stage.

However, as Mondial had shown with their superb double overhead camshaft machine, the two-strokes' days were numbered (strange when one considers what happened at Grand Prix level in the mid-1970s).

So Morini resolved quickly to enter the four-stroke field, first in racing, later for its street bikes, too. The first Morini four-stroke racer appeared in 1950, and featured a single-cylinder ohc 123.1cc (52×58mm), with four speeds. This won the Italian Championships, but in the World Championship series riders Matucchi, Zinzani and Soprani just could not live with the all-conquering Mondials.

For 1951 the chain-driven single overhead camshaft engine was refined and the power rose from 12 bhp at 9000 rpm to 14 bhp at 9200 rpm, which equated to a maximum road speed of close on 100 mph. The team that year consisted of Zinzani, Zanzi and Mendogni. Even though they did not win a single classic, they were much improved over the previous season. Luigi Zinzani came second at Assen and third at Monza, to finish fourth in the series, which now took place over five venues.

For 1952 yet more power was extracted mainly by way of converting to double overhead cam. And with 16 bhp available, Morini's new star, Emilio Mendogni, completed a truly sensational finale to the season by giving Morini their first ever Grand Prix victory — and what better than to

In the 1948 Dutch TT, Nello Pagani pilots his Morini two-stroke to second place in the 125cc event.

To combat the FB Mondial four-stroke, Morini introduced their own poppet-valve machine, one of which is shown during 1951.

The 175 ohc Settebello. Capable of both speed and reliability, this machine carved out a great reputation for the Bologna company during the late 1950s as a fast roadster or clubman's racer.

score this on home ground at Monza! Not content with this success, Mendogni made it two victories in a row by taking the final GP of the season, the Spanish, held over the twists and turns of Montjuich Park, Barcelona. Having beaten such stars as Carlo Ubbiali and H. P. Müller (Mondials) and Les Graham and Cecil Sandford (MV Agustas), Mendogni could rightly feel elated. However, with improved machinery from MV Agusta and the onslaught by the German NSU company, Morini were little seen in the championships during 1953, even though Mendogni won the Italian Senior championship once again for the Bologna marque.

On the production front Morini had been busy developing a new 175cc ohv model, which made its public début at the Milan Show in November 1952. This sported a unit construction engine, four-speed box, telescopic forks and swinging arm rear suspension. By the end of 1953 a similar model, but with a capacity of 160cc, had appeared. Unlike the racing models these bread-and-butter production models largely failed to catch the eye compared with more glamorous rivals from factories such as Parilla, MV Agusta, Mondial and Gilera.

In 1954 an enlarged version of the 125 racer was produced for Mendogni to win the 175cc class of the Italian Senior Championship. The factory gained commercially from his success by giving more attention to the production

machines, and with this in mind introduced the superb 175cc push-rod Settebello (seven of diamonds). This machine was a real fire-breathing street racer which looked low, mean and powerful. The Settebello proved an instant success both in production racing and the sales charts. In standard trim it came complete with clip-ons, a tuned engine, large Dell 'Orto carburettor, conical brake hubs, alloy wheel rims, a bulbous 18-litre fuel tank, sprint saddle and lightweight pressed-steel mudguards.

Hungry for even more success Morini then played their trump card, the Rebello (Rebel). Rebel by name, Rebel by nature, for whereas the Settebello, however much of a success, was still a humble push-rod design, the Rebello had technical features quite different from a conventional production-based motorcycle. At the time of its introduction, spring 1955, it was one of the most up-to-date designs anywhere in the world. With an increase in capacity and double overhead cams the basic Rebello design was to lay the groundwork for the fabulous 250 GP model, which came later. With a bore and stroke of 60×61mm the Rebello had a capacity of 172.4cc and its single overhead camshaft was driven by a chain on the off-side of the cylinder. It was also the first Morini to sport a five-speed gearbox. The frame was a single-cradle affair, with the engine employed as a stressed member, there being no bottom frame rail. The fully enclosed telescopic

1959 shot of the Morini race shop, showing a pair of the 250cc double knocker Grand Prix singles, with the company's chief designer Ing. Franco Lambertini.

forks and dual shock swinging arm rear suspension were of typical existing Italian design. The Rebello soon showed its worth by not only winning its class in the 1955 Giro d'Italia, but winning both its class *and* finishing second overall (behind a 500 Gilera four) in the Milano−Taranto event that year. The rider was Mario Preta. A Rebello also won its class in the 1956 Giro d'Italia, and a large number of lesser events throughout Italy during the mid to late 1950s.

At this time, Morini's best-selling roadster was the Sbarazzino (free-and-easy). This was a 98.125cc (50×50mm) ohv unit construction design with the cylinder inclined 15 degrees from the vertical. Ratios in its four-speed gearbox were 2.50, 1.54, 1.07, and 0.80:1, with primary drive by helical gear. Like the similar 173cc ohv touring model, the Sbarazzino was neatly presented, economical and reliable, but not really exciting, either in terms of performance or style. Morinis, except for the

racers, never seemed to make headlines during this period, even though they continued to sell steadily to those wanting value for money and practicability.

Mid-September 1957 saw the début of a new single-cylinder model which was clearly based around the Rebello, but meant for Grand Prix duty rather than production-type events. This was the prototype *Gran Premio*, which had itself been built from an enlarged Rebello tested during 1956. This first prototype had a capacity of 246.7cc (69×66mm) and produced 25 bhp (against the 175's 22 bhp). By the time the new machine appeared at Monza in September 1957 power was up to 29 bhp at 10,000 rpm. On the model as it appeared at Monza, the double overhead cams bore directly on the valve stems and were operated by a chain (as on the Rebello). Ignition was by magneto with twin spark plugs and the compression ratio was 9.5:1. Hairpin-type valve springs were used and these were exposed to the elements. The cylinder head, barrel and crankcases were all cast in alloy. Lubrication was of the dry sump type, as favoured by Morini for their racing designs. The large oil tank was placed under the saddle and a double gear pump circulated the castor-based lubricant. The crankshaft had inside circular flywheels and rotated on three ball race main bearings, one on the timing side and two for the primary drive side. Both the straight-cut primary gears and the multi-plate clutch were contained in an oil bath. The five-speed close-ratio gearbox was in unit with the engine and the pedal controlled from the offside. Carburation was by a remote float 30mm Dell 'Orto SS1 instrument. Unlike the Rebello the frame was of the double cradle type, but otherwise both in its layout and the suspension system employed closely followed the earlier design. Dry weight was 113kg (248 lb).

Very soon after the Monza début, Morini constructed a modified version. On this the camshafts were driven by spur pinions in place of the chain and coil ignition was fitted. The latter had double contact breakers under a circular cover on the off-side (timing side) of the power unit, a battery and two ignition coils, and it was in this form that Morini planned to use their new double knocker 250 in 1958. With Guzzi and Mondial both pulling out, it seemed that with a little more development Morini would have a world-beater on its hands. Strangely the Gran Premio did not race again until some 12 months later when a pair of the machines were entered once more at Monza for the Italian GP. Ridden by Emilio Mendogni and Giampiero Zubani they totally dominated the race, which included multi-World Champion Carlo Ubbiali and his MV Agusta. Mendogni won by over 16 seconds at an average speed of 104.52 mph.

Besides gear-driven cams and coil ignition the engine dimensions had been revised and were now 72×61mm and with the much shorter stroke the capacity was 248.3cc. The compression ratio had been upped to a heady 12:1 and the factory claimed 32 bhp at 10,200 rpm. Other significant changes were the substitution of a six- instead of a five-speed gearbox, and Electron, instead of alloy, crankcases.

After the Monza success there were many column inches devoted in the Italian press to just what Morini would be doing the following year. A rumour circulated that Mendogni was leaving to join Ducati and that former champion Geoff Duke would be joining the team. Finally it was revealed that Mendogni and Zubani were staying and, for selected meetings, would be joined by Derek Minter and the 1957 500cc World Champion and former Gilera star Libero Liberati.

A new dolphin fairing was tested in the famous Moto Guzzi wind tunnel at Mandello del Lario and the factory

Monza, September 1963. Provini waves to a jubilant crowd after winning the 250cc Italian GP. A happy Comm. Alfonso Morini looks on.

also prepared a special detuned version of their racer for Liberati to use for his training on open roads around his Terni home! A modified version of the Amadoro twin cam brake was tested, as was the use of Oldani assemblies and even experiments with a disc brake.

All seemed set for a fabulous season, when at the Senior Italian championship races at Modena on Easter Monday 1959, Liberati, in his first outing on the Morini, dominated the 250 final in the early stages, with Mendogni holding second place ahead of a star-studded field, which included MV teamsters Ubbiali and Provini. Liberati led for most of the race, followed in the later stages by Provini, Mendogni and Ubbiali. Then Provini, risking everything, swept past Liberati only to crash in the rain and both

After Provini left to join Benelli, the youngster Giacomo Agostini took his place as Morini team leader. Here 'Ago' is seen on his way to victory in the Shell Gold Cup at Imola, 19 April, 1964.

rain and both Liberati and Ubbiali had to retire at the pits, leaving Mendogni to win easily.

Missing out the Isle of Man TT, the Morini team made its classic début at Hockenheim, West Germany. Here Mendogni finished second behind race-winner Ubbiali, whilst Liberati was fourth. Making his début with the team, Minter came home third at Assen, behind the MV pair of Ubbiali and Provini, whilst at the final round at Monza the same rider was fourth and Mendogni third. At Monza Liberati débuted a 320cc Morini dohc single (an over-bored 250). Even though it produced a reputed 40 bhp it was not capable of matching the MV fours. Liberati had other problems too, as his engine seized twice, in practice and during the race. Morini's season had not lived up to expectations, mainly because the new twin-cylinder MV and the MZ twin two-stroke were producing more power and MV still had the best riders. The factory had also entered the trials arena, after an 'experimental' season in 1958. The machines were powered by modified versions of the 98cc push-rod model ridden by Azzalini Carlini, Cervia and Giuseppe Villa. Much of their backing came from Morini's Varese agent Premoli.

On the production front the Milan Samples Fair held in April 1959 had seen the introduction off the *Corsaro* (Pirate). Derived from the 98cc *Sbarazzino*, which had been a sales success for the company over the previous

three years, the Corsaro was a particularly attractive machine, which still managed to retain the looks of its other ohv brothers. Of 56×50mm, the 123.08cc power unit developed 7.5 bhp at 8000 rpm on a 6:1 compression ratio. Top speed was 63 mph and dry weight was 195 lb. Although it cost rather more than contemporary machines of similar capacity, many riders proved that they were prepared to pay for the quality and race breeding, and the Corsaro sold well, even at the 185,000 lire asking price.

At the end of 1959 came the sensational news that Tarquinio Provini was quitting MV for Morini! With this came a statement that the former 1958 250cc World Champion would be Morini's sole runner in the 1960 championship series. Two bikes were built over the winter. On these the duplex frame was appreciably lower than before. Previously it had consisted of two complete loops with the seat tubes of the rear sub-frame attached about an inch below the bottom of the tank; but now it had straight tubes running at seat level from the saddle to the steering head with the main frame members welded to them at the rear. To permit a really low Provini crouch, the top of the 12-litre (2.64-gal.) tank was deeply dished. Overall height had also been reduced by fitting 18in. wheels, compared with 19in. the previous year. Both carried 2.75 section tyres. Basically the twin-plug, dohc single with six-speed gearbox remained unchanged. But its optimum revs had

Easter 1974. Journalist Bob Currie on the very first Morini 3½ Strada to be imported into Britain.

been increased by 200 to 10,400 rpm, and power upped to 35 bhp (at the rear wheel). Despite the use of heavier alloy for the crankcase, instead of Electron, which had given a certain amount of trouble the previous year, the total weight of the machine had been reduced from 251.5 lb to 238 lb, complete with streamlining. The new Morini with Provini aboard made a stunning début at Cesanatico in early April, setting new lap and race records. Besides winning the 250cc race, Provini was also faster than Ernesto Brambilla on a 350 Bianchi twin, who won the 500cc event! But at the Imola Gold Cup in May, however, Provini, having swept past race leader Ubbiali, was forced to retire with gearbox troubles. Everyone expected the combination of Provini and the Morini single to be a constant thorn in the flesh of the MV pairing of Ubbiali and new boy Gary Hocking, but after finishing third behind the MV riders in the Isle of Man, Provini chose (or was he ordered?) to revert to Italian meetings for the rest of that year.

1961 was hardly much better, with three classic finishes in the first six, and a third in West Germany at Hockenheim was his best performance. Much the same happened in 1962, although both years Provini had the satisfaction of winning the Italian title. The most important technical change that year was to the oil tank location. This was

moved from under the saddle to under the crankcase to lower gravity. In addition, Oldani brakes were employed for the first time — 230mm front, 200mm rear. At the Italian GP at Monza in September 1962 Provini split the mighty Honda team to finish second behind the World Champion Jim Redman. On the strength of this, Alfonso Morini decided to let him make a bid for the 250cc World Championship in 1963.

'Provini Thrashes Works Hondas' — so read the front page headline of *Motor Cycling* dated 8 May, 1963. This was in response to the combination of Provini and Morini's first ever win over the factory Hondas in a World Championship race. This had taken place at the previous Sunday's Spanish Grand Prix, the first of the year's classics, over the tortuous 2.35-mile Montjuich Park circuit in Barcelona. The victory was no fluke. For lap after lap, Provini fought a great battle with reigning World Champion Jim Redman, while Tommy Rubb on a second Japanese four tried all he knew to close the gap that separated him from the leaders. In the process all three constantly shattered the old Honda lap record and Provini finally carved over two seconds off it to win at a faster *average* speed than the old lap record! If everyone thought it was Provini's riding ability rather than speed which had been entirely responsible for the win

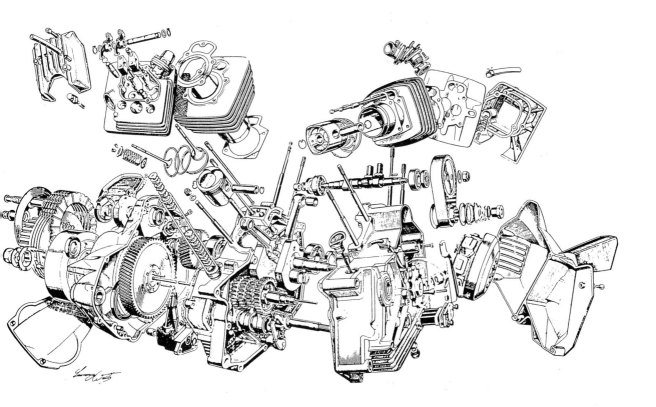

Exploded view of Morini V-twin engine. Note belt-driven camshaft parallel valves with Heron combustion chambers.

in Spain, a few weeks later at the end of May this theory was proved a myth, because again the Morini won, this time on the ultra-fast 4.8-mile Hockenheim circuit in West Germany. Once more the whole Honda team had to concede defeat to the flying Italian. At the end of the 20-lap, 96-mile race the victory margin was well over two minutes, with a new lap record of 118.27 mph.

Then came a spate of misfortunes. First the French GP was cancelled (due to fog and heavy rain) after Provini was clearly the fastest in practice, then Morini made what was to prove a fatal decision to give the Isle of Man a miss (which Redman won), mechanical problems surfaced in Holland (although Provini still finished third) and the inability to obtain a visa for East Germany did nothing to help matters. With a third in Belgium, second in Ulster, followed by wins at Monza and Buenos Aires, the 1963 250cc world title battle lasted to the final round at Suzuka in Japan with only two points separating title leader Redman from challenger Provini. All looked set for a blockbusting finish to the season, but, at least for Provini and Morini, things did not work out like that. After travelling half-way round the world to compete in the first ever Japanese GP, Provini was charged 270 US dollars

(nearly £100 at the time) for just one hour on the Suzuka circuit when he turned out on his Morini to learn the course prior to official practising. Even before this he had experienced problems. On board the aircraft he had developed ear trouble, causing terrible pain and total deafness which necessitated an operation in Japan. Then it took a week of arguing and pleading, supported by cables of protest from Italy and constant phone calls from the Japanese federation, to get his bike out of the customs. In the race his was the only non-Japanese machine and lined up against him were new, lower versions of the Honda fours ridden by Redman, Robb, Taveri and the Japanese rider Kasupa, plus the Yamaha twins of Ito, Hasegawa and Phil Read and a number of square-four Suzukis (two of which crashed in the race). Eventually Redman won, with Provini back in fourth place with his, and Morini's championship hopes dashed.

Almost a month to the day following the Japanese GP, Provini announced that he had quit Morini to ride Benelli's 4-cylinder model. This 'shock' announcement was not in fact really unexpected, because not only had Provini decided to leave Morini before the Japanese GP but had already turned down offers from the Yamaha and Kreidler

Larger version of the Morini V-twin appeared in 1977. In Britain it was sold as the Maestro by importers Harglo Ltd. Although not particularly quick, it was still a gutsy performer.

factories! The reason for the split was that Provini was no longer on the friendliest of terms with the man who had done much of the work to create the racing single-cylinder Morini into the force it had become, former rider Dante Lambertini. Together with engineer Biaveti (formally with Mondial, who specialized in cylinder head work), Lambertini had patiently developed the Bologna double-knocker machine into one of the most complete racing machines ever conceived. As a small family-owned factory, Morini lacked the resources to launch a full frontal attack on the might of the Japanese as 1964 would have demanded, with not only Honda, but also the new Suzuki square four and Yamaha RD56 twins making a bid for honours.

So Lambertini's Morini single reverted back to the Italian Championships, rather than the world stage for 1964. Their rider was a 22-year-old by the name of Giacomo Agostini and as he proved at Monza in September 1963, by lapping joint fastest in practice with Redman and Shepherd (MZ), he had real promise. In the race Agostini led for a period before finally having to submit to team leader Provini and Redman, and later still being forced to quit. Agostini had in fact done much of his early racing on Morinis, notably the ohv Settebello model. Finally, after a string of victories, he booked an interview with Alfonso Morini, in which Agostini asked if he could have a factory ride. When the answer was 'yes' the youngster was so taken aback that he promptly knocked a typewriter off a desk in the Commendatore's office! Agostini soon repaid this faith (and the cost of several typewriters) by showing real class in his first full season as a Morini works rider.

The 1964 West German GP was his first race outside Italy. At the Solitude circuit he not only finished fourth behind the Yamahas of Phil Read and Mike Duff and Redman's Honda, but also *beat* Provini on the Benelli Four! His only other classic ride that year was at Monza,

when he claimed another fourth spot behind the same three riders. By July of that year Agostini had already ended Provini's three-year reign as Italian 250cc champion, breaking many of his lap records on the way. All this had made a deep impression on Count Domenico Agusta, with the result that for 1965 Agostini was an MV rider and the rest is history. But remember the small Bologna factory played a vital role in Ago's rise to the top.

Following Agostini's departure to MV, the Morini single was 'retired' for a couple of seasons, but in 1967 it was raced again by the young up-and-coming Angelo Bergamonti (later to follow Agostini into the MV camp). Some ten years after its début, it proved itself still in the top flight by winning the 1967 250cc Senior Championship of Italy, beating the Benelli four and Montesa twin. When first produced the Morini had turned out 30 bhp at 10,000 rpm. In those ten years, without any major changes, the power output had been increased by 6 bhp, with a gain of 500 rpm without any mechanical danger, simply by minute attention to detail and continuous testing. During this time, in the endless search for power, development engineer Lambertini and his assistant Biaveti had tried both desmodromic valve operation and four-valve cylinder heads, but both had been discarded, as the modified engines produced *less* power than the existing double overhead cam two-valve version. Although capable of around 140 mph, the final version of the Morini racer was not quite deserving of the title 'World's Fastest Single', because, as lap times prove, the 1957 works 350 Guzzi flat-single was marginally the quicker. Even so it was most definitely the fastest ever quarter-litre four-stroke single and, like the Guzzi, a superbly complete motorcycle. It was this fine balance which gained its results, not just sheer speed, but reliability, exceptional roadholding and handling and not least a highly competitive power-to-weight ratio.

With the undoubted glamour of the illustrious racing exploits the production roadster side may seem somewhat dull and unexciting, but it should be remembered that without success in this field there is no money to go racing ... so the production models were vitally important to Morini. The 1961 Milan Show had seen the introduction of the attractive 175 Tressette Sprint. *The Motor Cycle* described it as 'the sort of model for which any red-blooded youngster in this country would cheerfully part with his eye teeth.' Unfortunately there was no British importer to test this statement.

Two years later and the theme for the 38th Milan Show in November 1963 was, as the American *Motorcycle World* summed things up: 'Fifties, Fifties, Fifties.' Morini's offering was the Corsarino, a four-stroke with three speeds and racy lines. The factory also displayed the latest version

This turbo prototype appeared at the Milan Show in November 1981, but never entered production.

of their ohv Settebello production racer intended for participation in FIM Sports category racing and a new dohc 175 based on the works 250 *Gran Premio*, with six-speed box which it said 'might' be available for private riders for the 1964 season.

Morini's main attraction at the 1965 show was the Settebello 250GTI, a touring model with four-speed 'box, deeply valanced mudguards, crash bars and high-and-wide 'bars' included in its comprehensive specification.

Founder Alfonso Morini died in 1969 and thereafter the factory was run by his daughter Gabriella. For 1970 the model range consisted of the ZZ50 roadster, Super Scrambler 50, Country 125, Sport Lusso 125, Super Sport in 125 and 150 versions, GT 150 and the Regolarita 125 and 160. The last-named were pukka competition bikes used in events such as the ISDT by not only the official Italian Trophy squad but also the Italian Army trials team. Based on the standard road-going ohv engine, the Regolarita came in two capacities: 123.08cc (56×50mm) and 163.9cc (60×58mm) and both proved Gold Medal winners in the ISDT during the late 1960s and early 1970s.

Morini had always produced quality motorcycles, but none of its designs were as innovative as the famous V-twin

line with which the company was to guarantee its commercial future throughout the 1970s and into the 1980s. The first of these, the 3½, was born in prototype form during 1971, and was the work of joint designers Dianni Marchesini (who was also the company's general manager) and Franco Lambertini Junior. Production commenced early in 1973 and with it a new era in the Bologna marque's history was born.

The basis of the new design was a brand new 72-degree V-twin with Heron combustion cylinder heads. The duo chose to use the Heron layout, not only because of its technical merit but also for its lower production costs. Although the system had been used in several engines in the car world, this was to be the first application in a production motorcycle. Essentially the Heron principle uses cylinder heads with a flat face and parallel, not inclined, valves, and the combustion recess is formed in the piston crown. This system was also used later by Moto Guzzi in their smaller V-twin engines. Heron heads had been used in the Repco Brabham racing car which had won the 1966 Formula One World Championship and also by Jaguar, Rover, Alfa Romeo, Audi and the Ford Motor Company. Like Ducati, Morini's choice of a V-twin was

350 KANGURO

MOTO MORINI

Best-selling Morini of the 1980s was the 350 Kanguro trail bike.

not only for reasons of character and smoothness, but also because the company could not afford the higher development costs of a multi-cylinder design. The parallel-twin route would also have meant problems of inherent vibration and there were already numerous middleweight parallel twins on the market.

The new Morini appeared in two guises: touring (Strada) and café racer (Sport). Both motorcycles were virtually the same except for cosmetics and minor changes to specifications such as compression ratio and front brake diameter. They not only offered a good blend of handling, braking and performance (by early 1970s standards), they were also to stand the test of time, with the basic engine still powering Morini models to this day. Several differences within the Morini power unit, besides the cylinder head and pistons, stood it apart from the mainstream bike design. These included the toothed belt drive to the camshaft, a forged one-piece crankshaft, transistorized ignition and a generally high level of castings. The 72-degree V-twin offered not only an acceptable level of vibration, but, unlike Ducati, who chose 90 degrees, it was an engine length which did not over-extend the wheelbase. It was angled so that the camshaft could be located high in the crankcase in the crutch of the vee. Even so, it was necessary to space the cylinders apart at the base to allow room for the camshaft. This method of off-set cylinders is known as *désaxé* and in the 3½ the effect was to give a positive bias on one cylinder and a negative on the other. Actual capacity was 344cc (68×57mm).

Even though they were able to take advantage of the lower production costs of the Heron layout, Morini still chose to forgo even higher savings by machining the concave piston crowns. This was to ensure an exact compression ratio. Ford, for example, in a cost-cutting exercise, has chosen to fit 'as cast' pistons, resulting in piston damage when used with inferior fuel. Another disadvantage of the Heron layout was that parallel valves had to be used and the head diameter was considerably smaller than with a conventional two-valve crossflow-pattern head with angled valves. The theory was that performance would be less, but there would be improved torque and fuel consumption. Somehow Morini engineers seemed to achieve all three. This was probably because Marchesini and Lambertini spent a lot of their time on the porting and combustion aspects of the design. Except for their compression ratios, 10 and 11:1 respectively, the engines of the Strada and Sport (both of which were on the market by the time the marque was first imported into Britain in 1974) were identical. These featured three-ring pistons, single-coil valve springs, split con-rods with big-end shells, short dural push-rods, helical primary drive gears and a six-speed gearbox, with dry multi-plate clutch.

Supplied by Ducati Electronica (not the same company as the bike builders), the capacitor discharge ignition was generated by the 6-volt alternator, not the battery. The alternator rotor was driven by the near-side end of the camshaft, whilst the stator mounting was slotted for timing adjustment. The range of the electronic auto-advance was from ten degrees after tdc (static) to 34 degrees at 6000 rpm, then backing off to 30 degrees at maximum engine revolutions. There were two transducers (which took the place of HT coils on a conventional points ignition system); one was slightly more powerful as it also provided current for the electronic tacho. Of the six coils inside the alternator, five were for lighting, the sixth for ignition. The Sport featured a tuned engine with 11:1 pistons and developed 39 bhp at 8500 rpm (the factory quoted a top speed of 108 mph for the Sport against 99 mph for the Strada) both with the rider in the prone position. Other changes on the Sport were the introduction of clip-ons, single racing saddle, hydraulic steering damper and a more sporting line to the tank and side panels. Its finish was fully in keeping with its sporting image, the bright Italian racing red of the tank and panels contrasting with the black frame and stainless steel mudguards and chain guard. The early Strada was available either in an ice metallic blue or metallic red, with a contrasting white line on the tank top sides. This tank was in fact best described as chisel-sided and differed from the later Strada models. In addition both the Strada and Sport had an abundance of polished alloy or chrome plate.

The Morini V-twin very nearly came to Britain a year earlier, when Ken Cobbing, a leading parts wholesaler, and myself almost became joint importers in the spring of 1973. But the idea was not proceeded with and it was left to the current importers, Harglo Ltd, to become the official Morini distributors for the British Isles. The first pair of bikes arrived during March 1974, a Strada and a Sport. These were loaned to leading journalist Bob Currie, who visited each of the Easter weekend's Anglo-American Match Races on one of them. An early development in the British Morini dealer network was the appointment, by Harglo, of Devimead Ltd as the official Morini Service Centre. Devimead's owner, Les Mason, was instrumental in producing a racing version of the 3½ Sport, but for the 500 class, with a capacity of 460cc. Even though this machine looked very pretty and was entered both in the 1975 and 1976 TT races it was not a success. The main problem centred around the con-rod and big-end assemblies, which had a nasty habit of failing. Even a special pressed-up crank with one-piece con-rods and Alpha roller big-ends failed to cure this weakness. Riders of this interesting addition to the race programmes were David Mason (Les's brother) and Nigel Rollason.

As a road-going engine the design was, however, much more successful, although it was unlike any of its predecessors and, at the same time, a simple design. Even the Morini designers were surprised that their handiwork was to embody the best features of Italian engineering and at the same time be such an economical engine to produce.

When it was launched, the Morini introduced several innovations to the bike world, certainly for production machines, with many ideas more akin to automotive than two-wheel practice, not just the Heron cylinder heads, but plain bearing big-ends (unusual for an Italian design at this time), toothed belt and electronic ignition. Like many other Italian manufacturers of the period Morini's main problems centred around items which were not their own products, but those of component suppliers. Until very recently the factory retained suppliers who were exclusively of Italian origin. The main list included Marzocchi suspension, Lafranconi exhausts, CEV electrical equipment, Ducati Electronica ignition equipment, Grimeca disc and drum brakes, Verlicchi controls and Fiamm batteries and horns.

The 1975 Milan Show heralded a new 250 single and 500 twin, both directly evolved from the 3½ V-twin. The latter was referred to in the issue of *The Motor Cycle* dated 29 November as 'one of the prettiest bikes at Milan'. I would agree, as this enlarged V-twin was a magnificent-looking machine. It differed from later bikes in having Guzzi Le Mans-type kinked spoke cast wheels, Brembo brake equipment and different styling. In my opinion this bike was one of the most attractive Morinis of all. The 500's specification included a capacity of 478.6cc, bore and stroke of 69×64mm, compression ratio of 11.2:1 and a power output of 46 bhp at 7500 rpm. The gearbox was a five-speeder and other details included cast wheels, triple disc brakes and an ultra-light weight for a half-litre bike at 336 lb dry. The new 250 single was half the 500, with a capacity of 239.3cc and power output was quoted as 18.5 bhp at 7000 rpm with a maximum speed of some 80 mph.

The Morini factory at Via Bergami 7, Bologna. The facilities were taken over by Cagiva during 1987.

As the 1980s dawned Morini began to add still more variations to the range. A 250 V-twin with a capacity of 239.496cc, bore and stroke of 59×43.8mm, was introduced. Although a unique machine, its high price and rather limited performance meant that it did not achieve the level of sales enjoyed by its forerunners, even though its rarity did ensure a number of satisfied owners. One model which did enjoy good sales, albeit on the home market, was a 125 single. This was again to make use of existing Morini technology, using essentially a combination of the earlier 250 single and the new 250 V-twin. Unlike the 250 single and 500 V-twin, it shared the 250 V-twin's 59mm cylinder bore, but its stroke was increased to 45mm, giving a capacity of 122.96cc. Power output was 13.75 bhp with maximum rpm of 9000. Maximum speed was a claimed 73 mph.

1981 saw most of the Morini V-twin models (except the 3½ standard) finished with striking red paintwork (including frame), black engine casings and exhausts and gold cast wheels. In 1982 a six speed version of the 500 was introduced and by then the range consisted of 500 (in Sport or Touring guise), 3½ Sport, 3½ Standard, 250 V-twin and 125 single. The 250 single had been dropped from the line-up, but a couple of enduro-style trail bikes had joined it. First had been the 500 Camel (known as the Sahara in the UK) with conventional twin shock rear and sixspeeds. Introduced at the 1981 Milan Show was the 350 Kanguro, with monoshock rear suspension. Both shared Marzocchi leading axle off-road front forks, 21in. front and 18in. rear motocross-section tyres, laced to Spanish Akront alloy wheel rims and 6-volt electrics. By now the 350/500 road-going models had 12-volt electrics, and when I tested the 500 Sahara I found this was perhaps its biggest disadvantage when compared to the 500 Maestro roadster.

Many Morini enthusiasts waited patiently for a production version of the much-heralded Turbo shown in prototype form at Milan in 1981, but at the time of writing it seems unlikely that this particular Morini V-twin will ever go into production. What did happen was a gradual changeover to what one might term Japanese orientated-styling, first seen with the introduction of the 350 K2 in late 1984. Having tested one I could honestly allay fears expressed by several die hard Morini enthusiasts about this line of development. As a motorcycle I found it superb and in many ways a genuine improvement over the earlier models, especially in the areas of the gearchange operation and detail points, but I can understand those who argue that Morini might well benefit by retaining its 'traditional' styling rather than substitute it with fashionable lines such as square headlights, belly pans or even fairings. The 1985 '500' (in trail guise only) had an improved cylinder head

layout. The valves were larger and further apart, the carburettors were larger and the cylinder bores increased by 2mm to give a capacity of 507cc. In standard trim it was good for 107 mph, which for a trail bike was an excellent performance. It may surprise the many Morini buffs that a 'mere' dirt bike-styled model should have been selected for this treatment first, but in its native land the best Morini seller was the 350 Kanguro trail bike. So it made sense when the Bologna company introduced an enduro-styled version of their 125 single, called the KJ. This looked very much like a miniature Kanguro and its 12.5 bhp output was good for almost 70 mph.

At the 1985 Milan Show the Morini stand displayed the 125KJ, 350K2, 350 Kanguro, 501 Camel and two brand-new US custom models, the 350 and 501 Excalibur. Garishly styled, these two bikes, except for their V-twin engines, could not have been any further removed from the original 3½ Strada and Sport models of 15 years before. By now many traditionalists were shaking their heads in disbelief. But more 'flying in the face of tradition' was soon to follow, not the least the takeover of the company in February 1987 by the Castiglioni brothers, owners of the Cagiva empire. This had come about due to a reluctance upon Gabriella Morini's part to mortgage the family's future upon the development costs of producing a much needed new water-cooled engine. Even though it was still profitable, Morini would have ultimately been forced to close if a new, quieter unit was not forthcoming, so Gabriella sold out.

Following the Cagiva takeover the Bologna factory was closed for a period of some six weeks, before reopening with the former Ducati chief executive Mario Scandellari in the chair. With Cagiva money, not only was Franco Lambertini given the authorization to proceed at full speed with his new 8-valve, 67-degree, narrow-angle, V-twin, but a retooling requirement programme was instigated. Instead of 3500 bikes leaving the factory during the final full year (1986) of Morini family tenure, the figure for 1988 was up to 8000. This had been helped by three new models which appeared at the Milan Show in November 1987, the racer-styled Dart, Caguaro trail bike and the New York custom. The Dart was essentially one of the old 344cc 72-degree V-twin engines slotted into the chassis of a 125cc Cagiva Freccia. Styled by the ex-Bimota boss, Massimo Tamburini, it instantly 'modernized' what was by now a rapidly ageing design. In their 12 October, 1988, test *Motor Cycle News* called the Dart, 'Short on rort, but big on refinement'. With 34.5 bhp, *MCN* put the Dart through the electronic eye at a one-way best of 102.55 mph, with tester Chris Dabbs's chin buried into the sculptured tank. The high-tech square-tube frame was painted steel, not alloy, and the

The first fruits of Cagiva ownership was the 350 Dart, which made its first appearance in public at the 1987 Milan show.

Marzocchi rising rate monoshock rear suspension was fitted with a softer spring than the original uncomfortable prototype. No one could dispute that its styling was startlingly effective. In Britain, with a price tag of £3995, the Dart was a poor substitute in the performance stakes to the similarly styled Honda CBR600, which was over 35 mph faster and cost £200 less!

Many still hankered after the more traditional Morini (read Italian!) style of the mid-1970s, and one company which responded to this demand was AMEX in West Germany, who in 1988 began to offer hand-built classically styled Morinis under the Rebello name in 396, 478 and 507cc versions. Built from the ground up these bikes featured special cams, cylinders and other internal components, as well as their own 1970s style. The AMEX Rebello V-twins were available with, or without, colour-matched fairings. As Morini's chief designer Franco Lambertini revealed, however, the company's real future did not rely on the now outdated 72-degree twin, but his new 67-degree vee, which is scheduled to go on sale in 1992. This new engine has several interesting features besides its water-cooling and eight valves.

It is very light and the prototype unit weighs in at only 110 lb. To counter vibration, off-set crank pins, as used on current Honda V-twins, are employed. This initial prototype, which has already been extensively tested, has a capacity of 720cc (84×65mm) and it is intended to increase this to around 750cc with probable dimensions of 86×64mm, before entering production. Its modular design means, like the existing Morini V-twins, that it can be increased or decreased (most likely) to provide a more comprehensive model range. As a guide to expected performance the prototype 720cc unit has already produced 84 bhp at 9200 rpm, with all legal exhaust and air filtration silencing fitted.

Each cylinder head of the new concept power unit had a single overhead camshaft. The drive to this could be either by belt or chain, as both have been tested. The four valves in each combustion chamber have an incredibly flat included valve angle of 23 degrees, more akin to existing Formula One car engines than the majority of current motorcycle designs. Facing each other, the inlet ports permit the use of a single twin-choke carburettor, or fuel injection to be fitted between the two cylinders. Ing. Lambertini sees the new 67-degree Morini V-twin holding the middle ground of the sports/tourer, rather than competing directly with the Castiglioni brothers' other V-twin company, Ducati, who he says will be aiming directly at the purely sports-minded rider.

For certain the Morini factory's future seems assured, something which did not seem likely a few short years ago when the cost of meeting forthcoming legislation seemed only an impossible dream. Now the small but enthusiastic Bologna marque can look forward to not only a new design but a new future.

CHAPTER 14

Motobi

One of the six Benelli brothers, Giuseppe, left the company in 1949 to begin work on an independent design. Known as the 'B', the original machine made its début at the Milan Spring Fair in April 1950. The newcomer was somewhat reminiscent of the German Imme of the same period. It was powered by a 98cc (48×54mm) horizontal single-cylinder two-stroke engine with a three-speed foot-operated gearbox in unit with the engine. There was swinging arm rear suspension controlled by leaf springs, with undamped telescopic forks at the front, to give it an up-to-the-minute appearance. The success of his new venture led Giuseppe Benelli to create a whole range of models powered by similar two-stroke horizontal power units, initially with 114 and 123cc single cylinders. Most exciting of all was a superbly crafted 200 *twin*, which was first displayed at the 29th Milan Show in January 1952. Once again this showed the preference by Giuseppe Benelli for the horizontal layout. The 196cc (48×54mm) engine was hung below the box-section 'backbone' frame. Cylinder heads and cylinder barrels were separate light-alloy castings finned longitudinally and contoured so that as *The Motor Cycle* show report put it: 'From a side view, the engine is Rugby football in shape.' As with the single-cylinder 'B' models, induction was now controlled by a rotary valve formed by a port in the engine's crankshaft. On this latest model there was extensive use of light alloys, for wheel rims, hubs, brake plates, engine covers, rear chainguard and many other components. As a result, the 'B' twin weighed only 100kg (220 lb), even though it was a relatively large machine for its class and was comprehensively equipped. The 1952 price was some 300,000 lire (around £175 in British currency at the 1952 exchange rate).

With its neat 196cc (later increased to 248cc) engine, the Spring Lasting, as it became known, soon proved a popular addition to the fast-growing line-up. This was no doubt because with its modern engine and equally modern suspension, twin shocks at the rear and hydraulically damped teles at the front, the Spring Lasting twin was at the very forefront of Italian motorcycle engineering.

An improved rotary valve layout was introduced in late 1952, but to start with was only incorporated in the 123cc single. The search for ways and means of improving the

performance of two-strokes had often been ruled out because the degree of complication entailed had often completely negatived any advantages gained. But Giuseppe Benelli's innovation was noteworthy in that it was shown to be both effective *and* still retain the characteristic two-stroke simplicity by the addition of no extra moving parts. The petroil mixture was induced into the crankcase through a rotary valve incorporated in the crankshaft. At low revs, it passed directly into the crankcase through a central diaphragm in the flywheel, induced, as was normal practice, by taking advantage of the partial vacuum formed in the crankcase as the piston rises. However, the flywheel on the induction valve side contained a number of channels, radiating tangentially from its centre in a manner of the spokes of a wheel. These channels connected to the hollow crankshaft. As the engine speed increased, centrifugal force acted upon the induction system and drew in a greater charge of mixture than could be inspired by conventional methods. At the upper end of the speed scale, all the mixture was distributed through the flywheel channels instead of through the diaphragm, by virtue of the force acting upon it. It was to be seen that the higher the engine speed the greater was the force, and, therefore, the breathing at higher revs was greatly improved when compared with conventional two-strokes, which utilize only atmospheric pressure as the induction medium. An ancillary effect, which was decidely interesting, was that centrifugal force broke down the petroil mixture, the oil separating itself from the petrol in the flywheel channels. The result was, of course, improved lubrication, and, as a result of the purer mixture reaching the cylinder, better combustion with consequent lowering of fuel consumption and an increase in power. Another improvement to the 'B' range was the adoption of twin-shock hydraulically damped rear suspension on the single, so all the 1953 range shared the same basic suspension layout.

The next real news did not come until the end of 1954. First came a name change. Hitherto the products of Giuseppe Benelli had borne the simple monogram 'B', but from then on were to be known as Motobi. The second and significant news was the replacement of the 200 model with the larger capacity 246cc. The top of the range was the superb 250 Gran Sport, which featured a deep, curvaceous

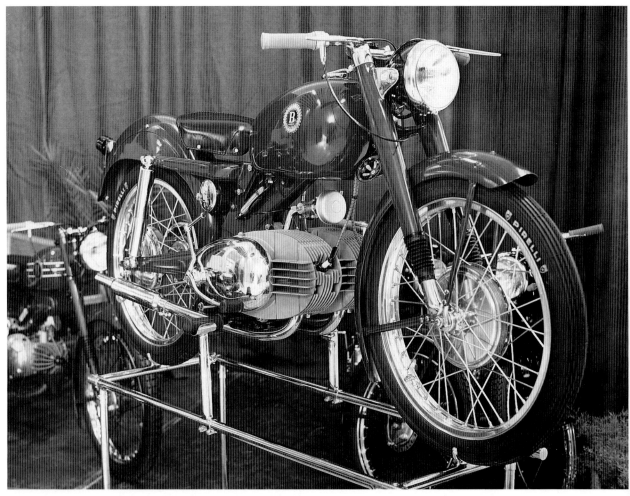

This superbly crafted 200 horizontal twin-cylinder two-stroke appeared at the Milan Show in January 1952. It was the work of Giuseppe Benelli, who had left his brothers to form a separate company, Motobi, in 1949.

tank, full-width highly polished brake hubs and a cleverly concealed front brake cam lever. It was a tuned version of this bike, the Gran Sport Speciale, which won its class in the Milano–Taranto in June 1955, ridden by Silvano Rinaldi at an average speed of 67.34 mph.

Giuseppe Benelli then made a move to enter the four-stroke field and for 1956 he designed a pair of new ohv singles, a 125 and a 175, which externally appeared almost precisely similar to the existing 'strokers. In fact, the only obvious differences that distinguished the four-strokes were the small oil sump below the crankcase and the position of the spark plug. The valve gear was enclosed by a cover finned to match the curvature of the finning of the cylinder head, barrel and crankcase. The smaller engine had a capacity of 123.67cc with square 54×54mm dimensions, whilst the larger push-rod model was 172cc (67×57mm). Called the Catria, the 175 was an instant sales

success and was available in a number of guises for both touring and clubman's racing. The spur-driven camshaft was located under the base of the cylinder barrel and the push-rods operated on each side of the cylinder itself. The camshaft also drove the gear-type oil pump, which worked in conjunction with a wet sump lubrication system. The engine was particularly quiet and vibration was well damped. In fact its biggest failing was the kick starter and rocker-type gear-lever, both of which were on the same spindle, so causing bottom gear engagement should the foot slip off the kickstarter!

By the end of the 1950s, Giuseppe Benelli had died, passing on the reins of power to his two sons, Marco and Luigi. 1959 saw a 175 Motobi win the Italian Junior racing championship for the first time in the hands of Ambrosi, a feat which was to be repeated another *nine* times until the last victory in 1972. By boring out the cylinder to 67mm, a

Later four-stroke models appeared, typified by the 200cc Catria, circa 1963.

203cc racer was constructed which did well abroad, in the United States, France and Belgium in particular. The early racing 175s developed 17 bhp at 9000 rpm, but this was later increased to 25 bhp at 10,500 rpm. On these machines all the very best equipment was used, such as Ceriani forks, Oldani brakes and Dell 'Orto SS1 remote-float carburettors.

Motor Cycling tested the Catria roadster in their 24 August, 1961, issue and found it capable of 67 mph and the standing quarter-mile speed of 52 mph was reached in 22 seconds. The brakes, handling and gearbox were praised in particular. The only real criticism was a tendency for the kickstart pawl to occasionally slip on the example tested. This bike had been loaned by the British importers, AJW Motorcycles of Pilford Heath, Wimborne, Dorset. It was also possible for the customer to stipulate particular requirements, including tyres, overall and internal gear ratios, a hotter camshaft and a differently angled carburettor. In the standard form tested, the price, including £49 10s. 0d. purchase tax, was £274 10s. 0d. At

The Swiss engineer Werner Maltry built a number of Motobi-inspired racers during the early 1960s, including this 490cc six-speed twin.

Race kitted 1970 Motobi 250 Super Sport as used in classic racing events by Terry Ives.

74cc two-stroke scooter. By 1963, with new importers, the latest version of Catria, now with a capacity of 198cc, cost £212.

The success of the racing ohv Motobi had prompted Swiss enthusiast Werner Maltry into building an interesting 490cc (57×74mm) racer based around the new 245cc Sports model which the Pesaro factory had introduced the previous year. Maltry's circuit racer attracted so much attention that soon he was offering both the 490cc and 350cc versions to order. Both these racers also sported the luxury of a Maltry-supplied six-speed transmission. Dry weight for either bike was 105kg (248 lb). Other details included 35mm Ceriani racing forks, Ceriani rear units, 240mm Oldani 2LS front stopper, a neatly crafted open frame and purpose-built tank and seat. Notable technical features included a dry clutch mounted on the offside, a pair of Dell 'Orto SS1 carburettors, with centrally mounted remote float chamber and specially constructed crankshaft and crankcases. The top end consisted of Motobi racing components as used on the Formula Junior racers.

The same year Motobi returned to the Benelli fold, but

this figure, the same as for many British 500s, very, very few Catrias were sold by AJW, who also offered one or two of the other Motobi models, including the recently released

After the death of Giuseppe Benelli, his sons took Motobi back into the Benelli fold; surprisingly the marque still retained a presence in the market, occasionally with autonomous models, such as this 1976 250 Café Racer.

still retained its individuality, as it did for many years to come. By 1966 the 175 had been dropped (except for road racing) and only the 123, 198 and 245cc horizontal ohv singles remained, the last-named now with five gears and in either street or scrambler (read *street* scrambler) form. The late 1960s saw Benelli themselves market the Motobi-conceived flat singles. For example, in North America, the Benelli importers Cosmopolitan Motors were offering five versions in 1968: the 125cc with four or five gears, the 200cc with four gears and the 250cc with four or five gears. *Cycle World* tested one of the 250s in their September 1968 issue (see Chapter 2) and were generally highly impressed. The venerable flat-single line remained until the de Tomaso era began following his takeover in 1972, but the Motobi name continued, now largely a matter of badge engineering with models such as the single- and twin-cylinder two-strokes and 650 Tornado four-stroke parallel twins. These were really Benellis, but available with the Motobi logo adorning their petrol tanks to capture a few more sales.

For 1976 Motobi enthusiasts had something of which to be proud, the exclusive 250 Café Racer. This was a specially prepared version of Benelli's 2C (and Guzzi 250TS) 250 twin. What made the Motobi version different was the outrageous style of the new tank, seat and special fairing. Finish was an equally striking red and white, with dual Brembo 260mm hydraulically operated disc brakes at the front and silver-painted cast alloy wheels. Underneath this brash exterior there lurked the same alloy barrelled piston-port two-stroke twin available for less money from the other two members in the de Tomaso motorcycle empire. In any event it was possible to buy a Motobi-badged standard bike if needed, and also ten other models from the Benelli two-stroke stable. The Café Racer was the last autonomous Motobi model offered, and after this all were simply Benellis with a different transfer and nothing else.

Although the Motobi had been created by a member of the Benelli family, it had achieved a marque loyalty through its high-quality design and manufacture, and owning a Motobi was *different* to simply owning a 'normal' Benelli.

A proud owner once summed things up in the following way: 'A Motobi has real class, whereas a Benelli is still only a Benelli.'

CHAPTER 15

Moto Guzzi

Moto Guzzi is probably the most famous name in Italian motor-cycling history, both on road and track. And the legendary Mandello del Lario company can justifiably be proud of their achievements. When the company retired from Grand Prix racing at the end of 1957 Guzzi had amassed an amazing total of 3327 international race victories, set 134 world speed records, taken 47 Italian championships, won 55 national titles, taken 11 Isle of Man TTs and perhaps, most important of all, had gained 14 World Championships (eight individual, six manufacturers'). On the street Guzzi was no less successful, with a whole host of interesting, often innovative designs which sold well both in Italy and around the world.

Moto Guzzi was started by the friendship of three men in the Italian Air Service during the final months of the Great War in 1918. This trio comprised two pilots, Georgio Parodi and Giovanni Ravelli, and their young mechanic/driver Carlo Guzzi. The latter was driven by a burning passion to design and construct his own particular breed of motorcycle. Ravelli, who was already an enthusiastic and pre-war race winner, soon found much to impress himself that the type of machine Guzzi was proposing made a lot of sense. Parodi, who was much less familiar with the ingredients which went into making up a powered two-wheeler, often sat watching the others in animated discussion, but was unable to grasp fully the technicalities. However, Georgio Parodi did have two vital qualities, a brain which had the potential for quick learning *and* a father who owned a corporate shipping line. A few days before the end of hostilities, Giovanni Ravelli was killed in a flying accident and so it was left to Guzzi and Parodi to turn the dream into reality.

The pair's first concern was finance, as without it the project would be stillborn. Here Parodi's father, Emanuele, came to the rescue, providing the necessary funds in January 1919 to enable the fledgling enterprise to begin its activities. This was in the form of a loan, which was ultimately repaid in full. With the money came an agreement that Parodi Senior would provide the new enterprise with his considerable entrepreneurial skills during its crucial first few months of trading. In fact, he provided much valuable advice on all matters of business for a considerable number of years. With the finance in

place, Guzzi then proceeded at full speed to transform his design, which had been approved by Parodi Senior, into reality. The creation that appeared a few months later was given the name GP (Guzzi-Parodi), but by the time the magazine *Motociclismo* published its first details of the new marque on 15 December, 1920, the name had been altered to Moto Guzzi. Out of respect for their late friend Ravelli, the now famous eagle emblem had been chosen, with its origins in the Air Corps, which all three men had served in. *Societa Anonima Moto Guzzi* was officially founded on 21 March, 1921. The first models offered for sale shared the prototype G&P's engine dimensions of 88×82mm, but unlike that machine featured two-valve push-rod ioe, rather than four-valve ohc.

A total of 17 bikes was produced in the first year, 1921, with a total of ten employees. The 498.4cc horizontal single, with its massive outside 'bacon-slicer' flywheel, semi-unit construction gearbox and magneto ignition mounted centrally above the engine/gearbox was to remain in production, albeit continually updated, until as late as 1976 and even then still retained the original 88×82mm bore and stroke measurements! Together with BMW's flat-twin it must rate as the longest-running engine configuration in continuous use by a motorcycle manufacturer, but the German design had numerous changes in engine dimensions along the way.

Right from the start, Moto Guzzi had realized that there was no better form of publicity than racing and as early as 1921 the company entered Aldo Finzi and Gino Cavedini in the Milano−Napoli long-distance road race on a pair of the new 500cc models. These first ever 'works' Guzzi riders both completed the course (quite an achievement in itself), Finzi in 20th place and Cavedini just behind in 22nd. Strangely it had been Giorgio Parodi, rather than Carlo Guzzi, who had urged the importance of competition participation. Although Guzzi eventually accepted the wisdom of this move he was always inclined to take a very back-seat view of the proceedings and be reluctant to take on board new responsibilities. This was in stark contrast to his innovative and aggressive approach to engineering challenges. While Parodi did not have any mechanical knowledge, he did possess the drive, determination and vision which was so vital to the company during its formative years. Others who played an important part in the fledgling company's early success were Parodi's cousin, Angelo, and Guzzi's brother, Giuseppe. A month after the Milano—Napoli came the Targa Floria, staged in Sicily. This heralded Guzzi's first ever victory and the rider was Aldo Finzi's brother Gino, who received an enthusiastic reception when he returned north.

The following year, 1922, Guzzi garnered still more success. Up to this time the machines were essentially carefully prepared and tuned standard models, but in 1923 the new Corsa 2V (racing two-valve) appeared. The biggest difference lay in the cylinder head, where the former inlet over exhaust layout had given way to a pair of parallel valves operated by exposed rods and rockers. Another change was to the rear section of the frame. The Corsa 2V was also the first Guzzi to be finished in red (the production Normale was green). The new machine made a stunning début by completely dominating the local Circuito del Lario, the Italian equivalent of the Isle of Man TT, staged over 50km of public roads near the factory base. Guido Mentasi swept all before him to score a great victory.

International fame came the next year, when the same rider triumphed in the European Championship race at Monza, and then Guzzi scored again a mere two weeks later, when Mario Ghersi won the German Grand Prix.

By now Moto Guzzi were rapidly becoming a major force, with not only race-track success, but an overflowing order book. The victories at Monza and in Germany had come from a yet further improved racer, the C4V. This was a readoption of the very first G&P prototype principle, with its single overhead cam and four-valve head. On the production front the Normale had been superseded by the Tipo Sport, featuring a tuned version of the original ioe engine. This developed 13 bhp at 3800 rpm and was good for 62 mph.

The year 1926 marked a milestone in the company's history. Not only did they produce something other than their by now familiar half-litre engine size, but they chose to throw the gauntlet down to the world leaders, the British, on their home ground! The machine was the appropriately named TT250 and the event the ultra-demanding Isle of Man TT. Assisted by his elder brother, Giuseppe, Carlo Guzzi had created a quarter-litre machine. Unlike its larger brother this featured square engine dimensions of 68×68mm, giving a capacity of 246.8cc. Even though the new bike was largely untried, Guzzi still felt it stood a chance of success and so the team, with rider Pietro Ghersi, set out on their long journey to Mona's Isle, and although he had never seen the circuit before, and was therefore under a considerable disadvantage compared to

The four-valve, sohc 500 Guzzi which won the European Championship in 1924, ridden by Guido Mentasi at Monza, on the outskirts of Milan.

the local riders, Ghersi proved just how competitive the new model was by finishing only a second behind race winner C. W. Johnson's Cotton. This outstanding result turned sour, however, when Ghersi was disqualified, of all things, for using a spark plug of a different make than that declared on his entry form! To have been knocked out by such a seemingly trivial item must have been extremely frustrating. It was not until another nine years had passed that Guzzi exacted revenge over the British on their own home ground. As with the bigger Guzzi racer, the TT250 was offered for sale to leading private riders.

In January 1928 the Mandello del Lario marque brought out its first motorcycle with a sprung frame. The Guzzi system, developed jointly by Carlo Guzzi and his brother Giuseppe, used a swinging arm supporting the rear wheel, with horizontal springs located underneath the engine which worked under compression through a pair of long rods and a front plate. The system was completed by two adjustable friction devices beside the rear wheel and offered a considerable improvement over the many earlier efforts from other manufacturers which had largely proved unsuitable. Although by no means perfect compared with machines of today, the Guzzi system worked, and to prove this Giuseppe Guzzi made a historic journey north through Europe and Scandinavia to the North Cape. This was instrumental in satisfying the doubters as to the soundness of the design and there after the GT springer was nicknamed 'Norge' in recognition of Giuseppe's lonely ride.

The same year also saw the launch of another innovative design from the Guzzi team, and one which was to prove an outstanding commercial success. This was the *Motocarri* (motorcycle truck). As the name implies this was essentially a cross between a motorcycle (the front half) and a lightweight truck. The first version, the Tipo 107, was offered for sale in early 1928, powered by the familiar 498.4cc horizontal single. But perhaps most amazing of all, the Motocarri 500cc was listed from then until 1980 (except for the war years), making it Guzzi's longest-running model of all time.

A whole succession of production models appeared during the late 1920s and early 1930s, even though Europe was gripped in the Great Depression, but the vast majority of these were for basic transport, of little technical merit, and usually were variants of existing designs. Guzzi even tried a supercharged four-cylinder 492.2cc (56×60mm) racer during 1930, but this project, which featured horizontal cylinders, was not proceeded with, although a prototype gave 45 bhp.

By late 1932 the effects of the Depression were beginning to wear off, and so Guzzi, like many other

Engine from the supercharged 500cc four-cylinder of 1930.

factories, began to think of a more prosperous future and the need to lay down new designs. Guzzi realized that this meant not only production roadsters but improved racing models. The highlight of this new wave was perhaps the *Tri Cilindri*. Powered by a 494.8cc (56×47mm) near-horizontal across-the-frame three-cylinder engine with partial unit construction, it was an outstandingly modern design. Running on a 4.9:1 compression ratio, it not only offered smooth flowing power from its 25 bhp engine, but exclusive motorcycling for anyone with a deep enough pocket. Price was the design's major handicap and there were very few takers, which meant that it was taken out of production at the end of 1933. Much more popular and therefore profitable were singles like the Tipo Sport 15, P175, P250 and the GTV.

However, as in much of Guzzi's history it was racing where the real headlines were made, and 1933 saw the first appearance of the *Bicilindrica*, a 120-degree, 494.8cc (68×68mm) V-twin, which in its original form pumped out 44 bhp at 7000 rpm. Essentially this used a pair of TT250 cylinders on a common crankcase. It was with one of the V-twins and its smaller 250 single-cylinder brothers that Guzzi was to set the 1935 Isle of Man TT series alight. With the services of the Irish star Stanley Woods, the Italian marque won the Lightweight (250) TT, its first ever TT victory and in fact the first one by a foreign marque since the American firm Indian took the Senior TT way back in 1911. Woods not only won the event, but also set a new class lap record, despite poor visibility on the Mountain section of the course. Two days after his historic Lightweight

Carlo Guzzi (far left, cap) and Georgio Parodi (shaking hands) congratulate Stanley Woods after he won the 1935 Lightweight event – Guzzi's first Isle of Man victory.

victory came an even bigger upset when, against all predictions, Woods took one of the new V-twins to a sensational win in the Senior TT. Norton's Jimmy Guthrie had actually been declared the winner when the Guzzi crossed the line to snatch victory by a mere couple of seconds – there were a large number of red faces in the organizers' office that day!

More records came two years later when Omobono Tenni became the first Italian to win a TT by finishing ahead of the field in the 1937 Lightweight event after an extremely well-judged ride. In the final year prior to the outbreak of war between Germany and the Allies, Guzzi fielded a very quick, but unfortunately far from reliable, supercharged version of their 250 racer. They also offered for sale the 500 Condor and 250 Albatros over-the-counter racers, both of which soon built up an excellent name.

Like the majority of Italy's motorcycle industry, Moto Guzzi was badly affected by the declaration of war by Mussolini in June 1940. In many ways Italy was totally unprepared for modern warfare and from September 1943 was effectively split into two opposing sides. At least Guzzi's rural surroundings on the shores of Lake Como meant that they were not a target of the Allied bombing campaign, which was directed against other concerns

based in cities such as Milan or Turin. The main model built for the military during the conflict was the *Alce* (elk), which replaced the long-running and successful GT17, which had entered service with the Italian army way back in 1932. Both models were powered by an ioe version of the trusty 498cc horizontal single-cylinder engine, as was the *Trialce*, which had twin rear drive wheels. A total of over 8000 *Alce* and *Trialces* were produced from 1940 to 1944 and these comprised the backbone of the Italian army motorcycle fleet during the hostilities. Generally the Moto Guzzi facilities escaped the war unscathed, and were therefore in an ideal position to capitalize on the situation when it became possible to restart production for peacetime purposes. In Italy the late 1940s was a time of unparalleled growth in the popularity of motorcycling.

Prior to the war motorcycles were ridden either by enthusiasts or for sport. But in the immediate post-war period, with the private car almost non-existent in a generally war-torn country, public transport in disarray and fuel strictly rationed, motorcycles at last came into their own. Of course the factory still continued to manufacture enthusiast-type machines, like the 250 *Airone* (Heron) and 500 GTV, but its most important model was without doubt the *Guzzino* (Little Guzzi), also known as the *Motoleggera*

The 1937 version of the long-running 500 V-twin.

The Mandello del Lario factory raced a supercharged 250 during 1938 and 1939.

(light motorcycle). This little machine designed by Ing. Antonio Micucci first appeared in 1946 and broke with Guzzi design tradition. It was a *two-stroke* with an innovative rotary valve, a three-speed gearbox and a very basic, but entirely practical, swinging arm rear suspension. Its 64cc (42×46mm) engine produced 2 bhp at 5000 rpm and it was built in vast numbers. It was the first Italian motorcycle which was really mass produced. In 1949 Guzzi organized a rally for owners of their little 65cc motorcycle and the result was incredible. Over 14,000 people on some 13,000 machines arrived at the tiny village of Mandello del Lario and the event caused a massive traffic jam in the entire lakeside area. Even today it remains probably the largest gathering of a single motorcycle model type in Italy. Customers used the tiny Guzzi for almost every task imaginable, even to haul lightweight sidecars, but perhaps the strangest modification of all was a conversion kit which transformed it into a four-stroke!

The success of their diminutive 'strokers helped Moto Guzzi reinforce its position as the premier motorcycle

The Airone 250 (shown) and Falcone 500, together with a gaggle of ultra-lightweight two-strokes, put Guzzi back on top in the sales league during the immediate post-war era.

producer in Italy. This in turn meant that the company was once again able to mount a challenge in the racing world, with the 250 single and 500 V-twin, both suitably updated. Much of the early design work in the immediate post-war period was by Ing. Micucci, who had joined Guzzi in 1942, and it was Micucci who was responsible for the various two-strokes, not just the 65 Guzzino, but later models such as the *Zigolo, Dingo* and *Trotter* and for the racing models in the period 1946-48. The first of these was an improved version of the 500 V-twin, using the old 120-degree engine with a 17kg weight reduction. Another Micucci design was the all-new 247.2cc (54×54mm) near-horizontal dohc twin. In many ways this was an excellent machine and deserved a better fate than being consigned to the scrap heap. For example, it immediately gave 25 bhp at 9000 rpm and could have no doubt been developed much more. It is also likely that it would have been better equipped to meet the challenge from NSU in the early 1950s, which effectively made the long-running 250 horizontal single obsolete. Designed in 1947 the 250 twin made its début in the hands of the Irishman Manliff Barrington in the 1948 Lightweight TT, but thereafter very little was heard of the bike. By 1949, the first year of the official World Championships, Guzzi chose to concentrate on the single.

A particularly interesting production model of the era was the *Galletto* (Cockerel), which had a horizontal push-rod motor. When it was first shown in public at the 1950 Geneva Show, it had a capacity of 150cc, but by the time

This 75cc record breaker set a host of new speeds for its class during 1950.

production started this had grown to 159.5cc (62×53mm). A strange mixture of motorcycle and scooter, it was nonetheless a popular bike and stayed in production, albeit with its capacity raised yet again to 192cc (65×58mm), until 1966.

The *Zigolo* (Bunting) was another top-selling commuter-style model. This was very much an improved and enlarged '65'. When it first appeared in 1953 it had a capacity of 98cc (50×50mm), but this was later increased to 110.3cc (52×52mm), by which time it had a chrome-plated alloy cylinder. *The Motor Cycle* called the *Zigolo*

Complex 500 in-line dohc four with fuel injection and shaft drive. Introduced in 1952 (1953 version illustrated), it never lived up to expectations.

'easy on the eye, fun to ride, yet not a bank-breaker' — a description which summed up the humble machine exceptionally well. Incidentally, it will be noted that the vast majority of Ing. Micucci's designs, both for road and racing, used square engine dimensions.

Together with the 250 *Aircone*, the range of 500 four-strokes continued. These now included the *Astore* (Goshawk), which made its bow in 1949, and probably the most famous of all roadster Guzzi singles, the *Falcone* (Falcon), the following year. Today the *Falcone* is universally regarded as the ultimate development of Carlo Guzzi's original single-cylinder family. There were very few changes to the GTV and *Astore*, but the *Falcone* was given a new look which can now be called classic. The narrow handlebar and revised riding position offered a definite sporting stance, while the engine was lightly tuned to provide 23 bhp (compared to the Astore's 19 bhp) at an equally low 4300 rpm. Its maximum speed of 84 mph could be upped almost 10 mph by fitting certain components from the *Dondolino* (rocking chair), which itself was a post-war development of the Condor production racer. From 1953, when the Astore was deleted from the catalogue, the Falcone was offered not only in 'Sports' style but also in 'Turismo' guise.

The only really 'new' Guzzi production roadster during the early/mid-1950s was the *Lodola* (Lark), which had its public début at the Milan Samples Fair in April 1956. This was a four-stroke with a near-vertical cylinder and chain-driven overhead camshaft. Up to 1958, the Lodola had a capacity of 174.4cc (62×57.8mm), but for 1959 this was increased to 235cc (68×64mm) and altered to ohv. Besides its standard and sportster variations it was a successful entrant in the ISDT for Italian team riders in 175, 235 and a special 247cc version, winning a whole series of gold medals. It was road racing with which Guzzi has really always been connected and its activities during the late 1940s and early 1950s in this sector of the sport were perhaps its greatest triumphs. This was in both the Isle of Man TT and the World Championship series, where the marque shared equal levels of success. In the former, the Mandello del Lario factory's policy of support was to be rewarded time and time again during these years with a whole host of TT victories, starting with their former star rider Stanley Wood's protégé Manliff Barrington's victory in the 1947 Lightweight race, the first post-war TT held. Maurice Cann, who also set the fastest lap at 74.78 mph, was second on another Mandello single. The following year Barrington, aboard Ing. Micucci's 250 twin, was by far the quickest in practice for the Lightweight event, but was forced to retire from the race, which was won by Cann.

The real news in 1948 was that Tenni set the fastest lap of the 1948 races in the Senior TT on his V-twin at 88.06 mph. The little Italian did not win as his Guzzi went sick and he eventually finished ninth, even though he led the race for the first four laps. Just over two weeks later tragedy struck the Guzzi camp when two of Italy's most famous riders, Omoboni Tenni and Achille Varzi, were killed while practising for the combined bike and car Swiss GP at Berne. Both were veterans, but both had shown riding ability to match that of anyone in the world, as Tenni had established by his TT performance. Back at the TT the following year Barrington regained the Lightweight title, whilst Tommy Woods won it in 1951 and Fergus Anderson in 1952 and again in 1953. These victories were followed by Bill Lomas's and Ken Kavanagh's, in the 1955 and 1956 Junior TT, respectively.

The new World Championship series had started in 1949 and Bruno Ruffo took the 250cc title for Guzzi in 1949 and 1951; Enrico Lorenzetti retained it for the marque the following year. Then came NSU's dominance in the Lightweight classes. Guzzi responded by going up to the 350cc category and Fergus Anderson promptly won in 1953 and 1954, Bill Lomas in 1955 and 1956 and, finally, Keith Campbell in 1957. It is true to say that it would take a book itself to cover these great victories in full, but just as significant as the results themselves were the men and machines which achieved these superb results. Today Ing. Giulio Cesare Carcano is the man largely credited with the design work during this great period in the company's history, but it should also be remembered that Micucci, Cantoni and Todero were all engineers who played a vital role. Another vitally important facet of the Guzzi post-war GP racing effort was the famous wind tunnel and the various streamlining which the Mandello team employed between 1953 and 1957.

Most enthusiasts think of the racing Guzzis as singles and certainly the ones which won the titles *were* singles. Technically, however, the multi-cylinder Guzzis were of most interest. Apart from the 120-degree 500cc V-twin and Micucci's parallel twin 250 already discribed, there were the in-line four and the fabulous V8. The 492.2cc (56×50mm) dohc in-line four was not created by Guzzi themselves as such, but commissioned by the Mandello management, and was the work of Ing. Carlo Gianini in Rome. It had been Gianini who had been responsible many years earlier, with Piero Remor, during the early development of the OPRA and Rondine ventures, which had led to the pre-war Gilera four-cylinder racers. The 500

Much of Guzzi's post-war racing success was gained by the singles. Here Enrico Lorenzetti pilots his ex-works 250 Guzzi against Carlo Ubbiali's MV during the Italian Championship round at Monza, 6 May, 1956.

Guzzi four was water-cooled, had fuel injection and the final drive was by shaft, so with a narrow frontal area from its in-line cylinders and partial streamlining it *looked* every inch a certain race winner. On its début day in early 1953 at Siracusa, however, it retired with unspecified mechanical trouble. Then shortly afterwards, with Enrico Lorenzetti in the saddle, it won its first race in May at Hockenheim in Germany, at an average speed of 107.5 mph. Fergus Anderson put in the fastest lap on another example at 113 mph and Guzzi seemed to have the makings of a world-beater. Somehow after this it never seemed to match expectations, even though by 1954 it was pumping out 55 bhp at 9000 rpm. One problem centred around the Hirth couplings forming the big-end journal of the massive built-up crankshaft. Another was the torque reaction from the shaft drive, which limited its roadholding abilities. Yet another was the engine speed clutch, which made it impossible to guarantee clean gear-changing at racing speeds. None of these three failings could be entirely cured and so after a couple of years it was wheeled away to be put under dust covers in the factory's museum.

Even though the in-line four had been retired, Guzzi knew that the days of their venerable flat singles were coming to a close, at least in Grand Prix events. So Ing. Carcano, by now the man in charge of the race department, designed what many still regard as the most magnificent Grand Prix motorcycle of all time, the fabulous 500 V8. I have chosen this machine to illustrate the amount of development and detail which went into a Guzzi racing design. The idea for this machine had come whilst Ing. Carcano was sitting quietly on the grass near the famous Parabolica bend of the Monza Autodrome watching the 500cc class practising for the 1954 Italian Grand Prix. From his trackside vantage point, Carcano was watching a rider of one of the rival fours making a major riding error while negotiating the bend and, even worse, showing no signs of any improvement on succeeding laps. Yet on consulting his stop-watch, Carcano discovered that the rider's lap times were far better than those of his Guzzi riders, who negotiated that bend with perfect technique, flat out on their singles. 'This is too much,' he exclaimed. 'We'll have to start with a clean sheet of paper and design a new multi-cylinder job.'

And so it was. The in-line four was abandoned at the end of that season (the single, on the contrary was kept in service with good results on appropriate tracks) and work started on a highly unorthodox mount, which featured eight cylinders arranged in two blocks of four, at an angle of 90-degrees. The axis of the engine was transverse to the frame to simplify the employment of chain final drive, which Carcano rated as more practical than shaft. The

reason for the complex design was that the cubic capacity of each cylinder could be reduced to a minimum, for very high rpm and consequent high power output. There was the added attraction that the originality of the design gave great possibilities of development in a new field (nobody had ever attempted such an arrangement before), and the overall dimensions, both longitudinal and transversal, could still be quite reasonable, so enabling the engine unit to be housed in a conventional double-cradle frame.

The project crystallized during the winter of 1954-55, in an atmosphere of the greatest secrecy. However, Carcano was not only a brilliant designer, and a champion yachtsman, but he also had a great sense of humour. As a vivid illustration of this, without adding any written explanation, he sent his friends in the press, who were clamouring for information, a drawing of his latest project seen from the right-hand side (off-side) and invited them to guess what it was. Not one journalist came up with the correct answer and one even went as far as suggesting that it was a turbine-powered machine! The Carcano masterpiece first appeared mid-way through 1955, at an Italian national meeting at Senigallia. The newcomer caused a great sensation in racing circles throughout the world, even though it was not raced that day. The same thing happened at its second appearance, during practice for the Italian GP at Monza later that year. The main teething problems encountered were with the carburation, the ignition system and crankshaft lubrication.

With bore and stroke dimensions of 44×22mm, giving each cylinder a swept volume of 62.31cc, the 498.48cc was oversquare, with a 0.932:1 bore and stroke ratio. During the early stages of development, power output of the V8 was about 65 bhp at 12,000 rpm, but gradually this figure was increased. By the end of 1957, when Guzzi unfortunately decided to withdraw from Grand Prix racing, it had been boosted to close to 80 bhp at 14,000 rpm, almost 10 bhp more than the most potent rival 500cc four-cylinder efforts, and unsurpassed until the 1970s. A point worth commenting upon is the fact that even at 14,000 rpm, the linear speed of the tiny pistons was lower than that of a single-cylinder 500cc racing engine of the period (such as the Manx Norton or Matchless G50) turning over at 7000 rpm! Owing to its cylinder arrangement, the engine needed water-cooling and the radiator was situated at the front of the crankcase. The water pump was driven by one of a train of six timing gears (housed in an oil bath on the off-side of the engine), which operated the twin overhead camshafts for each bank of cylinders. On the left-hand side of each inlet camshaft were two distributors, each with four contact breakers. The coils, one for each cylinder, were mounted in two clusters of four in either side of the frame's front down

The 1957 version of Guzzi's awesome 500 V8. It is still held by many as the most magnificent racing motorcycle of all time.

tubes. Dual 6-volt batteries were mounted either side of the rear frame section and the firing order was 1,8,3,6,4,5,2,7. To provide more space for the two valves per cylinder in their respective hemispherical combustion chambers, 10mm spark plugs were fitted. The short, massive forged nickel-chrome crankshaft, with circular flywheels, was supported by a total of five caged roller bearings, with split races between each throw. Split roller bearings were also used for the big-ends of the 90mm-long connecting rods. The crankcase was a truly superb one-piece casting in electron and the cast-iron wet-liner cylinders were finned at the top, within the water jacket, for more efficient cooling.

The valves, operating in split guides, were set at an inclined angle of 58 degrees to one another, with diameters of 23mm for the inlet and 21mm for the exhaust, each with dual coil springs, over which large tappets came into direct contact with the cams. The highly domed forged pistons, deeply recessed for valve clearance and also to provide a squish effect, carried two compression rings and a single oil-scraper ring. Following conventional Guzzi racing practice, the lubrication system was of the dry sump type, with the oil pump gear-driven at half engine speed. The oil tank itself was in the large-diameter top frame tube, with a capacity of five litres. Each miniature cylinder was fed by its own 20mm Dell 'Orto SSI carburettor, with two float chambers on the left-hand side of the engine each serving four carburettors. A single cable from the quick-action twist-grip operated the eight throttle slides with a clever linkage system, which reduced effort to a bare minimum.

MOTO GUZZI

Zigolo

World's most advanced Lightweight

SERIES I

£112 - 19 - 6 incl. P.T.

Complete with Speedometer

Much more down to earth, but perhaps more relevant to the company's well-being, were humble two-strokes such as this 98cc Zigolo of 1959.

The multi-plate clutch was located outside the crankcase and was of the dry variety. The primary drive, by means of two spur pinions enclosed in an oil bath casing, provided an engine-to-gearbox ratio of 2.75:1. Amazingly, there were four-, five- and even six-speed gear clusters available, depending on circuit or rider requirements. In practice it was soon discovered that, thanks to the tremendous torque generated by the eight-cylinder powerplant, the six-speed cluster was completely unnecessary. Incidentally, this high torque feature of the engine at low rpm made the V8 very useful on even the most twisting course. Secondary drive was transmitted to the rear wheel via a ⅝ × ⅜ in. chain which ran on the right-hand side of the machine.

The chrome-moly tubular frame was of the double-cradle type, with the pivot point for the round section swinging arm incorporated in the crankcase casting (as on the Ducati Pantah), to reduce the machine's overall wheelbase. As was the practice with the majority of post-war Guzzi racing bikes, the V8 employed leading-link front forks. However, in an attempt to cope with the awesome power output, additional exposed shock absorbers were fitted at the front. Besides being able to cope with the speed while in action, one must be in the position to decelerate. Here, the V8 had a massive 240mm drum front brake, which sported four-leading-shoe operation. The rear was a 220mm single-leading-shoe drum. Both brake drums were mounted on Borrani alloy wheel rims with a 3.00×19in. front and 3.25×20in. rear tyre. The fuel tank, like other works Guzzis of the period, was constructed from hand-beaten aluminium, as was the streamlining, at first a full dustbin, later a dolphin. The weight of 325 lb dry, complete with streamlining, is truly remarkable for such a complex machine and substantiates the claim that Carcano was perhaps the greatest of all motorcycle designers. Remember that the same man succeeded in putting it across the opposition with his 1956 and 1957 World Championship 350cc single, which tipped the scales at an amazingly low 225 lb. If Guzzi had not pulled out of GP racing at the end of 1957 who knows just what they might have achieved?

The actual racing début for the Guzzi V8 came during April 1956 at the Imola International Gold Cup event. Here Australian Ken Kavanagh demonstrated the machine's potential. In spite of atrociously wet conditions Kavanagh immediately went to the front at the start of the race and held the lead for the first six or seven laps. After breaking the lap record he was forced to retire because of a faulty water gauge. 1956 was considered by Guzzi as still part of the V8's development period and successes were few. The following year saw the V8 start well, with some successful

record-breaking exploits. Without any special tuning, or resorting to special fuels, Bill Lomas sprinted along the Terracina Straight to smash the world standing start 10km record at an average speed of 151.5 mph, a record which still stands over three decades later! 1957 also saw V8-mounted Giuseppe Colnago take the 500cc Italian championship and Dickie Dale the Imola Gold Cup title, beating all the top riders and bikes in the process. It was Dale who was chosen to ride the V8 in the Diamond Jubilee Isle of Man Senior TT. Although slowed by ignition troubles, which caused his machine to run on only seven cylinders for most of the race, he still managed fourth place. For the TT a dolphin fairing was used, but on the ultra-fast Francorchamps circuit for the Belgian GP the full streamlining was fitted and Australian star Keith Campbell finally showed the world the full potential of the Italian rocketship. Campbell thrashed all the opposition, showing a clean pair of heels to everyone else out on the circuit. Disappointment awaited the Guzzi team, however, as after recording the fastest lap of the meeting at 118.06 mph he was forced to retire with a broken lead from one of the batteries.

Racing accidents sidelined the top Guzzi riders for the final Grand Prix of the 1957 season, the Italian at Monza. This prevented the V8 from competing in the final classic of what many regard as the golden era of road racing. The Guzzi directors, together with those of Gilera and FB Mondial, had already made a secret pact jointly to retire from Grand Prix racing. This cut short the development of a machine which looked set to rule racing in the future. Sadly, the most famous machine of its time, perhaps ever, was destined never to be used in anger again. Today all that remains of the V8 is a complete machine and an engine unit, which are housed in the factory's museum in Mandello del Lario. As with Gilera and FB Mondial, Guzzi's reason for its withdrawal from the Grand Prix was for purely financial reasons. With ever more complex and expensive design work needed to achieve race-winning performances and less and less production roadsters being sold, the manufacturers simply could not balance the books and go racing as they had done previously.

By 1957, even with the introduction of the new *Lodola* model, Moto Guzzi were struggling to find enough customers. And in any case the roadsters had not benefited from the design innovation lavished on the racing machines. Well over 50 per cent of the factory's production was centred on small two-strokes, which by now comprised the *Zigolo*, *Zigolo Sport* and *Cardellino* (Gold Finch). The original 'stroker, the 65 *Motoleggera*, had been pensioned off in 1954.

The 1960s started with the introduction of the *Stornello* (Starling). This was a simple ohv single intended as a

One of the most important models in Guzzi's history, the 1967 700 V7. From it stemmed a vast range of models over the next two decades.

commuter rather than sportster, initially as a 125 (actually 123.1cc; 52×58mm) and later also as a 160 (153.24cc; 58×58mm). It was originally equipped with four gears, but both models were updated and fitted with five speeds before production came to an end in the mid-1970s. They were never machines to get excited over, but the Stornello played an important role in the company's strategy over the 15 years it was in production. A similar picture could be painted for almost all the Moto Guzzi line of 1965: *Zigolo* 110, *Lodola* 235, *Galletto* 192 and *Falcone Turismo* (the Sport had been discontinued in 1964), and the various three-wheel *Motocarris*, plus the Stornello 125 (the 160 version did not come until 1968). The only really new developments had come from the Carcano-designed V7 V-twin, a 700cc class machine still in the prototype stage

**GUZZI
"V7 special"**

V7 engine assembly — it was developed from an engine used to drive a military tractor during the early 1960s.

Nuovo Falcone. Introduced in 1970 it never lived up to the original and was discontinued in 1976.

and the Micucci-conceived *Dingo* range of 50cc two-stroke mopeds and ultra lightweight motorcycles which had first appeared in 1963.

These designs could not halt Guzzi's slide and by the time the last Lodolas, were coming off the production line in mid-1966 bankruptcy had only been avoided by using the entire Parodi family fortune; even so, later that year the company was forced into compulsory court administration (the Italian equivalent of receivership). The following year a trustee ship company called SEIMM had to be set up by the creditor banks and the IMI (state financing agency), who effectively assumed financial control over the company to enable Moto Guzzi to continue trading. In retrospect this state of affairs can be mapped out relatively simply. First came the massive race programme of the 1950s, then the slump in sales caused by the emergence of the smaller, cheaper automobile and finally the crisis created by particular events within the company's own senior management structure.

Emanuele Parodi, who had not only provided the original loan but much valuable business acumen, had died during the war, almost at the same time as his nephew Angelo. Then his son Giorgio had died suddenly in 1955, and to complete the gloomy picture, Carlo Guzzi, by then old and frail, died in 1964 at the age of 75, shortly after finally retiring from the company he had been instrumental in creating some 45 years earlier. By 1966, the only link was Giorgio Parodi's brother Enrico, who had himself joined Guzzi as late as 1942. Unfortunately for all concerned, he was not entirely suited to the task of running such a large company, and not only made a number of wrong moves but also brought the entire Parodi empire to the verge of collapse with a series of misplaced financial speculations that turned sour, just at the very time when the benefit of these investments was most needed. The result

was therefore inevitable, with a large number of workers being made redundant at Mandello, and with it a severe pruning of the model range, including the Lodola line and several of the two-strokes.

Ing. Antonio Micucci, then the designer director, was so disgusted that he resigned from the company, and in a recent letter openly stated, 'because of my disagreement with the new incompetent direction'. Ing. Carcano remained, and it was he who was responsible for the design of the V7 project for both military and civilian use. There is no doubt that without the V7, Moto Guzzi would most probably not have survived to see in the 1970s. Not long after the new management had taken control, Carcano finally decided to retire, his place being taken by Ing. Lino Tonti, formerly with a number of manufacturers, including Aermacchi, Bianchi, Gilera and Paton. Under Tonti the original ungainly V7 tourer was transformed into machines such as the V7 Sport, 750S/3 and finally to the Le Mans of the mid-1970s and beyond. Before all this a great deal of new design work was undertaken to both the engine and the running gear.

The first production V7 700 came in 1967. This had a 703.718cc (80×70mm) 90-degree V-twin push-rod engine which itself had its origins in the 3×3 military tractor-like vehicle conceived for the Italian Defence Ministry back in the late 1950s. The civilian V7 prototype had first appeared in public at the Milan Show in November 1965, where it had created a lot of interest. It had also won a fierce battle which was waged between Ducati, Gilera and Guzzi for the right to supply the next generation of military and police motorcycles for the Italian government. Perhaps even more significantly Tonti realized that the next generation of production roadsters would probably be not only of large capacity, but of a sporting nature. He therefore undertook the transformation of what had originally been conceived as purely a *touring* bike into a super sportster. He also appreciated, as he had shown at Aermacchi and Bianchi, the importance of publicity through motorcycle sport. Obviously Guzzi could not make a racing comeback, but it could go in for a spot of record-breaking with some lightly modified production models.

At Monza on 28 June, 1969, Remo Venturi, Vittorio Brambilla, Guido Mandracci and Angelo Tenconi rode a pair of specially modified and tuned production V7 Specials. One had a 739.3cc (82×70mm) engine for the 750cc class, while the other displaced 757.5cc (83×70mm) so that it was eligible for the 1000cc category. The team set new 750cc world records for the standing start 10 kilometres and the 100 kilometres, as well as the hour for the 750 and 1000 classes. On 30 and 31 October Tonti and his team of mechanics returned to Monza, but with a partly

Mk 1 version of the Le Mans. This sleek sporting V-twin first appeared in 1976.

The smaller V35/50 V-twin initially sold in quite large numbers, but their poor reliability record hit sales after 1981. Photograph shows a 1979 V50 Mk 2.

different set of riders (Brambilla and Mandracci had been joined by Pagani, Bertarelli, Patrignani and Trabalzini). The 1000-kilometre record for the 750 class was improved, and so was the 6-hour. In the 1000cc class records were set for the 100 kilometres, the hour, the 1000 kilometres and the 6- and 12-hour distances. By putting a third wheel on one of the machines eight sidecar records were also established. Finished in the famous lime green colour of the old factory racers, this record stint was successful in getting Guzzi's name amongst the headlines of the world press once again.

In 1971 the first real results of Tonti's labours on the production front made its appearance in the shape of the striking V7 Sport, now regarded as one of the classic machines of its period. This had a capacity of 748.388cc (82.5×70mm), a five-speed gearbox, alternator (in place of the earlier car-type dynamo) and a new double cradle frame which endowed the newcomer with low, lean aggressive looks. In contrast to the earlier V7 models, the Sport handled more like a racer than a heavyweight truck. This enabled Guzzi to offer a wide range of variations from one basic model. The 90-degree V-twin not only provided Guzzi with a positive means for survival, but a future too.

The SIEMM holding company's task was accomplished as the Mandello factory was now back on sound financial tracks and it was therefore in a position to offer the company for sale. A few months before Alejandro de Tomaso had acquired the ailing Benelli concern (see Chapter 3) and was already reshaping its fortunes. The SIEMM board entered into an agreement to sell Moto Guzzi to this aggressive and dynamic Argentinian of Italian stock when he came to their door. De Tomaso continued the rebirth of the marque even though certain moves were made with motives of profit rather than quality, such as the adoption of timing chains instead of the more expensive gears on the V-twins and selling badge-engineered Benelli 'strokers under the Guzzi label at a higher price.

Throughout the 1970 and 1980s the V-twin theme has endured through a whole succession of models: Ambassador, GT 850 (called Eldorado in North America), 850T, 850 T3 California, 850 T4, V-1000 Convert Automatic, 1000 SP (Spada in Britain), V1000 G5 (manual conversion of Convert), the various Marks of the Le Mans sportster and the truly vast array of smaller Vees sired by the original V35/50 of the late 1970s.

There have also been a number of other machines, such as the *Falcone Nouvo* (a largely unsuccessful attempt to re-create the aura of the original *Falcone*), the 254 (a four-cylinder 250 based on the Benelli design), a 125 twin and 350/400 versions of similar Benelli four-stroke multis. Then came, as already mentioned, various blatant badge-

engineering exercises with Benelli two-strokes in sizes up to the 250 twin-cylinder TS (Benelli 2C). Except for the V-twins none of these creations has been particularly successful, and of the vees there is no doubt that the larger 700, 750, 850 and 1000 class machines have been generally much better bikes than the smaller V35/50/65 series, the latter often let down by poor finish and less than reliable mechanics.

During the de Tomaso era there have been certain factors behind the scenes which have played vital roles. Some of these included a policy to build four-stroke engines at Mandello del Lario and two-stroke units at the Benelli facilities in Pesaro (with the recent sale of the Benelli factory all Guzzis are now built at Mandello). Under de Tomaso control the spares organizations of both companies were moved to a central location in Modena; an unsuccessful attempt was made to centralize design work for both Guzzi and Benelli at Modena and this resulted in a number of mistakes, such as the saga of the 16in. front

SP1000 – Italy's answer to the BMW R100RS. This motorway express was sold as the Spada in Britain.

1983 version of the Le Mans, by now the Mk 3, but still 844cc capacity, later upped to 949cc and Mk 4 form in 1985.

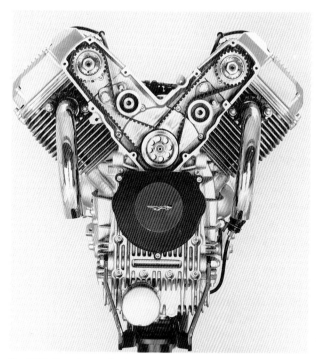

By 1988 Guzzi were in the process of developing a belt-driven ohc version of their long-running V-twin engine.

wheel farce of the mid-1980s. This was an attempt to 'modernize' various V-twins with smaller, more fashionable wheels. Unfortunately the result was bikes with poor ground clearance and equally poor road-holding and handling!

In an attempt to learn from these mistakes the Modena design centre was forced to take notice of the traditionalists at Mandello once again, with the result that all Guzzi V-twins now have 18in. wheels, some are finished in old-fashioned all red *Falcone*-style finish and some even sport wire instead of cast alloy wheels! The former Innocenti plant in Milan, where the V35/50 production took place in the boom years of the late 1970s, has been sold to General Motors and production concentrated at Mandello.

Like Ducati, Guzzi V-twins have been used successfully in the popular Battle of the Twins Series on both sides of the Atlantic. The American tuner known as 'Doctor John' was probably the most successful Guzzi tuner of the 1980s.

There has also been speculation of new models, even rumours of an imminent takeover, but as yet Moto Guzzi seems set to continue much as it has for over a decade, slowly refining the existing products. The only real developments have been fuel injection on some models and experiments with belt drive and overhead camshafts. A German company has even brought out a desmodromic cylinder head conversion. This is in strong contrast to its innovative designs, particularly in racing, from its earlier years. Currently, Guzzi seem to be stuck in a time warp, as a journalist for the British *Superbike* magazine vividly described his visit to the factory: 'As we walked the ten yards or so over to his (the export director's) enormous oak desk in the corner, overlooked by a bronze bust of Carlo Guzzi himself, I registered the embarrassment on his face. He knew he looked as if he had sat there since 1950.' How long can any factory, even one with its history steeped in tradition like Moto Guzzi, afford to stand still?

CHAPTER 16

Motom

Mention Moto Guzzi, Gilera, MV Agusta, Ducati — even Benelli, Bianchi or Parilla — and most motorcycle enthusiasts will know at least something of these marques. During much of the 1950s and 1960s, however, there was another important name, one which today is sadly all but forgotten: Motom. During the boom years of the early post-war period, the demand in Italy for cheap two-wheeled transport was tremendous. A Milan engineering company took full advantage, although it did not have a famous tradition or works four-cylinder racers. Instead it had an ultra-modern plant and produced small-capacity, cheap-to-buy four-strokes.

Motom Italiana SpA's production facilities at Via J Palma 27, Milan, were a model to which the rest of the Italian industry could only aspire — modern buildings, the latest machine tools, even its own extensive fully covered test track. Situated on the outskirts of the Milanese industrial sprawl, the company started production during 1947. Its initial design, like so many others at the time, was a 49.78cc (40×39.8mm) auxiliary engine unit complete with pedalling gear, carburettor and exhaust for slotting straight into a pedal cycle. With overhead valves, its only serious competitor was Ducati's Cucciolo, for all the others in the war of the micro-motors were humble two-strokes. Its other claim to fame was that it had been designed in 1946 by Piero Taruffi and some Lancia car technicians.

By the middle of 1948 Motom were offering their first complete machine powered by a version of the auxiliary unit. The overhead valve engine was mounted in a fabricated box-girder frame comprising a beam from the steering head to the rear wheel spindle and incorporating an engine support and bottom bracket lug, and the saddle support, all of which were unique among designs of the day. This formula soon became a top best-seller. The success of this early venture paved the way for the Milan company's next two-wheeler, a highly original creation called the *Delfino* (Dolphin). This half-scooter, half-motorcycle made its début at the 1950 Milan Show. The *Delfino* was very much in the vogue of the Guzzi *Galletto* and MV Agusta *Pullman*. Initially it featured a 147cc, four-speed, ohv, unit-contruction power unit. By the time the production version appeared a year later its capacity had grown to 163cc (62×54mm). In this form it gave 8 bhp at

6000 rpm, hardly earth-shattering today, but nonetheless was more than adequate for the time. Cooling was assisted by fan blades attached to the crankshaft-mounted magneto rotor: forced air circulated the partially enclosed head and barrel as on many scooter designs. Within the engine a forged, three-ring Borgo piston was employed together with coil valve springs, a pressed-up crankshaft with a caged roller big-end and phosphor bronze bush small-end. The push-rods were alloy.

The gearbox had four speeds and there was a multi-plate clutch in an enclosed oil bath. The engine was mounted in a full cradle frame with a massive single front down tube and a 'floor' for the rider's feet. The rear suspension was taken care of by a single horizontal shock absorber mounted directly underneath the engine. The specification was completed by a front fork of the leading-link variety with dual single-leading-shoe brakes. Fifteen-inch alloy rims were used with 3.50 section tyres. Front crash bars and a tyre inflator pump were standard equipment.

The very same year as the prototype *Delfino* débuted at the Milan Show, Motom had seen their machinery employed by racing enthusiasts in the very first attempts to create a 50cc category. This featured a hotted-up version of the company's well-known 49cc engine. In tuned form this produced 4.5 bhp at 9000 rpm. Other features included a high-compression, forged 11:1 piston and larger 14mm Dell 'Orto carburettor. It retained the normal three-speed gearbox and single-plate dry clutch.

The Motom was not only sturdy but could quite easily be made to exceed 50 mph, an outstanding speed at the time. For example, in 1952 the Italian rider Dalmasso averaged 46.5 mph over a standing kilometre and actually covered the last 500 metres at 58 mph to break the world record for the class. His team-mate Vasco topped 42.7 and 49.6 mph, respectively. It is also worth noting that no streamlining was used, although the rear wheel was enclosed by a large disc. The 50cc category for the 1953 Giro d'Italia (1900 miles in six days on normal roads) was won by Motom rider Giovanetti, who averaged almost 40 mph. Motom machinery reigned supreme in short-circuit events throughout Italy. Without doubt, the company's sporting peak came in 1958, when, during rain at Monza on

Mopeds by the hundred – literally. Part of the storage area at Motom's Milan factory in the early 1950s.

The Delfino. Half-scooter, half-motorcycle, it made its début at the 1950 Milan Show.

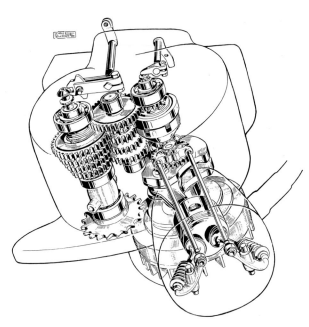

3 and 4 April, world record attempts with a production Super Sports model resulted in a 100-kilometre speed of 54.10 mph, 12 hours at 54.24 mph and 24 hours at 55.20 mph. In addition the one-kilometre standing start was covered at 52.23 mph. Riders for the successful record-breaking spree were: Passina, Saini (later a member of the Guzzi trials team), Pernigotti, Domenicali, Giuseppe Rosetti and his brother Gianfranco. During the whole attempt petrol consumption averaged an amazing 144 mpg!

The Milan company had launched perhaps its most exciting machine and certainly the one which was destined to receive the most publicity, when a brand new 98cc model made its bow on Friday morning, 12 April, 1955, at the opening of the *Fiera di Milano*. In their subsequent test in the 24 May, 1956, issue, *Motor Cycling*'s headline read: 'Italy's Most Advanced Lightweight.' There could be no doubt that at the time of its appearance the Motom 98TS really did rank among the world's most advanced lightweight designs, with a specification which read like something from a works racer rather than a humble commuter mount. Its technical features included a horizontal 98cc overhead cam engine with 'square' 50mm bore and stroke dimensions, ducted cooling, a unit

Delfino engine unit. Originally a 147cc ohv four-speed design with unit construction, by the time the production version appeared at the end of 1951 its capacity had grown to 163cc.

Hailed as Italy's most advanced lightweight when it first appeared in late 1955, the Motom 98TS had an extremely advanced specification.

During 1952 the Motom rider Dalmasso averaged 46.5 mph for the standing kilometre and covered the final 500 metres at 58 mph to break the world 50cc record.

construction four-speed gearbox, cantilever rubber-in-torsion swinging arm suspension at front and rear, pressed-steel frame with integral bodywork, fuel tank, battery, tool kit and other auxiliaries all built into a streamlined container.

The new Motom had attracted so much attention that *Motor Cycling* undertook the unusual decision to send a staff man to test one of the models on home ground in Italy (there was no British importer), and Motom sales director Signor F. Mariassy played host. Under very wet test conditions the maker's claimed 62 mph from the 6.75 bhp motor was not reached. However, the *Motor Cycling* man was generally full of praise for the highly unconventional design, in particular the high level of comfort. The 98's frame consisted of two steel pressings, centre welded. The same construction was employed for the front and rear swinging forks, and for the mudguards. Despite its seemingly complicated engine/gearbox assembly, Motom claimed it had been expressly designed for ease of production and was in fact cheaper to manufacture than its well-established 49cc moped unit.

In 1956 the price in Italy was 189,000 lire (£108 sterling) and the 98TS helped Motom into fifth spot in the

Departing from usual Motom practice, this new 92cc ohv model with vertical cylinder was intended as a commuter lightweight at the lower end of the price range. It made its bow at the Milan Spring Samples Fair in April 1961.

two-wheel-sales chart that year, behind Vespa, Lambretta, Moto Guzzi and Garelli, and in front of such well-know marques as MV, Gilera and Ducati.

The first British enthusiasts saw of Motom was when a moped version of the production 49 was displayed at the Earls Court Show in 1956. A year later the Milan concern released details of the 51 model. As its designation suggested, this had a capacity of 51cc (40.2×40mm), which, running on a compression ratio of 8:1, produced 2.5 bhp, giving a genuine 40 mph top speed. A de luxe version with a dual seat and larger tank was also listed. Both models, like the earlier 48, sported plunger rear suspension and three speeds. 1958 saw works racing Motoms sweep the board in every 50cc competition held in Italy. In addition a Supersport version of the 49cc was introduced. This had low 'bars', plunger rear suspension and miniature handlebar racing fairing, but still retained the three-speed box. Running on a compression ratio of 8.5:1, the Supersport's engine developed 2.5 bhp at 6800 rpm and was capable of nearly 50 mph, making it Italy's fastest moped. Its four-stroke engine also gave it the advantage of offering an easily achieved 200 mpg.

However, the end of the 1950s were tough times for the Italian motorcycle industry and the going was getting even tougher. As the new decade dawned, Motom were forced for the first time to actively seek export sales, together with a development programme of new models.

The make or break year was 1961. First came a serious export push. In Britain this was channelled through Morray & Co Ltd of London, SW1. There were full-page advertisements in the motorcycle press, road tests and even works support for a racing team. *Motor Cycling* tested a Motom 60S in their February 1961 issue, the 51cc ohv model, largely unchanged from the 1957 model 51. Tester Bruce Main-Smith was generally impressed. The 60S was comfortable, quiet, endowed with excellent handling and its price of £104 16s. including £18 purchase tax was not excessively expensive. The 48C and 48SS were also available from the importers, the latter claimed to achieve 47 mph. However, sales never materialized in Britain.

Neither, for that matter, did racing results, even though considerable effort was expended.

Motor Cycling called it the 'Battle of the 50s'. The Motom factory were reported to be sending over works machines for a 250-mile event at Snetterton on 7 May, but over the Norfolk circuit, the ohv challenge to the two-stroke domination was doomed to fail. Only one of the three works Motoms finished. Ridden by Jim Pearson and Peter Inchley, it came home in third spot. However, another ridden by Barry Smith and Roy Righini set a new lap record at 56.26 mph and led for the first 30 laps, only to retire with a sick motor. The other machine, ridden by Paul Wright (co-rider Roy Broom), crashed at the Esses while holding sixth place. Strangely the factory stayed away from the Coupe d'Europe, the forerunner of the world championship for 50cc machines which was due to start a year later in 1962. In Italian national events the marque still dominated.

On the production front, April 1961 witnessed the first of the promised new models, a 92cc machine marketed simply as the 92. It was a neat lightweight touring motorcycle with telescopic forks, swinging-arm rear suspension and pressed-steel chassis. Its engine, although completely new in design with vertical cylinder and four-speed gearbox, still employed overhead valves. Other details included deeply valanced mudguards, full-width alloy hubs and 18in. alloy wheel rims. Although offered at a highly competitive price, the 92 was never destined to sell in any numbers.

Following this costly experience, which also included a 100cc (52×47mm) version, Motom took the decision on financial grounds to use bought-in engines for the first time. By 1964 a 48cc model was being offered with a French Peugeot two-stroke engine. There were several versions, some with automatic gearboxes. Another Motom used a four-speed German 49cc Zündapp power unit, and this was also available in motocross trim. None of this activity could stop the company's downward spiral and, although they struggled on to the end of the decade, Motom were fated to join the long list of Italian motorcycle manufacturers who had already gone to the wall during the 1960s as an ever increasing number of Italians made the move from two to four wheels.

CHAPTER 17

MV Agusta

When it comes to the history of the World road racing Championships one company stands head and shoulders above the rest, MV Agusta. To trace its history one has to go to the year 1879, when Giovanni Agusta was born. Agusta could see a big future in aviation and became one of his country's true pioneers when he not only built, but successfully flew, his own prototype aircraft at Capau, just north of Naples, in 1907. In 1920, Agusta formed Costruzioni Aeronautiche Giovanni Agusta, a company incorporated for the construction, overhaul and repair of both military and civilian aircraft, with facilities in Tripoli and Benghazi. Three years later, in 1923, he returned to Italy and established his base at Verghera, a small village on the bleak Gallarate plain to the north of Milan, where Italy's international Malpensa airport has since been built. In 1927, Giovanni died prematurely at the age of 48, leaving the company in the hands of his wife, Giuseppina, and the eldest of his four sons, Domenico.

Throughout the 1930s, the company prospered on repairs and sub-contracted work for the civil aviation industry, and also managed to produce their own aircraft. With the outbreak of war, Agusta had to take on military work. During the dark years of the hostilities the Verghera concern carried out a number of tasks, from licence-built dive bombers to the manufacture and testing of tricycle landing gear for Fiat aircraft. As early as the autumn of 1943, following the removal of Mussolini, and even though the district around the factory was still within German control, the company began to consider a number of projects aimed at diversifying their activities in a post-war world.

Meccanica Verghera began trading in 1945 following an idea by Count Domenico Agusta in 1943 to build an ultra-lightweight 98cc two-stroke motorcycle, powered by a single-cylinder piston-ported two-stroke engine, with two (later three) speeds. It was to have been called the 'Vespa' (wasp), but Piaggio got in first with that name for their new scooter, so it became simply an 'MV' when Domenico changed the name of the company to Meccanica Verghera (after the place where it was sited).

Interest in motorcycle sport soon blossomed at Verghera. A sports version of the 98cc machine was introduced, with the engine tuned to churn out some 6 bhp,

three-speed gearbox and frame modified by using telescopic front forks and plunger suspension at the rear. With a top speed of around 56 mph, this little machine had many successes in the 1946 and 1947 seasons. In 1948, with 125cc racing becoming extremely popular in Italy and other European countries, the firm brought out their own 125, a two-stroke with heavily finned cylinder head and equipped with a four-speed gearbox. Its introduction brought them into contact for the first time with one of their fiercest rivals, Morini. The Bologna factory had a 125cc two-stroke, with three-speed gearbox, but slightly higher speed than the MV, and it nearly always had the edge over the Verghera model. At the Italian Grand Prix, however, held at Faenza because Monza was still not available, the tables were turned and Bertoni gave Count Agusta his first ever victory.

1948 had also seen the appearance on the scene of an overhead-camshaft four-stroke 125, built by the Bologna engineer Alfonso Drusiani and taken up by FB Mondial, who had already considered, but rejected their own racing two-stroke. From that moment it was realized that the two-stroke could no longer be taken into serious consideration for Grand Prix racing. In the meantime a certain young man from Bergamo, by the name of Carlo Ubbiali, was cutting his racing teeth with an MV and in September that year, switching from the road circuits to cross-country events, he competed in the International Six Days' Trial, held in Wales, and won a 'gold'. This was the first to be won by MV Agusta, who have only taken part in the trial on three subsequent occasions: in 1951 (three 'golds'), in 1952 (two 'golds', the only ones for Italy that year) and in 1954 (one 'gold').

During the winter of 1949/50, first Arturo Magni and then Ing. Piero Remor were persuaded to join MV from Gilera. Magni had been chief mechanic and Remor chief designer at the famous Arcore factory. Both men had played a vital role in the development of the post-war air-cooled four-cylinder Gilera Grand Prix racer. The new team working flat out built the first MV four from scratch in a little over six months. Unlike the Gilera, the MV had shaft drive and torsion bar suspension both fore and aft, and a unique feature was that it had a gear-change pedal on *both* sides. These were operated by the rider's heels, pushing down on the left side for upward changes and down on the right to change down. The gearbox was a four-speeder. MV said that the bore and stroke were square at 54×54mm, but suspicious members of the press alleged that the dimensions were in fact 52×58mm, the same as the Gilera design. This might also explain the shaft drive, as Remor could otherwise have been openly accused of taking his former employer's secrets to his new boss. So he chose to use a shaft drive when it would obviously have been better from a racing point of view to use the simpler chain and sprockets. Power output was a claimed 52 bhp at 9500 rpm and on its very first racing appearance at the 1950 Belgian GP the new four, ridden by Arciso Artesiani, kept going to finish fifth behind three Gilera fours and an AJS Porcupine twin ridden by Ted Frend.

Again perhaps proving that Remor leaned heavily on his Gilera work, the first MV four proved remarkably reliable and Artesiani finished the season with a fine third at Monza in the Italian GP behind winner Geoff Duke (Norton) and Umberto Masetti's Gilera four. Perhaps more significantly the MV rider beat the Gileras of Milani and Bandiroli. In fact this was easily the best placing in 1950 by an MV Agusta, because the new 125cc double-knocker singles were completely outclassed by the Mondials and Morinis that year, with a fifth at the Dutch TT being the highest they could achieve. At the Milan Show in November that year, MV stunned the press corps with a road-going prototype of their four-cylinder model. Called the Gran Turismo it was destined to remain a prototype and never entered production.

Realizing that what he needed was a top-class rider who was also capable of track testing the bikes, Count Agusta made a clever move when, late in 1950, he persuaded AJS team leader Les Graham to leave the British factory and join MV. Winner of the 500cc world title in 1949, Graham was just the man the Verghera factory needed. Despite the shortage of time, the MV four was a very different machine when it appeared for the first time in 1951. Telescopic forks replaced the torsion bar-controlled blades of the original design and orthodox hydraulic dampers took over at the rear. In addition the strange double-sided gear change was abandoned in favour of an orthodox system, though shaft drive was retained. It was to be a year of hectic development work rather than any real race-track success, with Les Graham leading a team of four riders in the classics. The Englishman also rode the latest version of the 125 dohc single. It was on one of these machines that he gained his best GP result that season, a third in the Dutch TT. With only a couple of solitary leader-board positions to show for all the effort (both scored by Bandirola who had defected from Gilera), observers could

Englishman Les Graham signed for MV at the end of 1950, and it was he who was largely responsible for the early race testing of the four-cylinder models. Graham is shown here at Marseilles in April 1951.

have been forgiven for thinking Magni, Remor, Graham and all the rest had picked a loser. This ignored what was going on behind the scenes. During the winter of 1951/52 completely new four-cylinder engines were under construction. These had a bore and stroke of 53×56mm with a carburettor for each of the four cylinders, tried on the original engines, though they had usually been raced with only two carbs. There were also new five-speed gearboxes, with chain drive to the rear wheel at last, which meant an instant improvement. Not only was the engine assembly re-vamped, but the running gear as well. At the same time, new frames were built and development work commenced with the type of forks which had recently been designed by Ernie Earles back in Birmingham, a close friend of Graham's. Known as the Earles-type fork, these were considered by the MV team leader to be superior to telescopics. An all-alloy frame was tried, also of Earles design. The power output had now risen to 55 bhp with the motor capable of spinning over at 10,000 rpm.

This new bike was an instant success. In the 1952 Senior TT, Graham fought a tremendous dual with Norton star Reg Armstrong, but eventually lost the lead when oil leaking from the engine smothered the rear of the MV. He still finished second, but would have won easily if the race had lasted a few more miles, as race winner Armstrong's primary chain snapped as the Irishman crossed the finishing line! The 1952 Isle of Man races were also significant because Cecil Sandford brought his 125 MV single home first in the Ultra Lightweight TT, the factory's first ever IoM victory. The man Sandford beat was Mondial team leader Carlo Ubbiali, later to carve out a legend for himself as an MV rider in the lightweight classes. Sheer bad luck robbed Les Graham of a win in Ulster when, after

leading for six laps, and with a new lap record at 105.94 mph already set, he was forced to retire with rear tyre problems caused by the tremendous leaps which the fastest machinery had to endure on the seven-mile straight of the old Clady Circuit.

However, all this was forgotten when, after finishing third in the 125cc event at Monza, he set a start to finish lead to win the 500cc Italian Grand Prix, with another lap record in the bag. In the final classic of the year at Barcelona Graham did even better, with a second in the 125cc race and another win in the 500cc. Although Masetti won the title for rivals Gilera, the warning from the MV camp was there for all to see, with Graham finishing the season in runner-up spot (only three points behind Masetti) with his four. Sandford also proved the work put in by the development team had not been wasted when he took the 125cc world championship, MV's first.

After three very satisfactory years as a Mondial rider,

1952 Senior TT Graham (17) leads the eventual winner, Norton-mounted Reg Armstrong, at Ramsey, the MV rider finally finishing second.

The 1953 version of the production sohc Competizione racing model for paying customers.

Carlo Ubbiali returned to the MV camp for 1953, but his only success that summer was a win at Schotten in Germany. This was the German GP in which rain made the course so slippery that many leading riders refused to compete; but the conditions failed to stop Bandirola from giving a winning début to the 350cc four, a scaled-down version of the 500 with 47.5mm bore and 49mm stroke, a maximum power output of 38 bhp at 10,500 rpm and a total weight of 325 lb. For 1953 the bigger 'four', which weighed about 10 lb more than the 350, had had its power output bumped up to 63 bhp, while the little 125cc single was churning out 16.5 bhp at 10,000 rpm.

A great loss for MV Agusta, and for the whole sporting world, was suffered in the Senior TT, with Les Graham's fatal crash. He had only just won the 125cc race, and the previous month had swept to victory in the 500cc race at Mettet in Belgium. The factory lost heart in the fight for the 500cc championship with Moto Guzzi and Gilera, whilst in the 125cc manufacturers' title, in the face of a rising challenge from NSU of Germany, MV and Sandford could only finish the season in runner-up spot.

In 1954 Domenico Agusta tried to fill the gap left in his team by Graham's death and signed up Bill Lomas and Dickie Dale as well as a quartet of Italians, headed by Bandirola, to ride the fours. Engine performances had all been stepped up: 17 bhp at 10,800 rpm for the 125, 40 bhp at 11,000 rpm for the 350 and 65 bhp at 11,000 rpm for the 500, but Gilera, Moto Guzzi and the other opposition was too strong. The only successes that year were a 125cc victory

Carlo Ubbiali testing the latest version of the works double knocker 125 single at Monza, 11 March, 1954.

for Guido Sala in the Italian GP (but NSU had withdrawn from the race following Ruppert Hollaus's death in practice) and a 500cc win for Dale in Spain (but Gilera were not there, as they had already won the World Championship).

Better results followed in 1955. Out went Lomas and Dale, and in came Masetti and Ray Amm, the fabulous Rhodesian, for the big machine team. In also came Luigi Taveri, to join Ubbiali, Alfredo Copeta and Sala on the 125s. The 500 was now blessed with a five-speed gearbox and another 2 bhp. The 350 had also been given a boosted performance, while there was a new (63×69mm) version of the 125 to provide a 27 bhp machine of 203cc capacity for the 250cc class. It weighed only 210 lb and could be fitted with either a five-speed or six-speed gearbox. The 125 itself was virtually unchanged, but Ubbiali managed to win the World Championship with it. Germany's Hermann Müller took the 250cc title on an NSU Sportmax, not a works racer, although MV Agusta took the manufacturers' award for this class. The only 500cc victory for MV came in the Italian GP, won by Masetti, and Ray Amm had crashed in the 350cc race at Imola and been killed.

For 1956 Domenico Agusta engaged another famous British rider, John Surtees. He made a big contribution to the improvement of the four-cylinder machines, now producing 44 bhp and 68 bhp, respectively, on which he was teamed with Bandirola, Forconi and Masetti. For the 125cc classes there was a line-up of seven riders, headed by Ubbiali and Taveri. The 125 had been given a shade more power, while the 250 had been brought up to full size with 72.7mm×60mm bore and stroke and was now developing 32 bhp at 11,000 rpm. Winning all the World Championship

events except the German, where he had to give best to Romolo Ferri on the Gilera 'twin', Ubbiali took the 125cc title, making it a double by also becoming 250cc champion. John Surtees made a brilliant start to his partnership with MV Agusta by taking the 500cc title with victories in the Isle of Man, Holland and Belgium and by giving the '350' its first Grand Prix win on the fast Francorchamps circuit in Belgium.

At the beginning of 1957 Count Agusta took stock of the fact that Grand Prix racing is an expensive business — 'one million lire a day' he reckoned it was costing — and that he was up against some very powerful opposition. Moreover, the Italian home market for motorcycles and scooters was beginning to wane, while he was beginning to take an increasing interest in the manufacture of helicopters, under licence from the Bell company of America. So he started the ball rolling for a limitation of racing activity by inviting the other Italian factories to consider withdrawing official support for racing at the end of the season. That year was not a good one for MV Agusta. Not a single world or Italian championship title was gained, despite almost frantic efforts by his riders, especially

Team manager and ex-racer Nello Pagani trying out an Earles-forked MV four with experimental streamlining during 1955.

1956 175 Sport model. Drive to the ohc was by chain. Somehow the roadsters never fully captured the spirit of the racing models, but were nonetheless an important source of revenue for the Agusta company during the 1950s.

MV riders Hartle (4) and Surtees (2) lead the field during the 1958 350cc Italian GP. At the finish their positions were reversed. Surtees went on to become double world champion that year.

Ubbiali and Surtees. The power output of all the machines had been considerably increased and the 500 was by then producing 70 bhp, but this had brought little success. So, considering that 1957 had done little good for his factory, Count Agusta played one of his master-strokes. Having put up the proposition that the Italian manufacturers should retire from the sport (to which his rivals had agreed) he now decided to stay on in the game.

So the most dangerous adversaries would not be present in 1958, and he could recruit the fabulous Tarquinio Provini from the now-inactive FB Mondial team. The only opposition came in the 125cc class from the Ducati factory's new desmodromic machines, but Ubbiali was still able to win the World Championship for that class. Provini became 250cc Champion and John Surtees, with a phenomenal seven wins in seven starts for each class, notched a richly deserved 350cc/500cc double.

The following year saw a repetition of the factory's sweeping successes. The only change was that Ubbiali added the 250cc title to his 125cc, after a season of such persistent rivalry with team-mate Provini that it was no surprise when Tarquinio transferred to Morini for 1960. However, the rising Rhodesian star Gary Hocking earned himself a contract ride for MV Agusta in the Italian GP and for the following season!

Ubbiali dominated the 125cc class in 1960, Hocking the 250cc and Surtees the two big machine classes. Towards the end of the season Hocking also got permission to race a 350cc 'fire engine'. Having had such a successful year, Domenico Agusta now decided, for the same reasons as before, to do what he had wanted to do, and retire from full support for racing. That year he conceived the Privat-MV idea: 350cc and 500cc machines were given to Gary Hocking, who won the world titles with them. Similar experiments in the smaller classes were less successful, so the 125cc and 250cc Privat-MVs were very soon withdrawn. Similarly, the 350cc model was quickly withdrawn from circulation in 1962, as soon as it was seen that the new Hondas were faster. However, the four-cylinder 500 'fire engine' continued on its winning way with Hailwood aboard after Hocking quit two wheels for four after the TT that year. True to form Hailwood was the 1962 500cc world champion.

The following year, in spite of the challenge from Geoff Duke's Gilera team, MV and Hailwood took the title once more. It was also rumoured in 1963 that the factory were pressing ahead with development of new lightweight machines: a 250 four and a 125 twin. Bruno Spaggiari was the likely pilot, but these smaller bikes were never to appear in anger. In March 1964 MV set up a new One Hour Record at Daytona, with Mike Hailwood again the

John Surtees receiving the winner's trophy after his victorious ride in the 1958 500cc Spanish GP on 14 October, 1959, from Señora Franco, wife of the Spanish dictator.

rider. Hailwood once again took both the individual and manufacturers' titles for his class for the Verghera company.

1965 was a highly significant year, for not only did MV take the 500cc individual (Hailwood) and manufacturers' titles for the seventh year running, but they also introduced a new 343.9cc (52×54mm) dohc three-cylinder racer and signed the Italian Giacomo Agostini as a support rider. The company also tested its first two-stroke racer since the late 1940s, when Walter Villa put in a few practice laps at

Mike Hailwood cranks over his 500 MV four on the way to winning the Race of the Year at Mallory Park, 26 September, 1965.

Cesenatico in early May on a 125cc disc-valve single designed by the West German Peter Durr. But perhaps most interesting of all was the firm's show-stopper at the Milan Show held that November. This was a new prototype 591cc four-cylinder roadster. The new model was powered by a transverse four, with twin overhead camshafts, five-speed gearbox and shaft final drive. Two carburettors with siamesed induction stubs fed each pair of cylinders. The bore and stroke were 56×60mm, compression ratio 9:1 and 52 bhp at 9000 rpm was claimed. Observers wondered if the world would ever see a production version after what happened to the Milan Show prototype 500 roadster four of the early 1950s. But this time MV *did* get around to offering small numbers for sale over the next six years or so. Besides the awkward engine size, the '600' four was a heavyweight touring bike and perhaps the ugliest Italian bike of all time. This I am sure was Count Agusta's way of making sure nobody attempted a racing version! Also announced at the same time was a new 247cc (53×56mm), push-rod, parallel twin. This replaced the 160cc twin introduced two years earlier but not produced.

In 1966 Hailwood left to join Honda and was succeeded as number one rider by Agostini. The final result at the end of the year was that Ago became 500cc World Champion but MV lost the manufacturers' title in the same class to Honda. The following year, 1967, MV and Agostini once again won the 500cc title, MV's tenth successive win! They also regained the 500cc manufacturers' award. By now the company had won 25 world titles in 15 years and a total of 165 World Championship races, 70 of them in the Blue Ribband 500cc class.

1968 saw the first deliveries of the 250 twin roadster, which had appeared at the Milan Show in late 1965, whilst in racing MV gained its first TT Junior and Senior double victory and the 500cc world title — thanks to Agostini. It also recaptured the 350cc World Championship it had last held in 1961 and to cap a truly magnificent year it took both the 350 and 500cc manufacturers' titles.

In March 1969, Count Agusta's latest racer appeared. This was a 350 six reputed to rev to 16,000 and produce 70 bhp. A 500 version was also said to be in the development

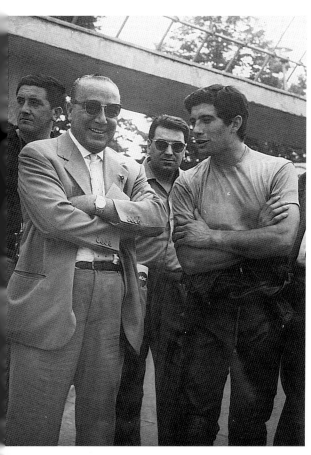

Giacomo Agostini succeeded Hailwood as team leader with MV. Here he chats to Count Domenico Agusta at the Italian GP, 3 September, 1967.

stage. However, again these projects never went beyond the prototype stage. Instead the year saw Agostini sweep all before him on his three-cylinder MV models, taking yet again the 350 and 500cc titles in both the individual and manufacturers' categories. On the production front a 'Street Scrambler' variant of the push-rod parallel twin made its bow, and at last Count Agusta relented and allowed his engineers to build a truly super sporting street racer, the 750S. This finally silenced those critics who had (rightly!) labelled the 600 four as staid, unexciting, or just plain ugly. By contrast the newcomer showed all the style, glamour and colour of the works GP racers. To achieve its 743cc capacity as opposed to the 600's 591.8cc, the cylinder bores of the 750S were increased to 65mm with the stroke remaining as before at 56mm. Higher compression three-ring forged Borgo pistons were used, with a ratio of 9.5:1. Carburation was again by 24mm Dell 'Orto instruments, but now they were four instead of two. Overall though its state of tune remained relatively low, with a maximum power output of 65 bhp at 7900 rpm. Making up for this

was the engine's high level of flexibility, which was outstanding compared to other multi-cylinder designs of the era. In typical Italian fashion of the early 1970s the 750S possessed a real Jekyll and Hyde character. The *Motorcyclist Illustrated Road Test Annual* summed it up thus: 'Its paint and chrome finish is poor, the electrical controls stupidly inadequate, but with the soul of a grand prix machine as well as the basic requirements of a fast roadster, the MV has, at grass-root level, a quality denied to almost any other machine. I will never agree to its generally lauded sophisticated or even civilized achievements. Its attraction lies wholly in its raw, almost crude, appeal of pure speed suitability. Perhaps the one word that sums it up is sensuality.'

The 1971 MV model line comprised 125 and 150cc singles in touring and sport form, 250 and 350cc twins in touring, sport and street scrambler guise, 600cc four tourer and the 750S sportster. The same year also saw the death in Milan, from a heart attack, of Count Domenico Agusta. Whilst MV rider Angelo Bergamonti was fatally injured racing at Riccione, Agostini once again dominated. By then his constant wins were beginning to bore the crowds. Almost everyone wanted to see the master beaten. But like the great professional he was, he continued to break records. In the 350cc title chase the talented Finnish rider Jarno Saarinen began to prove something of a menace, winning two Grands Prix in which Agostini either did not ride or did not finish and came second in the championship. Agostini also became the rider with the greatest number of titles with ten, overtaking Ubbiali and Hailwood, who each had nine.

In 1972 Ago took MV to their 15th successive 500cc world championship, with Alberto Pagani, signed as replacement for Bergamonti, taking second place. Their speeds, however, were often lower than those in the 350 class, in which Agostini found the going the most difficult since the withdrawal of Honda and Hailwood's retirement. At the first two rounds MV and Agostini were humiliated by the talent of Saarinen; at the Nürburgring the 'Flying Finn' beat the MV rider into second place, but worse was to follow in France with Agostini down in fourth spot. This prompted MV to build a new machine with which to counter the Yamaha threat, and so keep the title in Italy. The year saw Phil Read have his first rides for the Verghera concern, including a win in the 350cc East German GP at the Sachsenring. October 1972 saw Gus Kuhn Motors of 275 Clapham Road, London SW9, become the British importers. Five models were initially brought in: 250S, 350GT, 350S, 750GT and 750S. With a price tag of £2175, the 750S was the most expensive machine on the British market. When one realizes that a Honda 750 four was

Agostini on the new 500 three-cylinder model leads Pagani (Linto) and Stasa (CZ) during the Czech Grand Prix, 20 July, 1969.

around £800 at the time, the MV was clearly only for the extremely well heeled.

The first real effects of Count Agusta's death began to show themselves in 1973, when the Italian government effectively took control of the Agusta group with a 51 per cent share stake in the previously wholly family-owned enterprise. Much of this was due to the amount of capital needed to fund the long-term development of military helicopters, which were by now Agusta's main source of revenue. It is difficult to say if this would have happened had Domenico still been at the helm, but what is certain from subsequent events, the Count would most certainly have fiercely resisted the gradual rundown of the motorcycle side, at least the racing division. All this was not evident to the public at the time, as Phil Read had been signed for 1973, and together with Agostini dominated the Grand Prix scene once again. It must be said, however, that things might have turned out very different that year if Saarinen had not been killed at Monza in May. As it was Read took the 500 championship, Agostini the 350.

1974 was to prove a decisive year in MV Agusta's history. First Agostini left the company on which he had built his success for the Japanese Yamaha firm. This meant that the Englishman Phil Read was now MV's premier rider; he was joined by new signing Gianfranco Bonera.

With Agostini's departure MV pulled out of the 350cc class, concentrating its efforts on the Blue Riband 500cc category. This paid off, with Read taking the title, but only after a titanic struggle for much of the season with his former team-mate. Read ended the season with four classic victories, one of which was in the Belgian GP at Spa, where he set an absolute lap record at over 134 mph. It was also the company's 17th consecutive 500cc class victory in Belgium. Most significant of all, it was to be the last ever world championship title for the legendary marque. From then on it was largely downhill all the way in racing, with the only notable events being Read's gallant but ultimately unsuccessful attempt to retain his 500cc world title in 1975, when, although he won three races, the championship went to Agostini and Yamaha. The same year saw MV team manager Arturo Magni celebrate 25 years' service with the factory.

The following year MV quit racing on an official basis, but in a very strange set of circumstances Agostini rode 'privately' entered MVs backed by the Italian oil company Api. But although the company was not supposed to be taking a direct interest, there was still a full team of MV mechanics *and* a new 350 four! Although very fast the new bike was also, at least to start with, unreliable. It did score a sensational victory in the Dutch TT at Assen, MV's first

An array of MV models on the Gus Kuhn stand at the Sporting and Racing Show in London during January 1973. Left: 750GT; background 350 Sport; foreground 750S

New 350 Sport parallel twin, this is the original prototype first shown at Milan in Italy in November 1973.

350cc win since the Finnish GP back in 1973. Agostini also stunned the critics with a superb victory in the very last round of the 500cc championship at the Nürburgring, West Germany. British enthusiasts were to see Agostini and Read for the last time at Brands Hatch and Cadwell Park that autumn. Any more racing was barred by the accountants, who now effectively controlled the Agusta group's purse strings. For a time observers felt that Count Corrado Agusta might sponsor the race effort out of his own pocket, but this proved wishful thinking.

Had MV continued they might have used the 500cc flat-four boxer engine designed by Ing. Bocchi, who had joined MV in 1974 after posts at a number of Italian car companies, including Ferrari and Lamborghini. But again this is none too clear as another faction headed by team manager Arturo Magni preferred a more conventional flat-four with all the cylinders facing forward. In contrast to the new management's lack of interest in racing, they attempted to push ahead at full speed with the standard production motorcycles. The first 'new' model to make an appearance was a totally revised 350 Sport, which was displayed on the company's stand at the Milan Show in November 1973. Compared with the original model the newcomer had much more angular lines and a GT version followed later. Another move was into the American market, where MV hoped to sell a considerable number of its four-cylinder models. With this in mind, and following a meeting with a couple of American businessmen, the Italian factory decided to launch a new model appropriately named the 750 America (although the capacity had been upped to 790cc, 67×56mm). Finally came the 125 Sport, and if looks alone sold motorcycles the 1976 MV 125 Sport would have sold thousands; as it was its looks hid a rather lacklustre push-rod motor, and sales were never more than a trickle. All these machines used engines which were largely redesigns of the original units, a 124cc (63×56.2mm) ohv single, 349cc (63×56.2mm) ohv twin and 790cc (67×56mm) dohc four. All the range had five-speed gearboxes and multi-plate wet clutches, with wet sump lubrication.

The company also actively sought importers in various countries, Britain included. As early as late 1975 the

Final version of the four-cylinder racer, circa 1976. By then the two-strokes had the upper hand.

850 Monza (Boxer) on show at Earls Court, 1977. The machine was originally given the Boxer title, but protests from car makers Ferrari soon led to it being dropped in favour of Monza. This was the final production model from the Gallarate factory.

Coburn and Hughes enterprise, which already handled Ducati and Moto Guzzi, had talks at Verghera. But these came to nothing for C & H considered the prices too high. By December 1976 a new company headed by Peter Bate (his family then owned a large Saab dealership) was formed to handle MVs in the British Isles. The original importer, Gus Kuhn, had quit a couple of years before. Agusta Concessionaires (GB) Ltd were based at Beaconsfield Road, Farnham Common, Slough, Bucks, and initially they brought in two models, the 350S and 750 America.

The Motor Cycle tested both machines in their 26 February, 1977, issue and were impressed with both, with the test headlines reading: 'Harmony and speed from the MV 350S', and 'The Mighty America – class and charisma.' As tested both machines had the optional fairings; the 350 attained a best one-way speed of 106.4 mph, while the larger bike went through the electronic eye at 122.1 mph. If speeds were reasonable, prices certainly were not. As tested the 350 was £1412.40 (including the fairing at £113.40), whilst the 750 America cost a whopping £3,764.74. The fairing and cast alloy wheels cost £577.74. For a while everything looked from the outside to be going according to plan, but in reality sales never reached anything like the targets set by Agusta's financial parents, the governmental EFIM (Ente Finanziaria per le Industrie Metalmeccaniche) financial agency. During this period Luigi Ghisleri was the man in charge of MV's production side, with former Ducati director Fredmano Spairani

looking after the racing department. During 1977 even the production side began to be actively pruned back and the space formerly devoted to two-wheel activities turned over to helicopter manufacture. Motorcycle production finally came to a halt during 1978, but by then several key figures, including the long-serving Arturo Magni, had departed the scene.

Over the next few months several organizations, including the British importers and the wealthy Cagiva factory, attempted to purchase the rights to the MV Agusta name with plans to re-launch the marque, but ultimately nothing happened, because at the end of the day Agusta itself had not closed down, but only decided to concentrate its efforts upon the much more lucrative helicopter side of the business. The Agusta management feared that another company might tarnish MV's reputation.

In 1985 some of the famous racers were sold off to the American Team Obsolete, a group of classic racing enthusiasts, but the rest still remained under lock and key in the Agusta Museum in nearby Gallarate, perhaps a fitting tribute to the marque which could truly claim to have been the most successful ever in the history of motorcycle racing. In 25 years MV Agusta won 38 individual World Championships, 37 manufacturers' world championships and an incredible 270 Grand Prix races counting towards Championship points. Amongst its riders had been the very cream, including Graham, Ubbiali, Provini, Surtees, Hocking, Hailwood, Agostini and Read.

CHAPTER 18

Parilla

Giovanni Parrilla was the son of a Spanish family who emigrated to southern Italy in the 1920s and during the Second World War Giovanni had found himself a new home in the north, that industrial heartland, Milan, where he started up a small business specializing in the repair of agricultural diesel injectors and pumps.

At the end of hostilities much of the northern part of the country, including Milan, was left in a shattered state. Giovanni Parrilla was not only to prove himself a capable engineer, but a successful businessman in the immediate post-war era, because it was from his tiny Milan workshop facility in 1946 that he set out on the path which was to lead to fame, if not eventual wealth. With such humble beginnings the growth of Parilla (the second 'r' was dropped from the trading title), was truly sensational given its creator's lack of backing (unlike others such as Guzzi, Ducati or MV, for example).

Giovanni Parrilla's first motorcycle was a single overhead cam 247cc, which made its début as a racer in October 1946. This was very soon developed into the company's first production roadster, which created a lot of publicity in the Italian press when it was launched the following year. The reason for this huge outcry was simple; here was a brand new *real* bike amongst a horde of cheap and cheerful two-stroke commuters. Parrilla's concept was a thoroughbred sportster and, unlike the few other proper motorcycles, was not a rehash of a pre-war effort like the offerings from firms such as Guzzi or Gilera. This production sports roadster produced 17 bhp at 7250 rpm, a class-leading performance at the time which equated to almost 80 mph out on the road. Other features included unit construction, plunger rear suspension and leading axle telescopic front forks.

If the production machine caused excitement, the updated racing version which followed later that year caused a sensation, for Italians are in any case more than keen on anything which goes fast and performs on the race circuit. The newcomer did both and it also sounded superb with its deep, mellow note from the chromed, shallow taper megaphone which extended way back almost beyond the rear wheel. Besides the all-powerful Guzzi Albatros, no other production-based quarter-litre racer could compete on equal terms, certainly not an Italian in 1947. Power

output from the 66×72mm engine (dimensions it shared with its road-going brother) was a healthy 18.5 bhp at 7500 rpm. Dry weight was 98kg. The finish was in bright Italian racing red.

The company made an appearance at the local Milan Show at the end of November 1947. *Motor Cycling* had this to say about their effort: 'Another stand that was never without its crowd was the Parilla stand. This is a new firm specializing in racing and competition machines.' The journal went on to say 'beautifully finished in detail and with the largest brake drums that I think I've ever seen − 260×30mm. An example of the careful thought that has gone into its detail is the way in which the breather tubes from the gearbox and the oil tank are carried out to the very rear tip of the rear mudguard.'

A year later the Milan Show witnessed the launch of a completely new roadster and a double overhead cam version of the well-established racer. Both designs were the work of the designer Giuseppe Salmaggi, who had earlier been responsible for the creation of the Gilera Saturno. The roadster was Parilla's first two-stroke. The single-cylinder unit construction engine had a capacity of 248.9cc (65×75mm) and its flat top piston ran in a cast-iron cylinder. The alloy cylinder head featured a bronze insert for the 14mm spark plug. Lubrication was by petroil mixture at a ratio of 20:1. A form of rotary valve was used and the carburettor hidden from view under the offside outer crankcase cover. The gearbox was a four-speeder with foot operation and had its own separate oil compartment. Primary drive was by duplex chain.

Unlike previous Parillas, the rear suspension relied upon torsional coil springs at the pivot of the swinging arm, while there were girder forks up front. The wheels were interchangeable. These featured full-width light alloy hubs and 3.00×19 tyres. Finish was in a dark metallic grey, relieved with blue. Compared to the four-stroke models, the newcomer was much less sophisticated, but had the advantage of being considerably cheaper to produce and sell.

The other bike, the *Bialbeiro* (double cam), which contrasted sharply with the austerely packaged two-stroke, was to prove both successful and reliable for its intended purpose, road racing at national and international level.

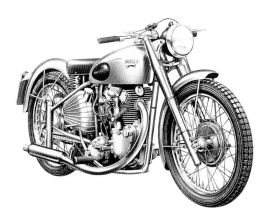

Giovanni Parrilla's first motorcycle was a single overhead cam 247cc, which made its début as a racer in October 1946. The following year this was developed into the 250 Sport production model.

Like the earlier version, the design of the Parilla Bialbeiro engine was not only particularly neat but also sturdy. The sleeved light alloy cylinder barrel was deeply spigoted into the unit construction vertically split crankcases. To save weight these were constructed from Electron. The vertical drive (like the sohc version) was by shaft and bevel gears operating by means of pinion gears, the inlet and exhaust camshafts. Each of these was supported by a roller bearing at the drive end and a ball race at the other. The cams themselves actuated the valves through flat top tappets, while the valve springs were of the hairpin type and left exposed.

The cambox was separate from the cylinder head, Manx Norton style. The top pair of camshaft bevels also drove the rev counter from a specially cast cover which housed the drive gears. A train of five gears joined the camshafts together with the driven bevels. The camshaft gears featured a peg-and-hole vernier arrangement for timing and shafts. A train of gears driven from a spur gear outboard of the camshaft bevel on the crankshaft drove the oil pump. Ignition was by a magneto mounted forward of the cylinder barrel atop the crankcase and actuated a single 14mm spark plug located in the nearside of the head. Although the compression ratio was a lowly 7.8:1 the forged, three-ring Borgo piston was still highly domed. The con-rod was a superb piece of workmanship, being double webbed for extra strength at both top and bottom. A caged roller big-end was employed together with a large-diameter crankpin, this being retained in the crankshaft flywheel by a pair of equally large nuts. Primary drive was taken care of by straight-cut gears directly on to the clutch drum, which in turn drove a close-ratio four-speed gearbox. A separate selector box was mounted on the offside of the engine unit and could be removed for any work that was needed. Lubrication by castor-based oil was of the dry sump variety, the lubricant itself being housed in

The work of the famous designer Ing. Salmaggi, Parilla introduced this new 249cc roadster in November 1947. It was the company's first two-stroke.

a finned tank aft of the massive remote float Dell 'Orto racing carburettor.

Where the double-knocker Parilla really scored was in producing effective power over a very wide range from 3500 rpm up to a maximum of 9000 rpm. In changing from single to double overhead camshafts the biggest improvement was not in maximum rpm, but in the fact that the power did not fall off as quickly after peak power rpm. Incidentally, much of the engine testing was done on the road, quite often public roads! In 1949 guise, the 250 Parilla single was capable of a genuine 100 mph for the first time. The running gear of the 1949 racer followed (as did the engine) much of that used by the earlier single overhead cam model. In other words there was a loop-type welded frame with single front down tube. Rear suspension, although of the swinging fork type, employed one compression spring in each plunger housing with the lower half of the piston used as a pneumatic rebound control. In addition there were conventional period Italian friction dampers with large adjusting knobs.

Although some of the earlier single overhead cam racers had used girders, the majority employed telescopics, and these were standardized for the Bialbeiro. These were not of the hydraulic type, however, but the far more primitive type using a plain spring fork with cone dampers and hand-adjustable dampers on top of each leg. Other interesting features of these bikes were the wide use of alloys, including both fuel and oil tanks, wheel rims, brake hubs and even sprockets. Strangely though, the mudguards were in heavier steel. The massive 10in. brakes are not fully evident from the illustrations, simply because of the 21in. rims (which were fitted with 2.75 section tyres). For 1950 a 350 version made its entry. This was a bored-out 250; with 30 bhp available it offered a superior power to weight ratio, but in practice it was not as successful as the smaller bike. The first race for the 350 was at Marseilles in the hands of the 1949 125cc World Champion Nello Pagani. Although showing a fair turn of speed, reported to be around 110 mph, this first outing ended with a sheared camshaft drive.

It was in Germany that the 250/350 Parilla singles were to really make their mark. In the spring of 1950 Roland Schnell, later to win fame with the Horex company, purchased a pair of Parillas to be ridden by Hermann Gablenz. In practice both Schnell and Gablenz put together a string of racing successes with these machines over the next couple of seasons. One of the first came on 4 May, 1950, at Hockenheim, where Gablenz narrowly missed out on victory in the 250 race because of mechanical problems. Just over a month later, on 11 June, the same rider made amends when, at the Nürburgring in front of an amazing

330,000 crowd, he brought his Italian machine home behind the super-quick privately entered Guzzi Albatros of winner Thorn-Pikker and the factory DKW twin of Siegfried Wünsche in the 85-mile 250 race. This three-cornered scrap was to be repeated throughout the long hot summer of 1950 in German events.

The following year both Gablenz and Schnell did even better with their Parillas, witnessed by the important Eilenriede-Rennen held at Hanover on 29 April. Here Gablenz won the 250 race, averaging 72.3 mph, from his arch rivals Thorn-Pikker and Wünsche. And to make it a real Parilla benefit Schnell won the 350 race from Baltisberger and Knees, both on AJS 7Rs. Schnell averaged 77.6 mph, with a fastest lap of 79.2 mph. Gablenz managed 73.7 mph on the smaller bike. Although neither Gablenz or Schnell achieved any real success in the classics that year they did venture abroad, with Gablenz taking victory in Madrid with the larger bike.

By now they had considerably modified their mounts and not just in the engine department. The major change

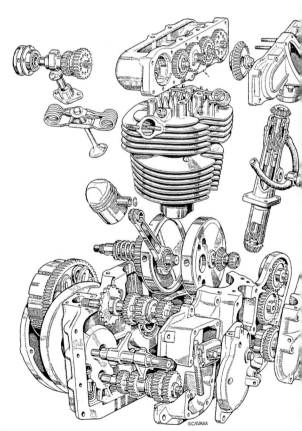

Exploded view of the 1949 dohc 250 racing engine. It never achieved the success of its main rival, the horizontal single-cylinder Guzzi Albatros.

Only built in prototype form the 1977 Laverda V6 was timed at 180 mph during the classic French Bol d'Or 24 Hours race.

The Laverda Montjuic 500 twin. Although these were usually finished in orange, British dealers, Lloyd Brothers, marketed a very attractive special edition in black and gold.

Angel Nieto with his Minarelli in the 125cc race at the 1978 British Grand Prix.

Another photograph from the 1978 British Grand Prix: Mario Lega in the 250cc race with his Morbidelli twin.

Bill Lomas with the 1957 Moto Guzzi V8 at the 1981 Surtees Day at Brands Hatch.

Giacomo Agostini with the 500cc MV Agusta 'four' at Bray Hill in the 1970 Isle of Man TT Senior race.

Expensive when new, the 1972 MV Agusta 750S; the asking price for a machine in first class condition is now £25,000.

The 1984 Moto Morini 500cc *Camell* marketed as the *Sahara* in the United Kingdom). It was a lively performer both on and off the road.

The most successful double knocker Parillas were those tuned by the German Roland Schell, who, together with Hermann Gablenz, put together a string of successes during 1950 and 1951. Photograph shows Gablenz winning the 350 class at Madrid in 1951.

was fitting stronger front forks and converting the rear suspension to full swinging arm with adjustable multi-rate dampers. The only Parilla rider to score points in the 1951 World Championships was the Italian Nino Grieco at the Swiss GP opener over the Bremgarten circuit with a sixth place in the 250 race. Although Gablenz scored an impressive win at the unofficial German GP in 1951, it was not until 1952 that Germany got back its classic status, when the event was staged at Solitude. By then Schnell and Gablenz had sold their stable of Parilla machines and begun their association with Horex. This was after the final Schnell development, which gave the Parilla a six-speed gearbox.

Back on the production front the 1949 Milan Show had seen a brand new 98cc two-stroke roadster appear on the scene. Unlike the larger 'stroker, this was of extremely modern appearance, with not only telescopic forks but full swinging-arm rear suspension. The four-speed gearbox was controlled by a left-hand twist-grip in the style of the Vespa and Lambretta scooters. From this was developed a very successful 125 version, which soon became the company's best-selling model.

The year 1950 saw the Italian two-wheel industry continue to boom in a most promising fashion, but even better was to come. Italian registrations of motorcycles, three-wheelers, scooters and cyclemotors reached record figures in 1951, amounting to a total of 1,112,500 — more than 400,000 up on 1950!

Obviously buoyed by this healthy state of the market, Parilla had decided the time was right for expansion and new models. These were launched at the Milan Show, which that year had been 'delayed' until mid-January 1952. The most exciting newcomer was a prestigious 350 parallel twin four-stroke. With an exact capacity of 348cc (62×58), it had separate cylinder heads (in light alloy) and separate cylinders (in iron). Interestingly the cylinder heads featured side exhausts, like the similar Gilera design which appeared later. The single camshaft was housed at the rear of the vertically split crankcases and each push-rod had its own separate tunnel at the rear of the cylinder castings. Primary drive to the four-speed foot-operated gearbox was by duplex chain. The tubular frame featured swinging arm rear and telescopic front fork suspension, the latter sporting rubber gaiters. Other details in the comprehensive specification included wet sump lubrication, full unit construction, conical brake hubs laced to 19in. alloy wheel rims, coil and battery ignition, touring bars and a sprung single saddle.

For 1951 the ISDT was held in Italy, based around the town of Varese in the north. A works Parilla entry was ridden by Britain's Olga Kevelos, who was the only woman among 221 entrants. This ride came about through Count 'Johnny' Lurani, the Italian FIM boss, who had introduced Olga to Signor Parrilla, who had immediately offered the Englishwoman one of his newly introduced 125 two-strokes. Interviewed recently, Olga Kevelos remembers the Parilla as, 'A great little bike, so much easier for me to handle day after day'. Previously she had ridden the much heavier British four-stroke singles, such as the 350 AJS and 500 Norton. Unfortunately, on the fourth day of the trial she was involved in an incident where the Parilla disappeared over the edge of a mountain road. It was totally wrecked and its rider left bruised and battered. However, grateful as he was for the publicity which had been accrued before the accident Giovanni Parrilla not only paid her a bonus but gave Olga a gold watch to make up for the gold medal that she might have won.

The following year, when the event was held in nearby Austria, Parilla again participated at factory level in the ISDT. This time there were both 125 and 150 two-stroke singles. Road-racer Nino Grieco was a member of the five-man Trophy Squad on his 150 Parilla, but both he and Olga Kevelos, again on a Parilla, retired on day two.

The end of 1952 saw the début, again at the Milan Show, of the unorthodox 175 Fox, a high-camshaft model, in which the valves operated through short splayed push-rods with the nearside of the engine being the timing side. With a capacity of 174cc, the engine dimensions were very slightly long stroke with a bore of 59.8mm and a stroke of 62mm. As mentioned the actual valve operation was by means of the ultra-short inclined push-rods from a single chain-driven cam, mounted at the top of the timing case, and this was kept in adjustment by a Weller-type tensioner. The valve included angle was 90 degrees. The four-speed gearbox had ratios of 7.5, 9.8, 14 and 29 to 1, with primary drive by helical gears. The 7:1 compression piston had four rings (two compression, two oil scraper). The pressed-up crankshaft featured a caged roller big-end and phospor bronze small-end, tappet adjustment was by a simple screw and locknut method and valve springs were of the coil variety. The gearchange and kickstart levers were both situated on the offside (right) of the machine. All this added up to 9 bhp at 6800 rpm and 65 mph out on the road.

The 'high-cam' concept was also seen by Parilla as the way for its racing efforts to go. And these, together with the roadsters, were largely the work of two men, Giuseppe Salmaggi and his younger assistant, Alfredo Bianchi (who later went to Aermacchi and was responsible for the Chimera and other flat singles from the Varese marque—see Chapter 1). Known in Italy as *camme rialzata* (lifted camshaft), the first prototype 'high-cam' works racer made its début at the *Gran Premio delle Nazioni* at Monza in September 1952. In this engine the cam drive tower was on the opposite side to all the subsequent racing *and* street Parilla models employing the high-cam principle. This design never went beyond the experimental stage, becoming the basis for a 125cc dohc single-cylinder Grand Prix racing prototype the following year. On this bike the camshaft drive had been relocated (as on the production Fox) to the nearside of the engine and utilized a triangular chain drive to the twin camshafts. This project was soon aborted.

In 1953, a second 250cc Bialbeiro works bike appeared. This was equipped with an Earles-type front fork assembly, similar to that used on several MV racers of the era. Piloted by regular Parilla jockey Nino Grieco this model, which featured a petrol tank with built-in fairing wrapped around the steering head, was only destined to race a couple of times. Alongside this works bike, a production 'over-the-counter' racer was built and offered for sale during 1953 and 1954. Called the 175 Competizione it only employed a single camshaft, yet still used the Earles fork from its senior brother. The American journal *Cycle* tested the first batch of Parillas to reach the States, including one of the Competizione boy racers. *Cycle* tester Bob Schanz was generally impressed, finding the bike fast on speed and acceleration and 'the fastest-stopping machine that *Cycle* has tested'. As delivered the Competizione came knitted out with clip-ons, rear-sets and alloy rims, but still with lights and silencer. Like the 175 roadsters, the bore and stroke were 59.8×62mm. Running on an 8:1 compression ratio, power output was 17 bhp at 9500 rpm, red lining at 9800 rpm and the power was delivered via a close-ratio four-speed box. The cam drive of the Competizione was different from the production roadster chain and for the racing model the camshaft was operated by a series of straight-cut gears. According to sources close to the factory the reason for this was that early high-cam engines had problems with chain tension, resulting in chains coming adrift. Even so the gear drive was much more expensive and not completely foolproof. Later on a modified design for cam chain tension largely rectified the problem and made gear drive unnecessary. The American importers then were Joe Berliner and Ernest Wise. At the time *Cycle* reported that 'twenty-five Competiziones were then in the United States and more are

Riding a works 125 Parilla two-stroke Britain's Olga Kevelos was the only woman among 221 entrants when the ISDT started on 18 September, 1951, based at Varese, Italy. She was forced out through an accident on the fourth day.

Another newcomer was the *Levriere* (Greyhound), a 153cc (60×54mm) two-stroke scooter with an engine closely related to the latest 150cc class motorcycle from the Milanese concern.

In a road test carried out by *The Motor Cycle* in their 7 April, 1955, issue, maximum speed was found to be 51 mph and unlike the Parilla motorcycles at that time there was a British importer. This was G. Nannucci of 58 Newman Street, London W1. Notable features of the *Levriere* were a four-speed gearbox with foot control by rocking pedal, Dell 'Orto MB22A carburettor, dual seat and Pirelli 3.00×12 tyres. The wheels themselves were built up with motorcycle-type spokes and alloy rims − unlike the usual scooter practice of pressed-steel bolted-up assemblies. The British price was £115 including purchase tax and the only listed extra was a windscreen at £4 10s. 10d. Finish was in beige.

The same month as *The Motor Cycle* test, Parilla announced that it would be entering a new 175 double-knocker sports machine in the Giro d'Italia. The prototype of this bike was shown to journalists at the Milan Industrial Fair which opened on 12 April. At the time a company spokesman said that its maximum speed was 94 mph. Called the 175 Sport Competizione Bialbeiro, this was the work of Ing. Salmaggi and can be considered as the last of the true Parilla works racers. Only a very small number (exact quantity unknown) of these were built and aimed at bringing the factory success in the important Italian Formula 2 racing class, which specified the use of production crankcases and very little else. Many F2 bikes of the era were in fact little more than full works racers with lighting equipment, and this was only fitted because in several cases the Giro d'Italia and Milano−Taranto long-distance events included night work. Compared to the customer Competizione models, the pukka racer had lots of differences besides its double overhead camshaft head. There were exposed hairpin valve springs, a remote float 27mm Dell 'Orto SS1 racing carburettor, a gearbox which sported five instead of four ratios and a dry sump lubrication system with a large oil tank mounted just in front of the rear wheel. Even the frame was different. This had two lower members to cradle the engine and twin front down tubes. Unlike the 'over-the-counter' Competizione, the Bialbeiro had 30mm telescopic front forks. The racing brakes had come from the abortive 125 GP bike. Of the three or four probably built only one of the 175 works double-knocker F2 bikes is known to exist. Currently this is owned by Italian Gianni Petrone, who is reputed to have located it in Sicily a few years ago in remarkably good condition. That so few were built is probably because, in its intended role, the F2 bike was just not competitive enough

on the way'. Recently interviewed, however, Wise stated: 'It was an exaggeration. Only five or six of both bikes (Competiziones and Turismos) ever came to the country at the time. They were given out to magazines for tests and later there were plans to race them. Who knows where the bikes went.'

Meanwhile, back in Italy the 1954 Milan Show had seen the introduction of the 49cc (38×44mm) Parillino. This was a two-stroke, three-speed moped in either Turismo or Sport specification. This meant a power output of 1.3 and 1.7 bhp respectively. Later a four-stroke version, still of 49cc, but 40×39mm, made an appearance. Both the two-stroke and four-stroke cylinders were inclined almost vertically. A brochure of the period proclaimed, 'The maximum production capacity is of more than 100 units per day − one Parillino 4-stroke, 3 gears each 5 minutes'.

There was much excitement in the Parilla camp when the company introduced this 350 parallel twin to an unexpecting press corps at the Milan Show, January 1952.

against the even more expensive and specialized machinery from the larger factories.

Although the 1955 Milan Show did not see anything startlingly new from Parilla, nonetheless the company had its largest display of different machinery ever, the main line-up consisting of no less than 16 models, ranging from 49 to 349cc. The full list comprised Turismo and Sport versions of both the two-stroke and ohv 49cc engines and a 98cc push-rod motorcycle, the *Fauno* (Fawn). This was capable of 50 mph and came into the tourist rather than sport category. Then came a quartet of two-strokes, three of 150cc, one 125cc. The smaller-engined bike was the Turismo Speciale, a long-running model which was based on the ISDT bikes of a few years previously. The trio of larger two-strokes were divided into three distinct categories: basic commuter (Turismo Speciale), racer style (Sport) and de luxe − the last-named was the interesting *Bracco* (Gun-dog). Although still a motorcycle this was obviously meant to appeal to someone wanting scooter-type comfort and protection, with its wide 16in. tyres, comprehensive deeply valanced mudguarding, leg shields and footboards. It also came equipped with a built-in parcel carrier mounted above the rear mudguard. Maximum speed was 56 mph (the same figure for the Turismo Speciale), while the Sport was good for 65 mph.

The *Levriere* scooter had been changed in minor detail, and now came with separate seats, whitewall tyres and a series of protection grilles for the formerly exposed middle section of the rear wheel. A series of extras was now offered for the Parilla scooter: rear number plate holder with built-in direction indicators, spare wheel, chromed luggage rack, chromed front bumper, chromed tubular framework for front shield and a chromed disc for spare wheel.

Next came five 175s: Turismo Specials, Lusso Veloce, Sport, Gran Sport (Derivato Serie), which effectively replaced the earlier Earles-forked Competizione, and the works Sport Competizione dohc racer. Finally the Gran Turismo 350 twin, which had seen very few changes since its début four years earlier, except minor styling changes, more vertical rear shock mounting, new silencers and a dual seat to replace the original sprung single saddle.

During mid-1956 an agreement was reached with the German manufacturer Victoria whereby the Milan company would supply quantities of the 175 high-cam engine for fitment into Victoria machines. These were

Cover of a special booklet which Parilla produced when it launched the Slughi 99 at the 1957 Milan Show. In concept and appearance the machine bore a striking resemblance to the Aermacchi Chimera, which had appeared a year before.

displayed at the Frankfurt Show held in October that year. Unfortunately this plan was doomed to ultimate failure due to the crumbling state of the German motorcycle industry at that time. At the Milan Show a month later the Parilla stand had nothing new, even though its rivals such as Ducati, Aermacchi, MV and Demm all had brand new machinery, but Parilla could at least take heart that its high-cam range was selling well both at home and abroad.

1957 saw Parilla achieve success in the nine-stage 1277-mile Giro d'Italia held from 6-14 April, when works-supported rider Giuseppe Rottigni won the 175 Production class with a Gran Sport. Rottigni's victory came under the MSDS (*Macchina Sport derivata dalle Serie*). This was a homologated production formula introduced in 1956 to keep out the pukka racing Formula 2 bikes. Rottigni's average speed for the whole distance was a respectable 60.78 mph. Out of the original 240 riders at the start in Bologna, only 100 finished.

Later that year one of the surprises of the Milan Show was the unorthodox *Slughi* (Desert Greyhound) 99. The work of Ing. Piero Bossaglia (both Salmaggi and Bianchi had left the company by then), the original concept called for a choice of two- and four-stroke engines, both of 98cc capacity. However, when the machine finally reached production during 1959, only a four-stroke was available in the original capacity. Later 125s in *both* two- and four-stroke versions were offered. The basis of the design was a fabricated pressed-steel backbone extending to form the base for the dual seat and rear mudguard. The horizontal engine was suspended from the backbone and detachable steel panels covered the sides of the power unit and continued rearwards beyond the hub. Movement of the tubular rear fork was controlled by a rubber block

concealed inside the frame backbone. In concept and appearance the machine bore a very striking resemblance to the Aermacchi Chimera, which had been the star of the 1956 Milan Show, even to the point of having a horizontal unit construction, four-speed, push-rod engine! Additionally, the Aermacchi Chimera had been designed by no less than Ing. Bianchi, who had previously worked for Parilla.

At least the Parilla design had the advantage of appealing to the commuter-type customer and so avoiding the poor sales performances, which was the fate of the Aermacchi bike. Additionally the major disadvantage of the Chimera, lack of decent weather protection, was looked after on the *Slughi* by the availability of elegant *and* efficient legshields and a large windshield, both of which could be fitted quickly. In any case, later on the majority of Slughi models came with the leg shields as standard equipment. Another major feature was the lockable hinged dual seat which gave access to the fuel filler cap and a useful storage cavity. The only drawback to this was fuel vapours escaping from the filler cap breather which tended to accumulate in the recess, so risking contamination of any luggage which might have been carried there. The engine on this first Slughi variant had a bore and stroke of 52×46mm, giving a capacity of 97.7cc. The maximum power of 6.5 bhp was produced at 7200 rpm. A four-ring piston gave a compression ratio of 7.2:1. Primary drive was by gears, with a multi-plate wet clutch and four-speed gearbox. Carburation was taken care of by a Dell 'Orto UA16BS instrument. Other details included a 6-volt 30-watt flywheel magneto, semi-hydraulic telescopic forks,

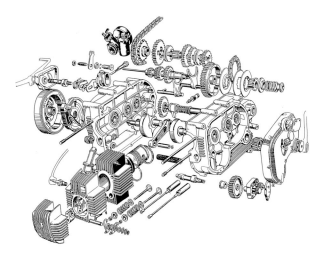

Details of the 97.7cc ohv engine used in the Slughi. Later a larger 125 two-stroke-engined version was also offered.

2.50×17 tyres, full-width brake hubs, a 6-litre fuel tank and a dry weight of 78kg.

When tested by Italian journalist Carlo Perelli for *Motor Cycle News* in October 1959, the Slughi 99 attained a maximum speed of 53 mph, while by adding the factory legshields and screen and with a pillion passenger, top speed dropped to 48 mph. Perelli also found that even under full throttle treatment fuel consumption never dropped below the 125 mpg mark. A criticism concerned the poor lights with the flywheel magneto, but there was an optional battery system which improved night navigation considerably.

The spring of 1958 saw the introduction of a new ohv 125 'Street Scrambler' intended for the American market, and a more conventional roadster version. And although the Milan Show was now a bi-annual affair, which meant no event at the end of that year, this did not stop Parilla making a considerable effort with several new or improved models for the 1959 season. Brand new were the two Olimpia models, essentially conventional motorcycles (except for an unusual frame) using some components (including the engine) from the Slughi, which itself was now available with a 125 (114cc actually) two-stroke power unit in addition to the 98cc ohv engine. The 125 and 175 Specials were sports roadsters derived from the earlier 124cc ohv and 174cc high cam models. A new larger-capacity Street Scrambler was added. The 175 Derivato MSDS was a Formula 3 racer with a top speed a shade over 90 mph − and a straight-through exhaust pipe. The 350 Gran Turismo twin, which had received yet another face-lift, including full-width brake hubs, was continued, together with the Parillino mopeds. And although the Levriere scooter survived, the 125/150 two-stroke motorcycles had been discontinued.

In February 1959 came the announcement of an official works Parilla trials team, using 125 four-stroke models. This was to compete in the Italian Championship, the ISDT and other important events. Ing. Bossaglia had prepared a new 125 dohc engine with square 54×54mm dimensions which was reported to be capable of revving to 12,000 rpm. Unlike the other earlier chain-driven GP engine, the Bossaglia motor featured gear drive. Not content with all this activity an improved version of the old 1949 dohc Bialbeiro motor had been prepared for motocross use. In this new role power output was between 26-27 bhp. Although little came of the motocross or road-racing effort, the Parilla trials trio, Reggioli, Tosi and Cornago, rode in the ISDT at Gottwaldov, Czechoslovakia. And although Reggioli and Cornago retired, Canzio Tosi won a gold medal, the first Parilla rider ever to do so.

By now Parillas were being exported all over the

Parilla works trials team for 1959. Left to right: Reggioli, Tosi and Carnago. Tosi won a gold medal in the ISDT in Czechoslovakia that year − the first Parilla rider to do so.

world, even to Japan! Parillas were displayed at the Tokyo Fair, held between 5-22 May, 1959, by the importer Yamada-Rinseikan Co Ltd. The company also had its own magazine, *il Levriere* (The Greyhound), the first edition of which appeared in July that year.

The 1957 Giro d'Italia victor Giuseppe Rottigni had emigrated to North America and won the 1959 Canadian 250cc road racing championship on a 175 Parilla.

Stationary engines had entered production; this diversification was needed to offset a decrease in the sale of two-wheelers on the home market. Parilla's first unit was a single-cylinder four-stroke with a capacity of 402cc and square 80mm dimensions, code named the MP8. When the 1959 Milan Show took place one of the visitors was Ernest Wise of Cosmopolitan Motors, the sole distributors for Parilla in the States, and a show highlight was Tosi's ISDT gold medal winner still covered in Czech mud. Besides the ISDT bike other models displayed were: Slughi 99 and 125, Olimpia 99 and 125, Special 125 and 175, 175 Derivato MSDS and 350 Gran Turismo. An agreement was signed in Milan during the show period whereby RAP Motor Co, of

1960 version of the 175 MSDS Formula 3 racer. Parilla claimed 88 mph, but with careful tuning it could be made to reach 100 mph.

Stoke Heath Works, Bromsgrove, Worcestershire, would act as British importers for the Parilla range, beginning with the Slughi 99 four-stroke model, which was to retail for £162 10s., including purchase tax. The importers formed a separate company to handle the Parilla side of their business, named Moto Parilla Concessionaires. Also in November it was revealed that Parilla's designer, Ing. Bossaglia, was working on a new 125cc two-stroke racing engine, inspired it was said by the success achieved by the East German MZ factory. It was hoped to have the new design racing the next year.

More details were released in April 1960. In some respects it did appear to have been influenced by MZ design, for it had rotary disc-type inlet valves in the crankcase, three transfer ports and a bifurcated exhaust port, but in another respect it was reminiscent of the works Moto Guzzi singles, with its horizontal cylinder and deep radial finning. The carburettor had a pronounced forward incline, while the skirt of the shallow-dome piston was cut away at the sides for the two symmetrical transfer passages and ported at the top for the third passage, which was diametrically opposite the exhaust port. The cylinder head was profiled to provide a squish-type combustion chamber with axial sparking plug, but its most striking feature was the layout of the massive fins. There were 28, all substantially radial. Four groups each comprised a one-

piece V-shape fin with two independent fins between the arms, and separating the groups were four batches of three independent fins. The fins in each of the eight groups were joined with an arcuate strip. While high-grade aluminium alloy was specified for the cylinder barrel and head, the ribbed crankcase was made of magnesium. There were five speeds and an exposed, dry clutch. Total weight of the engine-gearbox unit was a mere 33 lb. Ignition was by battery/coil. The power output was 23 bhp at 11,500 rpm. Experiments were also carried out with a disc front brake, although an Oldani drum was eventually specified.

At around the same time Parilla became involved with the sport of go-kart racing for the first time (later it was to feature heavily in the company's activities). Driven by Marino Innocenti, it came second in its first race at the Marina di Grosseto. The kart was powered by a tuned version of one of the earlier piston-ported 125 Parilla units.

At the Milan Samples Fair that spring Parilla displayed a prototype 160cc scooter, featuring a horizontal parallel-twin engine with double cooling fans working in reverse, so that air was not blown on to the engine but drawn through twin chambers located between the inner and outer walls of the crankcase. A four-speed transmission was employed with a primary drive, by duplex chain, and secondary drive through intermediary gears to the rear hub. An electric starter, bottom link forks and swinging arm rear suspension were featured. An attractive body had a hinged dual seat, hiding the tank and luggage compartment. However, this project did not reach the production stage.

1961 saw Parilla up the capacity of the 'high-cam' motor to first 199cc (64×62mm) and then 247cc (68×68mm), mainly it must be said for the American market. By now Cosmopolitan Motors were promoting Parilla in a bigger way across the Atlantic with the following model names: 250 Wildcat Scrambler, 175, 200, 250 Grand Sport, 175 and 200 Super Speedster, 100 Ramjet De Luxe (Slughi with legshields and panniers), 150 Greyhound (Levriere) scooter and 350 Clipper (Gran Turismo). Most of these models were exported to North America with high 'n' wide bars and very little other modification from the European specification.

The Wildcat Scrambler was the name given by Cosmopolitan to the new 250 motocross bike first shown at the Milan Samples Fair in April 1961. This was intended purely for competition, not as a street scrambler, and came with a megaphone exhaust, no lights, abbreviated mudguards, leading axle telescopics, large air filter, tuned motor, large rear wheel sprocket, tacho and knobbly tyres.

In Britain Moto Parilla Concessionaires were now importing eight models from the Olimpia 98 at £150 up to the Gran Turismo 350 twin at £278. However, in reality very few Parillas were ever sold in the British Isles over a six-year period. The most popular was the 175 Special and 125 Sprint and, unlike America, no 250 street bikes were imported, although a couple of the motocrossers were sold.

From early 1961 to late 1962 there were very few developments on the Parilla scene, except that the slow-selling 350 twin had been discontinued, together with the Levriere scooter and four-stroke mopeds. The model line-up had been trimmed back to nine machines for the 1963 season: two fifties, a step-thru moped and ultra-lightweight sports motorcycle; the 98 Slughi and Olimpia; the Sprint 125 and Special 175 sports roadsters aimed solely at the American market; the Cross 125 and 250 (with lighting equipment) and the Touring 250. Additionally there were now a total of four stationary engines and a purpose-built 100 kart engine.

October 1963 saw a change in British importers, with

Built mainly for the American market, the 246cc Wildcat motocrosser.

Capriolo Ltd of 66-68 Southbridge Road, Croydon, Surrey, taking over the Parilla concession. The 250 motocrosser was tested by Mike Bashford for *Motor Cycling* the same month. Bashford nicknamed the Parilla dirt racer the 'Italian Bronco' after its wild antics during the test session.

The only new Parilla on display at the 1963 Milan Show was a revised version of the 49cc two-stroke three-speed Sport, which now featured a tubular open frame rather than the pressed-steel item used previously. A re-styling job which included a sleeker tank and miniature racing saddle gave the revised bike much sharper lines. This lack of development stemmed from a financial crisis which threatened the whole company due to continuing poor sales on the home market and had resulted in Giovanni Parrilla being forced to quit the company he had founded nearly 20 years before, a sad and disillusioned man.

In January 1964 Ernest Wise, President of Cosmopolitan Motors, visited the factory in Milan and while there was able to view the assembly of the new five-speed experimental Grand Sport racer. This development was of great interest to the American importer because 1963 had seen riders such as Charles Foulkner, Roy Baumgarder, Jim Bassey and Tony Woodman all win in AMA (American Motorcyclist Association) 250cc races Stateside. This had coincided with the rival AFM (American Federation of Motorcyclists) making big steps with their road racing programme during 1963. A schedule of 15 races on different circuits throughout California had given AFM riders an extensive and varied season. The AFM, unlike the AMA at the time, followed FIM rules and encouraged *real* road racing for the first time in the United States. In the AFM 250 class the Parilla of Norris Rancourt was considered the fastest in its class, ahead of riders such as Tony Murphy's and Ron Grant's Hondas and Yamaha-mounted Don Vesco. Rancourt's Parilla was owned by Orrin Hall of Sacramento and had started life as a production model Grand Sport which Hall had acquired in 1958 and which had been painstakingly developed over the

years since then. Hall considered the basic Parilla engine with its 68×68mm and valves driven by a single lobe, high-cam to possess all the advantages of the full ohc system without any of the disadvantages. Besides a host of engine mods, including twin-plug ignition and Amal GP carburettor, the Hall Parilla sported a front brake from a Manx Norton. Another factor besides Hall's tuning talent and Rancourt's gritty riding were the advantages of minimum weight. Hall had liberally drilled just about everything on the bike. Hall's philosophy of 'nothing too small' meant that he invested an incredible number of hours on the bike and Rancourt got on with winning races.

Early February 1965 brought news that Giovanni Parrilla had privately developed the 125 disc valve racer first seen in 1960 and Giampiero Zubani, an ex-Morini-team rider, would race the bike in Italian meetings. Very little, if anything, seems to have come of this plan. In March 1964 the first United States Grand Prix counting towards World Championship points took place at Daytona. The race was won by British MZ star Alan Shepherd, but the second placed man was Ron Grant riding a Parilla, the nearest the factory ever got to a classic victory.

By 1966 models such as the Wildcat Scrambler and Olimpia 98 ohv were both still in the American distributor's line-up, but Cosmopolitan were now acting as Benelli importers and could obviously see that Parilla was getting further and further behind the opposition. This was borne out the following year when the company quit motorcycles completely, thereafter producing other products, including the kart engines, which proved popular until well into the 1970s. So Parilla became one of many pull-outs and closures in the Italian motorcycle industry of the 1960s which had already seen Bianchi, Rumi and Capriolo disappear from the scene. This, of course, had been jointly caused by the growth of the small car market and the equally rapid rise of Japanese motorcycle exports, both of which had been a feature of the decade.

CHAPTER 19

Rumi

Officine Fonderie Rumi was founded by Donnino Rumi in Bergamo, just prior to the outbreak of the First World War. During the 1920s the company manufactured, first, cast components for the textile machine industry and, very soon afterwards, complete machines. By the early 1930s Rumi had built itself an enviable reputation for both design and quality within the textile industry. During the Second World War, Rumi became engaged in a totally different engineering role, the construction of midget two-men submarines and torpedoes. With the conflict at an end there were obviously a dearth of contracts for any form of armaments, so Rumi looked at other ways of keeping their production facilities active. Besides general engineering, a decision was taken to diversify into motorcycles, then enjoying a sales boom.

By 1949 the Bergamo concern had created not only a sporty lightweight motorcycle of particular beauty, but one which was also wholly functional, powered by a 180-degree crankshaft, twin-cylinder, two-stroke engine far in advance of its time. It was this 125cc horizontal unit which was to characterize the marque throughout its 14-year reign as a motorcycle (and scooter) manufacturer. Another feature on all Rumis was the famous 'Anchor' logo, which reflected the company's recent nautical past.

The Rumi 125 horizontal twin employed 42×45mm bore and stroke measurements which gave 124.68cc and with a single Dell 'Orto UB carburettor this provided smooth, almost turbine-like performance. Other features of this very first Rumi motorcycle included cast-iron cylinder barrels and alloy heads, telescopic (undamped) forks, plunger rear suspension, full-width brake hubs and a frame which had the engine slung underneath it supported by two main points.

The first trip outside Italy for the marque was the 1950 Paris Show, quickly followed by the Geneva Fair. Rumi's competition début came during the 1951 ISDT, held in Italy that year, with Varese as its base. Thereafter the company became rapidly involved in a wide range of two-wheel sporting activities. In January 1952 (at a delayed Milan Show) the Bergamo marque presented a sleek super sportster version of their popular 125. Appropriately called the Supersport, this had all the usual Rumi features plus twin vertical racing Dell 'Ortos, additional engine

tuning and special patented bottom-link forks. With 8 bhp at 7000 rpm, Rumi claimed a maximum speed of 115km/h (72 mph).

The Supersport was only the beginning, for soon a whole string of new machinery with the anchor logo began to appear. Most of this activity was due to the genius of one man, the former FN and Sarolea designer Ing. Salmaggi, who was also responsible for several Bianchi and Parilla models around the same time. It was Salmaggi who created the exciting and innovative dohc GP racing twin which sported shaft drive, massive 230mm brake drums, swinging arm rear and bottom axle forks of a similar design to the Competizione 125 racing twin. But the main centre of interest in this unusual creation was its 247.34cc (54×54mm) engine, which featured its cylinders inclined 27 degrees from the vertical. Its double overhead camshafts were driven by a central gear drive.

Tested at Monza during April 1952 by Bruno Romano, the new 250 shaft-drive, double-knocker twin-cylinder Rumi was impressively fast, certainly fast enough to warrant the close attention of MV Agusta team leader and 1949 500cc World Champion Les Graham. However, although obviously costing considerable sums of lire to produce, the Salmaggi Rumi GP twin was never used in anger. The most probable reason is not so much that it was not fast enough, but quite simply Rumi just did not have enough financial resources to launch an all-out attack on the likes of the contemporary Moto Guzzi and NSU teams. Just to confuse matters still further another Rumi dohc engine existed of *different* design, and with chain final drive.

The 1952 ISDT saw the Rumi rider Carissoni selected to represent his country in the Trophy team, whilst the entire trio of Vase team members were Rumi-mounted: Riva, Romano and Strada. Only Riva (Silver) and Carissoni (Bronze) gained medals. Rumi were later to win the team prize at the 1954 ISDT.

No doubt inspired by the huge success of Innocenti (Lambretta) and Piaggio (Vespa), Rumi decided it had to have a scooter. The first effort, the Scoiattolo (Squirrel), fell somewhat short of the formula required for sales success in the scooter sphere. This was because, like the majority of other motorcycle manufacturers who had

Original 125 Rumi horizontal two-stroke twin motorcycle on display at the Paris Show in 1950.

entered the field, Rumi produced a machine which in many ways was more closely related to a motorcycle than a scooter. In fact not only was the same 125 horizontal parallel-twin engine used, but also the full-width brake hubs (laced to 14in. rims), and even motorcycle-type telescopic front forks and swinging arm rear suspension. The frame of the Scoiattolo was of monocoque construction, with the engine unit being mounted in such a way that the crankcase and gearbox assembly was at footboard level, enabling a conventional motorcycle-type gearchange and kickstart lever to be employed. The monocoque covered the top section of the crankcase and thus there was a definite raised section between the rider's feet. The fuel tank was also part of the monocoque, and was directly located between the rider's knees, motorcycle fashion, even though there was still a small gap left between the rear of the tank and the dual seat. The outer section of the legshields comprised a thick chrome-plated curved tube which also acted as a crashbar in the event of an accident. Initially the gearbox of the Scoiattolo was a three-speeder, but this later was replaced by a four-speed version. The same was true for the touring motorcycles using the horizontal parallel-twin 124cc engine (but not the sporting versions, which had four-speed assemblies from the start, such as the Supersport).

By mid-1953 the Rumi range consisted of four models: the Turismo, the Scoiattolo scooter, both of which featured three-speed gearboxes, the Sport and the new

Competizione, a four-speed racing version of the now discontinued Supersport. Initially the racer featured the same frame and suspension as the sportster, but at the 1953 Milan Show, a revised version made its bow. This now featured a completely new rear sub-frame with full swinging arm suspension replacing the previous plunger set up. The forks had been strengthened and now sported a large knurled hand adjuster at each side so their damping could be set up more accurately. Although similar, the streamlined fuel tank and front number plate assembly had been altered in style, larger Dell 'Ortos were fitted and finally a truly massive Marelli magneto provided the sparks in place of a much smaller flywheel-mounted magneto. Rumi's over-the-counter racer was exhibited at shows in both Geneva and Vienna in early 1954 and the Bergamo concern was, unlike many smaller Italian marques of the period, making a genuine attempt to export their products.

From the start, Rumis had figured conspicuously in the great inter-city road races so popular in Italy at the time; 1952 had seen an impressive third place in their class during the 870-mile, single-stage, Milano–Taranto and third the next year in the Giro d'Italia. 1954 brought the factory a gold medal in the important Liège–Milano–Liège. On the pukka racing front the Swedish Grand Prix that year saw eight of the first ten positions in the National Invitation event go to riders mounted on Rumi machinery, while the company was equally successful in the ISDT held that year in Wales, when four Rumi riders were selected to represent their country: Romano and Serafina (Trophy) and Riva and Carissoni (Vase). Three won gold medals, Carissoni, Riva and Romano, and another gold was won by the privateer Basso.

On the production front, 1953 had seen not only the new 125 Competizione production racer, but also 175 and 200cc variants of the horizontal parallel-twin theme. They differed from the smaller roadster models in having swinging arm rear suspension in place of the plunger type hitherto favoured and in the use of an extension of the petroil tank around the steering head as a housing for the headlamp. If 1953 had been interesting, then 1954 was commercially more important, as it was to witness the début of what many people still consider the definitive Rumi two-wheeler, the Formichino (Little Ant) scooter. In many ways it was an inspired design, once again the work of Ing. Salmaggi, and one which was ultimately to be produced in far larger numbers than any other Rumi, motorcycle or scooter! It was also built in Belgium by Sarolea and sold under the name of *Dijn* (Goblin). *The Motor Cycle* called the Formichino 'unorthodox', which is absolutely correct, because although it cleverly utilized the 124cc horizontal parallel twin engine from the motorcycle range (and for that matter the Scoiattolo scooter) it was considerably different in several other ways. There was no separate frame to carry the engine; instead, front and middle body sections, of cast alloy, were bolted to the power unit. The front section was split vertically and housed the steering head and fuel tank, while a further casting at the front carried the headlamp. The front mudguard and tail section were additional castings and the tail formed an extension of the body middle portion. A leading-link front fork was employed and the rear wheel was stub-axle mounted onto the cast-aluminium chaincase which formed a pivoted arm controlled by a rubber suspension unit. Wheels were of 8in. (later replaced by 10in.) diameter, with split rims, and carried 4.00in. tyres. An unusual feature was that the rear chain was tensioned by an eccentric swinging arm pivot shaft.

In its original form, the Formichino came with iron barrels, a four-speed box, 6.5:1 compression ratio, single 15mm carburettor and a maximum speed in the region of 55 mph. This was a higher performance than either of its Lambretta or Vespa rivals and much of this was due to its lower weight, 180 lb, helped by the wide use of alloys in its construction. The aluminium bodywork was produced by Rumi in their own foundry.

The first Rumis to be imported into Britain (a small batch of Formichinos) arrived in November 1955. The company involved were Scooters and Vehicles Concessionaires Ltd of 149 High Street, Harlesden, London, NW10. This firm were to remain the sole British importer until the Bergamo marque's ultimate demise.

The same month as the first Rumis were arriving in Britain, the 1955 Milan Show was taking place. The only really new design on the Rumi stand was the 175 ohv model. This sported a neat wet sump, push-rod, four-speed unit with typical Italian full unit construction, very similar in appearance to MV and Gilera roadsters of the period. However, it was destined to only ever sell in very small numbers and was soon discontinued even though a modified version appeared at the Milan Samples Fair the following spring.

In January 1956 it was announced that the Competizione racer was to be imported into Britain to sell for £348 inclusive of purchase tax. The first (and probably only) customer was Watford two-stroke racing enthusiast Jim Bound (later to become the Montesa importer).

The mainstay of Rumi sales were the Formichino scooter and the various variants of the 125 motorcycle (the 175 and 200 flat twins had by now been discontinued), which all used basically the same power-plant. A new trio of the latter, intended to help improve the Bergamo company's motorcycle sales, made their début at the 1956

Works rider Fumagalli at the 1951 ISDT.

Milan Show. Called the Junior, Bicarburatore and Diana these were all different expressions of the same theme, a smooth but powerful 125cc engine, with superb handling and braking. The top model (and the fastest) was without doubt the Junior. This was styled very much in the popular racing mould with a large 18-litre sculpted tank, narrow racing saddle, sprint-type mudguards, low 'bars', flyscreen and alloy wheel rims. With twin 18mm carburettors and 10.5:1 compression pistons, its engine would spin to over 8000 rpm on open pipes (7300 rpm with silencers). Power output in standard form (with silencers) was 9 bhp. Higher 11.5:1 pistons were available for anyone wishing to race their Junior. The Diana was intended as a de luxe touring mount, with styling akin to that of the 175 ohv model, with deeply valanced mudguards, flat bars, a 14-litre tank and 6:1 compression ratio. Maximum speed was 59 mph from its 6 bhp. The Bicarburatore used the twin carb (hence its name) motor from the Junior, but was very much the

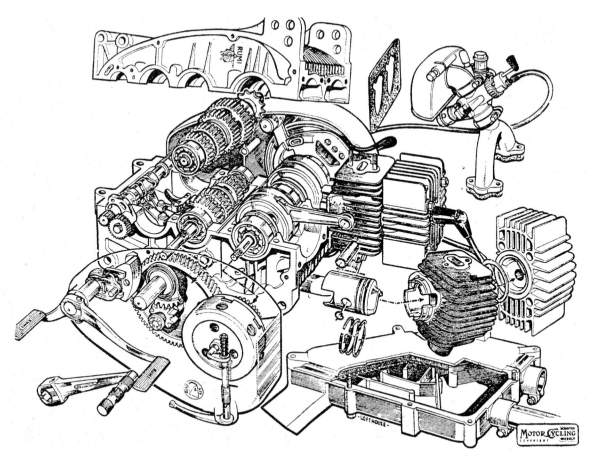

Exploded view of 124.68cc (42×45mm) Rumi engine. This formed the backbone of the company's production motorcycles and scooters for well over a decade. It was turbine smooth.

Tested at Monza during April 1952 by Bruno Romano, this 250 double knocker twin-cylinder Rumi was impressively fast. But lack of resources halted its further development.

economy sports model, with its old-fashioned plunger frame and spartan ancillary equipment.

The cylinder barrels on both the Junior and Bicarburatore were in alloy, with chromed bores. These were deeply finned and manufactured in West Germany by the KS company. Although allowing closer tolerances and being much lighter they had the disadvantage of not being reborable, and replacement barrels were expensive. It was the advantages of performance of these barrels which were to pay dividends with some fantastic performances put up by Formichino scooters in racing, notably the prestigious French Bol d'Or 24 hours staged at Montlhéry during the late 1950s. Rumi scooters entered by the Max Raudou Ecurie won their class in the Bol d'Or in three consecutive years. Without doubt their greatest moment of glory came in the 1958 event with a legendary victory over a mixed field of scooters *and* motorcycles. Riders Foidelli and Bois had by the end of the 24 hours covered 1302 miles, an average 54.258 mph. This was an overall average, including pit stops, refuelling and change of riders. The

French magazine *Le Scooter* speed-tested the untouched winning machine, after the event, and obtained 76 mph over 2548 metres and a maximum speed of 81 mph. The model used in the 1958 Bol d'Or was a Formichino Tipo Sport, fitted with twin carburettors. By now all the Formichino line had four-speed gearboxes, but only the Tipo Sport featured the aluminium cylinders with chrome-plated bores from the motorcycles.

The 1958 range comprised four scooters and two motorcycles: Formichino 125, Formichino 150 (149.490cc, 46×45mm), Formichino Tipo Sport (production version had single 22mm carburettor and 65 mph) and Formichino E (Economy). The latter featured cheaper pressed-steel panel work rather than the cast alloy bodywork of the other three scooters.

The pair of motorcycles were the Junior, now with Earles-type forks (telescopics were optional). The other machine was the Regolarita (All terrain). This was an over-the-counter version of Rumi's successful works ISDT bike. Engine specification was that of the Junior, but with lower 6.5:1 compression ratio and air filters which restricted performance somewhat. Even so, depending on the gearing the Regolarita was no slouch, top speed varying between a shade over 48 mph with the largest rear wheel sprocket, to around 62 mph with the highest gearing. The triangulated tube frame was completely different from the Junior and immensely strong; even the rear shocks for the swinging arm were inclined at a different angle. The wheelbase was on the short side to improve handling over the rough, an important design feature as it allowed a more erect riding position and played an important part in the control of the machine off road. Earles-type forks were chosen for their 'climbing steps' ability, but as was soon discovered braking was something of a problem (this is why these forks were soon deleted from the Junior and a return made to teles). Because of this problem even some of the Regolarita models were subsequently converted to the more conventional teles. The quickly detachable wheels were equipped with a waterproof version of the Rumi full-width alloy drum brake, reinforced steel rims and 2.50×19 knobbly tyres. As standard the Regolarita was provided with a special leather bag for tools, sparking plugs, schedule card and other necessary items. This bag was mounted atop the 18-litre steel fuel tank. For competition work the petroil mixture recommended by the factory was 10:1, causing something of a blue haze to emit from the twin upswept exhausts, which had silencers packed with glass-fibre wool. A socket plug was fitted for rapid disconnection of the electrical equipment.

Writing for *Motor Cycle News* in 1958, Italian journalist Carlo Perelli was enthusiastic about the Rumi

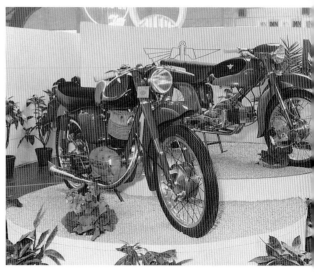

The company's stand at the 1956 Milan Show. Left: 175 ohv, a new design that year. Right: latest version of the long-running 125 horizontal two-stroke twin.

This Formichino scooter, produced in 125, 150 and 170cc engine sizes, was Rumi's top-selling model.

Regolarita which he owned. Even he, however, pointed out a couple of failings, 'The Rumi is heavy on fuel consumption, varying between 55 to 65 mpg. And, as already mentioned, the Earles forks created some problems; braking can sometimes be frightening as a result of the 'hunting' or waving action set up by the long fork

Rumi made their mark with some fantastic performances put up by Formichino scooters in racing, notably the prestigious Bol d'Or during the late 1950s. Then staged at Montlhéry, Rumi scooters won their class in the event for three consecutive years.

arms. Cure for this is wide throttle openings.' Which obviously when one was trying to slow down was not a very suitable solution!

1959 saw Rumi commemorate their achievement of winning the Bol d'Or by launching a scooter called simply 'Bol d'Or'. Finished in a spectacular gold and white finish, it came fully equipped with chrome bore alloy barrels, twin 18mm carburettors (22mm optional), low bars and a sports dual seat. With 8.5 bhp at 7200 rpm available, it could reach 75 mph, making it the fastest 125cc production scooter of all time. Perhaps the most amazing event in the company's history came in April 1960, when the Bergamo factory announced a completely new range of motorcycles and scooters powered by a modular engine concept in three capacities; 98, 125 and 175cc. The last was displayed in prototype form at that month's Milan Samples Fair, where it created a big stir.

Whilst the running gear of the motorcycle was similar to the then current Junior model, the scooter's lines were far more conventional than those of the revolutionary, but expensive to manufacture, Formichino and it was something of a cross between a Lambretta and a Vespa. What really startled observers were the engine-gearbox units. These were superbly crafted miniature 90-degree V-

twins. The engines were four-strokes of a very neat design with push-rod-operated overhead valves. Oil was contained in a finned sump cast integrally with the crankcase and was circulated by a gear-type oil pump to the main and big-end bearings and the valve gear. Like Ducati's later V-twins the 90-degree configuration was chosen because this provided the most perfect balance, and thus virtually eliminated vibration. A single vertical carburettor was mounted on a manifold on the left side of the engine and was fitted with an air filter and silencer. The kickstart lever was on the nearside and the gear-change pedal was on the off-side. Current for the ignition and lighting was provided by a flywheel magneto. Gear primary drive transmitted power via a multi-plate wet clutch to a four-speed gearbox. Final drive was by chain.

The trio of V-twin motorcycles were all of typically sporting Italian appearance, with clip-on bars and recessed fuel tanks (very similar in appearance to the famous Ducati 'Jelly mould' type as fitted to the 175 Sport and 200 Elite). Telescopic front forks and swinging arm rear suspension controlled by spring/hydraulic shocks were featured. The frame of a single-loop tubular pattern was common for all models. Bore and stroke of the V175 engine were 48×48mm (173.62cc) with a compression ratio of 8:1. The 19in. diameter wheels were fitted with 2.50 section tyres. For the V125 model the bore and stroke was again square at 43×43mm (124.862cc) for each cylinder and featured an 8:1 compression ratio. Wheel diameter was 18in., with 2.50 section tyres. Lastly came the V98 version. Dimensions of this were 40×39mm (97.968cc), providing 5.8 bhp at 7500 rpm and a maximum speed of 59 mph,

Rumi's stand at the 1960 Paris Show. In the foreground is the latest version of the ultra-sporting 125 Junior Gentleman. Race kitted it could exceed 100 mph.

LIGHT MOTORCYCLE "REGOLARITÀ" 125 c.c.

PERFORMANCES

Maximum speed 62.1/7 status miles per hour.
Average consumption 1 imperial gal every 113 status miles.
Maximum surmountable slope 25%.
Minimum steering radium 71''.

BRIEF SPECIFICATION

SUSPENSIONS: the front and back suspensions are by swinging fork with hydropneumatic shock absorbers.

WHEELS: spoke wheels. Rims in steel. Size of the tyres: 2,50 × 19''.

ELECTRIC PLANT: feed by alternator flywheel 6V - 30 W. Headlight with 3 beams and switch placed on the handle-bar, rear lamp, and horn.

TANK CAPACITY: 4 imperial gals of petroil.

ENGINE: cycle at two strokes. Two horizontal cylinders, side by side, with ignition at 180º. Bore 42 mm. Stroke 45 mm. Total cubic capacity 124,68 c.c. Number of revs per minute: 7.200. Compression ratio 1 to 6,5. Maximum power 7,2 H.P. Fiscal power 3 H.P.

GEARBOX: in block, 4 speed ratios, with constant mesh gears, front clutch. Control by double treadle.

rumi

125 Regolarita trials model. This was not only specially kitted out for off-road use, but even had a different frame from other Rumi models.

April 1960 saw Rumi announce a completely new range of motorcycles and scooters powered by a modular 90-degree V-twin, with push-rod operated valves. The motorcycles were the V98, V125 and V175 (shown). It is widely believed that the cost of developing these machines ultimately caused the company's downfall.

against 6.8 bhp and 65 mph for the 125 and 8.2 bhp and 71 mph for the 175.

The new scooters shared the same power units as the motorcycles. Starting was again by kickstarter on the left, but gear selection was now by a twistgrip on the left handlebar. Attractively styled, the bodywork and weathershield, with integral front mudguard, was formed from sheet-metal pressings with detachable side panels to give access to the engine assembly. Front suspension was by a leading link fork, while a pivoted fork was employed at the rear. The 10in. diameter pressed-steel split-rims were fitted with 3.50 section tyres.

These new designs were destined never to enter full-scale production, and certainly none were imported into Britain, even though the importers made a big noise about their imminent availability and even went as far as publishing a price list: the V175 was to cost £199 10s. 7d. One school of thought says that just prior to their introduction Rumi were offered a lucrative arms contract by the Italian government, whilst the other weight of opinion says that the development of this totally new range precipitated a final and most grave financial crisis for the small Bergamo factory. Either way the fact remains that Rumi officially went into liquidation during September 1962. As this was a mere two years from the first news of the V-twin range, there is evidence that all post-1960 machines were either old stock or built from reserves of

spare parts, so the second solution seems the most likely.

In any case, with the arrival of machines from Japan such as the Honda CB92, complete with an output of 15 bhp and such luxuries as electric starting, it is doubtful if there would have been enough buyers for the new Rumi twins, let alone the existing rawbone Junior street racer. The latter, now renamed Junior Gentleman, was also offered in over-bored 175cc form. As for the scooters, the 1960s heralded their rapid decline from favour, so their fate would have been sealed.

During 1960 and 1961 leading British rider John Dixon put up a number of impressive performances at circuits such as Mallory Park, Oulton Park and Scarborough with a race kitted 125 Junior Gentleman, quite often finishing in the top three at both national and international level on the British short circuits. Except for home-made expansion chambers his mount was surprisingly standard, proving just how good the little Rumi really was.

One of the very few tests ever carried out by the British press of a Rumi motorcycle was by *Motor Cycle Mechanics* with a Junior Gentleman in April 1962. The magazine was impressed by its performance, which was almost 80 mph in full road-going trim and a genuine 100 mph when race kitted. The test came shortly before the British Concessionaires finally quit the scene later that year, selling off the remaining stock of Rumis at knock-down prices. Responsibility for the marque (in Britain) then

British rider John Dixon put up a number of excellent performances with a race kitted 125 Junior Gentleman during 1960 and 1961. He is seen here in action during a British Championship meeting at Oulton Park.

passed to Alford Brothers of Wandsworth. Meanwhile the Hounslow firm of Multi-Motors geared themselves up for the production of pattern parts and even an interesting 200cc three-cylinder conversion kit. Plans were also made for the manufacture of a water-cooled four-cylinder engine, based on the original 124cc two-stroke, horizontal parallel twin Rumi crankshaft and piston sizes, using British-made clutches and gearboxes. In late 1962 Worminghall, Buckinghamshire, car dealer Jack West built a superb 250cc four-cylinder model. The cycle parts were MV, with the engine constructed from a pair of Junior twins. Four contact breakers, four Dell 'Orto carburettors and a Siba electric starter were fitted. A similar bike had been built in 1960 by Giuseppe Fabbri, a Gilera agent in Lugo di Ravenna, Italy. However, little appears to have come of these various projects and eventually it was left to the small Richmond firm of Stephen's Scooters to carry the Rumi banner, handling both spares and rebuilds. Eventually they

too closed, leaving the marque to be kept alive by a small but amazingly enthusiastic band of loyal followers around the world. However, in early 1967 Stefano Rumi, son of the founder, built a special 125cc for trials. This had a single-cylinder, two-stroke engine which offered 19 bhp and maximum revs of 9000. Although entered for the tough Valli Bergamasche Trial that year its development was not continued, and so the rebirth of the famous Bergamo marque came to nothing.

During my time as Editor of the magazine *Motorcycle Enthusiast* the huge amount of mail that flooded in after any Rumi feature never failed to amaze me. One reader who wrote in described the reason for such a large postbag: 'Enthusiasm for the marque is akin to Bugatti ownership.' Maybe he was right, for, like Bugatti, Rumi could never really be described as anything other than small production, but those motorcycles and scooters that were completed displayed a rare quality.

CHAPTER 20

Minor Marques

This chapter sets out to catalogue the truly amazing number of smaller Italian marques which have produced motorcycles since the end of the Second World War. To have included manufacturers before this date would have required simply too much space. As it is this chapter has almost 200 entries!

Adrictica 1979-80

Founded in 1979 to sell agricultural machinery, Adrictica decided to gain publicity by running a small racing team. It chose the 250cc class and engaged the services of the Dutch two-stroke wizard Jan Witteveen. The result was a 247.34cc (54×54mm) disc-valve twin which produced 65 bhp at 11,800 rpm. Riders included former world champion Walter Villa. The team was disbanded at the end of 1980.

Aero Caproni (see Capriolo)

Agrati (see Garelli)

AIM 1974-78

The company produced competition machines, mainly powered by bought-in Minerelli or Franco Morini engines up to 125cc.

Aldbert 1953-59

Interesting and well-built range of roadsters with a choice of 49 to 173cc two-stroke, or 174 to 246cc ohv four-stroke engines. The most sporting was the 175 Razzo (Rocket), which was capable of over 90 mph.

Alpino 1948-62

Most famous for establishing a number of world records both in Italy and Argentina during the early and mid-1950s with 49 and 74cc machines. Its production range included both two- and four-strokes ranging from 50 to 175cc. An early victim of the sales depression which swept Italy in the early 1960s.

Ambrosini 1951-54

German Sachs-engined 150cc scooter, with 3.00×12in. wheels and white-walled tyres.

Ancillotti 1967-85

The company concentrated upon off-road bikes, including moto cross, enduro and one-day trials machinery. Employed a variety of engines, including Sachs, Hiro and Franco Morini.

Aquila 1953-58

This Rome-based factory had no connection with the pre-war Turin company of the same name. It offered a wide range of models up to 175cc, including a 160cc prototype which appeared at the 1953 Milan Show. In late 1956 they became the first Italian manufacturer to offer a road-going motorcycle with a fully streamlined fairing.

Ardita 1951-54

Limited production of a wide range of models, including several mopeds and ultra-lightweights with two-stroke engines and a pair of 123 and 174cc ohv motorcycles of typical Italian design.

Aspes 1967-82

Most notable models were powered by the company's own 123.6cc (54×54mm) single-cylinder piston-port engine, with either five or six speeds. This was fitted to the RCC motocrosser and Juma sports roadster. In 1976 this latter machine produced 19 bhp at 9000 rpm and offered its rider a top speed of 85 mph, making it the fastest machine in its class. A racing version was also offered. This came with cast alloy wheels, a full fairing and expansion chamber — plus additional engine tuning. The dirt racer was marketed in Britain by Moto Aspes UK in Bournemouth during the late 1970s and was particularly successful in schoolboy events. The Aspes factory was located at Gallarate, not far from the famous MV Agusta works.

Aspes 125 Juma, one of the fastest and sleekest models in the class of 1976.

Aspi 1947-48

Produced an interesting flat-twin 150cc two-stroke with shaft drive. This prototype was the only venture into the motorcycle field by a factory well known for its stationary engines and pumps.

Astrá 1931-51

The trade name for a range of motorcycles produced by Max Turkheimer of Milan, who had been connected with the British Ariel concern. Their machines used a number of Ariel components, while the British Burman gearbox was made under licence by Fiat. Also offered a very neat 125cc two-stroke of their own design.

Atala 1954-77

Mainly concerned with the manufacture of accessories, Atala also built various small motorcycles over the years, all powered by single-cylinder two-stroke engines.

Bartali 1953-61

Named after the well-known cycle racer Gino Bartali, these machines were offered in a variety of engine sizes. Most notable was the 158cc Marziano, a semi-racer model with an ohv four-speed engine unit and nice styling.

Benotto 1953-57

Mainly used German Ilo engines, but also offered a few machines with own four-stroke unit.

Berneg 1954-61

Founded at the end of 1954, its first product was a superbly engineered 159cc vertical twin designed by Alfonso Drusiani, which was shown at the Milan Samples Fair in April 1955. The 160 was joined by a 172.78cc (50×44mm) version by the end of that year. The two models were essentially similar. There was duplex-chain drive to the overhead camshaft and single-chain primary transmission to a four-speed gearbox in unit. The cams operated the parallel valves through large-diameter tappets. A third bearing supported the crankshaft outboard of the camshaft and primary drive sprockets, whilst the contact breaker was operated from the off-side end of the camshaft.

By 1960 the top-of-the-range model was the 175 Fario Sport, but this, like the earlier models, only ever sold in limited numbers, due in the most part to its expensive price tag.

The factory was based at Caselecchio di Reno, Bologna, and was owned by Paride Bernardi and Corrado Menini. A 175 Berneg Formula 2 racer was entered for the 1957 Giro d'Italia, but was unsuccessful.

Bertoni 1948

Built a twin-cylinder 125 racer in 1948, but against machines such as the MV Agusta and Morini it was totally outclassed and was soon withdrawn.

Beta 1948-

Founded by Giuseppe Bianchi at Firenze in 1948, Beta still survives to this day as one of the most important smaller Italian marques.

By the mid-1950s Beta had quite an impressive range of nine models, including the Mercurio and Orione. These

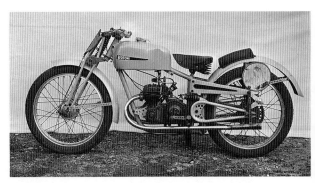

1948 Bertoni 125cc twin-cylinder two-stroke. Against machines such as the Morini and MV Agusta 'strokers it was totally outclassed.

Engine from Beta 246cc motocrosser of the mid-1970s.
Note German Bing carb.

had ohv four-stroke engines: 153.24cc (58×58mm) and 199.45cc (64×62mm) respectively and the semi-racing MT (Milano Taranto) 175. This latter machine used a specially tuned 172.3cc (59.5×62mm) version of the touring TV two-stroke model and was capable of 82 mph.

More recently the marque has been heavily involved in the off-road sector producing a number of specialized motocross, enduro and trials bikes. But roadsters have not been forgotten and as early as 1974 Beta offered a five-speed 48cc two-stroke trail machine. The late 1970s saw the introduction of a new 125 model in touring and sport guise, the latter sporting cast alloy wheels, dual disc front brake, clip-ons and an expansion-type exhaust.

Beta machines have been widely exported to a large number of countries, including North America and Britain, where the current importer is John Lampkin (trials machines only).

Two versions of 1981 Beta 125 roadster. The Sports model on the left had tuned engine, dual disc front brake, cast alloy wheels, expansion chamber exhaust and a more sporting riding stance.

Bimm 1972-78

Only produced off-road machines with 49 or 123cc Minerelli engines.

BM 1950-72

Originally using imported German Ilo two-stroke engines, the BM concern, headed by Mario Bonvincini, then began to use Italian power units, notably Franco Morini. But the best BMs were those equipped with four-stroke engines built by the works. Both ohv and ohc was tried up to 175, including a dohc racer in 1956.

Borghi 1951-63

Assembled Ducati Cucciolo, Garelli Mosquito and BSA Bantam-powered machines, the last known as the Olympia. Very limited production.

Breda 1946-51

Originally a leading arms company and aircraft manufacturer, Breda, like several others in similar industries, was forced to change to more peaceful pursuits after the war. But unlike marques such as Caproni (Capriolo), Aermacchi and Agusta (MV), Breda did not win any real acclaim or long-term success with their range of motorized bicycles powered by their own 65cc two-stroke power unit.

BRM 1955-57

Manufactured small-capacity two-strokes, mainly mopeds. Largely unsuccessful and soon disappeared.

Busi 1950-53

Range of attractively styled, two-stroke-engined machines ranging up to 200cc, but nonetheless could not command any real presence in the market and soon folded.

Capri (see Garelli)

Caproni−Vizzola (see Capriolo)

Carda 1946-50

Manufacturer of auxiliary engines for fitment into customer's own cycle.

Cardani 1966-68

A three-cylinder dohc Grand Prix racing project − the name of which was an anagram of the forenames of financial backer **Car**lo Savare and designer/builder **Dani**ele Fontata (the brake specialist). Designed to produce 75 bhp at 13,000 rpm the 496cc (62×55mm) engine had four valves per cylinder. Australian Jack Findlay was also involved in the project and helped with the frame layout, partly based on the famous McIntyre Matchless which he had ridden. Although similar in layout to the MV three's engine of the same period, the Cardani failed to shine and was soon discarded.

Carnielli 1951-81

Originally offered models with German engines, first NSU and later Victoria. Later manufactured the well-known Graziella folding moped.

Carrú 1953-55

First appeared at the Grand Prix of Nations at Monza in September 1953, the Carrú was a 497.73cc (65×75mm) chain-driven dohc vertical twin which was mainly used in the sidecar class. The cam boxes were heavily finned and fed with oil under pressure. Exposed hairpin valve springs were employed. A single carburettor supplied both cylinders through a Y-shaped induction pipe. A larger 599.35cc (67×85mm) version was also produced. Both were the work of Giuseppe Carrú, who had raced both solo and sidecar with a variety of machinery, including Norton and Harley-Davidson.

Casalini 1958-79

Originally produced small scooters, then later turned its attention to mopeds.

Ceccato 1950-63

Most famous of these superbly engineered machines were the 75 and 100 Sport models. These featured sohc unit construction engines, with the drive to the camshaft by a train of gears up the offside of the cylinder. The smaller 74.74cc (45×47mm) unit won the 75 Sport class of the 1956 Milano−Taranto, ridden by Vittorio Zito, whilst the larger 98cc provided a challenge to both Ducati and Laverda in the 100cc category.

The legendary Ducati designer Ing. Fabio Taglioni worked for Ceccato before joining Mondial and later Ducati.

Besides a wide range of four-stroke singles, some with ohv, Ceccato also produced, in 1952, a 200cc horizontal two-stroke twin.

CF 1928-71

Before the war CF (named after its designers Catelli and Fiorani) garnered much success in Italian racing circles with its fleet 173 and 248cc overhead cam singles. The factory was bought out in 1937 by Ing. Fusi, who had close ties with the Belgian FB marque. Post-war CF built smaller two-stroke models, but never recaptured its pre-war prominence.

Chiorda 1954-56

Originally offered 48cc ohv ultra-lightweights, but at the 1954 Milan Show displayed a smart little 100cc ohv twin called the Sparviero (sparrow), but this never reached production. Finally in 1955 began building 49cc Franco Morini two-stroke-engined models.

Cimatti 1937-84

Founded by Marco Cimatti − who had won a gold medal as a cycle racer in the 1932 Olympic Games − the Cimatti company began production in 1937, at the small town of Porta Lame. But although it prospered as a bicycle manufacturer, the factory was destroyed during the war years. However, undaunted Marco Cimatti restarted production and, in 1949, branched out into powered two-wheelers. This was during an era when motorcycles of any type found willing buyers. But Cimatti concentrated its efforts on smaller, cheaper machines, including mopeds. And during the late 1950s, while rival manufacturers, producing larger, more expensive machines went to the wall, Cimatti saw his company expand and prosper. The factory was relocated in 1960 at Pioppe di Salvaro, in the Apennines. During the 1960s Cimatti not only built a vast array of humble ride-to-work mopeds but won the Italian 50cc trials championship three years running, in 1966, 1967 and 1968. They also offered the 100 and 175cc Sport Lusso models for street use and the Kaiman Cross Competizione for motocross racing.

1972 saw a new 125cc motocrosser now with five-speed box and a roadster version. By 1977 production, including mopeds, was up to 50,000 units per year. But in the early 1980s demand fell alarmingly and Cimatti was wound up in 1984.

CM 1930-57

CM was the brainchild of the famous rider and engineer Mario Cavedagna and was based in Bologna. Cavedagna was assisted by Oresle Drusiani, elder brother of Alfonso, the creator of the all-conquering 125 works Mondial racers of the early 1950. Cavedagna sold out in the mid-1930s. The new owners continued to produce the line of ohc models in various capacities from 173 to 496cc, and also a new 496cc ohv single. There was also a competitive 348cc overhead cam racer, which, ridden by Guglielmo Sandri, was particularly successful.

After the war only the 500ohv single and a massive-looking 250cc single with chain-driven ohc continued and they were joined by a new range of two-stroke singles from 123 to 173cc from 1949 onwards.

At the Milan Show in November 1952 CM displayed a brand new 250cc two-stroke parallel twin, with slightly inclined cylinders. A sports version of this was subsequently entered in the long-distance road events such as the Milano−Taranto and was even kitted out as a pukka racer for short-circuit events. Its most successful pilot was Gian Emilio Marchesani.

CMP 1953-56

Used various Ceccato two-stroke engines and also a 48cc Sachs unit. Finally tried the Ducati Ceccato ohv engine, but none proved particularly good sellers.

Comet 1953-57

'One of the most interesting models on view,' was how *Motor Cycling* described the 175cc Moto Comet, in their Milan Show issue, dated 4 December, 1952. Built by Ing. Alfonso Drusiani this new Bolognese machine was of considerable technical interest. The engine was a vertical twin, with light alloy barrels and heads, the overhead camshaft being driven by a chain located between the cylinders. A particularly interesting feature was the use of overhung cranks − with gear primary and chain camshaft drives taken from the centre of the crankshaft. In unit with the engine, a four-speed gearbox drove an in-built distributor, a separate ignition coil for the flywheel generator being located in the tank cutaway. Telescopic forks and hydraulically damped rear shocks for the swinging arm completed an exceptionally neat package.

A sports version was introduced at Milan a year later in November 1953. And the same venue was chosen in 1954 to display an experimental Moto Comet. Alfonso Drusiani had dreamed up a 250cc four-stroke in which the *slide-*

valve principle was used. The barrel had three bores in line — a main cylinder between two smaller ones. Three crank assemblies were geared together, the 'valve cylinder' pistons operating at half engine speed.

More conventional was a new 250cc Moto Comet vertical twin, based on the existing 175s. Also introduced at the same time was a racing 175 single, with overhead camshaft, outside flywheel and dual ignition.

DE-CA 1954-57

The first model was a 48cc (39×40mm) ohv ultra-lightweight motorcycle. Soon followed by a 98cc ohv single and 123cc vertical ohv twin. None sold in any quantity.

Dei 1932-66

Founded by Umberto Dei, the Ancora factory produced a range of lightweights powered by bought-in engines, including Sachs and Garelli Mosquito units.

Della Ferrera 1909-48

Old-established factory named after the Della Ferrera brothers. Early bikes included the 498cc ohc V-twin racer of 1922. This featured chain-driven overhead cams and was successful in both road racing and hill climbs.

Large range of singles and twins built up to the beginning of the Second World War. The factory never really recovered post-war and closed in 1948. Its final model was a 499cc side-valve single, with unit construction engine.

Demm 1953-82

Although usually associated with mopeds during its final years, the Milan-based Demm concern — which was owned by Daldi and Matteucci — actually produced a vast array of machinery over almost 30 years. For example in the mid-1950s they offered a superbly crafted 175 — the TV (Turismo Lusso) and TL (Turismo Lusso) which had its overhead cam driven by shaft and bevels which ran up the offside of the cylinder and was almost out of sight within the engine's finning. Power output from the 60×61mm bore and stroke engine was 10.5 bhp (TV) and 9 bhp (TL), both at 7000 rpm. Primary drive was by helical gear. The gearbox was a four-speeder, with a heel-and-toe gear lever on the offside of the unit construction power plant.

Also offered at the same time were two 125s, the 2-stroke Normale Lusso and ohc Turismo. Both these machines shared essentially the same rolling chassis to

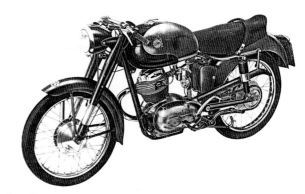

Details of the mid-1950s Demm ohc engine. In engineering terms it was the equal of any other production 175 roadster of its time, with a specification more akin to a racer than a roadster.

1956 Demm 175TV overhead cam single.

keep costs down. Like many other manufacturers Demm produced a range of *Motocarris* (three-wheel trucks), but strangely these were powered not by the four-stroke ohc unit but a totally different 175 two-stroke engine, with fan cooling.

On 7 November, 1956, at Monza, Demm broke a total of twenty-four world records in the 50, 75 and 100cc classes. The fully streamlined machine was powered by a 49cc two-stroke engine. Riders were Fausto Pasini and Franco Mauri.

Demm also supplied engines to other manufacturers, most notably Testi, with whom they had a close association for a number of years.

During the 1970s the British Demm importer was the

same company, the Heron Corporation, who also handled Suzuki. Only one model was offered, the Dove, a simple two-stroke step-thru moped. Previously in the late 1950s Demm had been imported by G. Nannucci of London W1, who offered a special 49cc Demm two-stroke racer at £125 and a 49cc four-stroke roadster at £95.

Devil 1953-57

Moto Devil SpA of Bergamo offered a comprehensive range of two- and three-wheelers using a variety of engines from 49 to 250cc. Their designer, Ing. William Soncini, created some interesting models, including the 125 ohv Sport Lusso, 125 two-stroke, 160 in either Sport Lusso or Sport Extra guise, the 160 Raid and the top-of-the-line 160 Sport Internazionale with its 12 bhp motor and 80 mph performance.

The company also built a 175 ohc single-cylinder racer for Italian Formula 2 events. This produced a healthy 20 bhp at 11,000 rpm and was good for around 100 mph.

Doniselli 1951-

Originally offered a line of motorcycles with either German Ilo or Alpino engine units from 65 to 175cc. But by 1960 concentrated exclusively upon mopeds and ultra-lightweight motorcycles with 49cc Franco Morini or Minerelli power.

DRS 1967-75

A 123.67cc (54×54mm) racer with rotary disc induction. Designed by the West German Peter Durr, it produced 20 bhp at 10,800 rpm. In 1974 a new version appeared which offered considerably more power (30 bhp), but no DRS achieved anything other than distinctly moderate success.

Eurocross 1969-70

Produced small numbers of motocross machines powered by 123cc Aermacchi two-stroke single-cylinder engines.

Faggi 1950-53

This small factory used exclusively British Villiers-engined machines of conventional appearance.

Falco 1950-53

Based at Vercelli, Falco built a range of lightweights powered by 98 and 147cc Sachs engines. Only limited numbers were ever sold.

FAM (see Motobi)

Franco Morini (engine manufacturer)

Fantic 1968-

Founded in 1968 by Henry Keppel Hesselink, a Dutch Italian, Fantic Motor have rapidly grown to become one of Italy's most successful small manufacturers, with a particular emphasis on trials and enduro machinery.

Their first model was a small child's bike powered by a four-stroke Aspera engine, called the Bronnco TXI. At the same time a prototype trike with the same engine appeared. These were soon followed by a succession of models, including the Caballero, Chopper and Super Six GT. On the dirt the 125RC enduro won countless medals, whilst Fantic even built a motocross version of this aircooled flier.

But it was in one-day trials where the Barzago, Como, factory was to really find its forté and during the later 1970s and early 1980s Fantic machines dominated this section of the sport, gaining the world championship in the process. The company is now led by Mario Agrati.

The French brothers Thierry and Frederic Michaud with the 1984 Fantic Trial 300 Professional. They won the world and French trials titles respectively that year.

FPM 1950-55

Of considerable interest, the FBM usually had partly pressed steel frames and flat single engines mounted directly to the swinging arm of the rear suspension. Engines included both two- and four-stroke, from 48 to 198cc.

Ferrari 1953-55

Not connected with the famous car marque of the same name, this small firm exhibited a chain-driven 200cc ohc parallel twin at the 1952 Milan Show. This was joined the following year by a smaller 175cc version. Neither enjoyed much sales success and the marque soon disappeared.

Fiorelli 1951-54

Another company which used imported German Ilo engines. Soon halted motorcycle production to concentrate on the production of components for other manufacturers.

Fit 1950-54

Yet another user of Ilo power plants, usually of 125 or 150cc capacity.

Focesi (see Gloria)

Fochj 1954-57

One of a handful of Italian companies which used German NSU engines, including the 247cc ohc Max unit.

Franchi 1950-58

Another assembler who used German power plants, this time Sachs two-strokes. Also marketed as Franchi-Sachs.

Frejus 1960-68

Built at a factory in Turin, Frejus offered mopeds and motorcycles, the largest of which was 200cc.

Frera 1906-56

Old-established marque, founded by Corrado Frera at Tradate, near Varese in northern Italy. Was particularly successful during the inter-war years of the 1920s and 1930s, when they built a wide range of singles and V-twins, the latter up to 1140cc.

Frera also competed in many racing events of the period with riders such as Acerboni, Fieschi, Macchi, Meyer and Ventura.

Just prior to the outbreak of the Second World War, Corrado Frera died, and even though the company survived it only offered smaller-capacity, mainly two-stroke, machines in the post-war period.

Frisoni 1951-57

Offered Villiers-powered motorcycles and a 160cc scooter. The latter made its début at the 1952 Milan Show, powered by an engine of Frisoni's own design.

Fuchs 1953-57

A bicycle manufacturer who also offered motorcycles with 124cc two-stroke and 159cc ohv engines, and in 1954/55 a 175cc racing model with unusual swinging fork front suspension.

Furetto 1947-49

Produced a nice-looking scooter powered by a 125cc two-stroke engine. However, it soon disappeared from the scene.

Fusi (see CF)

Gabbiano 1954-56

Limited production of a single model with 123cc horizontal single-cylinder two-stroke engine.

Galbusera 1934-55

Produced the sensation at the 1938 Milan Show with a prototype transversely mounted 498cc two-stroke V8. There was also a two-fifty V4 which was essentially half the larger engine. But neither of these exciting projects reached production.

Plinio Galbusera mainly employed imported Rudge Python engines from Britain for the motorcycles constructed at his Brescia factory.

Post-war production was concentrated upon smaller machines with Sachs two-stroke engines up to 175cc.

Ganna 1923-67

Based in Varese, the Ganna company was a high-quality machine which used a wide variety of engines, first British Blackburne and JAP, and after the war Minerelli, Puch and Sachs. But Ganna did design a notable engine themselves. This was a 500 four-valve ohc single in 1936, but for the most part it relied upon bought-in units.

Gerbi 1951-53

Small producer which used Sachs engines.

Gerosa 1953-75

This Brescia concern originally manufactured its own 125 and 175cc ohv engines, but later relied upon Minerelli.

Girardengo 1951-54

Small company which produced a range of small two-strokes of 125, 150 and 175cc.

Gitan 1950-66

First products were a range of motorcycles up to 200cc. Thereafter smaller, mainly two-stroke models, including mopeds. Notable was the Honda C50 Cub-type 49cc Grillo (Cricket) of the late 1950s. Factory located in the principality of San Marino.

Gitane (see Testi)

Giulietta (see Peripoli)

Gloria 1948-55

Gloria's chief designer was Ing. Alfredo Focesi. His first creation was a 48cc two-stroke which mounted on the swinging arm assembly. But the most interesting of Focesi's designs was the 100cc ohv model which first appeared at the Milan Show in 1953. The engine and gearbox unit were of typical Italian appearance and were shown in sports and touring guise. In the former case, a pressed-steel beam frame was employed, together with leading link front forks which had pressed-steel pivoting members. A further pressing, faired on to the front of the petrol tank, contained the headlamp. On the touring machine, however, the frame was of basically tubular construction and an Earles-type fork was employed.

Gori 1969-83

Founded by Giancarlo Gori, the company was mainly known for its off-road bikes, but also produced children's models and a couple of very sporting 125s – a pukka racer and a super sports roadster.

The racer, which used a specially tuned Sachs six-speed unit, was particularly successful in hill-climb events, which Guido Valli becoming Italian hill-climb champion in 1974 and 1975 on his 125 Gori. The company also offered a customer version of this machine. Its specification included: 123.6cc (54×54mm), 13:1 compression ratio, 34mm Bing carb, Motoplat ignition, Marzocchi suspension, 170mm Fontana front brake and was capable of 185 km/h (113 mph). Maximum power was 24.8 bhp at 11,600 rpm.

Gori also produced a small number of the 125cc Sport Valli Replica during 1975-76. This used the same (very slightly detuned) six-speed Sachs engine, but had a full fairing, twin front discs, cast alloy wheels and sharp styling. Although barely road legal, it was at the time the quickest 125cc street bike in Italy, with a claimed maximum of 92 mph.

Only the off-road machines were ever imported into Britain. The SWM company acquired Gori in 1980 and the firm was renamed Go-Motor, which ultimately collapsed with SWM in 1985.

Guido Valli, Italian hillclimb champion in 1974 and 1975 with a 125cc Sachs-powered Gori machine.

Grasetti 1952-65

Manufactured 125 and 150cc machines with their own two-stroke engines.

Graziella (see Carnielli)

Guazzoni 1949-79

Formerly with Moto Morini, Ing. Aldo Guazzoni set up his own factory at Via Alta Guardia 6, Milan, and very quickly built up an excellent reputation for innovation and quality.

Besides the staple diet of small two-strokes, Guazzoni found time to create a very smart 200 (191cc) ohc model in 1954. This featured telescopic forks, swinging arm rear suspension and a full duplex frame. A tuned version which produced 13 bhp took part in the long-distance events such as the Milano–Taranto.

November 1959 brought the news that the new Guazzoni 175 horizontal two-stroke single was to be imported into Britain by the Manchester-based DOT concern. This was followed in June the following year by a 125 Sports. This latter machine had an upright cylinder. There was also a 98 Sport, essentially the 125, but with a smaller engine.

Not imported was the 125/150 Modernly, an attractively styled on-off road machine.

Later, disc valve models appeared, notably a 60cc (45×41mm) racer in 1966, to be followed in 1969 by a 50cc version which took the Italian Senior Championship that year. This success brought about an exciting twin-cylinder 125 for GP events. But although it produced 32 bhp at 12,500 rpm it could not match machines like the Spanish Derbi, Japanese Suzuki or East German MZ, and was soon withdrawn.

During the 1970s Guazzoni concentrated its efforts on mopeds and 50cc motorcycles, before finally closing later in the decade.

Guia 1950-54

Small concern which assembled machines with a variety of Sachs two-stroke engines.

Guizzo 1955-62

Mainly a moped constructor, but also built a 150cc scooter in early 1960s. However, this proved a sales failure and the company was forced to close.

Harley-Davidson (see Aermacchi)

Hiro (engine manufacturer)

Almost a miniature Bimota – the 1985 HRD WH 125 Silver Horse.

HRD 1981-86

Almost the Bimota of small motorcycles, the Vittore Olana, Milan, factory created a number of inspired designs in the early 1980s, including the Silver Horse and Formula LS high-performance 125s. HRD also supplied machines to the Roth organization in Germany, which were marketed under the Horex label. In addition the company raced a 250 which used an Austrian rotary valve in-line twin engine. HRD was originally owned by Docc. Riccardo Canosci, but are now incorporated with the Kram-It concern, after being forced out of business during early 1986.

Factory brochure showing 1963 Guazzoni Modernly enduro bike, available with a choice of 125 or 150cc two-stroke engines.

Idroflex 1949-54

Used a 105cc two-stroke engine built in unit with the swinging arm. Its unusual design and higher cost restricted sales.

IMN 1950-58

Based in Naples, IMN (Industria Meccanica Neapolitana) originally manufactured torpedoes for the Italian navy, but after the war decided to produce a range of motorcycles from 49 to 248cc, all of which were two-strokes. But at the 1956 Milan show IMN displayed the sensational Rocket. This was a horizontally opposed twin-cylinder (like the BMW) with a bore and stroke of 52×46.5mm, giving a capacity of 199cc. The engine had push-rod-operated valves and with a compression ratio of 7:1 developed 11 bhp at 6,000 rpm. The frame was particularly noteworthy; not only was it of the tubular space variety, but the engine and gearbox were bolted up to form a unit and to the rear of the gearbox was bolted a substantial light alloy fork, the left arm of which housed the final drive shaft. The entire engine/gearbox unit pivoted with the rear wheel and the pivot spindle, which passed through bushes in an extension of the top of gearbox, was its only point of contact with the frame. So the front and rear wheels were connected only through a single half-inch-diameter rod!

Unfortunately the Rocket was not fully developed when it was put on sale in early 1957, and its unreliability, combined with high development costs, signalled the end of IMN as a motorcycle manufacturer.

Innocenti (see Lambretta)

Intramotor 1971-81

Besides trials and motocross machines, also produced mopeds, all with Minerelli engines.

Invicta 1951-54

Small company which offered a couple of two-strokes of 73 and 123cc capacity. Only limited numbers made.

Iprem 1977-81

This Pesaro company built only road-racing machines. Its creator was Enzo Ridolfi, who chose at first the 50cc class with a Kreidler-type 49.64cc (40×39.5mm) horizontal liquid-cooled single. It produced 16 bhp at 16,000 rpm. In 1977, ridden by Guido Mancini, it won the 50cc Italian Senior Championship. By 1980 the machine had been developed into a world-class bike, so much so that new rider Eugenio Lazzarini was able to clinch the 50cc World Championship title with wins in Italy and Spain, a second in Belgium and two thirds in Holland and Yugoslavia. Also in 1980 a 124.68cc (44×41mm) horizontal disc-valve twin

made its début. This was the work of Paolo Marcheselli with assistance from Lazzarini. Its first GP finish was in France that year, when Lazzarini came home ninth, then at Silverstone he finished an impressive fifth. But the team's best ever finish with the twin came the following year, when Lazzarini was fourth in the Austrian GP at the Salzburgring. But the Iprem could not afford to mount a sustained world championship challenge and Lazzarini left to join Garelli in 1982.

Eugenio Lazzarini with the works Iprem 125 twin, before the start of the 1980 Italian GP at Misano.

Iris 1952-53

Very limited production of German Ilo-engined machines of 123cc capacity.

Iso 1948-64

Founded by Renzo Rivolta at Bresso in 1939, Isothermos (abbreviated as Iso) had hardly begun trading when production plans were halted by the outbreak of the Second World War.

Re-formed in 1948 as Iso Automotiveicoli SpA, Rivolta then began to build autocycles and scooters.

With increasing sales Iso then introduced the famous Isetta micro car, with its own 236 ohv air-cooled engine. Originally this was a four-wheeler, with twin narrow-track wheels. Access was by a swing-up front door to which the steering wheel and column were attached. The Isetta went on sale in early 1954. It was also produced in a number of countries under licence agreement. The most successful of these was with the German BMW company. Production ceased at the parent company in Italy during 1956, but BMW offered the tiny car (often with three wheels) with its own 247cc engine (from its single-cylinder R26/27 motorcycle) until 1963; and from 1957 to 1964 the BMW type was constructed under another licence by Isetta of Great Britain Ltd. A total of some 36,000 Isettas were built worldwide.

Next came a series of motorcycles and scooters, including a development of the original Iso split single. This scooter-like machine was powered by a 124.7cc two-stroke. The cylinder had a pair of 38mm bores with a stroke of 55mm. From this came a whole range of machines, including the 125 Gran Turismo and 'E', 150 (with the dual bore increased to 41×2mm), a 250 (236cc, 48×2mm×64mm) and the latest version of the scooter. The 250 had in fact been developed from the earlier 200cc (44×2mm×64mm), which featured shaft drive.

1957 saw the appearance of the Milano scooter. Of much more modern appearance this used a completely new 146cc (57×57mm) single-cylinder two-stroke engine and looked like a cross between a Vespa and Lambretta. By 1960 this was being imported into Britain by Stuart and Payne Ltd of 6/7 Bankside, London SE1.

For 1961 the Milano was joined by a trio of new ohv four-stroke single-cylinder motorcycles, two 125s and a 175. The latter model offered 8.3 bhp at 6200 rpm from its 172cc (60×61mm) four-speed unit construction engine. One machine which was not to enter production was a 492cc ohv flat twin shown at the Milan Samples Fair in prototype form during April 1961. This featured a full duplex frame, electric starting, 26 bhp and a claimed 90 mph performance.

At the end of 1963 all two-wheel production came to a halt, and Iso went a totally different route by concentrating upon high-price, luxury cars. These included the Rivolta, which had made its début at the Turin Show late in 1962, and the Grifo.

After several turbulent years of automobile production Iso was finally declared bankrupt in 1975, and although a new company resumed production briefly things finally ground to a halt again in 1979.

Italemmezeta (see Italjet)

Italjap 1949-51

A Florence-assembled machine with an imported British 125cc JAP engine.

Italjet 1966-

Leopoldo Tartarini was born on 10 August, 1932, the son of Egisto Tartarini, himself a leading Italian road racer of the 1930s.

After obtaining an engineering degree at Bologna University, Tarterini Junior built a special using a British BSA 650 twin engine in a chassis designed entirely by himself. With a sidecar attached the machine won its class in the 1952 Milano−Taranto. The following year he achieved lasting fame by winning the Giro d'Italia outright on a 125 Benelli.

Right up to 1957 he kept racing, which included another outright victory in the Giro and at Montjuich Park, Barcelona, the home of the famous 24 *Horas* (24 hours) endurance race.

Then Tartarini went on an 'around-the-world' trip with a 175 Ducati (see Chapter 8), which took a year to complete. Shortly after his return his father was killed in a road accident, and Leopoldo became the owner of the large family business empire. Based in Bologna, this included farming and the Citroën concession for Italy. But his interest was really in motorcycles and so in the mid-1960s a completely new factory was built at the little town of San Lazzaro, some four miles from Bologna. Before this Tartarini had constructed machines under the Italemmezeta brand name, using East German MZ engines. But in 1966 Italjet was formed. At first these used 490cc Triumph T100SS engines in Tartarini-designed cycle parts, and there was also a 50cc racer called the Vampire. Next came the 649cc Triumph Bonneville-engined Grifon and the 125 America, the latter being powered by a 125 CZ motor.

During much of the 1970s Italjet production concentrated upon children's mini-bikes for both fun and sport. Not only this, but Tartarini himself employed his talent doing a number of styling exercises for several Italian car firms − and the local Ducati factory, perhaps the most notable examples being the 500 Sport Desmo parallel twin and Darmah models.

Then there was the Pack-A-Way, a fold-up 50cc powered machine which could be transported in a car boot. Italjet also used the Japanese Yamaha YASI-YAS3 series of 125 twins to power a line of sports roadsters. There was also a pukka racing version which gave 24 bhp at 12,000 rpm.

With a decline in the sales of kiddies' bikes, Italjet then turned their attention to full-size machines once again with a number of trials bikes; and the H & H 350, which used a 330.13cc (83.7×60mm) two-stroke enduro-styled trial machine. This engine was also used in a number of other models, including the Custom 350, Transafrica and the

Italjet 49cc Pack-A-Way bike, circa 1977.

radically styled Roadmaster. Besides its futuristic styling the Roadmaster was water-cooled, unlike the other models. An update of the 1950s clip-on cyclemotor theme appeared in the shape of the Tiffany, powered by a 49cc Piaggio engine.

Finally there was a 322cc (80×64mm) four-stroke single, with a four-valve head. This was used to power the Boss and Scott Excursion models, both of which were on-off road bikes. Tartarini is rumoured to have co-operated with Ducati in the manufacture of this engine, which was nothing new, as the majority of Ducati's mid-1970s parallel twins were built not at the famous marque's Borgo Panigale, Bologna, facilities, but the Italjet plant.

Italmoto 1952-54

Neatly produced 160cc ohv motorcycle, small production.

The weird if not wonderful Italjet 350 Roadmaster. It used a water-cooled single-cylinder engine, with six-speed gearbox. Manufactured during 1982 and 1983.

Itom 1948-67

The first Itom was a cyclemotor which was designed in 1944. Based in Turin the company soon built up an excellent reputation for its 50cc and later 65cc models, all powered by single-cylinder piston-ported two-stroke engines.

In the late 1960s the company became involved in the 50cc racing boom, which ultimately led to the class's acceptance for World Championship status in 1962. The early 'racing' models had a three-speed gearbox, geared primary drive and a hand-operated twist-grip gearchange. With the Mk VII there were four gears, and with the Mk VIII four gears with foot change. Although the factory itself never entered works machines, private Itom riders made up the majority of any 50cc race entry for several years (from the late 1950s to around 1963) before being totally outclassed by 'official' production racers such as the Honda CR 110 and the Kreidlers, let alone the full works bikes from Derbi, Kreidler, Suzuki, Honda and Tomos, amongst others.

The first woman rider to compete in the Isle of Man TT, Beryl Swain on her Itom in the 1962 50cc event.

In December 1965 *The Motor Cycle* put one of the 49cc (40×39.5mm) Competition models through its paces and were generally impressed enough to comment, 'It has disadvantages, true enough; but a remarkable, exceptionally smooth engine, allied with exemplary roadholding is compensation enough for any discomfort!' Cost of this fully road-legal sports 50 was £118 16s. 3d. from the British importers, A. H. Tooley, Station Garage, Opposite Lee Station, London SE12.

A few short months later the factory was forced to close through falling orders. Perhaps if they had responded to the needs of the racing fraternity in a more positive fashion things might have been different.

Kram-It 1981-

Offered a range of enduro and motocross machines, usually with monoshock rear suspension and water-cooled engines from either Minerelli (49.6cc) or Rotax (123.6cc, 244cc and 276.5cc). Also built their own 79.6cc (48×44mm) unit. A Rotax-powered Kram-It won the outright Italian Enduro Championship in 1987. Kram-It took over the ailing HRD company in 1986, and since then have expanded their activities considerably.

Lambretta 1946-

Ferdinando Innocenti established his own workshop at the tender age of 18. In 1922, then aged 31, he moved to Rome, where he developed ways of improving the manufacture of steel tubing and nine years later moved once again, this time to the Milanese industrial suburb of Lambrate, where he founded a steel company which was to be the basis of his future empire. But the Lambrate plant was almost totally destroyed during the war, so he was faced with the daunting task of not only rebuilding the plant but finding a profitable niche of the metal finishing market in which to sell his wares.

The result was to be one of the success stories of the post-war two-wheel sphere − Lambretta. The idea of making scooters came with the realization that Italy was devastated and that a simple, cheap form of transport was a leading priority, and also that there was already a proliferation of motorcycle manufacturers.

So Innocenti picked the motorized scooter and in 1946 introduced the first Lambretta, the model A. He also realized the importance of publicity to his fledgling two-wheel enterprise and authorized the construction of not only specialized record breakers, but a 123cc (52×58mm) single-cylinder two-stroke racing motorcycle, known as the 2T. This appeared in 1949. Features included a conventional piston port induction engine with offset Dell 'Orto carburettor, four-speed close-ratio gearbox and, most interestingly, shaft drive to the rear wheel.

By 1950 production at the via Pitteri, Milan, factory was up to 300 scooters per day and two new models, the 125 C and LC, had just been introduced. And the same year Lambretta took more records at Montlhéry in France. Early the following year rivals Vespa hit back, but then Lambretta re-took these with a specially constructed, fully streamlined machine ridden by Romolo Ferri, with speeds up to 121 mph — truly amazing for a 125 scooter!

At around the same time an agreement was concluded with the German firm NSU for manufacture of the Lambretta scooter in that country. This lasted until 1956, when NSU began making their own Prima scooter.

June 1951 saw a well-kept secret leak out. This concerned the existence of a 247.3cc (54×54mm) 90-degree, across-the-frame V-twin racing motorcycle. Drive to the ohc was by shaft and bevel gears. Other technical details included a five-speed gearbox with drive to the rear wheel by a coupling and a shaft. And although the crankcase assembly was heavily finned, it was a dry sump design, with separate oil tank.

The layout of the entire machine, the work of the famous designer Ing. Salmaggi, was extremely neat and compact, giving the Lambretta 250 V-twin an elegant line.

Although extensively tested at Monza Autodrome, the bike never raced in anger. A strong rumour, never to be officially confirmed, was that expecting that there might be competition in the scooter world from the larger motorcycle manufacturers such as Guzzi and Gilera, Lambretta built the racer to show that they, too, could make motorcycles — if necessary

At the 1954 Milan Show the company launched a 48cc two-speed moped with front and rear suspension. However, it never sold in the hoped-for quantities.

But it was really the millions of scooters which made the Lambretta reputation.

After the LC came the LD, but perhaps the most important model of all was the Li series, which came out in late 1958. These used a choice of either 124 or 148cc engines. Earlier that year the company had introduced the TV175, a luxury model with a 170cc power unit and a top speed approaching 60 mph.

After 1962 scooter sales, particularly in export markets, declined rapidly. Even though Lambretta tried hard to combat this trend by bringing in a host of new models, including the Cento 100, GT 200, SX 200 and 122cc Starstream, the rot continued.

Romolo Ferri during his record-breaking stint for Lambretta during 1951.

This fall from grace by the scooter did not matter too much, as from the mid-1950s Innocenti had three divisions, one building scooters, one making mainly tubing and the third specializing in machinery, including presses and machine tools. Much of the other two divisions' products went to the car industry — including not only the majority of the Italian ones, but also Ford and Volkswagen.

In 1961 Innocenti moved into car production itself, initially with licence-built British cars such as the Austin A40.

At the height of its industrial success the group employed some 7000 employees, but after the death in June 1966 of its founder Ferdinando Innocenti it lacked leadership, and by 1975 was in deep financial trouble. The result

Lambretta's 250 vee-twin. A potential threat to the products of established motorcycle manufacturers, it was tested in 1951 by Enrico Lorenzetti, but it was never raced.

was that Innocenti passed into the hands of the Italian government, and thence to a new management team headed by Alejandro de Tomaso. By the late 1970s at least one of Innocentis' production facilities in Milan was building Guzzi V35/50 V-twin engines for another section of the de Tomaso empire (see Chapter 15).

Meanwhile Lambretta scooters are still being manufactured today, albeit under licence agreements, in both Spain and India.

Legnano 1954-68

Produced only mopeds, using either Minerelli or Sachs engines.

LEM 1974-83

Offered a range of mopeds and ultra-lightweight children's motocross models, with either Franco Morini or Minerelli as engine suppliers.

Leprotto 1951-54

Nicely made lightweight motorcycles using 123cc two-stroke and choice of 158 and 198cc four-stroke ohv engines.

Linto 1967-71

The Linto was a 500cc racing twin intended for sale to privateers, and to keep development cost to a minimum, and the ultimate price low, many of the engine components were from the Aermacchi flat single. First tested during the

summer of 1967, the Linto project was the work of three men: Ing. Lino Tonti (hence the name), engineer Aleide Boitti and the former rider Umberto Premoli, who provided the financial backing. A 'space' frame housed the 496.7cc (72×61mm) ohv, almost horizontal unit construction engine, which produced 61 bhp at 9800 rpm.

There was a built-up crankshaft with 360-degree crank pins (at first 180 degrees had been tried, but this gave too much vibration and was soon abandoned) and running on four bearings.

Initially it sold well because of a significant increase in speed over the now ageing British singles. Factory development rider Alberto Pagani finished second in the 1968 East German GP and followed this up with a fourth on Italian soil at Monza.

These results convinced several leading 'Continental Circus' riders, such as Marsovsky, Findlay, Dodds, Ellis and Turner, to buy. However, although fast the 'production' Linto was also to prove depressingly unreliable.

Its only Grand Prix victory was with Pagani in the saddle at the 1969 Italian GP at Imola. By the beginning of 1971 the Linto had all but disappeared from the Grand Prix scene.

Lusuardi 1984-85

Claudio Lusuardi designed and built his own 50 and 80cc racing machines. The latter model used a water-cooled rotary disc valve single of 72.98cc (44×48mm). This bike won the 1985 Italian 80cc Senior road racing championships, ridden by Bruno Casanova.

Magni 1977-

For almost 30 years the leading figure responsible for the preparation of the legendary MV Agusta racing machines, Arturo Magni, founded Elaborazioni Magni di Magni Giovanni at the family home in Samerate during 1977. At first, the new company concentrated on the production and sale of cast-alloy wheels and in offering special tuning parts for the MV roadster fours. This was followed in 1978-79 by the first of the Magni frames and chain-drive conversion kits, again for MV machines.

In 1980, Magni took an important step in his evolution as a motorcycle manufacturer in his own right when he offered the MHl. This not only used a Honda CB900 engine, but the Japanese forks, swinging arm, shock absorbers, brakes and exhaust system. Built exclusively for export, in 1981 Magni produced a total of 150 MHIs and the later MH2.

Then, at the 1982 Cologne Show, the MB2 appeared.

Magni Classic Le Mans at the Milan Show in November 1987.

This was powered by a flat-twin BMW engine. The success of this venture led to the introduction three years later of the Magni Le Mans. This employed a Moto Guzzi 948.8cc V-twin, or to special order, and exclusive to Magni, a larger 1116.87cc version. An interesting feature of the Magni Le Mans was its double (parallelogram) swinging arm. This was to avoid the problems of torque reaction with shaft drive, the swinging arm working independently from the rear drive, which itself featured twin fully floating universal joints. Magni had previous experience of this system on the MV 500 four-cylinder racers when they used shaft drive in the early 1950s before going over to a chain. The Le Mans was available only as a complete machine, unlike the BMW-engined MB2, which could also be purchased as a frame kit.

As I said in an article published in the July 1986 issue of *Motorcycle Enthusiast* 'The Magni Le Mans cannot be said to be cheap, but for this sum you do get the chance to own one of the world's most exclusive *and* exciting motorcycles, built by someone who has managed to pack more motorcycle experience into his life than most of us can dream about!'

Maino 1902-56

In the veteran days this small factory built motorcycles powered by the Swiss Sovereign engine. Then after a long gap when it ceased production, the owner, Giovanni Maino, restarted after the Second World War by offering first Garelli 38cc Mosquito-powered autocycles and later lightweight motorcycles powered by German NSU (98cc) and Sachs (147cc) engines.

Major 1947-49

Designed by Ing. Salvatore Majorca, this was a 347cc ohv fully enclosed engined machine with shaft drive to the rear wheel. Its cost limited sales to very small figures.

Malaguti 1930-

This San Lazzaro di Saverna (Bologna) company was created in 1930 by Antonino Malaguti to manufacture pedal cycles and accessories.

In the immediate post-war period it began to fit these cycles with the famous Garelli Mosquito auxiliary engine. This was followed in the mid-1950s by several years when German 48cc Sachs engines were used. Then came Italian engines such as Franco Morini (a trend still maintained today). During the 1960s a number of both lightweight motorcycles, with engines up to 125cc, and mopeds were built.

In the following decade the decision was taken to

Malaguti's first powered two-wheeler. This 38cc Garelli Mosquito-engined machine was built in the immediate post-war period

The Malaguti 49cc Calvacone enduro-styled ultra-lightweight motorcycle of the mid-1970s. It was also offered in certain markets, including Britain, with pedals.

Hi-tech dirt bike for kids: Malaguti's 'Grizzly' RCW/4 of 1987 featured water-cooling, monoshock rear suspension and full-size motocross looks.

concentrate 100 per cent on the 50cc market – and actively seek export customers. This meant that Malagutis were seen in some numbers in countries such as Britain and France.

Today there are 150 workers on the payroll producing 25,000 machines annually. Malaguti's leading export market is Britain, where sales are handled by the Harglo organization, followed by Spain and Switzerland. There are plans to double production over the next few years.

Malanca 1956-86

Formed in 1956 by Mario Malanca in Pontecchio Marconi, Bologna. It was most famous for its long-running line of parallel twin-cylinder two-strokes for both road and racing use. The racer's hour of glory came in the years 1973-1976, when Otello Buscherini gained several wins and places in the 125cc Grand Prix series. His mount employed a water-cooled disc valve 123.5cc (43.8×41mm) twin engine which delivered 36 bhp at 14,000 rpm and was one of the very few machines to match the class-leading Yamaha and Morbidelli machines. Tragically Buscherini was to lose his life in an accident during the 1976 Italian GP while riding his own 250 Yamaha, and Malanca's challenge effectively came to an end with his death.

During the late 1970s and early 1980s Malanca's road-going 124.9cc (43×43cc) piston ported twins were well known for their excellent performance, particularly in water-cooled form. For example, the 'ob one 125' was 'il primo della classe' (first in its class) with 25 bhp and 94 mph maximum speed.

However, with the emergence of a new generation of high-performance 125s from Cagiva, Aprilia and Gilera,

Malanca's performance was outclassed and with it went its sales advantage. 1985 saw the company sponsor the up and coming Marcellino Lucchi on a special 250 twin-cylinder racer. Although successful the racing publicity could not stave off financial disaster and the factory was forced to close.

Mas 1920-56

Founded by Ing. Alberi Seilig the Milanese company Mas (Motoscafo Anti Sommergibile) not only built roadsters, but military machines and even went in for winning gold medals in the ISDT, with their range of 123cc ohv engined machines.

A vast number of different models were offered during the 1930s, ranging from a side valve 248cc to a side-valve 568cc single. Usually these featured inclined cylinders. Seilig left in 1938 to form the Altea factory, but this only lasted until 1941.

Meanwhile Mas supplied a number of 498cc ohv singles to the Italian army. Post-war the first new model was the 122cc ohv Stella Alpine with 'suction air cooling' as the *Motor Cycle* described it in their 1946 Milan Show report. It was a truly innovative idea. The cylinder was cast in the form of two concentric cylinders; inside the inner cylinder was joined to the outer one by a number of vertical fins in a single casting operation. The idea behind this, which was the work of its designer Ing. Guidetti, was to provide efficient cooling at low speeds – much the same way as a stationary engine needs to be kept cool, in other words the engine itself had to provide its own cooling. Ingenious as it may have been, the Stella Alpino was not a sales success. Next was a prototype 492cc parallel twin with single overhead cam, but this never made it to production. There were also ohv and ohc single-cylinder 175s during the early 1950s, but these failed to sell in any great number. And finally this once great marque was forced into selling 125 two-strokes and a 49cc scooter with bought-in Sachs units. The factory closed during 1956.

Maserati 1953-61

This famous Modena car factory entered the motor-cycle arena in 1953 with two basic machines. These were each shown in standard, de luxe and sports forms – six machines in all. One basic model was a 123cc (52×58mm) two-stroke, whilst the other was a 158cc (60×56mm) ohv with its push-rods enclosed in an integral tunnel and four-speed gearbox in unit. Full-width hubs and light alloy rims characterized the sports models of both types.

The following year these models were joined by a

brace of new larger-capacity ohv singles, a 175 and a 200cc, both of which closely resembled the 158cc machine.

Then at the Milan Show in late November 1955 Maserati pulled off a coup by offering what they claimed to be the world's first disc brake on a production motorcycle. This was mechanically operated, rather than hydraulic. The disc brake made its appearance along with a new 246cc (70×64mm) ohv single. Outstanding engine features were double-helical primary drive gears with a third outrigger crankshaft bearing and twin spark plugs. The sports version offered 13.6 bhp at 7000 rpm.

Later still there was a 49cc two-stroke road racer, but like the other models this was more expensive than the majority of the opposition and after 1961 Maserati pulled out of motorcycles to concentrate on the more profitable four-wheel side.

MBA (see Morbidelli)

MBA (Morbidelli Benelli Armi) 124cc twin-cylinder rotary valve over-the-counter racer. The model shown is of the type offered during 1981, 1982 and 1983.

MBM 1974-81

Offered a range of Minerelli-powered mopeds.

MDS 1955-60

Manufactured lightweight motorcycles with own ohv engines in various capacities from 60 to 80cc. Also offered a 65cc scooter.

Memini 1946-47

Very limited production of a 173cc two-stroke of their own design.

Meteora 1955-

Various models, including ones fitted with German NSU engines. Later built a number of Franco Morini-powered ultra-lightweights, including off-road machines.

MFB 1957-64

This tiny Bologna factory built 48, 74 and 124cc two-strokes and also a 174cc ohv model.

MG-Taurus 1933-56

Pre-war both two-stroke and four-strokes offered. After the conflict there were German Sachs-engined mopeds and push-rod models from 74 to 198cc.

Milano 1970-

Mainly off-road models which used Minerelli two-stroke engines.

Miller-Balsamo 1921-59

Founded in Milan by the brothers Ernesto, Edgardo and Mario Balsamo, the company was once a major force in Italian motorcycling. Its first machine was a 123cc two-stroke. Then came the popular 174cc ohv model, with a Swiss Moser engine. In the 1930s Miller-Balsamo built several models with British engines, notably the Rudge (Python), in capacities from 174 to 498cc. The company also competed successfully in racing and broke several world records – the latter with 174cc Rudge-engined machines.

Just before the outbreak of the Second World War, Miller-Balsamo built a brand new model which used their own 246cc ohv single, and another quite revolutionary model with full enclosure, powered by a 200cc two-stroke engine.

The marque was one of the first to resume production at the end of the war and one of the star exhibitors of the 1946 Milan Show was the Jupiter. This carried the fully enclosed practice further and used a 246cc ohv single-cylinder engine. And it was not just the enclosure which was different, as the Jupiter employed hydraulically controlled rear suspension and compressed air front forks.

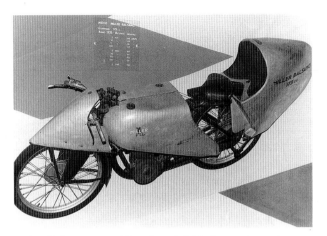

Miller Balsamo record-breaker of 1932 vintage. It used a 175cc single-cylinder overhead cam engine and comprehensive streamlining.

There was also a gear indicator. This was mechanically operated from the gearbox and a number came up on the instrument console to show the rider which gear he was in. Another innovation was a compression release, which was geared to the kickstarter so that it worked automatically when the pedal was depressed. In addition access to the mechanical parts was excellent, *The Motor Cycle* commenting: 'The usual bugbear of inaccessibility has been cleverly avoided. To remove the very large side panels it is necessary only to pull a large spring-loaded plunger for each! With the two side panels removed, which can be done literally in two seconds and without tools, the "works" are exposed as completely as with any normal machine.'

The other machines which made up the 1947 model year range were the Jupiter, together with a sports 'undressed' version, and the latest version of the pre-war 200cc model with enclosure.

By 1950 the range had changed to the Jupiter, plus conventional 125, 200 and 250cc two-strokes and a touring 250cc ohv.

Unfortunately try as they might Miller could not get back its pre-war success and even though a new 169cc ohc single appeared in the early 1950s the old firm finally passed into history during 1959.

Minerelli 1950-

Founded in 1950 by Vittorio Minarelli this famous Bologna engine manufacturer also built record-breaking machines in the 1960s and works' road racers in the late 1970s and early 1980s. The Spanish star Angel Nieto won the 1979 and 1981 125cc World Championships for the company on a water-cooled disc valve twin designed by the German two-stroke wizard Jorg Möller.

Giuseppe Ascareggi rode for Minerelli in the 50cc class during 1981 and 1982. The latter year saw him finish fifth in the world championship.

Mi-Val 1950-67

Metalimeccanica Italiana Valtrompia SpA of Gardone Val Trompia, Brescia, were essentially machine tool manufacturers who produced motorcycles for a number of years. At first they produced a 125 two-stroke and then in 1954 were granted licence rights to manufacture the Messerschmitt three-wheeler. In fact the Italian was considerably different from the German original; not only was the body design changed, but it also had a 172cc Mi-Val rather than 191cc Sachs engine.

The company made history in 1956 when it displayed a new 125 ohv model with a five-speed box, the first road machine of its type to be so equipped.

Mi-Val produced a number of competition machines in most branches of the sport. For example, in the 1950 ISDT they had entered a team which included sidecar racing champion Eric Oliver and the famous woman trials rider Olga Kevelos. In the long-distance road events such as the Milano-Taranto, Mi-Val fielded a fleet 175 model. But they were most well known and successful in motocross, producing throughout the late 1950s a range of dohc 250, 350 and 500cc singles, with five- or six-speed gearboxes.

In 1966, their last full year of motorcycle production, Mi-Val offered a total of ten two-wheelers, from the Presa Diretta commuter moped to the 200cc ohv Principe (Prince), plus the interesting Water Kart powered by a Mi-Val 125cc two-stroke engine.

The following year the company quit bikes to concentrate on the machine tool business.

MM 1924-57

The MM company of Bologna, the initials of which stood for the co-founders Mario Mazzetti and Alfonso Morini, began trading in 1924, with the launch of a neat and simple little 125cc road-racing two-stroke model.

This two-speed unit construction device was raced by Morini, who was not only one of the company's founders, but also the embryo firm's first official works rider.

Racing success was not forthcoming straightaway, but in September 1927, the 125cc MM caused a sensation when it won its class at the *Gran Premio delle Nazioni* (Grand Prix of Nations) at the famous Monza autodrome.

After 1930, the 125cc category was less important following a change to the Italian Highway Code, and MM switched its attention from two-strokes to four-strokes. The first of these new models, an ohv 175cc, soon became popular and was followed by a sports version with chain-driven overhead cam.

Also, from the early 1930s MM offered a 350cc side-

The local rider Terigi with his 175cc MM during the 1935 French Grand Prix at Montlhéry.

valve tourer and, a little later, a 500cc version intended for sidecar use. Both these larger-engined machines achieved considerable popularity, but even better things were around the corner when, in 1934, the Bologna marque introduced a 250cc single overhead camshaft sportster derived from the earlier 175cc machine. This was to remain, in developed form, a part of the company's line until their ultimate closure in 1957.

Alfonso Morini (see Chapter 13) severed his connection with MM in 1937 to start a rival business under his own name.

Throughout the 1930s the name MM was to be seen not only in the race programmes of the day but in the field of record breaking, where several world speed records were exceeded by MM riders. But the company was never a large organization as say the likes of Guzzi, Gilera or Bianchi.

During World War Two, MM suffered cruelly at the hands of allied bombing, and by 1945 were almost totally destroyed. But somehow Mazzetti managed to restart production in the face of tremendous odds.

The first models offered in 1947 were in the 350 and 500cc classes and were simply 'new' pre-war designs. By

1950 the 350 had telescopic forks and a plunger rear end. There was also an improved ohc 250.

But MM could never recapture their pre-war glory and finally closed in 1957.

Monterosa 1954-58

Very limited production of Minerelli-engined mopeds.

Monviso 1951-56

Sachs-engined lightweights of typical Italian design, with engine sizes from 98 to 173cc.

Morbidelli 1969-82

Giancarlo Morbidelli owned a successful wood-working tool business in Pesaro. He was also a great road-racing enthusiast. Many of his machines were built at the Benelli Armi factory (the former owners of the Benelli, Pesaro, motorcycle factory) in nearby Urbino.

The first time a Morbidelli appeared in a Grand Prix was when Lazzarini finished tenth in the 1969 Italian classic on a 50 designed by Franco Ringhini. The following year a water-cooled 124cc (44×41mm) disc valve twin made its début in France.

The larger machine was successful from the start, with works rider Gilberto Parlotti winning in Czechoslovakia during 1970 and at Monza in 1971. 1972 opened with two wins, a second and a third, but then tragedy struck and Parlotti was killed in the Isle of Man TT.

During 1973 and 1974 Morbidelli were largely recovering from the death of their star rider, even though there were occasional outings for riders of the calibre of multi-world champion Angel Nieto.

1975 was to see the start of a great run for the marque with the Morbidelli pairing of Pileri and Bianchi completely dominating the 125cc class, winning seven classics, while the West German rider Braun won an eighth for them. Pileri and Bianchi took first and second places in

Marco Lucchinelli with his Morbidelli 250 at Mugello, 2 October, 1977. His team-mate Mario Lega was world champion that year.

Morbidelli 500cc V-four of Graziano Rossi at the 1981 Dutch TT. The machine was very quick, but unfortunately not reliable.

the title chase and Morbidelli comfortably won the manufacturers' title. 1976 and 1977 proved repeat performances, except that Bianchi and Pileri reversed roles in the team from 1976. That year also saw a new '50', but ridden by Lazzarini it was less successful than its larger brother.

1975 had seen a brand new 250 twin. This was based on an enlarged version of the 125, with a bore and stroke of 55×52mm. Like the 125, it featured disc valves and water-cooling. Peak power was 61 bhp at 11,400 rpm. The cylinders were inclined forward at an angle of 45 degrees and the engine assembly was mounted in a Bimota chassis. The machine made its classic début in Belgium during 1976, when Pileri finished second.

Bianchi continued his winning ways by taking the 125cc world title again in 1976 and 1977, but perhaps most important of all was Mario Lega's 250 championship on the 250 in 1977, thus making Morbidelli double winners for the first time.

Morbidelli also built a 350cc four-cylinder, but this was never to achieve any real success, nor for that matter was one of the factory's final projects – a 500 four. But the fours absorbed vast amounts of money which eventually led to Giancarlo Morbidelli's withdrawal.

Their numerous 125 victories offered the chance of a commercial version and the company responded by offering an eighth-litre customer racer which swept all before it in GP events from 1976 onwards. And it was this same class of machine with which the new team of MBA carried on where Morbidelli left off in 1982.

Moretti 1934-52

Produced both bikes and cars. Giovanni Moretti used a variety of engines, such as DKW and JAP, in his pre-war motorcycles. After 1945 there were 125 and 250cc singles with ohc, a 125cc two-stroke racer in 1949 and finally a 246cc vertical ohc twin with a shaft drive.

Moto Bimm 1969-71

Built small numbers of off-road bikes – trials and motocross-with 49cc Minerelli two-stroke engines.

Motron 1977-

Specialist moped manufacturer which uses Minerelli engines.

MT 1949-52

Designed largely by Teresio Mutatore, the MT was an attractive and modern 248cc vertical twin with single overhead camshafts. Small quantities meant high production costs and therefore a high retail price tag. Also sold under the OMT label.

Müller 1950-79

Closely associated with the German manufacturer NSU, the factory's owner, Bruno Müller, insisted on only the best-quality materials. Therefore the 247cc ohc Max-powered Moto Müller was every bit as good as the German original. Later, with NSU's withdrawal from the motorcycle scene in the 1960s, Müller switched to Sachs, Hiro and Franco Morini engines. In its final days the company concentrated upon motocross and enduro machines with 123.6cc and 244.29cc Hiro engines.

MVB 1954-56

Very limited production of mopeds and lightweight motorcycles with bought-in two-stroke engines.

Nassetti 1951-57

Designer-manufacturer Ettore Nassetti produced a number of small-capacity two-strokes with much innovative engineering highlighted by the 49cc Pellegrina (Shoulder cape) with horizontal cylinder and friction drive.

Necchi 1951-53

Used British Villiers 98 and 123cc two-stroke engines; limited production.

Negrini 1954-

First models were roadsters with choice of 110 or 123cc two-stroke engines. Later offered a range of mopeds, children's motorcycles and miniature motocross models. Imported into Britain during the late 1970s by the Laverda importer, Roger Slater.

Nettunia 1950-53

Used Ing. Busi-designed 125 and 160cc two-stroke, unit construction, 4-speed engines.

Ocma (see Devil)

Ollearo 1923-52

Founded by Neftali Ollearo, the company mainly produced a range of single-cylinder ohv-engined machines which right from the start featured full unit construction *and* shaft drive to the rear wheel. There were also a few two-strokes of 131 and 173cc.

Post-war a 45cc 'clip-on' engine was manufactured together with several of the pre-war four-strokes.

Olmo 1951-61

Range of ultra-light mopeds and motorcycles. Their most popular model was powered by a 38cc Garelli Mosquito two-stroke engine.

Olympia (See Borghi)

OMA 1952-55

Interesting 175cc four-stroke singles with a choice of either ohv or ohc.

OMB 1947-48

A prototype 348cc model appeared at the 1947 Milan Show. Designed by Ing. Pedrini this was built at considerable expense by OMB of Bologna. It had both front and rear suspension − teles and plungers respectively − while the frame was most unusual with the fuel tank forming part of it. By removing only two nuts, the machine could virtually be divided into two parts to make major engine repair work a much easier job.

The valve gear was quite novel and incorporated a large cam-wheel turning at one-eighth engine speed and having the cam profiling cut internally on the underside of a toothed ring. Thus, the push-rods did not 'push' but 'pulled' the rockers. All bearings were of the roller type and with square bore and stroke measurements of 76×76mm, it gave 26 bhp at 7000 rpm.

A journalist of the period described the 350 OMB in the following fashion: 'A most interesting and unorthodox machine typifying the spirit of engineering adventure which is so strong amongst Italian technicians.' Sadly the high production costs meant the project was abandoned.

Omea 1950-53

Technically interesting machine because of its cast alloy frame, the Omea was the work of Ing. Carlo Bottari. It was powered by a 124cc single-cylinder two-stroke engine and featured leading link forks and swinging arm rear suspension.

Omer 1968-81

Offered a range of machines with 50cc Minerelli or Franco Morini engines.

OMT (See MT)

Orix 1949-54

The company used German Ilo two-stroke engines for both its motorcycles and scooters in capacities ranging from 125 to 175cc.

All Orix machines were the work of Ing. Amadeo Prina.

Oscar 1965-82

Small motorcycles and mopeds using mainly Franco Morini engines. First models were the College moped with carrier and pannier bags as standard and the racy-looking Sports, with a 49cc 4-speed Minerelli engine developing 3.5 bhp.

Paglianti 1958-66

Yet another small manufacturer who used bought-in Minerelli and Franco Morini power units.

Paton 1958-

The history of Paton dates back to the year 1957, when FB Mondial, together with Guzzi and Gilera, quit the racing scene. This move obviously meant that a number of very talented engineers suddenly found themselves idle.

Giuseppe Pattoni, as chief mechanic for the FB Mondial GP team, was one such person. Together with another former Mondial employee, the talented designer Lino Tonti, Pattoni created a 124cc dohc racer for sale to top-line (and well-off!) privateers for the 1958 season.

The Paton name was coined from PAttoni and TONti, although the pair soon went their separate ways − Tonti to Bianchi and then Guzzi, whilst Pattoni stayed and built a whole string of one-off racers over the next three decades. One of Paton's first customers overseas was Stan Hailwood, whose son Mike was just beginning to take his first step up the ladder to worldwide acclaim and a whole string of championships. Hailwood Junior brought his ⅛-litre Paton home seventh in the 1958 Ultra-lightweight TT.

Next came the twin-cylinder 250cc Paton − the first to be solely the work of Pattoni himself and with only his own funds. This appeared in 1963 and gave 33 bhp. It was then developed first into a 350, and later a 500. During the late 1960s and early 1970s Pattoni's racing was greatly helped by the sponsorship of Bill Hannah. Hannah was a Scot based in Liverpool, who ran a Grand Prix racing team with 350 and 500cc Paton twins under the Hannah-Paton tag. Riders were Angelo Bergamonti, Fred Stevens and Billie Nelson. Generally they were faster than even the best of the British singles and proved themselves reliable over several seasons' use.

1969 version of the 500cc Paton dohc twin engine.

The later 500s produced some 65 bhp in two-valve form, with the final version with 4-valve heads good for 70 bhp. Usually the Paton was second, but when Agostini's MV had its infrequent retirement the Paton riders were able to take victory.

In 1967, for example, Bergamonti even defeated the mighty combination of Ago and MV to win the 500cc Italian Senior Championship.

In the early 1970s Hannah hit financial trouble and withdrew his support. This meant that from then on Pattoni's efforts were largely restricted to domestic events. For example, Roberto Gallina (now a top team manager and tuner in his own right) rode the 8-valve Paton dohc to several leaderboard places in the Italian Senior Championship series.

But by the mid-1970s it had begun to be increasingly evident that it was necessary to go two-stroke. The result was a most incredible achievement for someone who had not only devoted his life to the four-stroke cause, but had to do the job out of his own pocket.

Pattoni's first attempt at his own four-cylinder 'stroker was as early as 1976, but results were none too encouraging. This 492cc (45×50mm) cross-port, water-cooled, six-speed unit had been built using a considerable number of parts from the RR250/350 Harley-Davidson (Aermacchi) two-stroke twins and mounted in a Bimota chassis.

But even though its rider was a certain young Virginio Ferrari, cost was a major problem for the team. But the really interesting Paton four-cylinder was the 4V115. This new bike was built in 1984 and was capable of well over 180 mph. It was a twin-crankshaft, close-coupled four essentially consisting of two 250cc twins mounted one above the other, with the cylinders spaced at 115 degrees to match the phasing of the Spanish Motoplat electronic ignition system. It produced around 120 bhp on the test-bed figure, which didn't give much away to the Japanese opposition. The problem however was to get this out on the circuit − not because of its technical refinement, but simply the high running costs of a full GP effort. And this is what finally caused Giuseppe Pattoni to make a (temporary!) retirement from the scene. He had the bike, but could not afford the running costs. But even so no one can say that Pattoni won't be back with another effort some time in the near future.

Pegaso 1956-64

Manufactured by SIM (Societa Italiana Motori) − not to be confused with the other SIM (Societa Italiana Motoscooters), the Pegaso used Motom 48cc ohv engines.

Peripoli 1957-80

Sold under the Giulietta name, and as AJW in Britain, Peripoli manufactured a wide range of mopeds and small motorcycles, usually powered by Minerelli two-stroke engines.

Perugina 1953-62

First appeared at the 1953 Milan Show with a neat 173cc single with vertical bevel shaft drive for ohc. The designer was Ing. Menicucci, who also created a 158cc two-stroke and later a larger 248cc version of the ohc model.

Piaggio (See Vespa and Gilera)

Piovaticca 1973-75

Egidio Piovaticci dreamed of winning races with his private Grand Prix team, but it ended in financial disaster and he was forced to sell out to the Spanish Bultaco company in early 1976, Bultaco ultimately winning four world championships to prove that Piovaticci had been going in the right direction. The machines in question were a 49cc (40×39mm) single and 124cc (43.8×41mm) twin. Both had horizontal cylinder, disc valve induction, water-cooling and six speeds. The 125 could top 135 mph, with the smaller bike good for 115 mph. Designers were the Dutch pair of Jan Thiel and Martin Mijwaat.

Pirotta 1949-55

Originally one of the many producers who built 'clip-on' engines for customers to fit to their own bicycles, Pirotta then switched to motorcycles. The 160cc two-stroke

The 1974 Piovaticci team. Left to right: Eugenio Lazzarini, Henk Ceulemans, Jan Thiel, Martin Mijwaat and Angelo Gerri.

model shown at Milan in 1954 was particularly interesting. Its extended fuel tank, with a wide window behind, allowed the headlamp to be fully enclosed yet still turn with the front wheel. The Pirotta designer was Ing. Gianfranco Viviani.

Polenghi 1950-55

Produced only mopeds and 48cc motorcycles.

Prina (See Orix)

Ringhini 1972-

Franco Ringhini was not only a rider of considerable note, but also a gifted engineer. He had amassed a considerable amount of experience with first Bianchi and later Guazzoni and Morbidelli. In 1972 he decided to build his own motorcycle. This was a 49.64cc (40×39.6mm) water-cooled racer, which produced 14 bhp at 14,500 rpm and was ridden to victory by Carlo Guerrini in the 1973 Italian Junior championship. A development of his machine was successful for several years thereafter in the Italian Junior and Senior championship series.

In 1979 Ringhini was the chief motivation in the RTM (Ringhini Torriani Motors). This was a 345.57cc (50×44m) four-cylinder two-stroke with disc valves and water-cooling. But although of considerable technical interest this 90 bhp machine never really made the grade.

Recently Ringhini has made a return to the scene with a 350cc twin-cylinder engine for Formula 2 sidecar use.

Rizzato 1972-79

Produced off-road motocross, enduro and trials bikes in limited numbers with 123cc Minerelli engines.

Romeo 1969-77

Mopeds and children's machines. Minerelli power.

Rondine 1951-54

Had no connection with the legendary forerunner of the Gilera racing four. This small company sold 124 and 147cc Sachs-engined lightweights designed by Martino Siccomario.

Rondine 1968-70

Yet another Rondine, this time created by the former MV works rider Alfredo Copeta. Specialized in competition mounts with 48cc two-stroke engines for road racing or motocross.

Rosetta 1950-52

Another small manufacturer who used British Villiers engines in the immediate post-war period.

Rossi 1950-55

Built in Parma, the Rossi used a 125cc German Sachs engine and was offered in either one-day trials or ISDT trim.

RTM (See Ringhini)

San Christophoro 1951-54

Early 1950s producer of two-stroke motorcycles up to 125cc.

Santamaria 1951-63

Employed a variety of engines up to 150cc from German companies, including Ilo, Sachs and Zündapp.

Sanverero 1980-83

The only European machine to win a 500cc road-racing Grand Prix since MV Agusta retired in the mid-1970s, the Sanverero concern's victory was a hollow one, with the Swiss rider Frutschi winning the very wet French GP at Nogaro in 1982 when the works riders staged a strike. But their 125cc wins with Bertin (Italy 1981) and Tormo (Sweden 1981 and Belgium 1982) were real enough.

Scarab (See Ancilotti)

Scarabeo (See Aprilia)

Segale 1981-

Luigi Segale is a perfectionist — and his various Japanese four-cylinder four-stroke-engined creations rival Bimota for quality. But outside Italy, unlike their much more famous rivals, Segale is virtually unknown. Also offers frame kits and tuning equipment.

Frenchman Guy Bertin in action with the Sanvernero 125 twin, 1981.

Sertrum 1922-51

This famous Milan factory originally manufactured precision instruments. But in 1922 its owner, Fausto Alberti, decided to enter the two-wheel world. The company's first design was a 174cc side-valve model, which was soon followed by a cheaper 119cc two-stroke.

Thereafter, throughout the mid- and late 1930s Sertrum manufactured a wide range of strong, dependable singles and twins with not only side valve, but ohv and even ohc.

The Milanese concern were also involved in motorcycle sport, most notably the ISDT and the long-distance road races, such as the Milano—Taranto.

After the war Sertrum were one of the first Italian manufacturers to resume production. And at the 1947 Milan show they were able to boast of being the only Italian company to support that year's ISDT. At the exhibition Sertrum were showing two basic models, a girder fork, rear-sprung, 250cc ohv single, and a similar 500. They also had a 500 vertical twin, but were undecided about production. The neatest bike on the stand was a new sports

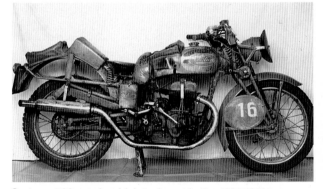

Sertrum 500cc twin which took part in the 1939 ISDT at Salzburg.

250 with a pressed steel frame.

The following year, together with Guzzi, Gilera, Bianchi and Parilla, Sertrum were responsible for 97.74 per cent of Italian registrations for motorcycles — with the remaining 33 producers having to divide a measly 2.26 per cent between them!

But from this high point sales declined rapidly, to a

point in 1951 where the company was forced to close its doors — the first major post-war casualty of the Italian industry.

Sessa 1950-56

Of unusual design these Ilo-powered two-strokes had a rear suspension controlled by a torsion bar, which also formed the pivot point.

Shifty 1975-78

Powered by a 907cc Fiat 127 car engine, the Shifty was of truly gargantuan proportions. It was hand built, almost to special order.

Siata 1946-51

Siata manufactured a very popular 48cc four-stroke, three-speed auxiliary engine, which at one stage was fitted to no fewer than 23 special bicycles of different makes.

SIM 1953-55

SIM (Societa Italiana Motoscooters) was formed in 1953, and its 150cc two-stroke Ariete (Ram) was hailed as one of the 'most unusual machines' of the Milan Show that year. It featured shaft drive and a single-sided support for the rear wheel. The massive swinging arm was of light alloy, and rubber was used as the suspension medium. However, sales never took off as expected and the whole venture failed after a couple of years.

Simonetta 1951-54

A 124cc two-stroke constructed at the San Christoforo factory.

Simonini 1970-83

Founded by Enzo Simonini, this factory produced some of Italy's finest off-road machines during the 1970s, including motocross and enduro models with seven-speed 248cc Sachs engines. Enzo Simonini sold out to Fornetti Impianti of Maranello (next door to Ferrari) in 1975.

In 1979 Simonini created an extremely neat prototype sports roadster, the SS125. This fully faired machine was powered by a six-speed engine and its specification included Ceriani forks, Campagnolo cast alloy wheels, triple Brembo discs and was good for 90 mph.

The Fornetti Impianti concern disposed of the

The excessively large Shifty on display at the Cologne Show in September 1976. It was powered by a four-cylinder Fiat 127 car engine.

Simonini SS125 prototype at Earls Court, 1979. Its specification included a 123cc single-cylinder engine, six-speed box, Ceriani forks and Campagnolo alloy wheels.

Simonini empire in 1981 to a new outfit who couldn't make a go of it, with the result that the marque just faded from the scene. The last Simonini motorcycle was produced in 1983.

Simplex 1921-50

Nothing to do with British and Dutch marques of the same name, the Italian Simplex was owned by Luigi Pellini. The company used both its own and other manufacturers' engines and built up a good name for quality. Offered ohv and ohc engines from 124 to 496cc. After the war production never reached anything like the earlier levels and the company soon disappeared.

Sparviero (See Chiorda)

Sterzi 1948-62

Produced at Palazzolo sull'Oglio, in the province of Brescia, Moto Sterzi's first effort was a two-stroke Sachs-engined machine in 1948. But it was best known for its range of four-stroke models, and in particular their 49cc Pony sports model, which won the marque the distinction of being the very first to offer a moped with an overhead cam engine.

SVM 1985-87

An unsuccessful relaunch of the SWM marque. Both companies had the same chief, Pietro Sironi.

SWM 1971-85

SWM (Speedy Working Motors) were one of the real success stories of the Italian motorcycle industry during the 1970s. With either German Sachs or Austrian Rotax engines it made some extremely competitive off-road machinery for both motocross and enduro use. But it was the latter machine which, together with KTM, became almost a cult with the more well-off Italian teenager during the late 1970s which led to SWM's rapid growth. Its purchase of the rival Gori concern in 1979 led to an over-capacity and when a market downturn came at the beginning of the 1980s SWM was left exposed. Company founder Pietro Sironi then had no option but to close the operation in 1985. Although he re-formed under the SVM title (see above) this enterprise too soon foundered.

SWM enduro with Sachs engine from the early 1970s

Tapella Fuchs 1957

Short-lived project to market Fuchs-engined mopeds.

Taurus 1933-66

Long-running factory who built a number of well-known machines, both two-stroke and four-stroke. Taurus also built a superb 499.34cc (85×88mm) dohc racing single in 1938. Unfortunately the machine's true potential was never realized as the company could not compete with the likes of Gilera or Guzzi.

Post-war the largest model was a 248cc ohv unit construction single.

Tecnomoto 1968-79

Originally built motocross and enduro bikes with Franco Morini and Zündapp engines. In the mid-1970s switched entirely to children's machines. Then in 1977 the factory was sold to an English company headed by John Rudge — and the location moved from Italy to Britain. But it soon ran into financial difficulties and closed.

Solid and staid, rather than swift and stunning, the Taurus 250 ohv single of the mid-1950s.

Testi 1951-83

This Bologna marque built a vast range of models in over 30 years of business, using a variety of engines from Sachs, FB Morini and Minerelli. Testi's most well-known models included the Trail King, Corsa 2000 and Champion Special. But the most interesting was the *eight*-speed Militar, which, as the name implies, was a fully equipped military machine with a fan-cooled 49.6cc Minerelli engine.

Testis were sold under the Horex label in West Germany by the Roth organization, and in Britain by the author's company, the Mick Walker Group. Also sold in certain markets under the Gitane label.

TGM 1974-

The Parma-based TGM factory concentrated upon competition bikes, notably motocross and enduro machines, using Hiro, Villa or similar engines.

Recently has had a working relationship with the Cagiva company.

Thunder 1952-54

Very expensive, but superbly executed 127cc ohv vertical twin. Its high cost limited sales to only a couple of hundred machines.

Super-ped, Testis Champion Special of 1979, had every extra as standard. In unrestricted form it could top 60 mph.

TM 1968-

Another small manufacturer who built only competition machinery. Their motocross bikes were particularly successful and often employed water-cooling. Displayed a neat single-cylinder 80cc road racer at the 1987 Milan Show, with disc valve induction, water-cooling and six-speed gearbox.

TM125 water-cooled single-cylinder racer at the 1987 Milan Show.

Torpado 1950-

First machines used 38cc Garelli Mosquito 'clip-on' engine, thereafter mainly Minerelli units.

Unimoto 1980-86

Comprehensive range of mopeds with Minerelli engines, including liquid-cooled 49.72cc Fox with enduro styling. Top of the range were the SK (road) and MTS (trail) motorcycles. Both used liquid-cooled 124.5cc, six-speed engine and modern styling.

UFO 1976-83

Mainly offered children's motorcycles, but also built an interesting (and fast!) 50cc racer with the help of Morbidelli. The UFO Morbidelli finished fourth in the 1976 world title chase ridden by Lazzarini.

Vecchetti 1954-57

Manufactured mopeds using German 49cc Victoria engines.

Verga 1951-54

This was a 73cc lightweight motorcycle, powered by a single-cylinder unit construction engine and mounted in a pressed-steel frame with swinging arm rear suspension.

Vespa 1946-

The Piaggio company was founded in 1884 in Genoa, making wood working machinery for the shipbuilding industry. In 1901 it turned to railway rolling stock and then aircraft. An aviation factory was built at Pisa before World War One and a car manufacturing plant was acquired at Pontedera in 1924, which was extended for aero-engine and aircraft production to such an extent that by 1939 Piaggio had 10,000 workers and had attained a leading role in the Italian aviation industry. Its most famous wartime type was the P108 — a four-engined heavy bomber, and the only such type manufactured in Italy during the hostilities.

By 1944 nothing was left but ruined buildings and a workforce trustfully awaiting their next meal ticket. With the design of a small two-stroke auxiliary engine and hardly any machine tools Doct. Enrico Piaggio decided that what he could best contribute to a practically derelict country was basic transportation. So he called his management team together and instructed them to produce something which would meet the bill. The result of this was the design of a two-stroke vehicle embodying the latest technology of motorcycle, automotive and aircraft engineering. And so the now legendary Vespa scooter was born.

Production began at the end of 1945, at the giant Piaggio works at Pontedera, less than half an hour's drive from Pisa on the Gulf of Genoa. By the early 1950s the Vespa was not only a familiar sight on the roads of Italy, but around the world. And a number of licence agreements had been signed — for example with Douglas in Britain and Hoffmann of West Germany.

There were also a number of world speed records with a fully streamlined 18 bhp, 123cc (42.9×44mm) machine.

Then on 28 April, 1956, came the millionth machine to

Typical Vespa product, the chic ETS scooter of 1985.

roll off the production lines, which by then were turning out 10,000 Vespas a month from a workforce of 4000.

Throughout its first 20 years Piaggio fought tooth and nail with its Innocenti rivals, who produced the Lambretta, for supremacy in the scooter sales war, and as Piaggio are still churning out many thousands of Vespas in Italy annually, it can be said in retrospect that they finally won the battle, even though Lambrettas (and for that matter Vespas) are still manufactured under licence agreements in certain other countries.

In 1979 Piaggio took over Gilera (see Chapter 10). Also in that decade the aviation side of the group, which had rebuilt successfully in the post-war era, was sold off. And Vespa added mopeds to its line-up.

For much of its life Vespa has consistently manufactured more two-wheelers than any other Italian company, and is without doubt the most successful Latin marque of the post-war era.

Viberti 1955-67

Not only built a neat 123cc ohv motorcycle, but a successful line of German 47cc Victoria-powered mopeds, under the Vivi name. Available in several guises, these were sold in Britain by the DOT company of Manchester.

Victory 1950-55

Used British Villiers engines for its range of lightweights.

Villa 1968-

Francesco Villa and his younger brother Walter were both road racers of world-class status. Francesco was also a gifted engineer, with a speciality for two-stroke engines.

When he started his own marque in 1968, Francesco had already played a leading part in the development of disc-valve racing singles and twins for FB Mondial and the Spanish Montesa company.

His first autonomous effort was the design of a fleet single-cylinder over-the-counter 125cc racer, with square bore and stroke measurement of 54×54mm (the prototype used 56×50mm). This seven-speed machine was water-cooled and employed disc valve induction. Power output was 30 bhp at 11,200 rpm, with a top speed of 118 mph.

This was soon supplemented by no fewer than seven rough stuff models. All were orthodox air-cooled singles with piston-controlled porting, available in trials or motocross form ranging from 50 to 250cc.

Other production Villa competition machines of the era included a purposeful disc valve single-cylinder racer of either 175 or 250cc suitable for the Italian Juniors class.

As if all this was not enough to keep the brothers busy there were also a 125cc narrow-angle 125 twin and a 250 four! Intended for Grand Prix events the larger machine soon became a victim of new FIM restrictions and the brothers decided to withdraw from direct involvement in Grand Prix events.

Villa machinery was ridden in the classics by not only the brothers, but riders such as Mandolini and the British rider Chas. Mortimer, which resulted in considerable publicity during the early 1970s.

Since then Villa has mainly concentrated its efforts on the manufacture of motocross and enduro machinery, latterly with water-cooling and monoshock rear suspension. Even so the Monteveglio company has also offered some street models, notably the 125 Daytona and Italia (roadsters), 125 Scrambler (trail) and the 350 Rommel (trail).

The off-road bikes were imported into Britain during much of the 1970s by the Cleveland-based John Burdon Engineering company.

Villiers Original 1950-51

The work of Giovanni Francesconi, this was a 123cc model powered by a Villiers engine, with telescopic forks and plunger rear suspension.

Vittoria 1931-72

Pre-war machines from this company used 98cc Sachs, 173cc and 248cc JAP, 346cc and 496cc Küchen and 499cc four-valve Rudge Python engines. After 1945 the company concentrated on mopeds and ultra-lightweights with exclusively two-stroke engines.

Wilier 1962-70

The company built only 49cc mopeds or motorcycles. Limited production only.

Zenit 1954-56

The machines used imported French AMC 123cc and 174cc four-stroke unit-construction engines, but only a small number built.

Zeta 1948-54

A scooter-like machine which used 48cc or 60cc Ducati engines.